W9-ASE-146

The Neuropsychology of Aging

UNDERSTANDING AGING
The Psychology of Adult Development

General Editor
James E. Birren

Editorial Advisory Board
Stig Berg, Dennis Bromley, Denise Park, Timothy A. Salthouse,
K. Warner Schaie, and Diana S. Woodruff-Pak

During this century life expectancy at birth has increased more for the average person than it did from Roman times to 1900: there are a greater number of old people today and they live longer than ever before. Within universities there is pressure to educate younger students about the scientific facts of adult development and aging as well as to train professionals to serve an aging society. The past twenty years have seen an exponential growth in material published.

This new series of modular texts has been designed to meet the need to integrate, interpret and make this new knowledge available in an efficient and flexible format for instructors, students and professionals worldwide. Each book will present a concise, authoritative, integrated and readable summary of research and theory in a clearly defined area. Bridging the gap between introductory texts and research literature, these books will provide balanced coverage and convey the excitement and challenge of new research and developments. The modular format allows the series to be used as a complete sequence in primary courses on aging, and also book by book in more specialized courses and in primary courses in other fields.

Published

The Social Psychology of Aging
Michael W. Pratt and Joan E. Norris

The Neuropsychology of Aging
Diana S. Woodruff-Pak

In preparation

The Psychology of Aging: An Overview
James E. Birren and Timothy A. Salthouse

The Cognitive Psychology of Aging
Denise C. Park

Personality and Aging
Jan-Erik Ruth and Peter Coleman

The Psychology of Aging and Mental Health
Michael A. Smyer and Sara H. Qualls

Gender and Aging
Nathan Kogan and Kathryn N. Black

The Neuropsychology of Aging

Diana S. Woodruff-Pak

BLACKWELL
Publishers

BOWLING GREEN STATE
UNIVERSITY LIBRARY

Copyright © Diana S. Woodruff-Pak, 1997

The right of Diana S. Woodruff-Pak to be identified as author of this work has been asserted in accordance with the Copyright, Designs and Patents Act 1988.

First published 1997

2 4 6 8 10 9 7 5 3 1

Blackwell Publishers Inc.
350 Main St
Malden, MA 02148
USA

Blackwell Publishers Ltd
108 Cowley Road
Oxford OX4 1JF
UK

All rights reserved. Except for the quotation of short passages for the purposes of criticism and review, no part of this publication may be reproduced, stored in a retrieval system, or transmitted, in any form or by any means, electronic, mechanical, photocopying, recording or otherwise, without the prior permission of the publisher.

Except in the United States of America, this book is sold subject to the condition that it shall not, by way of trade or otherwise, be lent, resold, hired out, or otherwise circulated without the publisher's prior consent in any form of binding or cover other than that in which it is published and without a similar condition including this condition being imposed on the subsequent purchaser.

Library of Congress Cataloging in Publication Data
Woodruff-Pak, Diana S., 1946–
    The neuropsychology of aging/Diana S. Woodruff-Pak.
      p. cm. – (Understanding aging)
    Includes bibliographical references and index.
    ISBN 1–55786–454–3 (hardback: alk. paper). – ISBN 1–55786–455–1 (pbk.: alk. paper)
    1. Brain – Aging.   2. Neuropsychology.   3. Geriatric neurology.   I. Title.   II. Series.
QP360.W64   1997
612.8 – dc21

                                                96-37330
                                               CIP

British Library Cataloguing in Publication Data

A CIP catalogue record for this book is available from the British Library.

Typeset in $10\frac{1}{2}$ on $12\frac{1}{2}$ pt Bembo
by Best-set Typesetter Ltd., Hong Kong
Printed in Great Britain by Hartnolls Ltd, Bodmin, Cornwall

This book is printed on acid-free paper

Contents

List of Figures   xi
List of Tables   xiv
Acknowledgements   xv

Part I   Introduction and Overview   1

1   Neuropsychological Approaches to Processes of Aging   3

Neuropsychology and the role of neuropsychologists   3
Relationships between neuropsychology and aging   4
What is aging?   8
   When and where does aging begin?   9
   Definition of aging   11
   A note on research methodology in neuropsychology and aging   12
   Definition of aged   15
Plasticity and compensation in aging   16
   Brain plasticity in aging   16
   Compensation in the aging brain   17
Neuropsychology: investigations using human and animal subjects   18
The neuropsychological approach to aging   21
Summary   22
Further reading   23

2   Neuropsychological Assessment in Adulthood and Aging   24

Problems in neuropsychological assessment of the aging   25
   Intelligence tests as a prototype   25
   Practical problems   26

Selected neuropsychological tests   31
   Mental status   31
   Attention   32
   Visuospatial ability   33
   Learning and memory   35
   Intelligence   39
   Language and communication   39
   Planning and executive function   40
   Depression   42
A sample neuropsychological test battery suited to older adults   42
Summary   43
Further reading   45

3   Methods for Assessing the Aging Brain   47

Categories of measures of the human brain   47
   Electrophysiological measures of the aging brain   49
   Event related potentials   51
   Computerized tomography   54
   Magnetic resonance imaging and functional MRI   57
   Positron emission tomography   58
   Histological techniques   60
Summary   62
Further reading   64

Part II   Aging and the Nervous System   **65**

4   Normal Aging in the Peripheral Nervous System   67

Sensory changes in adulthood and old age   68
   Touch   70
   Pain   71
   Balance   72
   Smell   72
   Taste   73
   Hearing   74
   Vision   76
The autonomic nervous system as an index of test anxiety and arousal   80
   Underarousal   80
   Overarousal   82
Summary   84
Further reading   85

5   Normal Aging of the Brain   86

General changes in the aging brain   87
  Cell loss   87
  Cerebrovascular changes   99
  Neurotransmitter systems   99
  Synaptic plasticity and molecular changes   105
Summary   106
Further reading   108

6   Neuropathological Brain Aging   109

A brief history of dementia and Alzheimer's disease (AD)   109
Late-life onset (sporadic) AD   112
  Diagnosis of AD   113
  Behavioral signs of AD   115
  Hypotheses about causes of AD   118
  Neuropsychology and AD   122
  Tests for the early detection of AD   123
Dementia resulting from single gene defects   126
  Huntington's disease   127
  Familial AD   127
Chromosomal aberrations and dementia   128
  Down's syndrome   128
Summary   129
Further reading   130

7   Emotion, Aging, and Brain Function   131

Depression in the elderly population   132
  Definitions of depression   132
  Suicide and depression   134
  Symptoms and diagnosis of depression   135
  Neuropsychological assessment of depression in the aging   136
Causes of depression in the elderly   138
  Neurobiological aspects of depression   139
  Psychological and social causes of depression in the elderly 140
  Psychotherapeutic treatments for depression in late life   141
The frontal lobes and emotion   144
Brain lateralization and emotion   147
Summary   148
Further reading   150

Part III Human Behavior: A Neuropsychological Perspective **151**

8 Arousal and Sleep   153

Sleep   156
Sleep stages   156
Sleep apnea   159
Arousal   160
Underarousal   161
Inhibition   164
A neurophysiological approach to inhibition and aging   165
A cognitive approach to inhibition and aging   170
Summary   171
Further reading   172

9 Response Speed and Timing in Behavior   174

Simple reaction time   175
Choice or complex reaction time   177
Search for the locus of reaction time slowing   178
Movement time   178
Sensory acuity   179
Conduction velocity   179
Synaptic delay   180
Central nervous system factors   182
Timing in cognition and behavior   187
Summary   188
Further reading   189

10 Intelligence   190

Defining intelligence   190
Psychometric assessment of intelligence   191
Intelligence tests and the assessment of normal aging   194
Causes of changing perspectives   196
Phase I: misperception of age-related decline   198
Phase II: stability versus decline   200
Phase III: optimizing intelligence in older adults   202
Phase IV: intellectual development and wisdom   205

Summary   207
Further reading   208

11   Learning and Memory   210

Brain memory systems   211
Declarative learning and memory   211
Declarative learning and memory in the adult years   212
Declarative memory deficits and the diencephalon   217
Nondeclarative learning and memory   220
Metamemory in older adults   228
Memory and life review   229
Summary   232
Further reading   234

12   Language and Communication   236

Brain and language: early perspectives   236
Broca's aphasia   238
Wernicke's aphasia   241
The Wernicke–Geschwind model of brain and language function 242
Language ability in normal aging   248
Age-related decline in selected linguistic functions   249
Locus of age-related impairment in language   250
Summary   251
Further reading   254

13   Executive Function, Attention, and Working Memory 255

Role of the frontal lobes   256
Executive function   257
Assessment of executive function   257
Executive function and aging   259
Working memory   262
Aging and working memory in nonhuman primates   263
Aging and working memory in humans   264
Attention   265
Selective attention and aging   265
Divided attention   266
Summary   267
Further reading   268

Part IV The Future   **271**

14   Prospects in the Neuropsychology of Aging   273

Some implications for new neurobiological knowledge   273
  Molecular genetics   273
  Tissue transplantation   274
  Neurotrophic agents   276
  Cognition-enhancing agents   276
Neuropsychology of aging in the twenty-first century   278
  Health and longevity   279
  Cognitive aging   280
Further reading   283

References   284
Index   336

Figures

1.1   The discipline of neuropsychology   5
1.2   Population in the United States by age and sex in 1950
     and 2030   6
1.3   Population of Asia and Europe by age and sex in 1995
     and 2025   7
1.4   Varying assumptions about future life expectancies   8
1.5   Plasticity in motor cortex resulting from finger stimulation   19
2.1   Clock drawing in neurological patients   36
2.2   Wechsler Memory Scale Visual and Verbal Paired Associates
     for 160 adults aged 20–89   38
2.3   Brain areas involved in language   40
2.4   Word fluency in normal aging and Alzheimer's disease   41
3.1   Changes in EEG alpha frequency between the ages of 79
     and 89 years   50
3.2   Composite evoked potentials in eight age groups in three
     sensory modalities   53
3.3   Computerized tomography (CT) scan of a 62-year-old patient
     who had surgical removal of a tumor in the left frontal lobe   55
3.4   Magnetic resonance image (MRI) of the same 62-year-old
     patient with left frontal tumor removed   57
3.5   β-amyloid plaques in cerebellum in AD and DS/AD   61
3.6   β-amyloid plaques in relation to cerebellar Purkinje cells
     in DS/AD   62
4.1   The human central and peripheral nervous system   68
4.2   Structures of the outer, middle, and inner ear   74
4.3   Components of the visual system   77
4.4   The autonomic nervous system: sympathetic
     and parasympathetic divisions   81
5.1   Alzheimer's brain at autopsy compared to a normal brain   91

5.2 Structural organization of the human hippocampal formation 94

5.3 Magnetic resonance images demonstrating hippocampal atrophy 96

5.4 Purkinje cell number in rabbits as a function of trials to learning criterion 98

6.1 Professor Alois Alzheimer 110

6.2 Auguste D., the first case diagnosed with Alzheimer's disease 111

6.3 Essential features of the acetylcholine synapse 117

6.4 Pupil dilation response and eyeblink classical conditioning scores for probable Alzheimer's disease patients and elderly control participants 126

7.1 Hypothetical trajectories of rod injuring Phineas Gage 146

8.1 Stages of sleep as identified by EEG 156

8.2 EEG, brain, and behavior of a cat from deep sleep to waking alertness 161

8.3 Evoked potential evidence for age-related decline in inhibition 167

9.1 Age differences in jaw, finger, and foot reaction time 180

9.2 Some possible mechanisms that could result in slowing of neural transmission across the synapse 181

9.3 Techniques for assessing the P300 and the resulting waveform 185

9.4 Sample event-related potential traces from normal control participant and patients with probable Alzheimer's disease 186

10.1 Schematic representation of the four phases of research on aging and intelligence 195

10.2 Figural Relations and Induction over eight retest sessions for older adults 204

11.1 Acquisition and retention on the California Verbal Learning Test in young and older adults 212

11.2 Mean recall and recognition scores as a function of age 215

11.3 MRI scan of the patient PS with a symmetrical bilateral thalamic infarction 218

11.4 The human cerebral cortex and brainstem and the regions essential for various forms of nondeclarative learning and memory 220

11.5 Experimental arrangement for classical conditioning of the eyeblink response in rabbits and humans 223

11.6 Trials to learning criterion in eyeblink classical conditioning over the life span in rabbits and humans 224

12.1 A nineteenth-century cartoon lampooning the "science" of phrenology 237

12.2 Geschwind's anatomical model based on Wernicke's ideas of brain and language function 240

12.3 The "cookie theft" picture used in testing for aphasia   241
12.4 Composite radioisotope brain scan of patients with Broca's,
      Wernicke's, conduction, and global aphasia   247
13.1 The Wisconsin Card Sorting Task   258

Tables

2.1 Clinical neuropsychological tests for assessment of attention 34
2.2 Brief battery for neuropsychological assessment of older adults 44
7.1 Summary of neuropsychological testing findings in geriatric depression 137
12.1 Samples of discourse illustrating disruption of macrolinguistic abilities 252

Acknowledgements

The author and publishers would like to thank all copyright holders who have kindly granted permission to reproduce illustrations from other publications. Every effort has been made to trace all copyright holders and the publishers would be grateful to be notified of any further copyright information that should be incorporated in the next edition or reprint of this book.

Part I

Introduction and Overview

1

Neuropsychological Approaches to Processes of Aging

What is neuropsychology, and why study it with regard to aging? The aim of this book is to answer these questions at length. A short answer is that the neuropsychology of aging involves scientific investigation and clinical assessment and treatment of brain function as it affects cognition and behavior over the adult life span. Neuropsychologists assess and treat individuals whose mental dysfunctions appear to be caused by damage or abnormalities in the brain. The basis of this form of assessment and treatment is neuroscientific research investigating brain and behavior relationships in human and subhuman species.

Neuropsychology and the role of neuropsychologists

The term "neuropsychology" is relatively new, having purely twentieth-century origins. The originator of the term may have been William Osler, an internist at Johns Hopkins University Medical School (Bruce, 1985). Ironically, Osler attributed aging of the brain to cerebrovascular rather than neural changes (Birren & Woodruff, 1983). The celebrated Canadian neuroscientist Donald O. Hebb used the term in 1949 when he published his influential book *The organization of behavior: A neuropsychological theory*. Although neuropsychology was not defined in Hebb's book, the term apparently originated as an attempt to represent a scientific domain combining topics of interest in neurology and physiological psychology (Kolb & Whishaw, 1995). Further visibility was given to the term when the Harvard University neuroscientist Karl S. Lashley's works were collected and edited by Beach, Hebb and others and published in 1960 under the title *The neuropsychology of Lashley*. Neuropsychology is defined as the investigation of brain function and behavior relationships. The perspective represented in this book is derived from Donald Hebb's meaning of the term "neuropsychology": the scientific study of brain function and behavioral relationships using experimental evidence from sub-human and human species as well as clinical evidence from human brain damage.

A more narrow definition of neuropsychology would limit the field to studies of human brain damage and the effects of brain damage on behavior. This aspect is a significant dimension of neuropsychology, and it includes the assessment and treatment of patients. The majority of individuals who classify themselves as neuropsychologists are trained and certified to practice clinical psychology. They may work in academic settings, but more likely they practice clinical neuropsychology in hospitals, clinics, or private practice. It is their role to identify the cause of cognitive or behavioral impairment in their patients through neuropsychological assessment techniques. They also treat patients or refer them for treatment.

The neuropsychologist Jenni Ogden (1996) provided a useful insight into the relationship of clinical neuropsychology to other disciplines as illustrated in figure 1.1. There are a number of disciplines that are closely related to clinical neuropsychology, and they can best be conceptualized as a continuum between brain and mind. Disciplines focused on the brain include neurology and neuroscience, whereas disciplines focused on mind include cognitive psychology and cognitive science. Neuropsychology integrates data from these sciences in the assessment, treatment, and understanding of brain and behavior relationships.

Relationships between neuropsychology and aging

Processes of aging affect brain function and behavior. Neurological, physiological, and psychological changes accompany aging. The neuropsychology of aging is expanding as a field because of rapid advances in neuroscience techniques and because the number of older adults in most countries in the world is increasing. Perhaps the most compelling reason for studying the neuropsychology of aging in the 1990s is the fact that there are so many more people who are elderly. With the alleviation of the high mortality rates of infancy and youth in the early twentieth century in developed nations, a much greater proportion of the population is surviving to old age.

Whereas the aged had comprised a relatively small proportion of the population of the United States in the early decades of the twentieth century, reflected in the more or less pyramid-like shape of the 1950 population in the United States, projections for 2030 resemble a pillar (figure 1.2; Quinn, 1996). Indeed, the population distribution in most areas of the world is

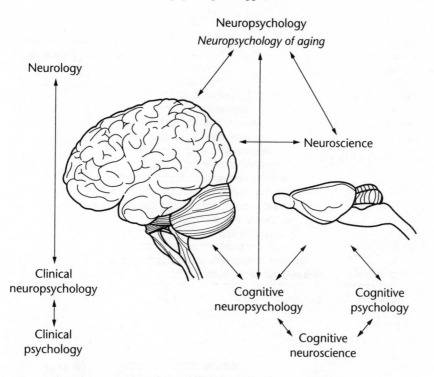

Figure 1.1 The discipline of neuropsychology and its relation to neuroscience, neurology, clinical neuropsychology and sub-disciplines in psychology and cognitive science
Source: Illustration by Michelle H. Pak

changing from a pyramid with few elderly at the top to a pillar with equal population size at all ages (figure 1.3; Holden, 1996). By the 1980s, 11 percent of the population was over 65 in the United States, and the percentage of older adults rose to 12 percent in the 1990s. With the aging of the post-World War II baby-boom generation, this figure may rise to 16 percent by the early twenty-first century.

Demographers cannot agree on projections for the size of the population over the age of 65 in the twenty-first century. Various assumptions about life expectancy in the future, differences in fertility rate, and patterns of migration result in a range of projections for the number of older adults in 2050 of between 50 and 100 million (see figure 1.4; Roush, 1996). In the absence of firm statistics on the size of the older adult population in the future, political leaders and economists are seriously challenged. Richard Suzman, Director of the Office of Demography of Aging at the National Institute on Aging, stated

Introduction and Overview

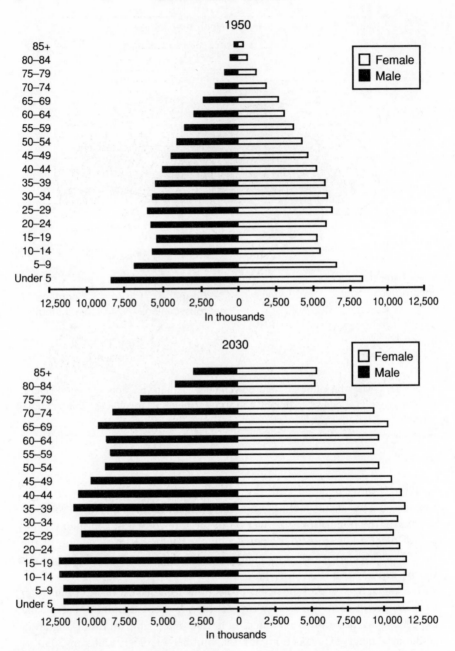

Figure 1.2 Population in the United States by age and sex in 1950 and 2030
Source: Quinn, J. F. (1996, August). Entitlements and the Federal budget: A summary. *Gerontology News*, Fig. 1, p. 3. Reproduced by kind permission of the National Academy on Aging

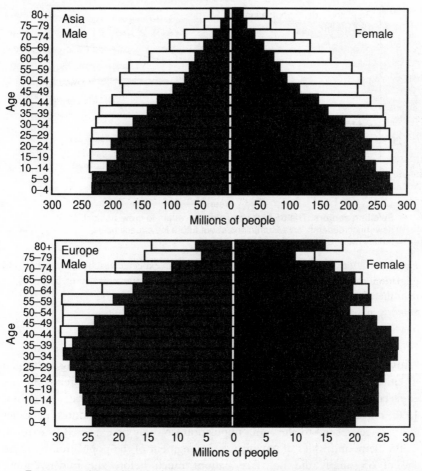

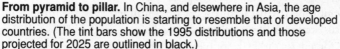

From pyramid to pillar. In China, and elsewhere in Asia, the age distribution of the population is starting to resemble that of developed countries. (The tint bars show the 1995 distributions and those projected for 2025 are outlined in black.)

Figure 1.3 Population of Asia and Europe by age and sex in 1995 (inside bars) and 2025 (outside lines). The population of undeveloped countries in Asia is beginning to resemble that of developed countries

Source: Holden, C. (1996). New populations of old add to poor nations' burdens. *Science, 273*, 46–48. Copyright © 1996, American Association for the Advancement of Science

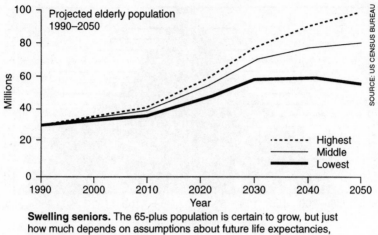

Swelling seniors. The 65-plus population is certain to grow, but just how much depends on assumptions about future life expectancies, fertility rates, and migration.

Figure 1.4 Varying assumptions about future life expectancies, fertility rates, and migration result in widely divergent projections about the number of adults older than the age of 65
Source: Roush, W. (1996). Live long and prosper? *Science, 273,* 42–46

"Anyone who gives you firm prognostications about what is going to happen is either a liar or a fool, because the uncertainties over trends in life expectancy, health and disability, and retirement are quite high" (Roush, 1996, p. 42). What is clear is that opportunities in careers addressing issues and services related to the aging population can only be expected to expand.

Problems and issues of having a major segment of the population over the age of 65 simply did not face nations much before the mid-twentieth century. Confronted with the prospect of continued growth in the numbers of individuals attaining their eightieth and ninetieth birthdays, social planners have been forced to direct resources into the study and care of an elderly population. This means that gerontology is an expanding discipline, and it will continue to offer career and service opportunities to growing numbers of individuals who become interested in answering the questions and addressing the problems of aging.

What is aging?

Where does aging begin and what does it encompass? This is one of the first and most often asked questions about aging, and the answer begins to illustrate the complexity of the issue. One of the first points necessary to establish is the fact that aging occurs on many levels. It can be conceptualized on at least three primary dimensions: biological, psychological, and social. Biological aging is conceptualized in terms of the nearness to death or the position of an individual relative to his or her potential life span. Biologists view adulthood and especially aging as a period of decline, and all biological aging functions as involving decrement or changes in the direction of less capacity. Biological development is seen as occurring until the organism attains maturity, and this is typically marked by the organism being able to reproduce. Aging begins after maturity has been attained. Psychological aging refers to the adaptive capacity of an individual as observed in terms of behavior. It may also refer to subjective reactions and to self-awareness. Social aging deals with the social habits and roles of the individual in relation to the expectations of various groups and of society.

When and where does aging begin?

With regard to the question of when and where aging begins, it begins at different points of the life span depending upon whether one is dealing with biological, psychological, or social age. If one is thinking in terms of catabolic processes and decline, then aging does not begin until some apex has been attained, whether it be at the point of 7–9 months in the fetus in terms of the total number of nerve cells which will ever exist in the organism, or at the age of 30 or beyond when physiological systems such as the cardiovascular, pulmonary, or nervous systems begin to show a loss in efficiency of approximately 1 percent per year. It could be argued that social aging begins at birth or perhaps at age one when certain social expectations and norms begin to be established on the basis of age. Psychological aging might be viewed to begin at a variety of different times depending on the behavior being assessed. One of the important differences between psychological age functions and biological age functions is that psychological age functions include the possibility of stability or increment, while biological age functions by definition involve decline. Psychological aging includes concepts of maturity and wisdom in addition to concepts of senility.

Psychologists have a more complex perspective than the simple biological decline model because behavioral change in aging is not only decline. Some behaviors such as response speed do decline in adulthood and old age. However, other behaviors continue to develop. One measure on intelligence tests which shows continued improvement in most individuals over the adult years is vocabulary. Our knowledge of the meaning of words, and the number of words we can define, increases as we get older. More unique to given individuals is expertise in a chosen field, which shows continued elaboration and improvement with age over the adult years.

Aging involves continued growth and differentiation over time. Human cognition and personality, to take two examples, do not stop differentiating at maturity. The thought processes of a 50-year-old executive have evolved considerably from the same individual's thinking patterns as a 20-year-old. Birren (1969) demonstrated the maturity of older executives' thought processes in an analysis of their decisions. The analysis suggested that the thinking of these individuals integrated more information. Young executives appeared to focus on small details, while older executives included broader concepts in their decision making. The older executives had developed fewer solutions with age, but the solutions were proven ones. Their integration was evaluated as a progressive manner of reasoning which they had gained through experience.

It seems quite plausible that after 30 years of experience, the older executive's capacity to make effective decisions expands. People in the adult years do not feel that their capacities are declining. They feel that they have improved with age. We asked adults in their mid-40s to answer a questionnaire assessing personal and social adjustment in the way they thought they had answered it 20 years before, when they were college students. The picture they presented of their younger selves was dramatically less well-adjusted than the picture they presented of their present selves (Woodruff & Birren, 1972).

The progressive elaboration of skills and capacities that accompanies maturation in adulthood undoubtedly has a neurobiological substrate. Brain plasticity is accomplished by changes at the neural synapse. Although brain plasticity is most obvious early in development, the brain remains malleable throughout the life span. Enriching experiences such as seeing Nureyev dance or eating gourmet meals can affect perception and synaptic connections. Even if this exposure occurs in old age, it changes one's later appreciation of ballet and food. There is a wealth of evidence demonstrating that placing mammals in an enriched environment results in a persisting increase in the structural complexity of neuronal elements in certain brain regions, and in improved performance in a variety of learning and memory tasks (Thompson et al., 1985). Such changes have been reported even when environmental enrichment is not initiated until middle age (Green et al., 1983) or old age (Diamond et al., 1985). Specifically, increased dendritic branching, spine densities, and spines (by implication, increased numbers of synapses) have been seen in cerebral cortex and cerebellar cortex in animals (usually rats, but also monkeys) raised in enriched versus individual-cage environments (e.g., Diamond et al., 1975; Floeter & Greenough, 1979; Turner & Greenough, 1985).

Physical as well as mental experience affects brain function in adulthood and old age. With a modified exercise program, even very old individuals can regain some of the physiological efficiency they had lost with advancing years. Indeed, Robert Dustman and his associates showed that brain function as assessed with evoked potentials was more efficient in a group of older runners compared to a control group of sedentary older adults. Neuropsychological test performance is also improved by older individuals completing a 4-month exercise program (Dustman et al., 1984). Sedentary individuals aged 55–70 years participated for 4 months, three times a week for 1 hr. One group received aerobic exercises consisting of fast walking or slow jogging. An exercise control group performed stretching exercises, and a non-exercise control group performed no activity. A battery of neuropsychological tests was administered before and after the 4-month program. Participants in the aerobic exercise group (but not participants in other groups) showed major improvement in physical fitness level, as well as mental functioning. Dustman and his colleagues noted that the pattern of results indicated exercise-induced changes in central rather than peripheral nervous system mechanisms. This interpretation was based on the fact that neuropsychological function improved, but there was no change in peripheral sensory thresholds. It was suggested that improved neuropsychological performance occurred as a result of enhanced cerebral metabolic activity.

Definition of aging

In this book, aging is viewed differently from biological, psychological, and social perspectives. Therefore, it is not specifically defined. It may seem unusual in a book about aging to avoid presenting a specific and quotable definition of aging. However, a major point to be made is that aging is no one process, but a number of processes which are not well understood. Furthermore, a definition of aging at one level may be inaccurate when applied at another level. To state, for example, that processes of aging begin at conception would suit some, but this statement would not be accurate for many phenomena which simply do not exist at conception or for many years after conception. Thus, we will consider components of aging, such as biological, psychological, and social aging, and refrain from specifically defining aging as a whole.

Another point which is important to understand when studying aging is that aging is simply a general marker term for something else. One of the goals of gerontologists is to eliminate the term "aging" altogether and replace it with the processes responsible for the change under examination. Aging denotes the passage of time and whatever processes occurring over time which result in change in the organism.

The term used to denote the scientific study of aging processes is gerontology. This term is more general than geriatrics because it is meant to encompass the entire scope of aging processes – normal and pathological. Geriatrics, on the other hand, is the study and treatment of pathological processes of aging. The medical model of aging, like the biological perspective, deals primarily in terms of decline. From this perspective, aging is viewed as synonymous with pathology.

A note on research methodology in neuropsychology and aging

The aim of neuropsychological research on aging is to evaluate changes in brain and behavior relationships as a function of age. This aim is problematic to achieve for a number of reasons, among them: a long period of time to be covered (60 or more years), tremendous individual variability, confounds with disease processes, and the uniqueness of each generation or cohort (group born around the same point in time). There have traditionally been two primary approaches used to study psychological aging. These approaches have involved research designs called *cross-sectional* and *longitudinal*.

Cross-sectional design.   This is a descriptive research design used to measure behavior as a function of age. Since researchers obviously cannot manipulate or assign participants to different age groups, this is a correlational design, and no inferences about causality can be made. The proper inference is that the participants are different in the different age groups (if indeed there are statistically significant differences in behavior in the results), rather than that they are changing with age. One of the most common errors made in the neuropsychology of aging is to interpret cross-sectional results as signifying age changes rather than differences between age groups. Age differences in behavior may be observed as a consequence of changes in the brain, but they also may exist because of differences in experience or genetic background in the various age groups assessed.

The cross-sectional design involves testing at least two age groups at one point in time and comparing the average scores of the two groups. Whereas a study can be a cross-sectional design by simply including two age groups, it is far more satisfactory to test at a minimum of three points in the adult life span (young, middle, and old adulthood) to examine when the age difference begins to appear. The goal of studies conducted using the cross-sectional design is to determine if differences occur between the groups as a function of age. The problem is that the groups may differ for many reasons in addition to age.

The cross-sectional research design is the most frequently used design in the neuropsychology of aging. In spite of its weaknesses and confounds, it is the quickest and most efficient means of gathering data in the adult age range. Most of the information imparted in this book is derived from the cross-sectional research design.

Longitudinal design. Like the cross-sectional design, the aim of studies employing the longitudinal design in the study of the neuropsychology of aging is to collect descriptive behavioral data as a function of age. The feature which is unique to longitudinal data is that it provides an insight about age *changes.* In the longitudinal design, one sample is selected and measured at least twice on behavioral dependent variables. Participants are tested at several ages at several times of measurement. Usually more than one dependent variable is used because of the major investment in time and other resources required to keep track of a longitudinal sample. Because of the extensive logistical and financial commitment required to undertake longitudinal research, relatively fewer longitudinal studies are carried out compared with the number of cross-sectional studies.

A modified form of the longitudinal design is the follow-up study. This is a study in which individuals who were tested at some point in time previously are followed up and retested at a later date. The original intent of the study was not to provide longitudinal data, but at some later point the original investigator or another investigator seizes the opportunity to gather longitudinal data.

Strengths and weaknesses of cross-sectional and longitudinal designs. Both cross-sectional and longitudinal designs are pre-experimental. They cannot be used to provide the inference that aging is causing any phenomenon to occur. However, they do provide insights about the descriptive nature of aging processes. They give us information about what may occur as we age.

Cross-sectional designs are appropriate for the purpose of immediate prediction and control. For example, in the case of the need to set immediate social policies based on the population of young, middle-aged, and old adults of the present, cross-sectional studies are extremely useful. However, when data collected cross-sectionally are used to predict the aging of subsequent cohorts, they may introduce biases. Cross-sectional studies are useful to provide normative characteristics of the population: to indicate trends of central tendency and variability. They are a very useful first step in the description of psychological aging phenomena because they may identify behaviors which vary between different age groups.

Unfortunately, in addition to their strengths, cross-sectional data also have serious limitations. For example, cross-sectional data are limited because they involve a between-subjects design and include interindividual variability. People in two age groups may differ for a variety of reasons apart from age.

They may have different educational levels, different socioeconomic status, different world views, and even different genetic constituency. For example, most members of the cohort born in the United States between 1942 and 1945 had fathers who were able to remain at home rather than being drafted or enlisted in the armed services and sent overseas during World War II. A large proportion of the potential contributors to the gene pool at that time were out of the country. This made the genetic composition (as well as the size) of the cohort born just after World War II different from the cohort born during World War II.

In addition to many sources for differences between cohorts, there may be so many interindividual differences within one age group that the existing age differences may not emerge when the two groups are compared. The vast diversity between humans provides a nuisance variable to cross-sectional designs: interindividual variability. When this interindividual variability is systematic according to the period in time in which an age group was born, it is called the *cohort* effect. Variance introduced with cohort makes it possible only in rare instances for cross-sectional data to be interpreted to reflect true age changes. For this reason we never call the results observed in cross-sectional studies *age changes*. We use the term *age differences* to remind ourselves that the results are probably not simply a function of aging.

One of the reasons longitudinal data are so useful is that the nuisance variable of interindividual variability is reduced considerably. The same individual is tested repeatedly, so individual identity is maintained and the same person is compared with himself or herself at subsequent times of measurement. Change can be observed. Another feature of longitudinal data is that they provide a picture of the temporal patterning of developmental and aging events. The rate of change and the actual shape of the individual growth curve can be observed. It is only with longitudinal data that the actual shape of the curve is apparent. To observe the patterning of relationships between variables over time, longitudinal data are essential.

Although they provide unique and valuable insights, longitudinal data are extremely problematic. There are several categories of difficulties with longitudinal designs. One has to do with repeated measures. By recruiting individuals into a longitudinal study and measuring them over and over, the individuals are changed. At each time of measurement, the participant is more test-sophisticated than on the previous occasion. Thus, confounded with the natural aging changes of the person are the changes occurring as a function of the testing. Control groups tested only once, or at less frequent intervals, can be employed to eliminate this problem, but they seldom are.

Another category of problems with longitudinal studies is that created by the long time-frames required to study adulthood. With time, a field changes. Advances are made in measurement techniques. This is especially the case in neuropsychology, as neuro-imaging has been available only in the last two decades. However, to assure comparability, the investigator is usually limited to the tools available at the time the study was initiated. New measures can be added, but they extend the time required for testing and lead to possible bias resulting from fatigue or boredom. Another problem introduced by the passage of time is the attrition of the sample. People move away, they lose interest, they become ill, and they die. All of these factors lead to a smaller and less representative sample. It is difficult to get a representative sample to volunteer to participate in a longitudinal study in the first place, and then attrition causes even more sample bias. This makes it more difficult to make valid generalizations to the general population. Furthermore, the cohort variable affects longitudinal data in that the generalizations based on longitudinal study of one cohort group may not be valid for another.

Responding to the seeming discrepancies in cross-sectional and longitudinal data, Schaie (1965) proposed sequential designs as an alternative. These designs have proved useful, but they have been applied in social and behavioral studies of aging rather than in neuropsychological studies. Warner Schaie himself may be the first to take a neuropsychological perspective in a sequential study, as he is currently attempting to use brain imaging as well as behavioral tests to assess cognition in aging in his Seattle sample assessed for over 30 years. He has also requested that his participants donate their brains for histological investigations.

Definition of aged

We will refrain from presenting a specific definition of aging, but it may be useful to consider some age as old. However, it seems that even this task of identifying an age when the term "aged" is appropriate presents a challenge. Chronological years are a relatively poor marker of normal aging, and some people are "old" at 55, whereas others are young at 75. In discussing humans in the mid- to late twentieth century, a commonly accepted age at which the term "aged" applied was 65 years. This age was set as the retirement age by the founder and first chancellor of the German Empire, Otto von Bismarck, in the late nineteenth century. He chose 65 arbitrarily as the retirement age because so few people in that period survived that long. Indeed, the age of 65 in contemporary society signifies something very different from what it indicated a century ago in von Bismarck's day. It must be made explicit that the acceptance of this number of years as the demarcation of an aged individual is arbitrary. Researchers often set the age of 65 years as the youngest age for inclusion into the older adult group. In this regard we will consider the age of 65 as an operational definition of aged. However, the age of 65 is quite young for the term "aged" to apply.

It is extremely important to stipulate that the aged are not a homogeneous group. Quite the contrary, individual differences increase with age, and many gerontologists have chosen to differentiate between the young old and the old old (Bengtson & Haber, 1983). Indeed, each decade beyond the age of 65 probably could be delineated as a new phase. The typical 65-year-old is quite different from the typical 75-year-old who, in turn, stands apart from the typical 85-year-old. Those in their 90s and beyond 100 are even more heterogeneous. Furthermore, those in their 80s and beyond comprise the most rapidly growing segment of the population of the United States.

For the most part, the neurobiological changes that take place in adulthood occur relatively late in life – in that most rapidly growing population in the 70s and especially in the 80s and older. Middle adulthood is normally a period of stability in the nervous system, with changes resulting in behavioral loss postponed until the decade of the 70s and beyond. Of course, there are exceptions to normal aging. Some individuals experience insults to the brain in middle and young old age from automobile accidents or cerebrovascular infarcts. The early onset of Alzheimer's disease or Parkinson's disease affects a small proportion of the population in the late 50s and 60s. These individuals, all suffering from some form of brain trauma and behavioral impairment, would likely be seen by neuropsychologists for assessment and treatment. The incidence of neurological and cognitive impairment in normal aging individuals increases in the decades of the 70s and beyond.

Plasticity and compensation in aging

Neuropsychological aging includes developmental progression as well as physical and behavioral decline. Biological aging includes the loss of neurons, and increases in abnormal substances in the brain such as β-amyloid plaque, Lewy bodies, and neurofibrillary tangles. The behavioral consequences of these physiologically based changes include slowed speed of responding and mild memory impairment. Yet, some aspects of psychological aging may be immune to the inevitable physiological changes that accompany biological aging, and other aspects may demonstrate less decrement as a function of compensatory mechanisms (Woodruff-Pak & Hanson, 1995). One goal of neuropsychologists working with elderly patients is to identify capacities that are retained and can be used to adapt and compensate.

Brain plasticity in aging

Because the vast majority of neurons do not divide after the birth of an organism, the concept of plasticity in the adult nervous system has met with severe resistance. Young (1996) pointed out that even a decade ago there was such deep pessimism surrounding the prospects for spinal cord regeneration that few researchers would have attempted the experiments reported by Cheng et al. (1996). These scientists presented the first evidence that true functional regeneration can occur in the adult spinal cord.

If the potential for plasticity in the adult nervous system has received relatively little research attention until recently, it is hardly surprising that investigators in the field of neuropsychology and aging have experienced strenuous resistance in promoting the occurrence of brain plasticity in older organisms. Until the late twentieth century, investigators did not include adult or older animals in their brain plasticity studies because they thought it was useless to even test plasticity in older organisms. This reluctance to investigate the effect of aging in studies of brain plasticity attests to the degree to which scientists form premature conclusions about adaptation in the older nervous system.

The continued expression of plasticity in the brains of adult mammals, including humans, has been documented by behavioral, biochemical, electro-physiological, and morphological evidence (Singer, 1992). By *plasticity*, we mean the adaptive capacity to change, including to perform complex cognitive processes. At the neurobiological level, plasticity can be supported by numerous mechanisms. For example, profound modifications in the responses of individual neurons recorded electrophysiologically are observed when pharmacological agents are applied to them. In this circumstance, plasticity might be changes in neuronal firing rates resulting from the increased availability of specific neurotransmitters. Morphological substrates of brain plasticity have been observed as increased density of dendritic spines in the cortex of animals exposed to an enriched environment (e.g., Turner & Greenough, 1985). Another physical form of brain plasticity occurs as functional reorganization after brain lesions. Cortical tissue adjacent to the zone of destruction can recover functions in a use-dependent manner (Singer, 1992). From the neuropsychological perspective, a discussion of plasticity includes the capacity for cognitive and behavioral change, along with the underlying chemical–structural–organizational changes that occur in the brain.

Compensation in the aging brain

Compensation is a term that denotes a response to loss or deficiency. When older adults compensate, the compensation must use the brain substrate that remains. In normal aging, there is a much greater brain substrate with which to work as compared to Alzheimer's disease that causes substantial neural loss.

Among the forms of loss affecting hundreds of thousands of adults each year are stroke and closed head injury. Deficiencies in the brain and in behavior result from these insults. Until quite recently, it was assumed that irreversible damage occurred in the case of stroke and closed head injury and that any improvement that was observed occurred simply as the result of a reduction in swelling or shock. Research and therapy are demonstrating, however, that the brain is capable of reorganizing itself, both in the case of experience and in the case of response to trauma. For example, electrophysiological mapping of the somatosensory cortex of the monkey identified a large region on the contralateral cortex where individual digits and the palm were represented (figure 1.5). After the middle finger was amputated, the somatosensory cortical receptive fields for the fingers of that hand were reorganized with the cortical representation of each adjacent finger expanded over the region previously representing the middle finger (Merzenich & Jenkins, 1993). In another experiment demonstrating the effect of experience, the monkey was rewarded with food for keeping two fingers in contact with a rotating disk. Electrophysiological mapping demonstrated that this type of stimulation expanded the cortical representation of the fingertip area of the stimulated fingers (see figure 1.5; Merzenich & Jenkins, 1993). Mechanisms are in place in the brain to reorganize on the basis of experience or to accommodate to structural loss and then to reorganize to preserve or adapt behavioral function (Kolb, 1995).

As measured on a behavioral level, processes of aging differentially affect various aspects of cognition. These effects will be explored in depth in chapters 8–13. For example, in the cognitive domain of learning and memory, some components of encoding and retrieval appear relatively spared, whereas other components are impaired in every individual who survives to the age of 60 or older. Identification of the components of learning and memory, and their underlying brain memory systems that are relatively spared, may provide insights about interventions for compensation in learning and memory in old age. The possibility exists that preserved components of learning and memory, and preserved structures of brain memory systems, might be used to compensate for the components particularly impaired by aging processes.

Neuropsychology: investigations using human and animal subjects

The body of knowledge that comprises what we know about the neuropsychology of human aging is derived from research using human and nonhuman subjects. There are two obvious features of animal models that

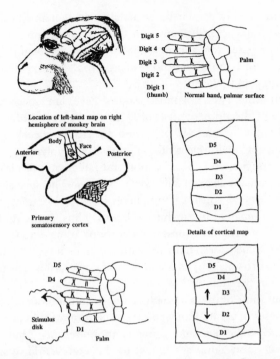

Figure 1.5 Plasticity in the brain. Illustration of the effect of stimulation on two fingers and the change in representation of those fingers in the contralateral motor cortex. *Top left*: monkey head and brain. *top right*: Palmar surface of the monkey's hand showing the five digits. *Middle left*: primary motor (anterior central gyrus) and somatosensory (posterior central gyrus) cortex with region representing monkey hand in box. *Middle right*: cortical map of digits before stimulation. *bottom left*: stimulation of digits D2 and D3. *Bottom right*: enlargement of cortical representation of digits D2 and D3 as a consequence of stimulation

Source: Original drawing by Michelle H. Pak based on Merzenich, M. M., & Jenkins, W. M. (1993). Reorganization of cortical representations of the hand following alterations of skin inputs induced by nerve injury, skin island transfers and experience. *Journal of Hand Therapy, 6,* 89–104

make them of invaluable assistance in research on neuropsychology and aging. First, the life spans of most animals are considerably shorter than the human life span, compressing the time required to observe processes of aging. For the rapid advancement of knowledge about brain and behavior relationships during aging, animal models are practical and expedient. Second, invasive and/or high risk observations and experimental manipulations are feasible with animals but not with humans. In many cases experiments can be performed on animals to demonstrate causal relationships between aging and behavior which simply cannot be undertaken in humans. Legal and ethical constraints on human experimentation lead us to use animals humanely in research as surrogates for human subjects. Thus, we begin here with the premise that animal models are an essential tool for the understanding of neuropsychology and processes of aging.

Along with their value, animal models have limitations in neuropsychology. One of the primary areas of focus in neuropsychology is language, yet only the human brain is organized to enable speech and language. Executive function, that aspect of cognition that involves planning, generation of new strategies, and co-ordination and integration of ideas, is far more developed in humans than in sub-human species. The specialization of the left and right cerebral cortical hemispheres is another feature of the human brain that is less apparent in sub-human brains. Thus, in the study of some of the highest of human functions, investigations using animal models have limitations. In some cases, humans with brain damage and normal adults assessed with neuro-imaging techniques are the primary means for investigating human neuropsychology.

Throughout most of the twentieth century, animal models have been used to study processes of aging. However, the utilization of animal models for the study of neuropsychology and aging is more recent. Animal models in neuropsychology and aging are linked to the post-World War II surge of research in psychology and aging, and to the even more recent advent of neuroscience research (Woodruff-Pak, 1990). The major portion of the animal model research on neuropsychology and aging has been published after 1980. This is a relatively new area of research — it is making rapid progress, and it holds promise for providing some strategies for optimization of some forms of cognitive capacities in aging humans that have parallels in animals.

For example, the neural circuitry for one significant form of learning, classical conditioning, appears to be similar for all mammals including humans. The pathways for classical conditioning of the nictitating membrane (NM)/eyeblink response in rabbits are almost completely identified, and the neural substrates of eyeblink classical conditioning appear similar in humans. To date, evidence is most consistent with storage of the memory traces in the interpositus nucleus of the cerebellum and possibly also in localized regions of cerebellar cortex. Eyeblink conditioning is affected dramatically by processes of aging in rabbits and humans, and drugs have been tested in older rabbits that ameliorate the deficit in eyeblink conditioning (Woodruff-Pak, 1995). These results demonstrate that animal models have utility in the neuropsychology of aging for the description and amelioration of age-related deficits.

The neuropsychological approach to aging

Aging is a complex process, involving both physiological and psychological changes. Some of these changes are positive and some negative. Neuropsychology attempts to document and to understand the effects of aging on both physiological and psychological structures and processes. In addition, a neuropsychological approach to the study of aging encourages an examination of how physiological and psychological factors interact to produce cognitive performance.

Assessment of physiological and psychological function and structure is a necessary first step in the study of aging. In chapter 2 we discuss the various methods, tests, and techniques used in the neuropsychological assessment of aging. These tests form the basis upon which the behavioral effects of aging are evaluated. Techniques aimed more at assessing physiological effects of aging are described in chapter 3. These techniques include measurement of electrical activity of the brain (electroencephalogram [EEG] and event related potentials [ERPs]) as well as brain imaging methodologies for neuroanatomical (magnetic resonance imaging [MRI] and computerized axial tomography [CT]) and neurophysiological (positron emission tomography [PET] and functional magnetic resonance imaging [fMRI]) assessment.

Based on the assessment techniques discussed in chapters 2 and 3, we describe what is currently known about the effects of aging on the nervous system. Normal aging effects are discussed in chapters 4 and 5, whereas pathological effects are examined in chapters 6 and 7. Chapter 4 focuses on the typical changes occurring in the peripheral nervous system over time, whereas chapter 5 examines differential patterns of aging in the neural systems of the brain. Neuropathological states (e.g., Alzheimer's disease, Parkinson's disease, cerebrovascular dementia) are discussed in chapter 6. The physiological, psychological, and social factors leading to age-related mood disorders are described in chapter 7.

A neuropsychological perspective of behavioral aging is presented in the third section of this book. Age-related effects on arousal and sleep (chapter 8), response speed and timing (chapter 9), intelligence (chapter 10), learning and memory (chapter 11), language and communication (chapter 12), and executive function, attention, and working memory (chapter 13) are described. Empirical work on behavioral aging and its neuropsychological basis as well as the theoretical and practical implications of this research are discussed.

Finally, in the last chapter of this book we examine how neuropsychology can be applied to future theoretical and practical issues in the field of gerontology. Progress in the neuropsychology of aging may help most older adults maintain intact cognitive functions until the very end of their lives.

Summary

Processes of aging affect brain function and behavior, and the neuropsychology of aging is at the exciting intersection of two of the most rapidly growing areas of science: neuroscience and gerontology. Although some perspectives limit neuropsychology to the investigation of brain damage in humans and its effects on behavior, the scope of this book is broader. Neuropsychology is viewed from the Hebbian panorama as an attempt to represent a scientific domain combining the provinces of neurology and behavioral neuroscience. Brain function in relation to behavior and aging as studied in nonhuman and human species is the topic of this book.

Aging involves change as well as stability over time at multiple levels: biological, psychological, and social. Psychological age functions in adulthood include both differentiation and increasing expertise as well as dedifferentiation and decline. A social definition of old age was the basis for retirement age: 65 years. However, chronological age is not necessarily a good index of neuropsychological aging. Furthermore, there are qualitative differences in the aged in the decades of the 60s, 70s, 80s, 90s, and older. The aged are clearly not an easily categorized, homogeneous group, and aging progresses at different rates in different brains.

Research methodology in the neuropsychology of aging has relied primarily on two designs: cross-sectional and longitudinal. By far the greatest preponderance of neuropsychological aging studies have been cross-sectional, comparing at least two age groups of participants on measures of brain and behavioral function. The differences between age groups observed by this research design may occur as a function of experience as well as a function of age. Longitudinal studies are valuable in that they assess change; however, confounds due to repeated testing, selective attrition, and changing techniques present limitations for this design.

Plasticity is an obvious feature of the brain, and it is prominent in late life even in the face of losses. Compensation and reorganization in response to trauma and cell loss are characteristic of the normal aging brain. Synaptic changes in response to the environment are a feature of the brain as long as the organism is living.

Animal models have utility in the investigation of neuropsychological aging processes, and they also have limitations. Among the advantages are the shorter life spans of animals and the possibility of invasive experimental treatments. Among the limitations of animal models is the fact that many neuropsychological aspects present in humans are not within the capacity of nonhumans.

This book is organized into three major sections. The section providing an introduction and overview orients the reader to the neuropsychology of aging and focuses on behavioral assessment and neuro-imaging. A second section covering aging and the nervous system addresses normal and patho-logical processes of aging in the nervous system. The section on a neuropsychological perspective of human behavior follows various behavioral processes and their neural substrates over the later adult years. The final chapter examines prospects for neuropsychology in the future. Taken to-gether, the overall aim of this book is to provide the reader with a perspec-tive of the theoretical, empirical, and applied neuropsychological aspects of gerontology.

Further Reading

Birren, J. E., & Warner Schaie, K. (Eds.). (1996). *Handbook of the psychology of aging* (4th ed.). San Diego, CA: Academic Press.

The rapid advances in many behavioral domains in the psychology of aging are provided here.

Parkin, A. J. (1996). *Explorations in cognitive neuropsychology*. Oxford: Blackwell Publishers.

An excellent overview of the investigation of the consequences of human brain damage.

Kolb, B. (1995). *Brain plasticity and behavior*. Mahwah, NJ: Lawrence Erlbaum Associates.

A scholarly view of the complexities of research on plasticity that is filled with neuropsychological examples using the case-study approach.

Cytowic, R. E. (1996). *The neurological side of neuropsychology*. Cambridge, MA: The MIT Press.

A useful study on the neurobiology of behavior.

Cheng, H., Cao, Y., & Olson, L. (1996). Spinal cord repair in adult paraplegic rats: Partial restoration of hind limb function. *Science, 273,* 510–513.

A study on a research breakthrough on central nervous system plasticity in adult animals.

2

Neuropsychological Assessment in Adulthood and Aging

A central operation in neuropsychology is the assessment of cognition and behavior as it is related to brain function. There are several goals of neuropsychological measurement. Whether the older adult is referred to the neuropsychologist as a patient with impairment or whether the person is recruited as part of neuropsychological research on aging, the first goal is to identify the strengths and weaknesses of the person on cognitive and behavioral measures. Neuropsychological assessment includes a battery of measures designed to evaluate capacities with diverse neurobiological substrates. If the older adult has come to the neuropsychologist as a patient, the second goal is to interpret the outcome of testing diagnostically. This means using the neuropsychological test results to identify those aspects of cognition and their supporting brain regions that may be impaired. A third goal with clinical cases is to make recommendations for treatment. Thus, some neuropsychological assessment is limited to the first goal of measuring the cognition and behavior of the older adult, whereas in the case of clinical neuropsychological assessment the additional tasks of diagnosis and treatment recommendations are carried out by the neuropsychologist. In many cases, the neuropsychologist also treats the older adult client.

Successful categorization of patients into diagnostic criteria is frequently quantified using the terms *sensitivity* and *specificity*. The sensitivity of a test is its success rate in correctly assigning patients into their diagnostic criteria. For example, we used an experimental test on 20 patients diagnosed with probable Alzheimer's disease (AD) and picked a criterion for cutoff for AD. In our initial study, 19 of the 20 probable AD patients fell below our cutoff, giving our test a sensitivity of 95 percent (Woodruff-Pak et al., 1990). The specificity of a test is its success rate in correctly assigning normals to the normal category. With our test, 13 of the 20 normals fell above our cutoff, giving our test a relatively low specificity of 65 percent. Three-year longitudinal data on these participants revealed that five of the "normals" who fell below our cutoff developed dementia ($n = 4$) or died ($n = 1$; Ferrante & Woodruff-Pak, 1995). Our test was actually more sensitive to dementia than a mental status examination (the Blessed Information Memory Concentration [Blessed IMC] test discussed below).

The theory on which neuropsychological assessment is based is that cognitive and behavioral measures provide insights about neurological functions. A majority of neuropsychological tests are derived and validated using comparisons between patients with circumscribed brain lesions (lesions limited to certain regions or lobes of the brain) and control subjects matched in age, educational background, and gender. The organization of this chapter reflects the fact that neuropsychological assessment is based on brain function. Neuropsychological tests useful for the assessment of older adults are described in terms of the cortical region they assess. Initially, we will discuss special issues of testing in adulthood and aging that affect most neuropsychological testing situations, and then we will examine some neuropsychological tests useful in assessing older adults.

Problems in neuropsychological assessment of the aging

One of the major limitations of most neuropsychological tests is that they were created to assess young adults. If older adults' performance on these tests is different from the performance of young adults, it is assumed that the older adults are deficient. Any deviation from the standard derived from 20-year-olds is automatically considered abnormal. This limitation of psychological tests in gerontology first became apparent in the literature on assessment and aging with tests of intelligence.

Intelligence tests as a prototype

Intelligence tests are used by neuropsychologists to evaluate participants' general level of functioning. In the manner that we have defined neuropsychological assessment – as a measure of cognition and behavior in relation to brain function – global intelligence measures do not qualify as neuropsychological tests. IQ is not a measure of any specific region or structure in the brain. Indeed, intelligence tests were not developed to assess behavioral capacity as a function of the brain. The IQ test was created to predict a child's success in school. As such, intelligence tests are quite irrelevant for the assessment of older adults. For decades researchers assessing intelligence in older adults have questioned the utility of considering older adults impaired when they deviate from patterns observed in children and young adults (e.g., Baltes, 1993; Baltes et al., 1984; Birren, 1959; Kuhlen, 1940; Labouvie-Vief, 1985; Marsiske et al., 1995; Schaie, 1978; Woodruff-Pak, 1989).

Contemporary gerontologists have re-examined the psychometric approach in an attempt to determine what are the most appropriate tests of intellect in later life. The ecological validity of traditional intelligence tests was questioned in the case of the aged (Schaie, 1978). In this regard, Sternberg's (1985) triarchic theory of intellectual development is relevant. One of the three components of the triarchic theory is the context in which intelligence is expressed. Different contexts foster the expression of different abilities. Hence, what intelligence tests measure may not relate to the context of older adults' lives. Berg and Sternberg (1985) examined applications of the triarchic theory to adulthood and aging and emphasized the role of intelligence in successful adaptation to the environment. Since the contextual aspect of the three-part theory highlights differences in the environment for different age groups, the resulting implication is that different measures of intellectual competence should be used for older adults.

The capacity for continued improvement in intellectual ability is an underlying assumption of many gerontologists (Cerella et al., 1994; Dixon & Backman, 1995). Characteristic of this perspective is the notion that intelligence is dynamic over the adult years and that certain abilities change and even improve with age. This perspective is relatively absent in the neuropsychology of aging, which is tied more closely with the medical model of aging with its focus on decline. Brain changes with aging are viewed as unidirectional and negative.

There are no intelligence tests specifically designed for older adults. Beginning with the assumption that intelligence develops during the adult years, one of the tasks of researchers is to begin somewhat in the manner of Piaget to observe carefully the behavior of older problem solvers to discover what is unique about their approach. A complementary approach would be to use Sternberg's (1985) componential analysis to identify the information processing strategies used by adults in middle age and later life. This approach is exemplified in the work of Salthouse (1984), who has analyzed behavioral components in task performance of younger and older typists which explain their expert performance. The important point is to develop theory and methods which are based on observations of older adults.

Practical problems

Apart from general issues of theory of test construction, there are specific and practical problems for research and clinical neuropsychologists when they administer tests to older adults. The following seven problems are common limitations experienced in neuropsychological assessment of older adults. In some cases, progress is underway to alleviate the problems. However, these problems are contemporary limitations encountered when making neuropsychological evaluations of the elderly.

Norms for the old-old. Very few neuropsychological tests have norms for older adults. When norms are available, they may extend only to the age of 75. As discussed in chapter 1, those over the age of 85 make up the most rapidly growing segment of the population in many developed countries. It is these elderly adults that are often the most in need of neuropsychological evaluation. At present, there are 3.3 million people in the United States aged 85 or older. It is likely that a number of these individuals will require evaluation by a neuropsychologist. Yet it is extremely difficult to evaluate their performance because there is no context available in which to place an 85-year-old's cognitive and behavioral profile.

A concrete example of this problem is illustrative of the dilemma facing neuropsychologists. The norms published with the revised Wechsler Memory Scale (WMS-R), the most widely used neuropsychological test of memory in adults, extend only to the age of 74. WMS-R norms available for individuals aged 80 and older and published separately (Spreen & Strauss, 1991) are available for some subtests (e.g., Personal and Current Information, Orientation, Mental Control, Memory Span, Logical Memory, Visual Reproduction) but not for others (e.g., Paired Associates Visual, Paired Associates Verbal). Consider a client aged 89 years who is tested on the WMS-R subtests of Visual and Verbal Paired Associates. She achieves a score of 4, but the norms for individuals aged 70+ indicate that 8.77 is the normal mean with a standard deviation of 1.01. The client is clearly below the normal range for people aged 70 and older, but is her performance deficient considering that she is almost 90 years old? On the basis of that test, one simply would not be able to determine if she was failing or normal. Unfortunately, even if her performance on an entire neuropsychological battery were tested, there would be little context in which to evaluate her cognitive and neurological status.

Tremendous individual variation. As emphasized in chapter 1, the aged are not a homogeneous group. Individual differences increase dramatically with age. This means that the variability on neuropsychological test performance is greater in older adults than it is in young or middle-aged adults. This can also mean that there is a wider range in older adulthood of what is normal than at other points in the life span.

There are ceiling effects on some tests that blur the distinction between normal aging and early dementia. The Alzheimer's Disease Assessment Scale (ADAS) was designed to detect AD (Rosen et al., 1984). It has proved to be more sensitive to AD-related changes than a variety of mental status tests including the Blessed IMC (Christensen et al., 1991). However, there is a "ceiling effect" on the ADAS for very early AD patients who make only a few errors on this test (Zec et al., 1994). Stern et al. (1994) reported that very mild AD patients with low error scores display only a very modest decline on the total ADAS score over a period of 24 months. To enhance the ability of the ADAS to detect early AD, seven additional subtests and two modifications were made to create the extended ADAS (Zec et al., 1994). Error score is increased from 70 to 170, and the subtests enhanced the ability of the test to measure cognitive deficits in early AD patients.

Neuropsychologists are often called upon to test older adults who are severely demented. The problem with variability that extends into the demented range is that the neuropsychological tests do not have floors low enough to measure differences. For example, the Blessed IMC test (Blessed, et al., 1968) is a brief cognitive test that screens for dementia. One way to score this test is to count the number of errors made by the respondent, and 33 is the highest score indicating the greatest degree of dementia. However, one demented patient might be profoundly demented far beyond what a score of 33 indicates. Another demented patient might be just at the 33 score level. Although they score the same, the potential for remediation in the second patient might be greater than the potential in the first patient. Tests with "deeper" floors would detect these differences.

As treatments increasingly become available for cognition-impairing diseases such as AD, it becomes important to be able to detect cognitive changes in dementia. At present, it is most difficult to assess variation within the demented range. Most neuropsychological tests are not sensitive several standard deviations below the norm.

Test anxiety and discomfort in the testing situation.   Contemporary older adults grew up in the first half of the twentieth century in a period in which attitudes toward psychological abnormalities were less understanding than they are at present. Having values that revile emotional and cognitive dysfunction, older adults are reluctant to consider that they themselves might have such problems. For example, many older adults consult their physician about physical symptoms when they are, in fact, depressed. They have substituted somatic complaints for emotional ones. When they are referred to a neuropsychologist for evaluation, they are uncomfortable and anxious.

Researchers at Duke University actually quantified this test-taking anxiety as an unexpected incidental observation in an investigation of learning and arousal (Larry W. Thompson, personal communication). As part of an experiment to assess relations between learning and arousal level, lipid mobilization (a biochemical measure related to sympathetic nervous system function and arousal) was measured. Blood levels were sampled throughout the learning procedure which meant that a catheter had to be inserted into a vein in the arm of participants. Another sympathetic nervous system measure, galvanic skin response (GSR), was also assessed throughout the experiment, and the GSR electrodes were attached before the experimental procedure was described to the young and older adult participants. The experimenters were surprised to observe that when they told the older participants that they would have to learn and remember some words, GSR measures showed that the older adults were anxious. However, when the experimenters mentioned that a catheter would be inserted into a vein in the arm to take blood samples, the older adults were relatively relaxed. Young adults had the opposite reaction: they had no GSR response to the information that a learning and memory test would ensue, but they had a strong GSR response (indicating their anxiety) when told that a catheter would be inserted to take blood samples.

Many older adults become anxious when they feel that their mental capacities are going to be tested. This anxiety may arise from a concern that mental capacities decline with age. Some older adults become anxious because they feel that the evaluation will reveal their inadequacies. Of course, it is often the excessive anxiety rather than any age-related problem that contributes to impaired test performance. Thus, it is important for neuropsychologists to be aware of the tendency of older adults to suffer from test anxiety. For accurate evaluation, discomfort and anxiety must be reduced to a minimum.

Excessive test difficulty. Because some neuropsychological tests are simply too difficult for elderly adults, tests typically included in neuropsychological batteries for younger adults are not administered in batteries for older adults. An example of a classical test given to young adults that is excluded or modified significantly for elderly adults is the Wisconsin Card Sorting Task (WCST), a measure of executive or frontal lobe function. An excellent test of learning and memory, the California Verbal Learning Test (CVLT) is another test that is modified or omitted from batteries testing elderly adults.

When neuropsychologists evaluate participants, it is essential to maintain rapport. Participants are often reluctant to subject themselves to evaluation, and they become distressed when they perceive that they perform poorly or fail. Tests that challenge the participant beyond his or her capacity can cause embarrassment and even refusal to continue. Executive function and learning and memory are behaviors that are affected by processes of aging. Tests such as the WCST and CVLT that are designed to assess optimal executive and memory function in young adults frequently cause distress and failure in older participants. Less challenging tests of executive function (e.g., Trail Making Test) and memory (e.g., Logical Memory subtest of the WMS-R) are substituted and provide valid assessments of these functions without being too difficult for the elderly participant.

Decreased stamina. The classical neuropsychological test batteries, the Halstead–Reitan Neuropsychological Battery and the Luria–Nebraska Neuropsychological Battery are extremely lengthy tests. In older adults, even the shorter Luria–Nebraska battery takes 3 hr to administer, and the Halstead–Reitan battery takes 5–8 hr in young adults. Neuropsychologists use subtests from these batteries to evaluate older adults, but the full batteries are excessively long for the elderly. Test fatigue occurs sooner in older participants. Because of decreased stamina, a battery that takes approximately 1 hr 30 min is considered appropriate for older clients. Another alternative, if more extensive testing is deemed desirable, is to ask the client to return for several sessions scheduled within the same week.

Sensory and motor deficits. Over the adult years there are quite evident changes that occur in the ability to sense and perceive the world. Age changes occur in all of the sensory modalities, but the most apparent changes are manifest in vision and hearing. It is more or less an expected landmark that reading glasses or bifocals are required in the mid-40s. The use of hearing aids is less universal, but quite common after the 60th birthday. Thus, some of the major and general changes in the sensory systems with aging are familiar to laypeople as well as to gerontologists.

Hearing acuity is affected in most older adults, and visual acuity is affected by aging as well. For neuropsychology, this means that test stimuli must be designed to be appropriate for the elderly. The examiner needs to consult with the client to ensure that the instructions are heard and understood. Practice tests are desirable so that the neuropsychologist can be sure that the older adult understands how to perform the test. Printed material must use enlarged letters to ensure legibility. Tests that require drawings need to be evaluated within the context that the hands may be arthritic or that tremor may impair the drawing.

Inappropriate or irrelevant tests. This issue was addressed at the beginning of this chapter in our discussion on intelligence testing. From the domain of intelligence testing, it has been learned that tests are more useful when they assess capacities that are utilized at present. The daily activities of older adults who are typically retired and engaged in leisurely pastimes are not likely to involve performance of skills tested on intelligence tests. To motivate the older adult and ensure optimal performance, the test must engage him or her.

Selected neuropsychological tests

Mental status

To evaluate whether an older adult is cognitively intact, mental status examinations are used. These tests have in common with intelligence tests the fact that they assess a variety of mental abilities. As such, mental status tests do not focus on any one part of the brain but rather contain assessments of many different cortical areas. Typically, mental status examinations are brief screening devices taking 10 min or less to complete. In a short period of time, these tests provide information about whether the participant has normal cognitive ability or whether he or she is mildly, moderately, or severely demented.

The Mini-Mental State Exam (MMSE; Folstein et al., 1975) provides gross estimates of cognitive function and is the most widely used mental status examination for older adults. Scores range from 0 to 30, with points subtracted for each error. Thus, the highest score is 30, and scores in the range of 27–30 are considered normal. Hospitalized patients ($n = 206$) with a number of diagnoses, including dementia as well as normal adults ($n = 63$) were used for test standardization. When the test was standardized, the mean score for normal adult participants was 27.6 (range = 24–30), whereas the mean score for patients with dementia was 9.6 (range = 0–22). These results led the test designers to use scores of 22 and below as suggestive of dementia.

The MMSE consists of ten questions assessing orientation. There are three words used to measure immediate and delayed recall, and there are measures of attention, calculation, simple language ability, and visuographic skills. Because the item measuring visuographic skills involves drawing, it is problematic for older adults with severe arthritis or with hand tremor.

Wide usage of the MMSE has led to the recognition that some aspects of the interpretation of results are problematic. In a general adult population (including adults of all ages), the test has adequate reliability (scores obtained are consistent and repeatable) and specificity (normals consistently score in the 27–30 range or at least 23 and above in the case of older adults; Roca, 1987). However, older and poorly educated individuals often score below the cut-off of 23. Almost 21 percent of older, community-residing adults scored 23 or below in a large epidemiological study, and in a third of these low-scoring participants there was no sign of neurological or psychiatric disorder (Folstein et al., 1985).

The Blessed Information Memory Concentration (Blessed IMC) test is a brief cognitive screening technique for dementia. It examines the orientation, remote memory, recent memory, and concentration of the subject. The scoring for this test involves counting the total number of errors among a possible 33 points. A score of zero indicates full cognitive capacity. A score of 7–12 on this measure indicates mild dementia. This measure correlated highly with the number of senile plaques and neurofibrillary tangles seen at autopsy in a sample of elderly subjects that included individuals diagnosed with AD (Blessed et al., 1968).

Although the MMSE and the Blessed IMC have utility as an initial screening, it is clear that these instruments are inadequate for diagnosing brain impairment. Rather, they should be viewed as a first step in neuropsychological assessment. Particularly if the neuropsychologist is planning to administer a battery of measures, brief screening devices used at the beginning of the session can orient the tester to the functioning level of the client. In this manner, tests can subsequently be selected on the basis of the individual's ability that neither overly tax nor underrate cognitive capacity.

Attention

The part of the brain essential for attention is the frontal lobes. Subcortical structures included in the ascending reticular arousal system also participate in the multidimensional capacity called attention. There are a number of components of attention, some of which are confounded with memory and executive function measures, that make attention a complicated aspect of cognition to assess. Pure measurement of attention is relatively difficult to achieve, even in an experimental laboratory setting. In the clinic, it is almost impossible to adequately assess attention.

Among the components of attention are: concentration, search, divided attention, selective attention, attention switching, and vigilance (Stankov, 1988). Concentration involves the ability to sustain attention over a period of time. It includes the ability to focus and ignore stimuli other than the ones relevant to the problem. Search includes the ability to locate certain signals in an array of many signals. Finding hidden figures within an array of lines is an example of this attention feature. Divided attention is the ability to carry out two or more tasks at the same time. Reading the newspaper while watching television is one example of divided attention. Selective attention is the ability to focus on one aspect and screen out other potentially interfering information. Conversing intently with one person in a crowded room filled with others talking exemplifies selective attention. Attention switching or flexibility is the ability to think fluidly and change attention from one aspect of the stimuli to other aspects. The Stroop Color-Word test (Golden, 1978;

Stroop, 1935) requires participants to work with stimuli that are color words (e.g., red, green, blue) that are printed in ink that is different from the color of the word (e.g., "red" written in green ink). The task involves alternation between *reading* the words and *saying the color* of the ink for the words. This is an example of attention switching. Vigilance is the ability to detect rarely occurring signals in an array over a long period of time. Air traffic controllers' jobs involve vigilance; they must identify and attend to certain blips on their radar screen over long time-periods.

Clinical tests of attention are not well developed, and consequently this aspect of cognition that shows significant age-related changes is evaluated by neuropsychologists in a superficial way (La Rue, 1992). Rather than using formal assessment procedures, examiners frequently rely on subjective impressions of the patient's ability to direct and sustain attention. Also, clinicians frequently intervene to redirect attention rather than assessing the deficit. Procedures that are used are not "pure" measures of attention. They are confounded with other cognitive processes. For example, the revised Wechsler Adult Intelligence Scale (WAIS-R) Digit Span subtest is often used to assess attention, but this measure confounds attention and primary memory. Furthermore, repeating strings of digits is a highly practiced skill that remains constant over most of the adult life span (e.g., Schaie, 1990). Thus, this test is relatively insensitive to mild impairment.

Other commonly used clinical tests of attention include the Mental Control subtest of the Wechsler Memory Scale (WMS) or revised WMS (WMS-R). This test involves counting backward from 20, reciting the alphabet, and counting forward by threes. It has many of the same limitations as the Digit Span subtest, along with the additional limitation that calculation skills are confounded with this measure of attention. Table 2.1 identifies additional clinical tests of attention, along with La Rue's (1992) critique of them.

Visuospatial ability

The ability to draw from a model or from memory, the ability to make patterns with objects such as blocks, the ability to reason about spatial relations among objects, and the ability to read and follow maps are all components of visuospatial ability. Visuospatial ability is associated with the parietal lobe, in particular the right parietal lobe. Adults with lesions in the right parietal lobe show significant impairment on visuospatial tasks (Coslett & Saffran, 1992). Inasmuch as attention and vision are involved in visuospatial ability, the frontal and occipital lobes are also engaged. Deficits in visuospatial ability associated with normal aging are relatively large.

The Boston Diagnostic Aphasia Examination (Goodglass & Kaplan, 1972) contains a series of brief tests that identify impairment when the parietal lobes

Table 2.1 Clinical neuropsychological tests for assessment of attention[a]

Measure	Description	Comments
Digit Span (WAIS or WAIS–R)[b]	Repetition of strings of numbers, forward and backward.	*Pros:* Brief; age norms available. *Cons:* Insensitive to mild impairment; confounds attention and primary memory.
Mental Control (WMS or WMS–R)[c]	Counting backwards from 20, reciting alphabet, counting forward by 3's.	*Pros:* Brief; age norms available. *Cons:* Same as for Digit Span; also requires skill in calculation.
Attention/Concentration Index (WMS–R)	Combination of Digit Span, Mental Control, and Visual Memory Span (repetition of block-tapping sequences).	*Pros:* Measures both verbal and nonverbal attention; age norms available. *Cons:* Same as for Mental Control; also requires intact visual perception.
Digit or Letter Cancellation[d]	Crossing off of specified digits or letters on printed pages; number of targets and total response time varies for different versions.	*Pros:* Provides a clinical index of vigilance; easy and difficult versions available. *Cons:* Age norms limited; requires intact visual perception.
The "A" Test[e]	Patient indicates each occurrence of a specified letter in a random series of spoken letters.	*Pros:* Oral analogue of digit cancellation. *Cons:* Age norms limited; lack of standardization.

[a] See text for additional references.
[b] Wechsler (1955, 1981).
[c] Wechsler (1945, 1987).
[d] Lezak (1983); Moran & Mefferd (1959); Ruff, Evans, & Light (1986).
[e] Strub and Black (1977).

are damaged. Most of these tests assess visuospatial functions: drawing certain simple figures when asked to do so, copying simple 2- and 3-dimensional figures, constructing designs from blocks and sticks, identifying and naming one's fingers, pointing to the left or right, showing a location on a map, drawing clock settings.

In particular, clock drawing has been identified as a task useful in differentiating normal aging from dementia (Tuokko et al., 1992; Wolf-Klein et al., 1989). There are three basic components to the Clock Test, and any one may be administered without the other two (Watson et al., 1993). Part 1 involves drawing a clock. The participant is either given paper with a pre-drawn circle or given a blank sheet of paper. Part 2 entails drawing the hands on a clock that is printed on the paper. The participant is asked to draw the hands at a specified setting, for example, 20 minutes to 8. Part 3 requires the subject to tell the time from a completely printed clock that has marks at the number locations but has no numbers. In 312 geriatric patients administered the Clock Test, the sensitivity for AD was 87 percent and the specificity was 97 percent. Comparable sensitivity and specificity for the Clock Test were reported for a completely different sample of normal older adults and demented patients (Tuokko et al., 1992). Figure 2.1 shows some clock drawings by older adults.

Other tests that have been used widely for the assessment of visuospatial function in aging are Performance subtests of the WAIS or WAIS-R and, in particular, the Block Design subtest. La Rue (1992) pointed out that the Block Design subtest is one of the most informative Performance subtests for neuropsychologists because it examines both visuoperceptual and visuoconstructive ability. To perform well, the older participant must adapt to the novelty of the task, organize a series of responses, and perform self-monitoring of each step to ensure accuracy. The Block Design subtest of the WAIS has been identified as an "age-sensitive" test (Botwinick, 1984). That is, this test shows rather dramatic age-related impairment.

Learning and memory

Previously in this chapter we pointed out that tests of learning and memory challenge older adults and cause them emotional distress. They become anxious just at the suggestion that their learning and memory abilities are going to be tested. Older adults perceive that their ability to learn and remember is not what it once was. An important role for the neuro-psychologist in administering these tests is to make the participant comfortable and alleviate stress.

It would be inaccurate to present older adults as always insecure about their learning and memory skills. Research on metamemory has indicated

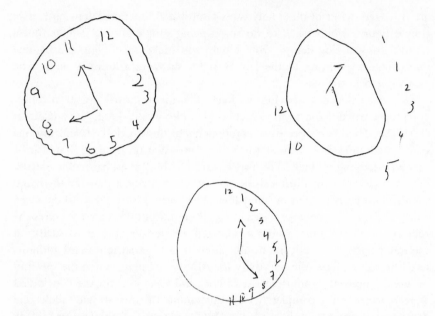

Figure 2.1 Example of the way older adults draw when asked to draw a clock and then place the hand at 5 minutes before 8. The clock on the top left is characteristic of an elderly adult with Parkinson's disease and no dementia. Although the drawing is impaired due to some hand tremor, it is essentially correct. The clock on the top right is like a drawing of an older adult severely demented with Alzheimer's disease. Numbers are placed outside the clock face, and the hands do not point to any time. The clock on the bottom is characteristic of an older adult who had a stroke affecting a large portion of the right parietal lobe. The left half of space is ignored

that older adults sometimes overestimate their skills. Murphy et al. (1981) gave young and older adults a memory task, but the investigators also gave participants as much time as they wanted to study and rehearse the lists. Older participants spent considerably less time studying the series of items than did young participants, and older participants' performance was much worse. The older adults apparently underestimated the time needed to study and learn the lists, and they overestimated their own competence.

A widely used test that provides assessment of learning as well as memory is the California Verbal Learning Test (CVLT; Delis et al., 1983). Although this is an excellent measure and is effective with community-residing healthy older adults (e.g., Woodruff-Pak & Finkbiner, 1995), the 16-word lists are too long for elderly residents of nursing homes. One modification of the test is to reduce the number of words on the list to eight or ten.

The CVLT is an orally administered test of verbal learning and memory.

Test stimuli comprise two word lists: a test list and an interference list. One valuable feature of the CVLT is its relevance to everyday life. Subjects are informed that they will be playing a memory "game" for which they will attempt to learn and remember a series of everyday shopping items. The experimenter then reads the 16-word list at a rate of about one word per second. Prior to the second trial, the experimenter gives these instructions: "I'm going to repeat the Monday shopping list in exactly the same order as before. I'll ask you again to repeat all the items in any order, and be sure to include the items that you have already told me."

After the final immediate recall trial (i.e., trial 5), the experimenter asks the subject to suppose that this time they are going shopping on a Tuesday. The instructions for Tuesday's list presentation and recall are identical to those above. There is no mention that the Tuesday (interference) list is presented only once. Immediately following free recall of the Tuesday list, 2-min free recall is measured by asking subjects to recall as many of the Monday items as they can. Cued recall is then measured by providing the four taxonomic categories (e.g., fruits) as cues for the Monday list. Next, subjects are involved in unrelated tasks for about 30 min, after which free and cued recall are measured using the same procedures as described above.

In our assessment of the CVLT in 40 young adult (age range = 17–29 years) and 40 older adult (age range = 63–80 years) community-residing participants, free recall was poorer for older adults at all retention intervals tested (immediate, 2-min, 35-min, 24-hr; Woodruff-Pak & Finkbiner, 1995). Even immediate recall testing after learning showed age effects. The largest decline for older as well as younger subjects occurred in the interval between immediate- and 2-min recall. Older adults showed a more rapid loss of recall ability when compared to younger adults. Age differences in recall performance were paralleled in recognition measures of memory.

Perhaps the most appropriate learning and memory test for older adults is the Logical Memory subtest of the WMS. In this test, two stories are presented orally and immediate recall is tested. On the WMS-R, delayed recall (after 30 min) of the story is also tested. A major advantage of this test is that old age norms are available. The test is problematic for clinical application with some subjects because very elderly and poorly educated participants score so poorly.

Paired Associate Learning subtests (Visual and Verbal) of the WMS are other commonly used memory tests for older adults. For the Visual Paired Associates subtest, cards with line drawings are shown one by one, and each is paired with a color. The drawings are shown a minimum of three times. The subject's task is to say the correct color when the line drawing is presented. Recall is tested immediately after learning, and 30 min later. For the Verbal Paired Associates subtest, the procedure is similar except that eight

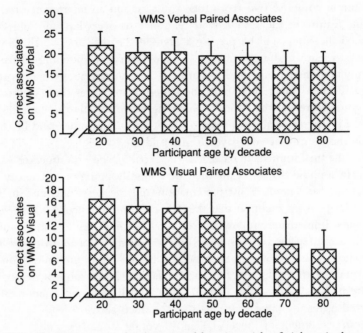

Figure 2.2 Top: Mean score for three initial learning trials of eight paired associates (total possible score of 24) on the Wechsler Memory Scale (WMS) Verbal Paired Associates for 160 participants in the decades of the 20s through the 80s. Error bars are standard deviation. *Bottom*: Mean score for three initial learning trials of six paired associates (total possible score of 18) on the Wechsler Memory Scale (WMS) Visual Paired Associates for 160 participants in the decades of the 20s through the 80s. Error bars are standard deviation. (Data collected by D. S. Woodruff Pak)

word-pairs are presented. Some of the pairs are easy to associate, and some are difficult. In this manner, errors are informative. The tests have norms available for old age, but the difficult pairs are seldom learned by elderly and poorly educated participants.

The WMS Visual and Verbal Paired Associate tests were among the assessments made on 200 participants ranging in age from 20 to 89 (see figure 2.2). On both of these subtests there were significant age effects beginning in the decade of the 60s. That is, adults aged 60–89 performed significantly worse than adults aged 20–39, but the performance differences between adults in the age range of 40–59 years and younger adults did not attain significance (Woodruff-Pak & Jaeger, 1997). Similar age–functional relationships are presented in Spreen and Strauss (1991), with relative stability through the decade of the 50s.

Intelligence

Earlier in this chapter, we used intelligence testing as a prototype of what can go wrong with assessment of the elderly. Here we will cover intelligence only briefly.

With all of its faults and in the absence of ties between its subtests and brain function, the WAIS or WAIS-R is the most widely used assessment of older adults. Clinicians favor this test because so much data have been collected with it. Scores on the WAIS can put the patient into perspective, in the mind of the neuropsychologist. Often the full test is not given, but subscales are administered to assess specific abilities.

An alternative to administering the entire WAIS or its subscales is to measure IQ using a short intelligence test. It is very useful when screening older adults for participation in research, as well as for obtaining an initial perspective during the clinical neuropsychological interview, to assess intelligence quickly. One such test that is easy and pleasant to use with older adults is the Ammons Quick Test (QT; Ammons & Ammons, 1962). The QT is an orally administered picture vocabulary test and takes only 5 min to administer. The test provides tables for converting QT scores to Wechsler verbal IQ equivalents.

Language and communication

Although it is probably an oversimplification, it has been suggested that hearing loss may be the sole mediating factor in age differences in comprehension of language (Sheridan, 1976). Slowing of response speed with age may also contribute to older adults' performance in language comprehension, as increasing speech rate decreases comprehension in the elderly (Konkle et al., 1977; Peach, 1987). Nevertheless, some measures of language function are the best preserved of functions.

Vocabulary remains stable over the life span or increases (Schaie, 1994). It is in the decade of the 70s that vocabulary may begin to show some age-related impairment (e.g., Balota & Ferraro, 1993). The shift from well-preserved functioning to significant decrement is so apparent that the years between ages 65 and 74 have been called "watershed for decremental changes" (Giambra et al., 1995). The brain site implicated in these changes is the posterior superior temporal lobe in the region of Wernicke's area. Figure 2.3 illustrates the human cerebral cortex showing Wernicke's area.

In general, language functions are well preserved in old age and neuropsychological evaluations for older adults may limit the number of assessments in this area to save time for assessment of functions that are more

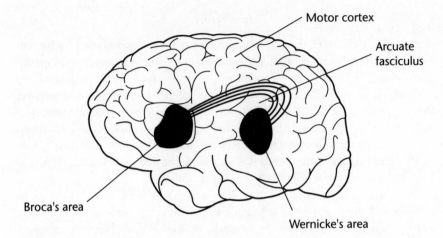

Figure 2.3 Drawing of left cerebral hemisphere showing major landmarks, including Wernicke's area involved in comprehension of speech

impaired. Tests of naming and verbal fluency may be all that are necessary to administer. The Boston Diagnostic Aphasia Examination (Goodglass & Kaplan, 1972) is the assessment most commonly used when more complete language assessment is required.

Planning and executive function

The assessment of frontal lobe function, the brain area possibly most impaired in normal aging, is problematic because the measures are so difficult for older adults. The Wisconsin Card Sorting Task is the test most associated with frontal lobe assessment, but many geroneuropsychologists eliminate this test from their battery because it causes too much failure for their clients.

The Trail Making Test is a brief test of sequencing and shifting between sequences. There are some age norms available, and the advantage of this test is that it is not overly stressful for elderly adults. Among its limitations are that it confounds cognitive flexibility with scanning and motor speed (La Rue, 1992). On the first part of the test (Form A), participants must draw a line connecting a series of numbers that are scattered out of sequence all over the page. The numbers must be connected in sequence. The second part of the test (Form B) involves drawing a line connecting numbers and letters. This is a more difficult task as the subject must alternate between numbers and letters. It is challenging to keep track of the last number or letter while searching and connecting in alternation.

Another aspect of frontal lobe function is divergent thinking. The ability to generate ideas, categories, words, and so forth relies on intact frontal lobes. Word fluency is a typical measure of this aspect of frontal lobe function. The client is asked to write as many words as possible in a 5-min period starting with a given letter (e.g., "b"). After completing that task, some constraints might be added by asking the client to write as many four-letter words as possible starting with a different letter (e.g., "t"). As shown in figure 2.4, a normal young-old adult is fluent in word generation even though he is

b	t	B (5 min)			T (4 min)	
baby	tape	Bank	bicker	belatedly	tank	ties
book	tar	Band	bread	bicycle	tent	task
body	tin	Bag	broad	biker	this	tame
bad	tear	Bed	back	basket	that	
boots	take	Bath	bat	base	thus	
bird	tie	Bad	batter	back	then	
beauty	thimble	Bud	~~brick~~	battle	tand	
big		Beg	blind	bait	thin	
by		Bin	blank	blank	tint	
bottle		Bat	banter	boss	talk	
		Back	bird	bustle	tell	
		Bet	bend	busy	toll	
		Biscuit	bang	bleed	tous	
		Brick	boy	brood	tall	
		breath	boast	blood	tale	
		Brink	bet		take	
		~~band~~	beset		took	
		Black	besiege			

Figure 2.4 Word fluency as an assessment of integrity of the frontal lobes. Clients were asked to write as many words as possible that begin with the letter b, and they were allowed to generate words for 5 min. Next they were asked to write as many four-letter words as possible that begin with the letter t. They had 4 min for this task. At the left are the words as they would be produced by an older woman in the early stages of Alzheimer's disease. She generated a limited number of words and could not constrain herself to four-letter words in the second condition. On the right are the words produced by a normal 63-year-old man who generated a large number of English words in both conditions, even though he is fluent in four languages

multilingual, but an elderly client in the early stages of Alzheimer's disease had a much more limited production of words.

Depression

The reason that it is extremely important to assess depression during a neuropsychological examination is that depression can impair cognition. This issue is discussed in detail in chapter 7 on emotion, aging, and brain function. Scales that are sensitive to degrees of depression in depressed elderly patients are inappropriate to administer to healthy adults. Conversely, those scales appropriate to identify depression in a healthy population do not detect subtleties important for clinical assessment.

The Center for Epidemiologic Studies–Depression scale (CES–D; Radloff, 1977) is a self-report measure of depressive symptomatology appropriate for the general population. Over 70 percent of depressed patients score above 16 points on the scale, whereas only 21 percent of the general population score in the same range.

The structured interview technique provided by the Schedule for Affective Disorders and Schizophrenia (SADS) appears to be one example of a reliable assessment tool for depression in the elderly. An observer rating scale (23 items) which has been used in a number of studies involving older patients is the Hamilton Psychiatric Rating Scale (Hamilton, 1967). This scale is useful for patients who deny or lack awareness of depression, but scores are often inflated for older patients because of the inclusion of somatic items.

A sample neuropsychological test battery suited to older adults

When administering a neuropsychological test battery, it is important for the neuropsychologist to remain flexible and receptive to altering the tests administered as the session progresses. For example, we mentioned that most neuropsychological assessments for older adults include limited assessment of language. If, however, the client has difficulty at naming items shown in pictures (naming or confrontation naming task), additional aphasia tests are warranted. The neuropsychologist is required to follow leads provided by the assessment session.

One of the first things essential in neuropsychological assessment of older adults is the establishment of rapport. Most neuropsychologists develop rapport by asking the client about his or her life at the beginning of the session. History-taking is a critical and central feature of neuropsychological assessment. By interacting with the client and taking a history, the neuro-psychologist is provided with many insights about the client's cognitive capacity. It is essential to establish whether the client has suffered from traumatic injury to the head, has experienced seizures, has been alcoholic, is taking medications affecting cognition, or has other conditions that may affect test performance. Simple questions such as "Have you ever had an EEG taken or a brain scan?" can elicit information critical to the evaluation. During this initial interaction which can last 30 min, the neuropsychologist may also revise the initial plan of assessment to better evaluate the capacities and deficits of this particular participant.

The battery shown in table 2.2 is provided as a guideline for an assessment that might take about 90 min to carry out after the history of the client has been taken. By no means is this particular battery presented as a mandated protocol. It is simply a set of measures relatively appropriate for older adults that cover a number of neuropsychological domains. One of the most valuable attributes of a clinical neuropsychologist assessing older clients is flexibility and an ability to adapt and restructure the assessment configuration based on the client's history.

Summary

Assessment of cognition and behavior as it is related to brain function is a central feature of neuropsychology. The goals of neuropsychological assessment using measures of diverse abilities include: identification of the client's cognitive and behavioral strengths and weaknesses; interpretation of the outcome of testing diagnostically; recommendation of treatment strategies. Neuropsychological research is limited to the first goal of measuring the cognition and behavior of the older adult, whereas in the case of clinical neuropsychological assessment the additional tasks of diagnosis and treatment recommendations are carried out.

When dealing with older adult clients, there are special issues that affect most neuropsychological testing situations. One of the major limitations of most neuropsychological tests is that they were created to assess young adults. When older adults perform in a different fashion, it is called decline. In addition to inappropriate assumptions about aging and abilities, there are at least seven of the following practical problems encountered when assessing older adults.

1 Very few neuropsychological tests have norms for the elderly. When norms are available, they extend only to the age of 75, but adults over the age of 85 are in the most rapidly growing segment of the population in many countries.

Table 2.2 Brief battery for neuropsychological assessment of older adults

Recommended tests	Functions evaluated	Findings that raise a question of impairment
Mini-Mental State Examination	Cognitive mental status	Scores ≤23[a]
WAIS or WAIS-R Vocabulary	Verbal intelligence; semantic memory	Perseveration, paraphasia, marked circumlocution
Digit Span	Attention; primary memory	Forward span <5; backward span <3
Block Design	Nonverbal intelligence; visuospatial abilities; nonverbal problem solving	Stacking or stringing of blocks; grossly inaccurate designs
Digit Symbol	Speeded perceptual-motor integration; sequencing and cognitive flexibility	Inaccurate copies of symbols; inability to adhere to specified sequence
WMS or WMS-R Logical Memory	Narrative recall	Complete recall failure; confusing details from the two stories; major extrastory intrusions; marked decline on delayed recall
Visual Reproduction	Recall of designs	Complete recall failure; rotations, perseverations; gross distortions; marked decline on delayed recall
Object Memory Evaluation[b]	List learning and recall	≤7 items stored by Trial 5; ≤2 items consistently recalled per trial; multiple intrusion errors; marked decline on delayed recall
Boston Naming Test	Naming; object identification	Perseveration, paraphasia, marked circumlocution, frequent perceptual errors
Controlled Oral Word Association Test	Verbal fluency; semantic memory	Severely reduced output (≤7 items per letter); loss of set; perseveration or paraphasia
Trail Making Test	Speeded perceptual-motor integration; sequencing and cognitive flexibility	Severe slowing (>2 minutes to complete Trails A, ≥5 minutes Trails B); any error on A, multiple errors on B

[a] Adjust for age and education (see text).

[b] For high-functioning patients, substitute the Selective Reminding Test, Auditory Verbal Learning Test, or California Verbal Learning Test; for low-functioning or uncooperative patients, the Shopping List Test or Delayed Word Recall Test can be substituted.

2 Individual differences increase dramatically with age, making a wider range in older adulthood of what is normal. Ceiling and floor effects are more likely in older adult groups where the range of ability is so great.

3 Test anxiety is a problem for many older adults who feel that their mental capacities may be declining. Sometimes the excessive test anxiety rather than any age-related problem contributes to impaired test performance.

4 Some neuropsychological tests are simply too difficult for elderly adults, and the neuropsychologist must gear tests to the client's abilities.

5 Test fatigue occurs sooner in older participants. Because of decreased stamina, a shorter battery is considered appropriate for older clients. Another alternative, if more extensive testing is deemed desirable, is to ask the client to return for several sessions scheduled within the same week.

6 Sensory processes decline with age, and this means that test stimuli must be designed to be appropriate for the elderly. The examiner needs to consult with the client to ensure that the instructions are heard and understood. Practice tests are desirable so that the neuropsychologist can be sure that the older adult understands how to perform the test.

7 Tests are more useful when they assess capacities that are utilized at present. The daily activities of older adults, who are typically retired and engaged in leisurely pastimes, may not demand intense cognitive rigor. To motivate the older adult and ensure optimal performance, the test must engage him or her.

Neuropsychological assessment is based on brain function. Tests useful for the assessment of older adults are described in terms of the cortical region they assess. Selected neuropsychological tests useful in the assessment of mental status, attention, visuospatial ability, learning and memory, intelligence, language and comprehension, planning and executive function, and depression in older adults are described. Finally, history-taking and a prototypical neuropsychological assessment battery are discussed with an emphasis on flexibility on the part of the neuropsychologist in adapting the assessment to the older client.

Further Reading

LaRue, A. (1992). *Aging and neuropsychological assessment.* New York: Plenum Press.
A clinical neuropsychologist's perspective of aging including comparative evaluation of neuropsychological tests.

Spreen, O., & Strauss, E. (1991). *A compendium of neuropsychological tests: Administration, norms, and commentary.* New York: Oxford University Press.
A useful collection of neuropsychological tests including normative data on older adults for a variety of tests.

Poon, L. W. (Ed.). (1986). *Handbook for clinical memory assessment of older adults.* Washington, DC: American Psychological Association.
Reviews perspectives on memory assessment and function in older adults from a multidisciplinary perspective.

Storandt, M., & VandenBos, G. R. (Eds.). (1994). *Neuropsychological assessment of dementia and depression in older adults: A clinician's guide.* Washington, DC: American Psychological Association.
A clear and practical guide on differentiating psychological disorders from normal aging.

3

Methods for Assessing the
Aging Brain

Measures of the aging brain and nervous system can be made using a variety of techniques that assess a variety of brain activities or qualities (e.g., electrical activity, neurotransmitter function, blood flow, glucose and oxygen metabolism). The measures we utilize for evaluating the functioning human brain are most often non-invasive; that is, we make the assessments from outside the brain. Like a chest X-ray, these measures provide us with a picture of internal structures, yet no surgery has been involved. It is only with animal subjects (and occasionally with human patient populations who will have therapeutic surgery) that we use invasive techniques to measure the living, responding brain.

Categories of measures of the human brain

The earliest modern measure of the living human brain is the electro-encephalogram (EEG). This is a physiological or functional measure that assesses ongoing brain activity. It is a dynamic measure in that it can assess changes over short (minutes in the case of the waking EEG) and longer (hours in terms of the sleeping EEG) periods of time. A measure derived from the EEG is the event related potential (ERP). Both the EEG and ERPs rely on brain electrical activity as a means to assess function. Hans Berger discovered the EEG in humans early in the twentieth century (Lindsley, 1960), and this measure has had diagnostic utility for many decades. It was the first of the non-invasive brain measures to be widely used in humans. In the evaluation of sleep, the EEG is still a measure that has the greatest utility in documenting sleep stages. ERPs represent an advance over the EEG in the sense that these brain potentials can be associated with sensation, perception, and cognition.

Brain imaging with X-ray beams (computerized tomography [CT]) and magnetic fields (magnetic resonance imaging [MRI]) are techniques of the late-twentieth century that have significantly advanced diagnostic capacity for neurological disease. CT and MRI have also expanded knowledge and diagnostic precision in neuropsychology. These images of the brain are like photographs – they provide a static view of the neuroanatomy. CT scans were the first images available, and they have been in widespread use by radiologists for about two decades. MRI scans represent an advance over CT scans in that the resolution of neuronal tissue is much greater. Brain structures central to cognition such as the hippocampus can be visualized with MRI scans but not with CT scans. These techniques provide images of the brain useful in the identification of tumors, cerebrovascular trauma, neuronal degeneration, and other brain abnormalities.

Other brain imaging techniques can be compared to video images. They provide information about ongoing brain processes – about brain *function*. With these measures, ongoing behavior can be observed in relation to brain function. In this sense the newer imaging techniques are comparable to the EEG and ERPs. However, the newer techniques have advantages over the electrophysiological techniques because the brain generators of neural activity are more clearly identifiable. One relatively new imaging technique is called positron emission tomography (PET). PET scans are useful in diagnosis, but they are also of great scientific value in providing insights about brain function in relation to behavior. Often the PET scan is overlaid with an MRI of the individual so that the brain structures that are imaged can be clearly identified. The MRI technique, with its excellent resolution, has been elaborated to provide ongoing, functional records. This form of MRI is called functional MRI (fMRI). Many researchers and clinicians predict that the fMRI will eventually replace PET, primarily as a result of the superior resolution of fMRI.

Another means of assessment that has great utility in the understanding of the brain in normal and pathological aging is post-mortem examination using histology. Whereas the resolution of MRI and PET scans has been improved to encompass as small an area as a few millimeters, such resolution is not nearly fine enough to envision individual cells or to view phenomena intracellularly. It is only by examining neural tissue under a microscope that cell abnormalities can be detected. Thus, at present the positive diagnosis for Alzheimer's disease (AD) can only be carried out post-mortem. This diagnosis is made by taking brain tissue samples from a number of sites and conducting a microscopic quantitative analysis of the number of plaques and neurofibrillary tangles in the various regions (Khachaturian, 1985).

Electrophysiological measures of the aging brain

The brain is composed of billions of nerve cells called neurons. The electrical activity of hundreds of thousands of neurons can be recorded by attaching electrodes to an individual's scalp and amplifying the tiny electrical signals roughly a million times. The characteristic oscillating pattern of electrical activity recorded in this manner is the EEG, and it has been used as a clinical tool to identify abnormal brain activity and as an experimental tool to examine brain and behavior relationships. Since it is not feasible to invade the human brain with electrophysiological probes as is done in animal brains, the EEG is used to measure human brain activity. It was the first non-invasive brain measure and is still often used as a first step in the assessment of neuropathology.

There are at least four identified rhythms in the EEG. The alpha rhythm is in the 8–13 cycle per second (c.p.s.) range and is the dominant or modal brain wave frequency. Behaviorally, it is associated with a relaxed but alert state and is most prominent in the back parts of the head, especially when the eyes are closed. Beta activity is a faster rhythm, above 13 c.p.s., and is associated with an alert, thinking state of consciousness. Theta activity is in the 4–7 c.p.s. range and is associated with day-dreaming and drowsiness. Activity in the 1–3 c.p.s. range is called delta and occurs during sleep. Thus, faster brain waves are associated with alertness and arousal, while slower rhythmic patterns are related to drowsiness and sleep. Clinical uses of the EEG include the identification of tumors and areas of pathology in the brain, which manifest themselves as areas of localized slowing of EEG activity. Thus, slowing is associated with drowsiness, sleep, and brain pathology.

The dominant brain wave rhythm of young adults is 10.2–10.5 c.p.s. (Brazier & Finesinger, 1944). One of the best-documented findings in the psychophysiological literature is that this dominant brain wave rhythm slows with age (for reviews see Obrist & Busse, 1965; Woodruff, 1985). By the time an individual reaches the age of 60–65, the dominant brain wave rhythm is probably around 9 c.p.s. Although some 80-year-olds have brain wave patterns similar to those of 20-year-olds, the normal pattern in even the healthiest of aging individuals is for EEG slowing to occur with age.

Obrist et al. (1961) demonstrated that the slowing of the EEG alpha rhythm is a reliable phenomenon occurring in longitudinal as well as cross-sectional studies (see figure 3.1). Over the 10-year period of the Obrist et al. (1961) longitudinal study, two-thirds of the subjects manifested slowing of the dominant rhythm. Since this slowing has been related to pathology, the subjects may have had some kind of disease, such as cerebral arteriosclerosis, which would cause a slower metabolic rate in the brain and lead to slower

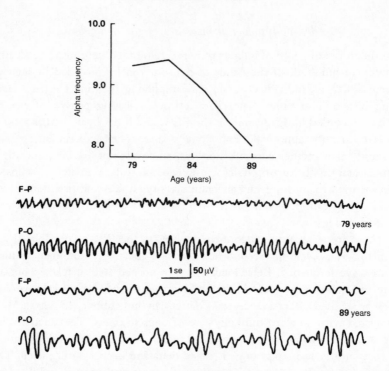

Figure 3.1 Alpha frequency plotted as a function of age for a normal older adult tested when he was 79 (*top tracing*) and 89 years old (*bottom tracing*). The bottom EEG was associated with mild signs of intellectual impairment. Electrode placements are: F-P = fronto-parietal; P-O = parieto-occipital

Source: Obrist, W. D., Henry, C. E., & Justiss, W. A. (1961). Longitudinal study of EEG in old age. *Excerpta Medical International Congress*, Serial No. 37, 180–181

brain wave rhythms. It has been demonstrated that senile patients and patients with arteriosclerosis or severe brain atrophy, have very slow brain wave rhythms. One of the studies which convincingly demonstrated that alpha slowing occurs in even the healthiest of aged individuals was reported in a book by Birren et al. (1963). An extensive study was undertaken to examine biological and behavioral changes in 47 old men chosen because they were in optimal health. Obrist examined the EEGs of these men and found that even in the healthiest aged there was a slowing of the EEG alpha rhythm to 9 c.p.s. Thus, alpha slowing is a phenomenon associated with normal aging and is not necessarily the result of disease.

The slowing of the dominant EEG rhythm is part of the legacy of descriptive studies of aging, and this finding is cited, along with numerous others, to support the biological decremental model of aging. While there are at least 20 studies documenting deleterious age changes in the EEG, the actual significance of this age-related change for behavior has not been identified. Most likely the slowing of the EEG alpha rhythm has significance for the slowing of behavior (Woodruff, 1985).

Event related potentials

Brain electrical responses to specific stimuli are usually not apparent in recordings of ongoing EEG, but by taking a number of epochs in which the same stimulus event has occurred and summing or averaging across these epochs, the activity related to the stimulus becomes apparent. The assumption is that random activity not associated with the stimulus cancels to a flat voltage pattern, while activity time-locked to the stimulus cumulates and emerges from the random background "noise" of the ongoing EEG. A number of different bioelectric signals exhibit stable temporal relationships to a definable external event, and these can be elicited in most of the sensory modalities. Most research involves auditory, visual, or somatosensory stimulation. The general term for these signals is event related potentials, and a number of categories of ERPs exist.

Brain stem auditory evoked responses. While we still do not have concrete information about the specific location of the neural generators of most of ERPs, a type of potential has been identified in the decade of the 70s which can be linked to specific generators and thus provides direct information about the intact nature of the brain pathways. This potential is the very early potential generated in peripheral sensory pathways. The visual and somatosensory pathways have been studied with this method, but the greatest amount of research and excitement has been generated in the auditory modality by potentials which have been named brain stem auditory evoked responses (BAERs). These very small (measured in tenths of millivolts) potentials provide information about hearing acuity, about the functional capacity of the auditory pathway through the brain stem, and about the speed of conduction of neural impulses through this pathway.

Anatomical mapping of the BAER waveforms in animal and human autopsy data indicates that wave I originates in the auditory nerve, wave II is from the cochlear nucleus, waves III and IV are in the pons, wave V is in the inferior colliculus, and waves VI and VII are in the thalamus and thalamic radiations, respectively. Wave V is particularly well-correlated with the intensity of the auditory signal in normal and pathological ears, and therefore it is useful diagnostically. At higher intensities the latency of wave V is shorter, and when the signal is not detected by the nervous system, the wave does not appear.

Studies of the BAER in old age suggest that wave V latency does not change dramatically in old age (Harkins & Lenhardt, 1980; Rowe, 1978). Rowe (1978) demonstrated about 0.3 ms slowing in all BAER waves when he compared 25 young (mean age 25.1 years) and 25 old (mean age 61.7 years) subjects with normal hearing. BAER data in older adults support the impression gained from other data sets in psychology and aging that at peripheral levels, the older nervous system performs about the same as the younger nervous system. It is when brain potentials are recorded from structures at higher levels of the brain that the slowing is significant.

The gerontological applications of the BAER are primarily clinical. The BAER is clearly of significance in the evaluation of hearing ability, which declines in a significant proportion of the elderly population. The BAER is particularly useful as a diagnostic tool for hearing in patients who are unable to respond. In addition to its clinical usefulness in hearing assessment, the BAER is a neurological assessment tool in that it provides a measure of the intact nature of the auditory pathway. Brain stem lesions can be detected with this painless measure, and the BAER is an improvement over the EEG in the assessment of brain death.

Sensory evoked potentials.   The most comprehensive study of sensory evoked responses has been carried out in the Salt Lake City laboratory of Dustman and Beck who, with Schenkenberg, measured auditory, visual, and somatosensory potentials in males and females over the life span (figure 3.2). This research began to appear in 1966 (Dustman & Beck, 1966), and was followed by a series of reports (Dustman & Beck, 1969; Schenkenberg, 1970; Schenkenberg, Dustman & Beck, 1971). The major change which the Salt Lake City group identified was a greater latency in the waveforms of older subjects, particularly in the later waves appearing after 100 ms. Amplitude in the later waves also decreased in old age. A change limited to the visual evoked response was an increase in amplitude in an early component. General hypotheses were advanced to explain these age changes. The slowing in the aged nervous system was associated with latency increases, and decreases in the amplitude and latency of the later components were associated with age changes in the secondary system – the ascending reticular arousal system (ARAS) – perhaps involving age changes at the synapse. To explain the increase in visual evoked response amplitude in early components, it was suggested that a decrease in inhibition was occurring.

Long latency potentials related to complex psychological variables.   The P300 wave of the ERP is prominent only when the stimulus which has elicited the ERP has some meaning or significance to the subject. A number of studies have indicated that the amplitude of the P300 component, regardless of the

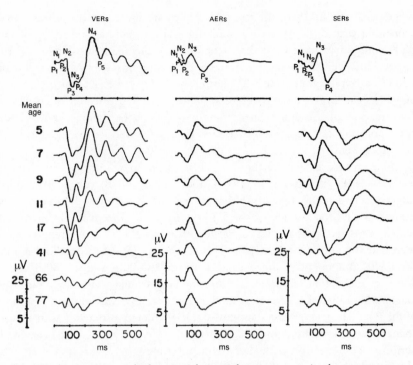

Figure 3.2 Composite evoked potentials in eight age groups in three sensory modalities: visual (visual evoked responses, VERs), auditory (auditory evoked responses, AERs), and somatosensory (somatosensory evoked responses, SERs). Evoked response plots for each age group represent a composite of 20 participants, ten male and ten female. VERs are from left occipital scalp; AERs and SERs are from left central scalp. P = positive peak; N = negative peak

Source: Dustman, R. E., Beck, E. C., & Schenkenberg, T. (1977). Life-span changes in man. In J. E. Desmedt (Ed.), *Cerebral evoked potentials in man: The Brussels International Symposium*. London: Oxford University Press. Reproduced by kind permission of Oxford University Press

stimulus modality, is inversely related to the degree to which the subject expects the stimulus to occur (e.g., Duncan-Johnson & Donchin, 1977). The factor which appears to determine the latency of the P300 component is decision time; more specifically, the time required for the subject to perceive and categorize the stimulus according to a set of rules (e.g., Kutas et al., 1977). When task difficulty is increased, subjects have prolonged processing times and longer P300 latencies. The P300 has received a singular amount of attention in research on aging (Bashore, 1993, 1994; Schroeder et al., 1991).

Comparisons of the P300 in young and old subjects have led gerontologists such as Thompson and Marsh (1973; Marsh & Thompson, 1977) to suggest that the ERPs of the two age groups are more similar during active processing than during passive stimulation. The amplitude and shape of the P300 component have been similar in many of the age comparative experiments. However, the result which has been consistent since the first report of P300 research in aging (Marsh & Thompson, 1972) is the fact that the latency of P300 is delayed in older subjects. Thus, the P300 research offers direct confirmation of the aging phenomenon to which behavioral studies have been pointing for decades. Processing time is slower in the aged central nervous system.

Using a task in which the subject is asked to count the number of occurrences of an infrequent tone, Goodin et al. (1978) tested 40 healthy subjects between the ages of 15 and 76 years. The primary finding of this study was that the latency of the P300 component systematically increased with age. Regression analysis indicated that the P300 component latency increased at a rate of 1.63 ms/year. This results in almost a 100 ms increase in the P300 component in the decades between the 20th and the 80th years. Some of the other components increased in latency with age, but the magnitude of these latency increases was not more than half of the magnitude of the P300 latency increase. Goodin et al. (1978) demonstrated that these age changes were not a function of auditory sensitivity by noting that behavioral performance (detection of higher frequency tones) was equal in young and old, all subjects reported that they could hear the tones clearly, and the N1 component which is dramatically affected by tone intensity was only different by 6 ms between the young and old subjects. Thus, ERPs provide differential information about the effects of aging and auditory acuity.

Because there have been a number of studies on P300 and aging carried out in the last two decades, it is now possible to undertake meta-analyses of these studies to evaluate the locus of behavioral slowing. Meta-analyses using P300 latency and reaction times of subjects performing the task to assess P300 have resulted in the conclusion that response-related processes show much more age-related slowing than stimulus-related processes (Bashore, 1993, 1994). That is, the central decision-making time it takes to respond is slower in older adults than is the assimilation of the stimulus information needed to make the decision. From this perspective, age-related slowing is not a global or general phenomenon affecting all processing components equally. Rather, aging has a localized effect, affecting response-related processing components more than stimulus-related processing components.

Computerized tomography

Another brain measure which has primarily clinical applications is the CT scan (figure 3.3). Just two decades ago, the assessment of patients with

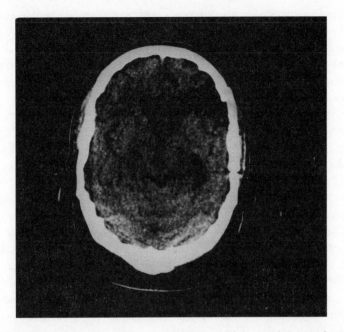

Figure 3.3 Computerized tomography (CT) scan showing horizontal view of a 62-year-old male patient who had surgical removal of a tumor in the left frontal lobe. Left side of brain is shown on CT scan as right

behavioral disorders involved indirect measures of nervous system function or dangerous invasive techniques that involved risks and potential complications to patients (e.g., angiography, pneumoencephalography). The first CT scanner was designed by G. N. Hounsfield in the 1960s who used mathematical techniques originated by A. M. Cormack. The 1979 Nobel Prize in Medicine and Physiology was awarded to Hounsfield and Cormack for this invention that revolutionized the assessment of the human brain.

The CT scan is a safe and painless procedure that provides a picture of the living brain. It is a method of visualizing cerebral structures including the ventricular system and cortical sulci. The value of this technique in neurological assessment of patients of all ages is so great and was recognized so rapidly that many hospitals throughout the country installed the relatively expensive apparatus required for this procedure, even though it became commercially available only in 1973. The CT scan has been used in most hospitals in the United States to assess geriatric patients showing symptoms of cerebral impairment.

The CT scan involves a rotating X-ray source that takes tens of thousands of readings in a few minutes. This usually consists of a scan that has viewed two contiguous slices of brain tissue in a transaxial plane at the selected level of the brain. The entire procedure takes less than half an hour. Readings are processed by a computer which calculates thousands of absorption values for each brain slice. The computer calculates the density of tissue scanned by the X-ray beam, and different densities of tissue are translated into lighter or darker areas.

The resultant photograph is essentially a picture of a transaxial slice of the brain. Bone and calcified areas that are dense look white in the CT scan, grey matter of the brain looks grey, and the least dense areas, the ventricles, look almost black. As mentioned previously, the resolution of CT scans is poorer than the resolution of MRIs.

Huckman et al. (1975) were the first to devise and validate specific quantitative criteria for evaluation of cerebral atrophy and dementia in older adults. They indicated that both enlarged ventricles and enlarged sulci were necessary for a reliable diagnosis of dementia, and they provided numerical standards for the width of the ventricles at two points and for the width of the four largest sulci that were considered atrophied. The criteria applied to CT scans yielded results as reliable as assessments based on pneumoencephalographic examination and pathologic examination at autopsy (Huckman et al., 1975).

CT scans have been used to diagnose AD and to identify geriatric patients with treatable brain pathology (Huckman et al., 1975). In the diagnosis of probable AD, the CT (or MRI) scan is used to rule out other neuropathology such as infarcts or tumors. This technique has also been used in conjunction with behavioral assessment to determine the relationship between behavioral capacity and brain structure. Kaszniak (1977) assessed the memory of 50 patients for whom a CT scan was available, and he demonstrated that CT scans predict behavioral changes. However, the correlations were moderate, and other evidence indicates that the severity of dementia cannot be predicted by CT scan data (Fox et al., 1979; Kaszniak et al., 1979). In 78 hospital patients aged 50 years or older with suspected changes in mentation in the absence of focal or other organic brain disease, EEG slowing was the strongest and most general pathologic influence on cognition (Kaszniak et al., 1979). Physiological functioning of the brain as measured by the EEG rather than neuroanatomical structure as measured by the CT scan was the best correlate of cognitive function. Thus, while the CT scan is a powerful tool in evaluating patients with dementia and can be used to rule out potentially treatable disorders, it is not terribly useful in demonstrating the severity of dementia or the ultimate prognosis.

Ford and Pfefferbaum (1980) correlated ERP changes with structural changes in the brain as assessed by the CT scan. Among the findings was a high correlation ($r = 0.77$) between a CT scan index of a decrease in brain tissue and longer latency P300 waves. This result linking decreases in brain tissue with longer latency P300 waves is in accordance with other data indicating that P300 latency increases dramatically in dementia patients. Ford and Pfefferbaum also found a high correlation (r = 0.81) between more negative slow waves recorded over the frontal area and less brain tissue. Behavioral, neuroanatomical, and ERP data converged to suggest a deficit with age in the frontal lobes – a topic that will be addressed more fully in subsequent chapters.

Magnetic resonance imaging and functional MRI

Working on a principle entirely different from that used in CT scanning, MRI scans are derived from signals emitted by atoms (usually hydrogen atoms) in response to strong magnets (figure 3.4). Mathematical reconstructions of slices of the brain are the outcome measure of MRI scans, and because the signal is generated from the neural tissue itself, the resultant scan is remarkably clear. The MRI technique involves the use of radio-frequency energy in a strong magnetic field to generate atomic signals from the nuclei of neurons. For this reason, the technique was initially called *nuclear magnetic resonance* (NMR). However, clinicians soon realized that the fear engendered by the word "nuclear" did a great disservice to the technique. Patients were afraid to submit to the scans because they thought that nuclear radiation was involved.

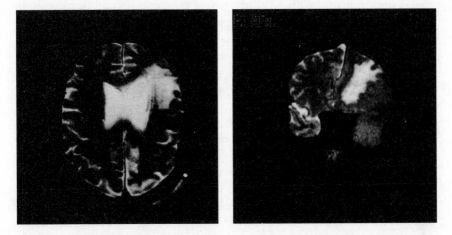

Figure 3.4 Magnetic resonance image (MRI) of the same 62-year-old patient for whom a CT scan is shown in figure 3.3. Resolution of the MRI is superior to the CT scan. *Left*: horizontal view as in the CT scan above. *Right*: coronal view of same surgically removed tumor. MRI right side is left side of brain

Just as the CT scan was the sensation of the 1970s, MRI became widely used and highly valued in the 1980s. In addition to the better resolution provided by the MRI scan, this technique has other advantages over the CT scan. No X-ray beam, with its risk of ionizing radiation, is used in an MRI scan, making it safe to use repeatedly. It is completely non-invasive. Technically, the MRI scan can be made at any angle, whereas the CT scan is limited to the horizontal plane. Three-dimensional images of the brain can be reconstructed from MRI data but not from CT data. The only limitation of the MRI scan for researchers, clinicians, and patients is the expense. MRI scans cost three to five times more than CT scans due to the more sophisticated equipment and training of staff required to produce an MRI scan.

The superiority of MRI scans over CT scans in diagnosis was recognized almost immediately. For example, in attempting a differential diagnosis of cerebrovascular dementia and AD, the MRI scan provides resolution suffi-cient to see arterial impairment that is simply beyond the power of the CT scan. Comparing the diagnostic utility of CT and MRI scans in AD, it was demonstrated that the MRI scan had greater utility (Growden et al., 1986).

In addition to its superiority as a neuroanatomical measure of the brain, the MRI technique has been elaborated to generate functional as well as static images. The fMRI technique is in use at present, but it is still being refined and enhanced. Measuring both blood flow in the brain and oxidative me-tabolism, this functional measure can be related to cognitive assessments on line – that is, brain and behavioral activity can be assessed concurrently. In the past, functional imaging was limited to PET scans. On the one hand, the data and insights provided by PET scans are remarkable. On the other hand, PET scans have relatively poor resolution of brain structures.

Positron emission tomography

Physiological response of the brain as it engages in cognition is the function assessed by the PET scan. For several decades this technique has been used to elucidate brain and behavior relationships more clearly than they have ever been visualized before. A PET camera is a donut-shaped set of radiation detectors that circles the head of the participant (Posner & Raichle, 1994). First, the subject is positioned in the machine, and then the experimenter injects a small amount of water labeled with the positron-emitting radioactive isotope oxygen-15. Within the next minute, the radioactive water accumu-lates in the brain in direct proportion to the local flow of blood. That is, whatever structures are physiologically activated will be identified by the radioactive water. The greater the blood flow, the more the PET will detect radiation. Higher radiation is indicated by brighter colors (red, orange, yellow), whereas lower radiation is indicated by darker colors (green, blue).

Radioactivity decays relatively rapidly during the PET scanning procedure. By the end of two minutes, radioactive decay has caused half of the radioactivity that was administered to disappear. Ten minutes after the injection of radioactive water, virtually all of the radioactivity has decayed. This means that the amount of exposure to potentially harmful ionizing radiation is relatively minimal.

A common tracer that is used in PET scans labels glucose. When cells are activated in a cognitive task and utilize glucose for their metabolism, the labeled marker (fluorodeoxyglucose, FDG) collects in the brain structures performing the task. Over the course of the few minutes that the cognitive task is carried out, the active parts of the brain accumulate more FDG than the regions that are less active. A scan of the patterns where FDG collected then provides an illustration of where brain activity occurred in relation to that particular cognitive task. FDG is only one of a number of tracers that are used to generate PET images. Examination of patterns of different neurotransmitters can be made by injecting tracers specific for those neurotransmitters.

PET studies are elucidating the brain mechanisms involved in age differences in cognition. For example, a PET study comparing healthy young and older adults on encoding and remembering faces revealed significantly different brain patterns in the two age groups as they performed the identical task (Grady et al., 1995). Young adults showed increased activation in the right hippocampus and left prefrontal and temporal cortices during encoding, but older adults showed no activation in these regions during encoding. In the recognition phase of the study, the brain activation patterns of young and old participants were more similar, with both age groups showing activation in right prefrontal and parietal cortex. The investigators concluded that age-related differences in performance on the task may be related to a deficiency in encoding in older adults. This was reflected in the lack of cortical and hippocampal activation in the encoding phase of the study.

A PET investigation of age differences in retrieval of words encoded with perceptual or semantic instructions revealed comparable hippocampal engagement in young and old, but age differences in activation of frontal cortex. Younger but not older adults showed bilateral blood-flow increases in anterior prefrontal cortex (Schacter et al., 1996). Older adults showed more posterior frontal lobe activation on the left (Broca's area) during attempted retrieval of words. The investigators concluded that the hippocampus activations may reflect a common means of remembering past events among young and older adults. However, the differences in frontal activation may reflect age-related differences in retrieval strategies, with strategies in older adults being less effective. The combined results of PET studies of memory by Grady et al. (1995) and Schacter et al. (1996) suggest that the hippocampus carries out different functions during encoding and retrieval. Whereas hippocampal functioning in older adults during encoding seemed impaired relative to younger adults (Grady et al., 1995), there were no differences in hippocampal activation during retrieval (Schacter et al., 1996). Bilateral anterior prefrontal cortical activation apparent during retrieval in young adults was absent in older adults whose performance on the retrieval task was impaired relative to young adults.

The fMRI scan has the advantage over PET in that it has greater resolution. Another significant advantage is that fMRI is not invasive. The injection of a tracer substance is a central component of the PET methodology. Whereas the injection of a positron-emitting radionuclide carries relatively little risk, the non-invasive fMRI technique carries no risk.

Histological techniques

The cellular and molecular structure and function of the nervous system are still only accessible through histological techniques. Using a microscope, neuroscientists and pathologists examine phenomena that cannot be detected with computerized brain imaging techniques. Although the resolution of CT, MRI, fMRI, and PET scans continues to improve, the computerized images cannot approach the fine degree of analysis provided by the light and electron microscope. Neurofibrillary tangles, β-amyloid plaques, and Lewy bodies, all found in the brains of normal elderly adults, and to a greater degree in the brains of patients with AD or Parkinson's disease (PD), cannot be seen in computerized brain images. The understanding of the consequences of these diseases may be obtained by viewing neuro-images, but an understanding of the causes of the diseases is more likely to be derived from microscopic examination.

In order for brain tissue to be viewed clearly under the microscope, it must undergo a series of processes. It must be fixated, that is hardened to a consistency so that it can be handled and cut. Fixation may involve soaking the tissue in formalin, freezing the tissue, or embedding it in paraffin. After it is hardened, the tissue is sliced with an instrument called a microtome into extremely thin slices (ranging from 4 to 80 μm) and mounted on glass slides. The tissues are then stained. Staining dyes the tissue to highlight the selected aspects. Different stains highlight different components (neurons versus glia, cell bodies versus fibers of passage, different types of cells). Techniques for staining of neural tissue have been progressing for 150 years and, currently, immunohistochemical techniques use monoclonal antibodies to create very specific stains highlighting cellular proteins.

The kinds of questions neuroscientists can ask with these techniques push the frontier of understanding of brain and behavior relationships. For example, research with the model system of eyeblink classical conditioning has mapped the circuitry for the learning and memory of this behavior (Thompson, 1986). This form of learning is significantly impaired in normal aging (e.g., Durkin et al., 1993; Solomon et al., 1989; Woodruff-Pak & Thompson, 1988) and it is abolished in an initial session in probable AD (Solomon et al., 1991; Woodruff-Pak et al., 1990) and Down's syndrome with AD (called DS/AD; Woodruff-Pak et al., 1994). The pathway for the tone conditioned stimulus (CS) involves pontine mossy fibers that synapse on cerebellar granule cells, and the granule cell axons synapse on Purkinje cell dendrites as parallel fibers. Using immunohistochemical techniques to stain β-amyloid plaques, we replicated previous observations of a significant number of β-amyloid plaques in the cerebellum of DS/AD brains but many fewer in AD brains (figure 3.5). In the DS/AD brains, these plaques were extensive in the molecular layer of cerebellum where the parallel fiber-Purkinje cell dendrite synapses occur. The β-amyloid plaques possibly impaired eyeblink conditioning by blocking the CS input to Purkinje cells.

Novel immunohistochemical double-staining techniques were developed by Young-Tong Li in John Trojanowski's laboratory, and Dr. Li took serial sections of cerebellum in DS/AD brains and examined the morphology of the Purkinje cell dendrites in relation to β-amyloid plaques (see figure 3.6; Li, Woodruff-Pak & Trojanowski, 1994). Purkinje cell dendrites did not

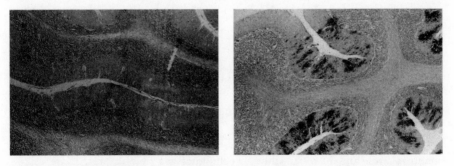

Figure 3.5 Left: cerebellar tissue of an 80-year-old male patient with Alzheimer's disease immuno-stained for β-amyloid protein showing relatively few β-amyloid plaques. *Right*: cerebellar tissue of a 54-year-old male patient with Down's syndrome and Alzheimer-like pathology immuno-stained for β-amyloid protein showing numerous β-amyloid plaques mostly confined to the molecular cell layer

Source: unpublished data from Li, Y.-T., Woodruff-Pak, D. S., and Trojanowski, J. Q. (1994). Amyloid plaques in cerebellar cortex and the integrity of Purkinje cell dendrites. *Neurobiology of Aging, 15*, 1–9

62 Introduction and Overview

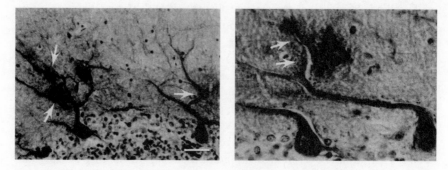

Figure 3.6 Left: Purkinje cell dendrites penetrating β-amyloid plaques look normal. Purkinje cells were stained with RMdO20, and β-amyloid was stained with $\beta A4_{2332}$. The scale bar is 40 μm. *Right*: Purkinje cells and their dendrites stained with PKC gamma (PKC66 neat) also look normal as they penetrate β-amyloid plaques (arrows) *Source*: Li, Y.-T., Woodruff-Pak, D. S., & Trojanowski, J. Q. (1994). Amyloid plaques in cerebellar cortex and the integrity of Purkinje cell dendrites. *Neurobiology of Aging, 15*, 1–9

appear impaired by the β-amyloid plaques. The investigators concluded that AD neuropathology in the form of β-amyloid plaques in DS/AD cerebellum does not appear to impair Purkinje cells or cerebellar cortical function beyond the effects of normal aging. In AD, there is less cerebellar β-amyloid plaque than in DS/AD. The conclusion from this investigation was that cerebellar neuropathology could not account for the extreme deficit observed in eyeblink conditioning in AD and DS/AD. Other brain structures were implicated.

Summary

The 1990s have been designated as the decade of the brain, and the techniques available to measure brain structure and function in humans offer significant insights to neuropsychologists in the assessment of behavior and brain relationships in older adults. Techniques available at present are relatively safe and non-invasive. These techniques can be thought of as photographs and video images of the living brain.

A technique available for much of the twentieth century is the electroencephalogram (EEG) that provides a record of ongoing brain activity related to states of arousal. The EEG is particularly useful in research on sleep. Among the major results of EEG research in normal aging is the observation that the dominant EEG frequency, the alpha rhythm, slows with age. Event related potentials (ERPs) are computer-averaged measures of EEG that show brain activity in relation to specific behaviors such as sensation, perception, and cognition. Research with the P300 component of the ERP indicates that central decision time slows with normal aging, and this slowing is exacerbated in Alzheimer's disease.

The computerized tomography (CT) scan is a safe and painless procedure that provides a picture of the living brain generated by an X-ray beam. It is a method of visualizing cerebral structures, including the ventricular system and cortical sulci. The value of this technique in neurological assessment of patients of all ages is so great and was recognized so rapidly that it became widely used within a few years of its discovery. The CT scan has been used in most cities in the United States to assess geriatric patients showing symptoms of cerebral impairment.

The magnetic resonance imaging (MRI) technique involves the use of radio-frequency energy in a strong magnetic field to generate atomic signals from the nuclei of neurons. Because the signals creating the MRI scan emanate directly from neurons, the resulting image is much clearer than the CT scan that simply measures tissue density. Although the MRI is preferable in its greater resolution, its higher cost puts some limitation on its use.

Physiological response of the brain as it engages in behavior and cognition is the function assessed by the PET scan. For several decades this technique has been used to elucidate brain and behavior relationships more clearly than they have ever been visualized before. However, PET technology is extraordinarily expensive and limited to centers in major research institutes and universities. Resolution of the brain structures generating PET images is somewhat limited, and PET is often used in conjunction with MRI to identify the locus of activity. PET studies in aging are contributing to the resolution of long-debated questions such as whether age differences in learning and memory reflect deficiencies in encoding, retention, or retrieval. PET scan data indicated that during encoding of unfamiliar faces the right hippocampus as well as left prefrontal and temporal cortices were not activated in older adults who performed poorly on the task. These structures were activated in younger adults. During retrieval of recently learned words, the hippocampus was equally activated in young and older adults, but bilateral anterior prefrontal activation appeared only in younger adults who performed better on the task.

The functional MRI (fMRI) scan has the advantage over PET that it has greater resolution. Another significant advantage is that fMRI is not invasive. Tracer substances are not injected for this technique as they are for PET. In the case of assessment of the elderly, this is a decided advantage. However, the fMRI technique is sufficiently new that few studies in the neuropsychology of aging have been carried out with this technique.

The cellular and molecular structure and function of the nervous system are still only accessible through histological techniques. Using a microscope, neuroscientists and pathologists examine phenomena that cannot be detected with computerized brain imaging techniques. Although the resolution of CT, MRI, fMRI, and PET scans continues to improve, the computerized images cannot approach the fine degree of analysis provided by the light and electron microscope. Neurofibrillary tangles, β-amyloid plaques, and Lewy bodies, all found in the brains of normal elderly adults, and to a greater degree in the brains of patients with AD or PD, cannot be seen in computerized brain images. An understanding of the consequences of these diseases may be obtained by viewing with scans, but an understanding of the causes of the diseases is more likely to be derived from microscopic examination.

Further Reading

Grady, C. L., McIntosh, A. R., Horwitz, B., Maisog, J. Ma., Ungerleider, L. G., Mentis, M. J., Pietrini, P., Schapiro, M. B., & Haxby, J. V. (1995). Age-related reductions in human recognition memory due to impaired encoding. *Science, 269,* 218–221.

Schacter, D. L., Savage, C. R., Alpert, N. M., Rauch, S. L., & Albert, M. S. (1996). The role of hippocampus and frontal cortex in age-related memory changes: A PET study. *NeuroReport, 7,* 1165–1169.
Two significant studies demonstrating the utility of the PET technique in answering questions about learning, memory, and aging.

Posner, M. I., & Raichle, M. E. (1994). *Images of mind.* New York: Scientific American Library.
A beautifully illustrated book by two leading researchers in cognitive neuroscience about the utility of brain imaging in understanding cognition.

Growden, J. H., Corkin, S., Buonanno, F., Davis, K., Jacob Huff, F., Beal, M. F., & Kramer, C. (1986). Diagnostic methods in Alzheimer's disease: Magnetic resonance brain imaging and CSF neurotransmitter markers. In A. Fisher, I. Hanin, & C. Lachman (Eds.), *Alzheimer's and Parkinson's diseases* (pp. 191–204). New York: Plenum.
Research comparing the efficacy of CT, MRI, and other techniques in diagnosis of neurodegenerative diseases of the aged.

Polich, J., Ladish, C., & Bloom, F. E. (1990). P300 assessment of early Alzheimer's disease. *Electroencephalography and Clinical Neurophysiology, 77,* 179–189.
Research suggesting the utility of the P300 wave of the ERP as a diagnostic indicator of dementia.

Part II

Aging and the Nervous System

4

Normal Aging in the Peripheral Nervous System

The consequences of normal aging in the peripheral nervous system are becoming evident as society adapts to the increasing size of the older adult population. In Florida, where the population has more than 16 percent of its residents over the age of 65, the State Transportation Department has a program to make road signs larger to accommodate diminished eyesight. Space pavement reflectors are 40 ft apart rather than the standard 80 ft, and paint lane strips are 6 in. long rather than the standard 4 in. (Navarro, 1996). Accidents statistics from the Florida Department of Motor Vehicles show that people aged 85 and older are second only to teenagers in accidents. This outcome does not occur because elderly adults speed: changes in sensory systems of the peripheral nervous system affect their ability to see and hear.

The sensory receptors and their peripheral pathways to the brain are components of the peripheral nervous system. Another major segment of the peripheral nervous system is the autonomic nervous system (ANS). Figure 4.1 illustrates the structure of the nervous system, showing sensory and ANS components. Age-related impairment in sensory systems can affect neuropsychological test performance as well as the quality of life of older adults. ANS activity can also affect test performance when an individual is over- or underaroused in the testing situation. It is important to determine whether an elderly person's cognitive performance is affected by sensory limitations or abnormal ANS responsivity. Identification of the cause of impaired performance is the aim of neuropsychology. Whereas neuropsychological tests assess cognitive and neural function, sensory impairment and level of emotional arousal also play a role in the testing environment.

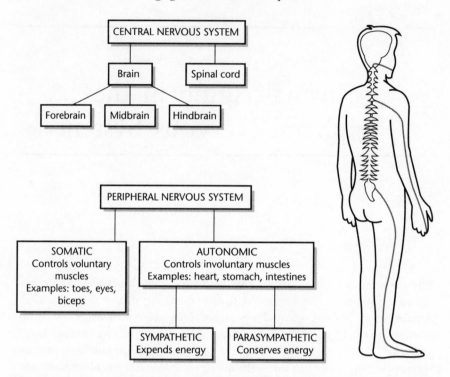

Figure 4.1 The human nervous system showing the major divisions into the central and peripheral nervous system. Sensory input from the environment enters the nervous system via the peripheral spinal and cranial nerves on its way to the brain in the central nervous system. The autonomic nervous system comprises the sympathetic and parasympathetic systems that respond to stress and express levels of arousal

Sensory changes in adulthood and old age

One of the more evident features of normal aging is the change that occurs in the individual's ability to sense and perceive the world. Age changes occur in all of the sensory modalities, and these sensory changes affect behavior in a variety of ways. Taste and smell affect the appeal of food, the sense of balance determines the incidence of falls and dizziness, hearing acuity affects the comprehensibility of language, and visual acuity affects the ability to read, watch television, and move around in the environment. To the extent that these senses are impaired, the quality of life and the life satisfaction of an older adult can be affected. Performance on neuropsychological tests and even the ability to perform certain tests at all can be impaired by sensory deficits in older adults.

A vast array of sensory information constantly bombards the individual. People learn to selectively attend to some stimuli and filter out most of the rest, or they are overwhelmed with too much input to integrate meaningfully. There are a number of dimensions of sensory stimulation. However, all sensory information, whether it is the wavelength of light, the frequency of a tone, or the intensity of pressure, is transduced by sensory receptors into neuronal signals. The world is never perceived directly. It is interpreted through the nervous system.

To optimize neuropsychological assessment in older adults, it is important to be aware of the changes which occur in the peripheral nervous system during adulthood. At the same time, changes in peripheral sensory systems are not the only possible locus of age-related changes that affect sensation and perception. The nervous system at and beyond the level of the sensory receptor is implicated in age differences in sensation (Fozard, 1990). For example, in the auditory system, neural changes in the brain along the auditory pathway at the level of the inferior colliculus, medial geniculate nucleus of the thalamus, and primary auditory cortex affect the quality of hearing.

The peripheral nervous system interfaces with the environment using a variety of sensory receptors. Cutaneous processes are registered by sensory receptors in the skin and involve sensations of touch, pressure, temperature, and pain. Kinesthesis includes coordination and the maintenance of posture. The kinesthetic receptors are located in the muscles, tendons, and joints. The sense of balance is mediated in the vestibular system by a group of receptors located in the inner ear. This system is intimately tied to the visual system. Olfaction or smell is input to the nervous system via receptors in the nose. Gustation or taste involves sensory receptors in the mouth (primarily on the tongue in adults), and taste and smell sensations are integrated to affect responses to food. Audition or hearing is mediated by sensory receptors located in the outer, middle, and inner ear. The most complex of all senses is vision. Sight begins at the eye, and a great amount of processing occurs right at the retina. The information is then sent to several relay stations in the brain where it is processed further. The simplest sensory modalities such as touch are the earliest to develop, whereas the more complex sensory systems such as vision are not fully functional at an adult level until well after birth. The most complex and latest developing senses are the most affected by processes of aging.

Many of the sensory changes that are concomitants of normal aging occur independently. That is, there is no one process of aging that drives all sensory changes. Rather, the changes occur independently of one another in the different sensory modalities. Indeed, some of the changes in a given sensory receptor such as the eye are independent of one another. This is because the eye itself is complex and has many functioning components. Thus, the loss of muscle fibers in the iris and the increase in the thickness of the lens occur as independent phenomena in the aging eye. On the other hand, the net effect of each of these changes is similar: the amount of light reaching the retina is reduced. We will begin with the simplest of sensory systems and the proximal senses, and proceed through the sensory modalities as they increase in complexity and include the distal senses.

The proximal senses are the earliest senses to develop and tend to be simpler in their organization. This means that the receptor responds to stimuli which actually have contact with it or are near. The sense of touch is called a proximal sense, along with the other cutaneous senses and the sense of taste. The distal senses such as audition and vision respond to stimuli which are distant from the sensory receptor. These two senses are also the most complex in terms of their sensory receptors and brain representation. They are the last senses to develop, and since they are so complex, they are the most likely to be impaired in later life.

Touch

The sensory modality of touch is affected by poor circulation in late life, perhaps more than any other normal aging process. Touch receptors are located under the surface of the skin. The blood supply to these areas comes through small capillaries which can become occluded in old age. The number of receptors is less in later life, and the threshold for the sensation of touch – that is the smallest amount of energy or change in energy which can be detected – is higher in old than in young individuals. In one study which suggested a parallel between the age differences in concentration of touch receptors and age differences in tactile sensitivity, Ronge (1943) counted the number and concentration of touch receptors in segments of the skin of the index finger in subjects ranging from 1 to 80 years of age. He found a decrease in the density of receptors (Meissner's corpuscles) in the first two decades of life due to the increase in size of the finger. An age difference was also found over the adult life span, presumably due to the loss of receptors in later life. Bolton et al. (1966) observed a decrease in the number of Meissner's corpuscles in the skin of fingers of older individuals, and Thornbury and Mistretta (1981) reported rather substantial age differences in the sensitivity of the index finger. Counts of touch receptors can be carried out only at autopsy, while measures of touch threshold are made in living subjects. Thus, there is at present no means to assess tactile sensitivity and count Meissner's corpuscles in the same individuals. Nevertheless, because the number of touch receptors declines around the same age that there are age differences in tactile thresholds (during the decade of the 50s), it is assumed that the sensitivity changes result from the loss of Meissner's corpuscles.

Few neuropsychological tests are directly affected by the sense of touch, but a decline in the sensory input to the brain from touch receptors could have an indirect effect on performance. Lindsley (1960) was one of the first to document the inverted U-shaped relationship between arousal and behavioral performance. The optimal level of performance is achieved when a person is at a middle level of arousal, neither over- nor underaroused. Sensory input to the ascending reticular arousal system (ARAS) plays a role in brain levels of arousal. If there is significantly less sensory input from the peripheral receptors, the central nervous system may be underaroused. The decline in the number of touch receptors, along with deficits in many of the other sensory modalities may have the cumulative effect of reducing central nervous system arousal level in older adults. That is, the cerebral cortex itself may receive less stimulation from the ARAS due to sensory deficits. Meanwhile, at an ANS level, the sympathetic nervous system may be hyperactive in older adults as part of the anxiety response they have to the testing situation.

Pain

There has been general interest on the subject of whether pain sensitivity changes with age. Since old people are likely to suffer from at least one chronic disease, and since they often adapt to it and continue to function, it has been speculated that pain sensitivity declines. Although a number of studies have been undertaken to answer this question, they have not provided compelling evidence either way. Early studies of pain perception used the technique of painting a black circle on the forehead of the subject with India ink, shining intense lights on the circle, and determining the amount of light energy required to elicit pain. Several of these studies found stability in pain thresholds over the adult life span (e.g., Birren et al., 1950), but Schluderman and Zubek (1962) found stability in pain threshold until late in the decade of the 50s. Using a different technique, electrical stimulation of electrodes attached to the teeth to produce dental pain, Harkins and Chapman found no adult age differences in pain perception in either men (1976) or women (1977).

The majority of research studies of pain sensitivity in adulthood and old age suggest that it remains constant. Clinical evidence implies that older people feel pain less than the young. They appear to respond less to pain. One interpretation of these results is that pain tolerance increases with age while pain sensitivity remains relatively stable.

Balance

The receptors involved in the sense of balance and the ability to maintain upright posture are called the vestibular apparatus. These receptors are located in the bony labyrinth of the inner ear. They consist of three semicircular canals, along with the saccule, and the utricle. Falls and dizziness are a common complaint of older persons, and these problems may be related to changes involving the vestibular apparatus. Postural dizziness is common in the aged and is present in the majority of adults over the age of 65. Dizziness probably results more from transient circulatory disturbances occurring during changes in body position than from age changes in the vestibular apparatus. The vestibular apparatus is located on the side of the head in a position where the cerebral arteries make the sharpest bends. Blood supply to the vestibular apparatus is likely to be adversely affected as the arteries harden with age, and it is likely that circulatory insufficiency impairs vestibular function. The fact that increases in body sway along with falls and dizziness are almost universally present in older people suggests that it is also possible that the vestibular apparatus itself changes adversely with age.

Smell

In a thorough review of the literature on olfaction and aging, Engen (1977) asserted that the data on age changes in the sense of smell are sparse and contradictory. On the basis of existing data, Engen concluded that the sense of smell is not seriously affected by age. Rather, in those studies in which there were large age differences in olfactory sensitivity, the health of the older sample was poor.

A comprehensive study of the sense of smell was carried out by Rovee et al. (1975). One hundred and twenty subjects ranging in age from 6 to 94 judged the intensity of seven different concentrations of an odorant. Two groups of older subjects aged 60–70 and 80–90 actually demonstrated more sensitivity than subjects in the age groups between 20 and 50. Thus, there was no evidence of any decline in olfactory sensitivity with age. Since olfactory sensitivity is particularly salient in neonates, the investigators suggested that senses developing very early in life may be the senses showing the greatest stability over the life span.

In contrast to these results, more recent investigations identify robust age-related changes in the ability to perceive odors (Doty, 1991). Age-related impairment has been reported in olfactory sensitivity, odor discrimination, odor identification, odor recognition, odor memory, and the perception of odor pleasantness (for reviews see Doty, 1990; Murphy, 1988). It is not clear whether age-related decline occurs as a gradual loss of the ability to smell throughout life or whether it reflects a precipitous loss after the age of 60 (Cain & Stevens, 1989; Wysocki & Gilbert, 1989).

In Alzheimer's disease (AD), olfactory function is significantly decreased relative to healthy age-matched control subjects (e.g., Corwin et al., 1985; Doty et al., 1987). This impairment is present at the earliest stages of the disease and is related to the severity of the dementia (e.g., Murphy et al., 1990). Talamo and associates (1989) demonstrated that peripheral olfactory neurons in the nose (neurons of the olfactory epithelium) of AD patients contained pathologic changes. Examining the next level of the olfactory system, the olfactory bulb in the brain, Hyman et al. (1991) found global atrophy. We mention this sensory deficit in olfaction in AD here, because in general AD is not associated with sensory impairment. The olfactory system appears to be selectively impaired in AD. It has been suggested that tests for the early detection of AD might utilize samples of the olfactory epithelium (Talamo et al., 1991).

Taste

The evidence for age changes in the sense of taste are somewhat mixed, but the majority of studies suggest that there is some decline in taste sensitivity in later life. In the early studies in which small amounts of various sweet, bitter, sour, or salty substances were mixed in water and tasted by subjects, older subjects required higher concentrations of the substance to detect it (e.g., Byrd & Gertman, 1959; Cooper et al., 1959). Using a different method, Hughes (1969) applied a weak galvanic current to the tongue which produced a taste sensation. The amount of current necessary to elicit taste sensation in young subjects was lower than that required to elicit a response in older subjects.

Most of the studies that have been carried out on taste sensitivity over the adult life span concur in indicating that there is a decline in taste sensitivity with age. However, in a review of the literature on this topic Engen (1977) cautions that this conclusion should not be accepted as a certainty without further research on taste preference as well as taste sensitivity over the life span. Indeed, since Engen made his caution, Grzegorczyk et al. (1979) measured sensitivity to salt taste in subjects ranging in age from 23 to 92 and found that threshold increases over the adult life span existed but were smaller than indicated by previous studies.

Hearing

The auditory apparatus is complex, and age-related changes can occur in peripheral components involved in sound transmission as well as in the neural structures. Nevertheless, the cochlea, located in the inner ear, is the part of the auditory apparatus that appears to be most affected by processes of aging. The auditory apparatus is illustrated in figure 4.2.

There are probably as many studies on hearing acuity that include extremely large samples as on any measure of human sensory capacity. Tens of thousands of adults of all ages have had their hearing tested with traditional audiometric techniques as they apply for jobs in some large corporations or as they continue in the work force. These large data sets have been combined and analyzed with the results indicating that hearing acuity begins to decline mildly in the decade of the 20s with some hearing loss apparent beginning in the decade of the 30s (around the age of 37 for women and 32 for men). Impairment occurs mainly at the upper end of the frequency spectrum, and hearing impairment fitting this pattern is called presbycusis. Presbycusis is

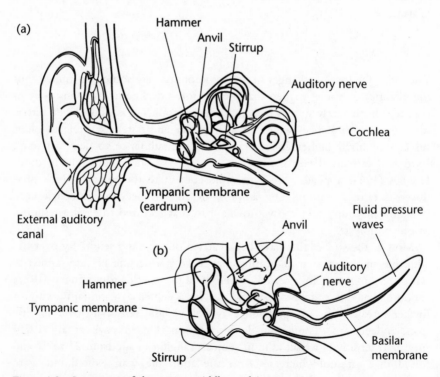

Figure 4.2 Structures of the outer, middle, and inner ear

characterized by a progressive bilateral loss of hearing for tones of high frequency due to degenerative physiological changes in the auditory system as a function of age (Corso, 1977).

The typical pattern is for individuals to lose the most acuity for the very high frequencies, and thresholds for frequencies below 2,000 Hz show no significant deterioration. The loss in the 4,000–6,000 Hz frequency range is greater than in any other frequency range. Hearing loss occurs earlier in men than in women, with women retaining more acuity than men. The magnitude of hearing loss over the adult years for low frequencies such as 250 Hz is relatively small (at most 35 dB), but the loss at higher frequencies such as 8,000 Hz is greater (as much as 100 dB). Longitudinal data on auditory acuity collected in the Baltimore Longitudinal Study of Aging now confirm what the cross-sectional data have been illustrating for years. There is almost a complete overlap between the longitudinal data and cross-sectional data on hearing loss associated with normal aging (Brant et al., 1986).

Some studies have demonstrated a shortening of the loudness scale in older subjects. This is called recruitment. Because of recruitment, older subjects perceive an increase in the intensity of an auditory signal as being much more rapid than it actually is. Perception does not always correlate perfectly with the physical qualities of a stimulus, and in the case of recruitment, the discrepancy between the perceived and physical qualities of the stimulus is greater than normal. What this means for the experience of the older adult is that noise is louder and more bothersome. For example, attempting to interact in a crowded room filled with people having conversations is more challenging for an older adults. He or she perceives the conversational noise as significantly louder than it seems to younger adults.

Almost all older individuals show some degree of hearing loss and 13 percent of the population over the age of 65 have advanced signs of presbycusis (Corso, 1977). Hearing disability can impair an individual's capacity for social interaction, as it interferes with the ability to understand conversation. Consonants are particularly difficult to understand when hearing loss is present, and women's higher frequency voice is less intelligible than the deeper tones of men. Speaking in lower frequencies to one suffering from presbycusis may be as helpful as speaking more loudly. Hearing loss has even been associated with lowered intelligence test scores in the elderly (Granick et al., 1976; Schaie et al., 1964). In both of these studies there was a statistically significant correlation between hearing acuity and intelligence test score. Granick et al. demonstrated in two very different samples that the relationship between hearing loss and performance IQ score was greater than the relationship between verbal intelligence and hearing loss. The implication was that hearing loss might have served as an index for some general aging factor in the individual.

Vision

Vision is the most complicated of the senses. The retina is like a little brain sitting on the periphery of the nervous system (figure 4.3 illustrates the visual system). Vision is the last sensory capacity to develop, and it is the sense with the most components to go wrong. A number of deleterious changes occur in the eye to make it function less efficiently in older adults. The crystalline lens of the eye thickens and yellows, scattering light as it enters the eye so that more light energy is required to permeate it. The muscles responsible for pupil accommodation lose fibers and cause the pupil to narrow. This again means that more light must be present to register on the retina. Because of these non-neural changes in the eye, it has been suggested that no increase in the magnitude of light energy of the stimulus can equate the old to the younger eye. It has been estimated that the retina of a 60-year-old receives approximately 30 percent of the amount of light reaching the retina of a 20-year-old. Clearly, neuropsychological tests should be administered to older adults in a well-lighted room.

Visual acuity with and without correction was measured in the Baltimore Longitudinal Study of Aging in several hundred men and women ranging in age from 20 to the late 80s. Results from previous cross-sectional studies were confirmed by both the cross-sectional and longitudinal data in the Baltimore study. In 587 men representing the age decades of the 20s to the 80s, 10-year longitudinal changes in acuities revealed significant declines in corrected as well as uncorrected acuity. Declines were greatest in men initially in their 60s and 70s (Fozard et al., 1986). The researchers felt that their data were consistent with the hypothesis that less light reaches the retina of individuals as they age. As expected, uncorrected distance acuity declined precipitously between the 40s and 50s, reflecting the age loss in accommodation.

Dark adaptation is the process by which the eye changes its capacity to respond as the level of illumination changes. Everyone has had the experience of walking from a brightly lit lobby into the darkness of the movie house and being temporarily blinded by the absence of light. Within a short period of time, some degree of dark adaptation occurs, and it is possible to see enough to get to a seat. For our eyes to become totally adapted to the absence of light, it takes 40 min. Numerous studies have illustrated how much more sensitive the eyes are to pinpoints of light after dark adapting for 40 min as compared to the sensitivity at the beginning of the waiting period when the eyes were adapted to bright light. For half a century, studies have demonstrated that the ability of the eye to adapt to darkness declines over the adult life span.

Birren et al. (1948) examined 130 men between the ages of 18 and 83

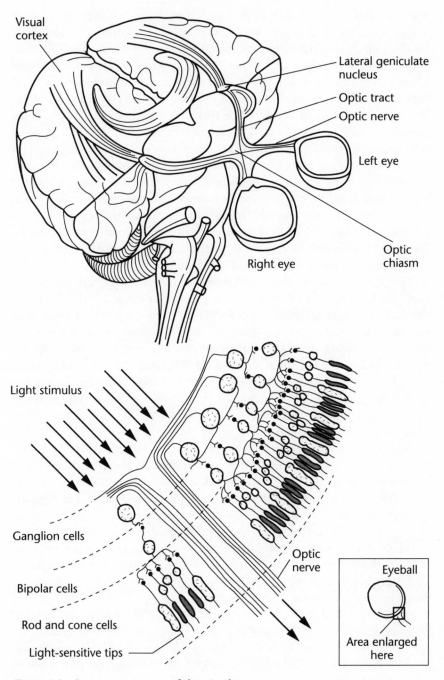

Figure 4.3 Some components of the visual system

years and found a significant decline with age in the sensitivity of the dark adapted eye. The decline was most marked in subjects beyond the age of 60. Smaller pupil size in the older subjects did not account for the age differences in sensitivity. McFarland and Fisher (1955) observed a correlation of 0.89 between age and the final point of dark adaptation. The intensity of illumination at threshold levels almost had to be doubled for each 13 years of age between the ages of 20 and 60. The dark adapted threshold was so closely related to age that McFarland and Fisher were able to take a given individual's threshold score and predict the person's age with an accuracy of ±3 years. A striking feature of the data was the magnitude of the difference in sensitivity between the very old and the young. For example, at the second minute of dark adaptation, young subjects were almost five times more sensitive than the very old. At the fortieth minute the young were 240 times more sensitive. The decrease in sensitivity to light was so apparent over the adult life span that McFarland suggested that the decrease in sensitivity to light might provide an index to the aging process.

The implications of these studies are considerable. In addition to the theoretical significance of the relationship between age and dark adaptation, the decline in light sensitivity with age has relevance to activities engaged in by many older individuals. For example, it is a common experience to enter a dimly lit restaurant with an older person and hear him or her complain that it is too dark to see the menu or the food. This ordeal for the older person is unpleasant, but it is in no way dangerous. However, there are activities in which the decline in light sensitivity in darkness are life-threatening. An obvious example of an activity involving risks for the elderly due to changes in the eye is driving at night.

Neuropsychologists are sometimes asked to assess elderly adults for competency hearings. One dimension of competence is the ability to drive. Neuropsychologists are sometimes consulted in the determination of whether an elderly person's driving license should be taken away. Typically, the neuropsychologist is brought in to assess the cognitive capacity of the person to determine if he or she can make appropriate decisions while driving. In addition to these cognitive considerations, sensory acuity, light sensitivity in darkness, and susceptibility to glare are significant factors that may weigh the decision toward revoking the driver's license or at least limiting the elderly driver to daytime driving.

Color vision is also affected by aging of the eye. The amount and spectral distribution of light reaching the older retina decrease. The changes in spectral distribution reaching the older eye appear to affect perception of short wavelengths of light. Older individuals have greater difficulty in discriminating blues and greens. The practical limitations imposed by this age-related change in vision are negligible; however, the neuropsychologist must be aware of this age-related sensory deficit when using colored test materials.

An obvious functional change in vision over the life span is presbyopia – the impairment of the ability to focus on near objects. A normal eye at rest can focus objects at virtually an infinite distance, and it accommodates to focus near objects by shortening the focal distance of the lens. Maximal focusing accommodation is attained around the age of 5 years, with a gradual decline in accommodation beginning in early adulthood and continuing to around the age of 60 years, after which there is no further decline. The progressive decline in the focusing function results mainly from a loss of elasticity of the lens (McFarland, 1968). Thus, most people become farsighted as they grow older, a decline that can even begin in childhood. Because most of this inability to focus near objects can be corrected with convex lenses, it presents a nuisance rather than a major problem for visual perception in middle-aged and older individuals. However, the neuropsychologist should always consider compensating for this normal aging phenomenon by having testing materials printed in enlarged letters.

The problems of visual acuity documented in research are also personally perceived by older adults themselves. Common complaints indicative of greater problems in the elderly were revealed in a survey of people aged 18–100 years (Kosnik et al., 1988). Five dimensions of visual functions were identified as relatively impaired: visual processing speed (e.g., reading speed), light sensitivity (seeing in twilight and dark), dynamic vision (reading scrolling TV displays or digital displays), near vision (reading small print), and visual search (locating a sign). Visual processing speed and near vision clearly impact neuropsychological test performance, and some tests (in particular, automated tests) may also be compromised by dynamic vision and visual search deficits.

The discussion of age changes in visual sensory capacity would not be complete without mention of two abnormal but common effects of aging on the eye. These are cataracts and glaucoma. While both of these afflictions are pathological and not components of normal aging phenomena, they affect a large number of older adults and impair vision and the ability to see neuropsychological test materials.

The name "cataract" was given to this pathology because an advanced cataract is white and frothy like a waterfall. A cataract is any condition in the lens which makes it cloudy and less able to transmit a sharply focused image to the retina. The symptoms of a cataract involve a blurring of vision and susceptibility to glare. The prevalence of cataracts in the United States has been estimated as 5 percent in individuals aged 52–62, and 46 percent in those aged 75–85 (Schwab & Taylor, 1985). Cataracts can be removed by trimming away the ectodermal opacity, and the procedure is performed more than 300,000 times annually in the United States (Roberts, 1987). However, cataracts are not removed until they start to produce some significant disability. After surgery the lens is usually replaced with an artificial clear plastic lens that eliminates the need for contact lenses or thick glasses.

Glaucoma is a general term for an elevation of pressure within the eye such that damage to the nerve cells in the retina is caused. There are a number of causes of this build up of pressure. However, glaucoma is rarely seen before the age of 40 (Anderson, 1987). When there is prolonged or severe pressure in the eye, nerve cells leaving the eye undergo progressive damage. The optic disk is damaged, and the outer areas of vision are affected first. When diagnosing glaucoma, the ophthalmologist studies the level of pressure, the appearance of the optic disc and retina, and the ability of the patient to see at the edges of the visual field. Early diagnosis is important because glaucoma is the leading cause of acquired adult blindness.

Treatment for glaucoma is through a number of modalities. The first step may by eye drops. Next may come oral medication, laser treatment, and surgery. Usually the patient does not notice any symptoms of glaucoma until the disease has progressed significantly. Thus, periodic eye examinations are strongly indicated for individuals over the age of 40.

The autonomic nervous system as an index of test anxiety and arousal

The autonomic component of the peripheral nervous system includes sympathetic and parasympathetic branches. These complementary components of the nervous system regulate viscera and glands and perform functions essential in homeostasis (parasympathetic) and stress and action (sympathetic). Figure 4.4 illustrates the ANS, and shows the sympathetic and parasympathetic divisions and their connection to the central nervous system. Emotional arousal is expressed in the ANS. Because anxiety and arousal level affect neuropsychological test performance, we will discuss aging in these systems from the perspective of arousal.

Underarousal

Early empirical investigations of the relationship between underarousal and aging were carried out in the 1950s and involved the galvanic skin response (GSR; Botwinick & Kornetsky, 1960). This research initiated a series of studies carried out in several laboratories over the next two decades, which related ANS activity to underarousal and poorer behavioral performance in the elderly. Much of this literature was reviewed and integrated into perspec-

Parasympathetic division   **Sympathetic division**

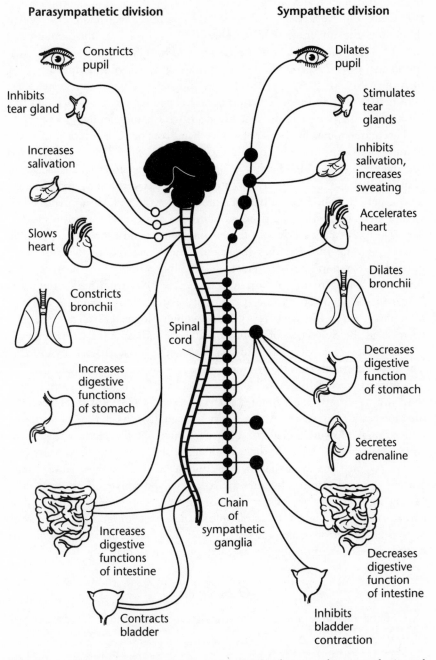

Constricts pupil

Inhibits tear gland

Increases salivation

Slows heart

Constricts bronchii

Spinal cord

Increases digestive functions of stomach

Increases digestive functions of intestine

Chain of sympathetic ganglia

Contracts bladder

Dilates pupil

Stimulates tear glands

Inhibits salivation, increases sweating

Accelerates heart

Dilates bronchii

Decreases digestive function of stomach

Secretes adrenaline

Decreases digestive function of intestine

Inhibits bladder contraction

Figure 4.4 The autonomic nervous system (ANS) showing the sympathetic and parasympathetic divisions and their connections to the brain and spinal cord in the central nervous system

tives of arousal level and aging (Marsh & Thompson, 1977; Woodruff, 1985). Botwinick and Kornetsky used a classical conditioning paradigm in which shock was the unconditioned stimulus (US), a tone was the conditioned stimulus (CS), and GSR was the response. The GSRs of the elderly men (mean age, early 70s) conditioned less readily and extinguished more quickly than the GSRs of the younger subjects, and older subjects also showed less GSR responsivity in the habituation period. The investigators concluded that autonomic reactivity was significantly decreased in the elderly.

The underarousal hypothesis has also been supported by studies of autonomic reactivity in the aged during vigilance tasks. Surwillo (1966) reported age differences in GSR, heart rate, and skin temperature which occurred while young and old subjects monitored a Mackworth clock over an extended period. (The minute hand of this clock would move normally every second, but occasionally the hand would move ahead two seconds instead of one. The participant's task was to remain vigilant and report every double tick.) In several other studies in which young and old participants were instructed to report the occurrance of a double advance on the ticks of a clock over a long period of time, the latency of GSR to critical stimuli was longer in the aged (Surwillo & Quilter, 1965a) and the frequency of GSR responses was less (Surwillo & Quilter, 1965b). Slower GSR latency and a decrease in the frequency of GSR response are indicative of lower arousal.

Heart rate reactivity has also supported the underarousal hypothesis. Thompson and Nowlin (1973) found heart rate deceleration to be much less in a warned reaction time task for the old subjects than for the young. This result was replicated and extended (Harkins et al., 1976). Taken as a whole, the bioelectric measures of ANS activity indicate that the old are in a state of underarousal. However, many of the studies involving bioelectric measures of ANS arousal have been boring to subjects and have involved relatively passive responses to the experimental conditions. Few of these studies supporting the underarousal hypothesis have involved active information processing in tasks that are anxiety-provoking or stressful for the older adult participants. In conditions of active information processing, older individuals have been shown in many cases to be equally aroused in comparison with young subjects, or more highly aroused and anxious than the young.

Overarousal

One of the first gerontologists to articulate the overarousal hypothesis was Alan Welford (1965) who stated:

> Reduced activation would tend to lower both signal and noise, the former probably more than the latter, rendering the organism less

sensitive and less responsive than it would otherwise be. At first sight the changes with age in neural structures make it seem obvious that older people would be likely to suffer from under-activation. Yet both clinical and everyday observations of middle-aged and older people often point rather to *over*-activation resulting in unduly heightened activity, tension and anxiety (Welford, 1965, p. 14).

The data that have been used most frequently to support the overarousal hypothesis involve the measurement of lipid mobilization, a biochemical measure related to sympathetic nervous system function. It had been demonstrated that the level of free fatty acid (FFA) in the plasma component of blood was intimately related to the level of ANS arousal (Bogdonoff et al., 1961; Bogdonoff, Estes et al., 1960; Bogdonoff, Weissler & Merritt, 1960). To obtain this measure an indwelling needle is placed in the subject's forearm and sequential samples of blood are collected during the experimental session. Thus, regardless of the behavioral measure being assessed, there is a certain amount of stress involved in this technique associated with the drawing of blood. As pointed out in chapter 2, the stress and anxiety produced by the blood sampling procedure probably elicited greater responding from young adult subjects rather than older participants.

In the studies that have used the FFA measure, results indicated that during serial learning and stressful monitoring tasks emphasizing information overload, aged subjects had initially higher FFA levels, showed increases comparable to the young while performing the tasks, and continued at a significantly higher level for a minimum of 1 hr following the behavioral tests (Powell et al., 1964; Troyer et al., 1966). On the basis of these data, Carl Eisdorfer concluded:

> It has been implicitly assumed, however, that the aged are at a resting state of low internal arousal and sustain a low drive state. Our contention is that the aged may not be at a low state of arousal. Once aroused autonomically, perhaps because of a faulty ability to suppress end organ response or because of an altered feedback system, aged *Ss* [subjects] appear to function as if in states of high levels of heightened arousal. In any event, increasing anxiety or further exogenous stimulation has a detrimental effect on performance, as opposed to the incremental effect that we would anticipate from an organism stimulated at lower levels of arousal. It would be predicted, then, that where arousal or anxiety is diminished by experimental manipulation, older persons should improve their performance (Eisdorfer, 1968, p. 215).

An experimental test of the underarousal hypothesis was undertaken by Eisdorfer et al. (1970). They administered an adrenergic blocking agent (propranolol) to one group of older subjects and a placebo to another, and found fewer errors and lower FFA levels when the experimental subjects performed the serial learning task. They concluded that autonomic end organ arousal accounted for the learning deficits in the placebo-treated group and asserted that the results supported the overarousal hypothesis. Unfortunately, a young control group was not tested, so the effect of the drug on subjects who would not be expected to be overaroused by the testing situation was not assessed.

An attempt was made by Froehling (1974) to replicate these results, and her study required repeated visits to the testing environment. Results did not support the hypothesis that overarousal was associated with learning decrement in the elderly. With repeated visits to the testing environment, older adults' anxiety diminished. If emotional overarousal exists in the elderly, it may be a transitory phenomenon occurring only in the older subject's first visit to the laboratory. These results assessing peripheral nervous system function in older adults suggest that neuropsychologists should test older clients in settings with which they are familiar and comfortable.

Summary

Neuropsychological test performance can be affected by age-related impairment in sensory systems as well as alterations in the autonomic nervous system (ANS). When evaluating an older adult, it is important to determine whether his or her cognitive performance is affected by sensory limitations or abnormal ANS responsivity. Identification of the cause of impaired performance is the aim of neuropsychology. Whereas neuropsychological tests assess cognitive and neural function, sensory impairment and level of emotional arousal also play a role in the testing environment.

One of the more evident features of normal aging is the change that occurs in the individual's ability to sense and perceive the world. Age changes occur in all of the sensory modalities, and these sensory changes affect behavior in a variety of ways. Sensory changes that are most likely to affect neuropsychological test performance are in the domains of audition and vision. It is essential that test stimuli be well above sensory threshold so that they are seen and heard well by elderly clients.

Emotional arousal is expressed through the ANS. Because anxiety and arousal level affect neuropsychological test performance in older adults, they are factors that must be considered and offset as part of the total evaluation. Bioelectric measures of ANS activity, assessed typically when participants were carrying out rather boring tasks, indicated that older adults were in a state of underarousal. Few of the studies supporting the underarousal hypothesis involved active information processing in tasks that were anxiety-provoking or stressful for the older adult participants. In this sense, the studies may not have simulated the evaluative environment more typical of the neuropsychological testing situation. In conditions of active information processing, older individuals have been shown in many cases to be equally aroused in comparison to young participants, or more highly aroused and anxious than the young. If the neuropsychological testing environment is overarousing to the older adult, it is likely to interfere with optimal performance. Making the older adult comfortable during the testing sessions is an important aim for the neuropsychologist.

Further Reading

Fozard, J. L. (1990). Vision and hearing in aging. In J. E. Birren & K. W. Schaie (Eds.), *Handbook of the psychology of aging* (3rd ed., pp. 150–170). San Diego, CA: Academic Press.

A definitive current review of the cross-sectional and longitudinal research literature on the two major sensory systems.

Kosnik, W., Winslow, L., Kline, D., Rasinski, K., & Sekuler, R. (1988). Visual changes in daily life throughout adulthood. *Journal of Gerontology: Psychological Sciences, 43,* P63–P70.

This article reports on a large survey of individuals reporting their personal experience with age-related changes in visual perception.

Prinz, P. N., Dustman, R. E., & Emmerson. R. (1990). Electrophysiology and aging. In J. E. Birren & K. W. Schaie (Eds.), *Handbook of the psychology of aging* (3rd ed., pp. 135–149). San Diego, CA: Academic Press.

The arousal hypothesis along with electrophysiological aspects of sleep and wakefulness, and changes during physical exercise and aging are reviewed in this chapter.

5

Normal Aging of the Brain

Unlike the predictable sequence of development of the nervous system, aging processes are relatively random. Processes of aging do not occur at a demarcated rate or sequence, and age-related brain changes begin and progress at different rates in different individuals. Aging in the nervous system cannot be described as occurring in systematic and predictable phases such as is the case for cell development in the nervous system. Instead, a number of structures change in the nervous system with age, and the magnitudes of these changes vary among individuals.

One of the most generalized findings in the literature on aging in the nervous system is the observation of fewer cells in older brains. This result has been interpreted to demonstrate cell loss or brain shrinkage, an interpretation based on some questionable assumptions, as described later in this chapter. The findings of neuron loss in the brain are typically interpreted to signify loss of capacity, but more recent conclusions have been that cell loss in some cases may improve functioning in the brain (Mesulam, 1988; Woodruff-Pak & Hanson, 1995). The central nervous system is composed of at least ten billion neurons, and it undoubtedly includes some redundancy. By eliminating some of the neurons, the system may be more finely tuned rather than impaired. The analogy which has been used is that of a sculpture. The young brain is like the uncarved piece of rock. Experience and aging sculpt the unformed brain into a finely tuned piece. The rough edges are removed and the core is honed into a representation.

With regard to the interactive changes in the aging nervous system, numerous investigators have emphasized the existence of compensatory processes. For example, Bondareff (1980) demonstrated that reorganization of the dentate gyrus occurs in senescent rats. Loss of both excitatory and inhibitory synapses results in the aging animal's ability to maintain an adaptive level of function. Compensatory mechanisms occur that may result in organization at a new functioning level.

General changes in the aging brain

Although the onset and rate of nervous system aging varies among individuals, some age-related changes occur in everyone if he or she lives long enough. These are normal aging changes. Other changes are caused by pathology that is restricted in incidence to a subset of the population. For example, Parkinson's disease (PD) affects only a limited number of older adults. Estimates of the incidence of PD range from 0.1 to 1.0 percent of the population, and the incidence rises sharply in old age (Kolb & Whishaw, 1995). Clearly, only a small percentage of older adults suffer from PD as it is a disease rather than a normal aging phenomenon. The neural pathology of PD involves the substantia nigra, a nucleus in the brain stem that supplies the neurotransmitter dopamine to the basal ganglia and cerebral cortex. The substantia nigra is almost obliterated in PD. Before the disease is even diagnosed, 85 percent of the cells in the substantia nigra are lost, and more substantia nigra cells are lost as the disease progresses. The magnitude of loss of cells in the substantia nigra in normal aging does not approach the loss occurring in PD.

Changes discussed in this chapter are those that are likely to occur in all individuals as they age. These changes are normative. Only subsets of the population suffer from dementing diseases causing extensive neuropathology. Among these neuropathological diseases are AD, PD, Huntington's disease, and cerebrovascular dementia. Pathological changes associated with neurological diseases that increase in incidence with aging are discussed in chapter 6.

Cell loss

At a cellular level, the most evident change that has been thought to occur in the aging nervous system is that nerve cells or neurons are lost. Neuronal loss is not unique to aging. More cells are lost in fetal and neonatal development than at any other point in the life span. In past decades we associated neural cell death with processes of aging. In reality, neuronal death is most closely associated with early development. Fewer neurons die in the brains of older adults than in the brains of fetuses. Neuron death occurs only in limited areas of the brain in normal aging, if it occurs at all, whereas in fetal development neuronal cell loss occurs in all parts of the brain.

The older brain retains the capacity to change as a function of experience;

it retains plasticity even toward the end of life. Behavioral, electrophysiological, and morphological evidence documents the continued expression of
plasticity in the brains of adult mammals, including humans (Singer, 1992).
The term *plasticity* is used to represent adaptive capacity to change, including
to learn and remember. At the neurobiological level, plasticity can be supported by numerous mechanisms. For example, profound modifications in
the responses of individual neurons recorded electrophysiologically are observed when pharmacological agents are applied to them. In this circumstance, plasticity might be changes in neuronal firing rates resulting from the
increased availability of specific neurotransmitters. Morphological substrates
of brain plasticity have been observed as increased density of dendritic spines
in the cortex of animals exposed to an enriched environment (e.g., Turner &
Greenough, 1985). Another physical form of brain plasticity occurs as functional reorganization after brain lesions. Cortical tissue adjacent to the zone of
destruction can recover functions in a use-dependent manner (Singer, 1992).
Discussion of plasticity includes the capacity for behavioral change as represented in new learning and memory, along with the underlying chemical–
structural–organizational changes that support learning and memory.

   After the massive cell loss occurring primarily in fetal but also in neonatal
development, neural cell numbers remain relatively stable during childhood,
adolescence, and early adulthood. The rate of neuronal loss may accelerate in
late adulthood in the decade of the 60s, but it is difficult to determine the
life-span developmental trajectory of neural loss because cell counts cannot be
undertaken in longitudinal studies of the same individuals. All studies of
neuron numbers are cross-sectional, comparing organisms that died at different ages. Most neuroanatomical studies of cell loss have relatively small
sample sizes, with a few individuals representing each age period. Given that
there is large individual variation in cell numbers in the brain in early life
(e.g., Woodruff-Pak et al., 1990), it is not a certainty that the differences
between cell numbers in young and older brains actually reflect age-related
changes. As discussed in chapter 1, cross-sectional studies reflect differences
between age groups, but the cross-sectional research design does not accurately reflect *changes* with age. However, with few exceptions (e.g., West,
1993b), the published literature describing cross-sectional studies of neural
cell numbers in adulthood and aging has been almost universally interpreted
as representative of age-related changes. Terms like "loss" and brain "shrinkage" were used to interpret the data, but now these interpretations are
coming into question (Wickelgran, 1996). These interpretations rely on
several types of assumptions that are not necessarily accurate.

   Accurately pinpointing the number of neurons in the aging nervous
system has been difficult for several reasons. There is no technique currently
available to examine or count neurons in the living brain. As discussed in

chapter 3 describing methods of assessing the aging brain, computerized scans do not have the resolution to detect individual cells. It is only with post-mortem brain tissue and microscopic analysis that cell counts can be carried out. Counts must be undertaken upon autopsy and so can be done only once – after the death of the individual. Since there is variability in the number of cells in human brains, it is difficult to estimate how much has been lost when an accurate count of what was present in earlier years is simply not available. Estimates of amount of loss are based on cell counts in brains of individuals who died at a younger age. There is no guarantee that the different age groups examined all started with equal numbers of neurons at birth.

Any cultural or environmental phenomenon that may have affected the number of brain cells in fetal and neonatal life could alter the number of adult brain cells for a whole generation. The following is a hypothetical scenario: consider the fact that progress has been made in obstetric and pediatric medicine such that an understanding of optimal nutrition during pregnancy has advanced significantly in the twentieth century. Facts about proper vitamins and diet have been widely disseminated since the mid-twentieth century. It has been documented that malnutrition reduces the number of neurons in fetal and neonatal brains. It is also possible that optimal nutrition during pregnancy advocated in the mid- and late-twentieth century produces brains with significantly more neurons than the less optimal nutrition that pregnant women in the early decades of the twentieth century may have had in part due to lack of awareness of the importance of optimal nutrition. This cultural difference could result in the fact that children born between 1900 and 1930 might have had fewer brain cells than children born between 1960 and the present. Comparisons at autopsy between the brains of older adults born between 1900 and 1930 and young adults born beginning in the 1960s might be interpreted to indicate cell loss in the older brains, when in fact the older brains began life with fewer neurons.

Another technical problem with making inferences about cell loss with human brain tissue is that removal of the brain does not occur immediately after death as it does in animal research. In the intervening time between death and the removal of the brain and tissue fixation, changes can occur in the brain which would render the resulting data inaccurate. Furthermore, tissue fixation affects young and old brains differently, affecting estimates of cell density.

In spite of the difficulties in carrying out cell counts in the human brain, a number of these types of studies have been conducted, and until recently, they concurred in the conclusion that neurons were lost in the aging brain. However, new techniques involving unbiased stereological methods have been developed that are now required for publication of research articles about the number and loss of neurons, glia, synapses, and other structures

(West & Coleman, 1996). The aim of mandating the use of these techniques is to establish more consistency in the reports about aging and cell loss.

The scientist best known for the initial research on estimating the number of cells in the aging brain is Harold Brody (1955, 1978). He performed some of the first hand-counts of brain cells in adults, using accident victims as his subjects. He found differences in the number of cells lost in different areas. The greatest loss was found in the top part of the temporal lobe, which is the superior temporal gyrus. All six layers of the cortex were affected, but the loss was greater in some layers than in others. In the last decade, new methods have been employed in which the cell counts can be automated. Research using the machine-counts corroborated the earlier work. The numbers of neurons in the brains of animals were also found to decline with age using the older techniques. In general, the results from hand-counts, machine-counts, and counts of animal cells indicated that there was a 20–40 percent loss with age in the numbers of neurons in selected regions of the brain.

These conclusions are now being challenged. In the last decade, techniques to detect neuropathology in humans have become more sophisticated. Earlier studies of "normal" aged brains may have inadvertently included patients with early AD or other dementias known to cause extensive neuron loss. A leading neuroscientist investigating AD, Robert Terry, said "Brody is an excellent scientist, but I'm confident that he included Alzheimer's cases and that these lowered his cell counts" (Wickelgran, 1996, p. 49). An Alzheimer's brain has extensive neuronal loss in areas identified by Brody (1955) as having loss due to normal aging. Normal older brains may not have such loss at all (figure 5.1).

We will examine three brain regions that previous investigators have identified as particularly affected by age-related neuron loss. Cognitive capacities affected in normal aging have been related to changes in these regions. Frontal lobe deficits have been associated with age-related impairment of executive functions, attention, and working memory. Hippocampal impairment is implicated in age-related deficits in declarative learning and memory. Cerebellar cortical Purkinje cell loss has been correlated with age-related impairment in a nondeclarative form of learning and memory, classical conditioning. Normal age-related cell loss in these regions may not be as extensive as previously thought, but these brain regions do show changes associated with normal aging that may affect behavior.

Frontal lobes.   The frontal lobes have been characterized as the part of the brain that most distinguishes primates, and especially humans, from other species. Operations carried out by the frontal lobes are called executive functions because they are thought to coordinate and control other cognitive

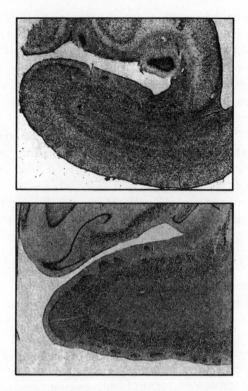

Figure 5.1 An Alzheimer's brain (*above*) shows extensive neuronal loss in the entorhinal cortex compared with a normal brain (*below*)
Source: Hyman, B. T., cited in Wickelgran, I. (1996). For the cortex, neuron loss may be less than thought. *Science, 273,* 48–50

functions. Among the capacities attributed to the frontal lobes are planning, attention, inductive thinking, and working memory. In chapter 4 we emphasized that sensory systems that are the last to develop (distal senses) are the most complex. These senses, vision and audition, are also the most likely to suffer impairment in normal aging. The frontal lobes are the last cortical region to develop, and this "highest" of brain regions is likely to be one of the earliest and hardest hit by processes of aging.

Investigations conducted both in nonhuman primates and in humans have documented neuronal loss in the frontal association cortex (Flood & Coleman, 1988). Alterations in frontal cell morphology have been documented in older monkeys (Brizzee et al., 1980) and humans (Brody, 1955). For example, the total volume of the frontal lobe in humans aged 70 years and older was 17 percent less than frontal lobe volume in young adult humans (Haug et al., 1983). Cortical thickness of the midfrontal area was less in older brains, and there were fewer numbers of large neuron types but greater numbers of small neuron types (Terry et al., 1987). The increased ratio of small to large neurons was interpreted by Terry and his colleagues to represent neuronal shrinkage. The numbers of terminals on presynaptic neurons in the frontal cortex was 23 percent less in subjects over 60 years of age (Masliah et al., 1993). These representative morphological studies, carried out post-mortem, converge to document significant differences in the frontal lobes of older brain.

Neuroanatomical imaging studies in living humans are consistent with the post-mortem data. Comparing all lobes of the cerebral cortex in a cross-sectional study using MRI imaging techniques, it was reported that the greatest differences between young and older subjects were evident in the frontal lobes (Coffey et al., 1992). The volume of tissue in the frontal lobes of older adults was more different (and less) than was any other region. The investigators interpreted these results as indicative of age-related shrinkage in frontal lobes. Comparing various regions of the frontal lobe in adults of different ages, it was concluded that the dorsolateral prefrontal cortex showed the greatest effects in old age (Raz et al., 1993).

PET studies added to the body of evidence indicating that the frontal lobes show some of the greatest differences in the brains of older adults. The mean rate of blood flow in the grey matter of the frontal cortex was less in older adults, and this age difference appeared in the fifth decade (Mamo et al., 1983). Comparable results were reported in a study that used PET and compared young and older subjects (Tachibana et al., 1984). One of the few PET studies to report longitudinal as well as cross-sectional data found consistent blood flow reductions in prefrontal cortex (Shaw et al., 1984). These investigators collected annual PET data over a 4-year period in older adults and found some decreases in blood flow in the prefrontal cortex even in this relatively short time-span. PET studies of memory comparing young and older adults demonstrated less activation in older adults' left prefrontal cortex including the orbitofrontal, inferior, and middle frontal gyri during the encoding phase of a face recognition task (Grady et al., 1995) and less bilateral anterior prefrontal activation during retrieval of words (Schacter et al., 1996).

There is a convergence of evidence from morphological studies carried out post-mortem and imaging studies of neuroanatomical (MRI) and physi-ological (PET) function in the frontal lobes in aging. The components of the frontal lobe most associated with executive function in patients with frontal lobe lesions, the prefrontal cortex, is smaller in volume and less activated in older adults. Many of the age-related deficits in cognition can be interpreted to occur as a consequence of the observed deficits in the older frontal lobe.

Hippocampus. The human hippocampus may be particularly vulnerable to processes of aging. Research has continually demonstrated in several mammalian species that the hippocampus is a brain structure impaired by normal aging processes (Barnes, 1983; Mani et al., 1986; Scheibel et al., 1976). At the same time, it has been pointed out that changes in the hippocampus with normal aging tend to be circumscribed rather than completely global (Barnes et al., 1991). In the aging mammalian nervous system, the age-related changes show regional selectivity, even within a given structure such as the hippocampus.

In particular, a number of studies are consistent in indicating that processes of aging affect hippocampal pyramidal cells. In humans, the pyramidal cells in the CA1 region of the hippocampus are lost with age (Flood & Coleman, 1988). Studies of the CA1 region in the hippocampus of humans, monkeys, rabbits, and rats have reported age differences between pyramidal cell numbers in young and old organisms to fall within the relatively narrow range of 15–19 percent (Coffin et al., 1996; Brizzee & Ordy, 1979; Knox, 1982; Mann et al., 1985; Miller et al., 1984; Mouritzen Dam, 1979).

In the face of apparently uniform documentation of age-related loss in the CA1 hippocampal region, one recent study is discrepant. Using newly developed stereological analyses techniques West (1993a) reported that unbiased estimates of the total number of neurons in the CA1 and CA3 regions of human hippocampus were not significantly different in 32 men aged 13–85 years. Comparing five regions of hippocampus (granule cell layer, hilus of the dentate gyrus, CA3-2, CA1, and the subiculum), significant age differences were observed in the hilus (31 percent fewer cells in older subjects) and subiculum (52 percent less cells in older subjects; West, 1993b; see figure 5.2). It was concluded that the loss of neurons in the hilus and subiculum qualify as potential morphological correlates of senescent decline in memory.

The functional organization of the hippocampus involves a unidirectional system of hippocampal subdivisions in which information flows from the dentate gyrus to the subiculum. Neurons of the hilus participate in the flow of information through the initial portion of circuitry. West (1993b) suggested that a reduction in the number of cells in the hilus would be expected to reduce the associative capacity of the dentate granule cells and the amount of resolution of the information sent to CA1. The loss of cells in the subiculum was interpreted to represent a more profound deficit, first because of the magnitude of the loss and, second, because of the position of the subiculum at the end of the unidirectional system of fiber connections within the hippocampus. Output from the subiculum flows to the entorhinal cortex and hence to other cortical regions. It is this system that is likely involved in the formation of long-term memories (Squire, 1992).

The disparities between the observations of West (1993b) and a large body of studies reviewed by Flood and Coleman (1988) probably result from differences in cell-counting techniques, sampling error, and other metho-

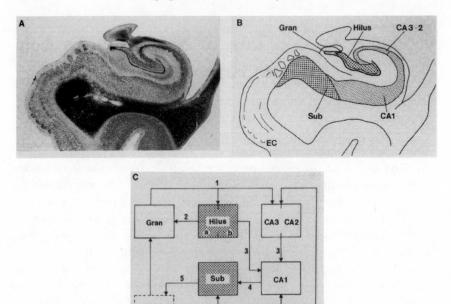

Figure 5.2 Structural organization of the human hippocampal formation. (a) Histological section through the dorsal-medial part of the temporal lobe of the brain showing the transverse organization of the architectonic subdivisions of the hippocampal formation. Medial to the left. Micrograph width = 2 cm. (b) Delineation of the subdivisions of the hippocampal formation in which estimates of the total numbers of neurous were made. *Gran*, the granule cell layer of the dentate gyrus. *Hilus*, the hilus of the dentate gyrus which contains both neurons of the polymorphic layer and the pyramidal neurons of the inner cellular layer. *CA3–2*, the layer containing tightly packed cell bodies of the large pyramidal neurons of the hippocampus proper. *CA1*, the layer containing the cell bodies of smaller, radially dispersed pyramidal neurons of the hippocampus proper. *Sub*, the subiculum, a thick zone of pyramidal neurons organized in two layers. The dotted subdivisions, hilus and sub, are those in which there were significant age-related losses of neurons. Estimates were not made in entorhinal cortex, EC, which has been illustrated for the sake of the discussion of the results. (c) Diagrammatic representation of the major connections of the sub-divisions. Axons of the granule cells (1) synapse on the polymorphic neurons of the hilus (a) and pyramidal neurons of the hilus (b) and CA3. The polymorphic neurons of the hilus (a) provide both excitatory and inhibitory feedback connections to the dentate granule cells (2). The pyramidal neurons of the hilus (b), like those of CA3 project to CA1 (3). The pyramidal neurons of CA2, which were included in the same zone as the pyramidal neurons of CA3, similarly project to CA1 but unlike the pyramidal cells of CA3, do not receive input from the granule cells. The pyramidal neurons of CA1 project to the subiculum (4), which in turn, projects to

dological variations. The techniques advocated and used by West (1993a,b) are currently accepted as the most reliable techniques for assuring valid cell counts. In terms of the implications for neuropsychology, memory impairment would be the consequence of any disruption of the unidirectional flow of information in the system of fiber connections within the hippocampus. Thus, whether it is CA1 pyramidal cells that are lost or neurons in the hilus and subiculum, the net result is to impair the major circuit that translates recent sensory and perceptual experiences into long-term memories.

More direct association between atrophy in the hippocampus and impairment in memory was provided in an imaging study in which brain scan data and memory test performance in the same individuals were assessed (Golomb et al., 1993). Of course, because this study used computerized imaging techniques, the resolution was not at a cellular level. Gross indices of hippocampal atrophy were used that could not possibly differentiate between regions of CA1, hilus, or subiculum. Of the 154 participants ranging in age from 55 to 88 years, one-third had radiographic evidence of hippocampal atrophy. That is, visual inspection of MRI or CT scans indicated reduced volume in the hippocampus (see figure 5.3). The prevalence of hippocampal atrophy increased significantly with age and was more common in male than female participants. Declarative memory, that is memory for events and facts, was significantly impaired in the participants who had hippocampal atrophy.

Cerebellar cortex. The discussion on aging in the cerebellum is based on published studies on humans, monkeys, rabbits, and rats. The focus is on Purkinje cells, the only output cells of cerebellar cortex, and on the major sources of input to Purkinje cells.

A painstaking count of human cerebellar Purkinje cells carried out early in the twentieth century yielded the first and often-replicated result that Purkinje cell numbers decrease with age in adulthood (Ellis, 1920). There was greater loss in the cerebellar anterior lobe than in the hemispheres. Harms (1944) reported that in the human cerebellum up to 25 percent of the

◀ ──

Figure 5.2 (continued) parahippocampal cortical regions, including the entorhinal cortex (5). The entorhinal cortex, in addition to having reciprocal connections with a wide range of cortical association areas, is the major source of extrinsic afferents to the dentate granule cells and pyramidal cells of the hippocampus proper. The age-related losses of neurons in the hilus and the subiculum (shaded regions) compromise the processing of information within the hippocampal formation and the transmission of hippocampal information to other cortical areas

Source: West, M. J. (1993b). Regionally specific loss of neurons in the aging human hippocampus. *Neurobiology of Aging, 14,* 287–293. Reprinted with kind permission from Elsevier Science Ltd, The Boulevard, Langford Lane, Kidlington, OX5 1GB, UK

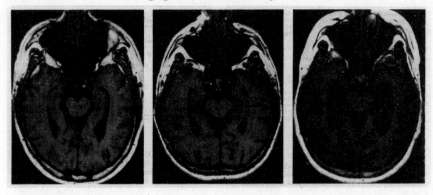

Figure 5.3 Magnetic resonance images demonstrating gradations of hippocampal atrophy (HA) as assessed in the axial plane. *Left:* cognitively normal 66-year-old man with no evidence of HA. *Center:* cognitively normal 70-year-old man with questionable right-sided and mild-to-moderate left-sided HA as indicated by a dilated cerebrospinal fluid space medial to the hippocampal body. *Right:* 71-year-old demented man with a clinical diagnosis of probable Alzheimer's disease and bilateral, severe HA. Note the temporal lobe sulcal prominence and enlarged temporal horns indicative of neocortical atrophy

Source: Golomb, J., de Leon, M. J., Kluger, A., George, A. E., Tarshish, C., & Ferris, S. H. (1993). Hippocampal atrophy in normal aging. *Archives of Neurology, 50,* 967–973. Copyright © 1993, American Medical Association

Purkinje cells were lost in very old patients. This result has been verified using more recently developed techniques by Hall et al. (1975). In the Hall et al. study, 90 normal cerebella were assessed in subjects ranging from childhood to over the age of 100 years. Wide individual variations were found at all ages, but a mean reduction of 2.5 percent of the Purkinje cells per decade was found which represents a 25 percent reduction over the 100-year period of life which was studied.

A 44 percent decrease in the number of Purkinje cells in the left cerebellar cortex of 20-year-old rhesus monkeys as compared to 4-year-old monkeys was observed (Nandy, 1981). The numbers of granule cells in the same area were relatively equal in the two age groups. Rogers et al. (1984) reported neuroanatomical changes in Purkinje cells in older rats. In Golgi–Kopsch sections, many 26-month-old Purkinje cells appeared defoliated, with small distal dendrites and spiny branchlets being the most affected. There was a significant decrease in the mean Purkinje cell area between 6-month-old rats and 26-month-old rats. The authors suggested that the morphologic changes might be the hallmark of dying cells. In every vermis lobule examined, there was a significant senescent decrease in Purkinje neuron density. The mean number of Purkinje cells/mm of Purkinje cell layer declined from 16.6 cells/

mm in young rats to 12.5 cells/mm in old rats. Related to the Purkinje cell loss was a loss in synaptic density.

We examined Purkinje cells in sections of rabbit cerebellar cortical areas including the vermis and area HVI (Woodruff-Pak et al., 1990). The two groups of rabbits had mean ages of 3 and 40 months. Comparisons of the total number of Purkinje cells counted for each age group revealed a highly significant difference, with the older rabbits having fewer cells. Cell counts in the molecular layer in the same animals indicated no age differences. Age differences in cell number were limited to the Purkinje cells. This result suggests that differential tissue shrinkage in young and old brains was not affecting age difference in Purkinje cell number. The correlation between Purkinje cell number and age was −0.79 ($p < 0.001$; see figure 5.4).

Using immunohistochemical staining techniques, Coffin et al. (1996) reported Purkinje cell counts for 25 rabbits ranging in age from 3 to 85 months. There were significant age differences in Purkinje cell populations with older rabbits exhibiting substantially fewer cells. Individual section counts of cells in the cerebellar cortical region called lobule HVI ranged from 52 to 326 Purkinje cells. Clearly, there was considerable variability in individual cell counts. Across the age-span that was studied (representing about 89 percent of the rabbit's 96-month or 8-year life expectancy), there was a 50 percent difference in mean Purkinje cell number. In general, older rabbits had fewer Purkinje cells. The correlation between age and Purkinje cell number was $r = -0.82$.

We interpreted these results as indicative of a "loss" or "change" in neuron numbers in the aging brain. As mentioned previously, the research design was cross-sectional, and the results could not directly assess cell loss. The most compelling evidence for cell "loss" in this study was the frequent appearance of gaps between cells in the cerebellar cortical Purkinje cell layer in older rabbit tissue. Cerebellar Purkinje cells lie in a single row between the granule and molecular cell layers. At the light-microscopic level, Purkinje cells in young and young adult rabbit tissue were tightly packed and evenly spaced. In middle-aged tissue samples, gaps appeared between some cells. In the oldest tissue samples, there were fewer cells and the Purkinje cell layer was interrupted with frequent gaps. The consistency of this pattern, coupled with the lower numbers of neurons counted in aged rabbit brains, suggests that gaps between neurons may appear as the result of age-related cell loss.

In addition to anatomical differences in young and older Purkinje cells, other measures of Purkinje cell efficiency have given evidence of age differences. Assessing Purkinje cell electrophysiology in Sprague–Dawley rats, Rogers et al. (1980) identified a number of cell firing parameters which were affected by age. In particular, increasing numbers of aberrant, very slow-firing

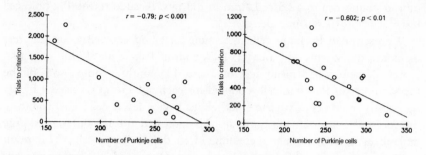

Figure 5.4 Number of Purkinje cells in rabbits plotted as a function of trials to learning criterion. *Left*: in 12 rabbits ranging in age from 3 to 50 months, the correlation between Purkinje cell number and trials to learning criterion was -0.79 ($p < 0.001$). *Right*: in 18 rabbits of a similar age (3 months old), the correlation between Purkinje cell number and trials to learning criterion was -0.60 ($p < 0.01$)

Source: Woodruff-Pak, D. S., Cronholm, J. F., & Sheffield, J. B. (1990). Purkinje cell number related to rate of eyeblink classical conditioning. *NeuroReport, 1,* 165–168

cells were encountered in older animals. Purkinje neurons from old rats were significantly less sensitive to locally applied neurotransmitters than neurons from young rats (Marwaha et al., 1981). Marwaha et al. (1981) hypothesized that there was a senescent postsynaptic change in noradrenergic transmission in Purkinje cells.

Evidence for loss of synapses in the cerebellar cortex of the rat has been provided by Glick and Bondareff (1979). Numbers of synapses were compared in the cerebellar cortex of 12-month-old and 25-month-old rats, and the total number of axodendritic synapses was found to be 24 percent lower in the older rats. While there were no age differences in synapses on dendritic shafts, there was a 33 percent decrease in synapses involving the spines in older rats. Glick and Bondareff hypothesized that granule cells, the axons of which form the majority of synaptic contacts with dendritic spines of Purkinje cells, may be preferentially impaired. The age-related loss of axospinous synapses may also depend upon the involvement of a specific population of postsynaptic cells (i.e., Purkinje cells), which are known to decrease with age.

Undertaking a comparative neuropathological study of aging using the brains of 47 species of vertebrates, Dayan (1971) observed that changes in the cerebellum generally resembled those seen in other parts of the brain. However, the loss of Purkinje cells was readily apparent. Indeed, Dayan concluded that there is a generalized loss of neurons in the brain "most easily detected as fall-out of Purkinje cells from the cerebellar cortex" (Dayan, 1971, p. 37).

It is not possible to assess Purkinje cell number *in vivo*, but MRI investigations of the cerebellum corroborate the post-mortem studies indicating that there is tissue loss in human cerebellar cortex. Measuring cerebellar vermis in human aging, Raz et al. (1993) demonstrated age-related regional differences in cerebellar vermis. Total area of the cerebellar vermis was significantly reduced in size, and it was the region of dorsal vermis (declive, folium, and tuber) that showed the greatest aging effects. This region of cerebellum is the most recently evolved and therefore likely to be of particular significance in human behavior. Because the cerebellum is increasingly thought to play a role in cognition, the fact that the "highest" regions of cerebellar cortex show age-related impairment has significance in the neuropsychology of aging.

The loss of neurons is one of the most significant age changes in the nervous system. There are a number of other changes as well, including changes in some of the components comprising the neuron, such as the membrane and nucleus, a build-up in all parts of the neuron interior of a substance called lipofuscin, and an increase in the number and density of support cells (glial cells).

Cerebrovascular changes

An age change which may have significant impact on the sensory capacities of the organism actually occurs outside the nervous system. This is the change which occurs in the arteries supplying blood to the brain and nervous system throughout the body. The arteries throughout the body lose elasticity and become more rigid and narrow in older adults. Arteries first begin to harden in the decade of the 30s and very gradually they become more rigid. This process is a part of normal aging. The elastin tissue in the arteries is replaced by collagen which is a stiffer, more rigid fiber. This constricts the arteries and often results in an increase in blood pressure as well as a decrease in blood flow. The process is exacerbated in the case of arteriosclerosis. When neurons receive less oxygen supply from blood they function less efficiently and will die if the oxygen reduction is significant. Thus, the loss in sensitivity in some of the sensory modalities may be a result of insufficient blood supply to the receptors.

Neurotransmitter systems

The chemicals stored at axon terminals and released when neurons fire are called neurotransmitters. Brain neurotransmitter systems typically have their cells of origin located in nuclei in the brain stem. Axons from these nuclei project to designated regions, activating specific postsynaptic structures. We have already discussed one such neurotransmitter system, the dopamine system with its origin in the substantia nigra. Neurotransmitter systems interact with one another rather than functioning independently. In the following, we will discuss how various neurotransmitters interact to affect learning and memory. Although several neurotransmitter systems affect learning and memory, certain neurotransmitter systems have been associated with other specific cognitive functions. In general, the neurotransmitter acetylcholine is associated most closely with learning and memory, dopamine is associated with executive function and motor control, norepinephrine is associated with arousal and depression, and serotonin is associated with sleep and wakefulness. Changes in these neurotransmitter systems with age affect cognitive processes.

Neurotransmitter systems may be compromised during the aging process by several mechanisms: (a) loss of cells of origin; (b) alterations in neural projections; (c) changes in metabolic activity; (d) changes in synthetic capacity; (e) alterations in catabolic activity; (f) increases or decreases in receptor density; and (g) alterations in both firing rate and postsynaptic responses. These mechanisms are interactive, with changes in one likely affecting the status of the others.

Acetylcholine and medial-temporal lobe memory circuits.   In describing the history of the cholinergic hypothesis, Geula and Mesulam (1994) noted that experiments in the early 1970s demonstrated that cholinergic blockade with scopolamine caused memory loss in young human subjects resembling the memory loss seen in normal aging and early AD. Acetylcholine is widely distributed throughout the central nervous system. Its source of origin in humans is in the nucleus basalis of Myenart, and ascending cholinergic projections synapse in most regions of cerebral cortex and in limbic structures known to be involved in learning and memory.

In both humans and monkeys, aging impairs the efficiency of the cholinergic neurotransmitter system affecting processes of memory (Bartus et al., 1987). Age-related declines in cholinergic receptor binding have been observed in rats (Lippa et al., 1980). The cholinergic neurotransmitter system is severely impaired in AD (Coyle et al., 1983). Muscarinic cholinergic receptors are largely preserved in AD, whereas nicotinic cholinergic receptors are reduced in number (Whitehouse et al., 1986). Cholinergic reductions in cerebral cortex have been attributed to atrophy of cholinergic cells in ventral forebrain nuclei, especially the nucleus basalis of Myenert (Mesulam et al., 1987).

There is considerable evidence from both animal and human studies that the cholinergic system is involved in memory processes and that age-related changes compromise the system to some degree (Court et al., 1993; Bartus et al., 1987). Furthermore, in basal-forebrain-damaged rats and patients diagnosed with AD, decline in memory function is exacerbated (for a review see Kesner, 1988). However, age-related declines in monoaminergic systems, and subsequent impairments in cognitive performance, have also been reported (Gold & Zornetzer, 1983).

Zornetzer (1986) pointed out that while the cholinergic system has taken "center stage" with regard to the attention focused upon its role in memory loss in normal aging and AD, it is unlikely that any one neurotransmitter system could account for the effects of aging and disease on learning and memory. Other neurotransmitter systems such as the catecholamines and opioids have been implicated in normal memory processes. These and other neurotransmitter systems must be studied with animal models if we are to understand more fully the effects of aging and pathology on learning and memory.

Dopamine and the prefrontal cortex. The catecholamine, dopamine, is found in the highest levels in the monkey cortex in the prefrontal region. Many areas of the frontal lobe are innervated with neurons using norepinephrine as their neurotransmitter as well (Levitt et al., 1984). The presence of catecholamines, particularly dopamine, appears to be essential for the prefrontal cortex to function properly (Brozoski et al., 1979). Biochemical analysis of neurotransmitter levels in the brains of "young-old" rhesus monkeys (aged 10–18 years) revealed substantial depletions in cortical catecholamine levels (Goldman-Rakic & Brown, 1981). Of the many regions studied, only the prefrontal and temporal cortices showed large depletions of dopamine of 50 percent or more. The older the animal, the greater were the dopamine depletions. Bartus et al. (1983) did not observe any cognitive improvement in Cebus monkeys over 18 years of age when they administered various doses of the dopamine-enhancing drug clonidine. On the other hand, research by Arnsten and Goldman-Rakic (1985) demonstrated that 18–30-year-old rhesus monkeys that were impaired on frontal tasks benefitted from treatment with clonidine. Robust improvements in delayed response performance were observed in a dose-related manner. At the most effective dose level, a majority of the monkeys were able to achieve near perfect performance. While the neurochemical mechanisms underlying the ability of the drug to ameliorate performance are not understood, the dose–response curves are consonant with clonidine having actions at postsynaptic receptors.

Norepinephrine. Central norepinephrine systems are derived mainly from the locus coeruleus, a prominent nucleus located in the brainstem reticular formation at the level of the isthmus. These norepinephrine-containing locus coeruleus cell bodies are highly collateralized, projecting to virtually all areas of the central nervous system. Small caliber, slow conducting norepinephrine axons from locus coeruleus cell bodies connect with the amygdala, hippocampus, hypothalamus, thalamus, and cerebellum. In addition, the locus coeruleus is believed to be the only source of norepinephrine fibers for most of the forebrain.

The first report of significant cell loss of locus coeruleus neurons in aged human brain was presented by Vijayashankar and Brody (1979). In their preparation, a 40 percent decrease in locus coeruleus neurons occurred by the ninth decade. In a similar study conducted by Tomlinson et al. (1981), results were more variable, with some subjects exhibiting a 30–40 percent loss of locus coeruleus neurons by the eighth and ninth decades. In this same study, a comparison between normal aged and AD revealed a further decline in locus coeruleus neurons in 50 percent of the AD cases. Bondareff et al. (1982) found significantly fewer locus coeruleus neurons in AD cases as compared to normal aged brain. In addition, a portion of the AD cases, characterized by a high dementia score, exhibited an 80 percent loss of locus coeruleus neurons.

It has been suggested that impaired cognition in aged humans may be related to a decline in the amount of norepinephrine synthesized by locus coeruleus neurons. This decline could be due to damage to the neurons or reductions in their numbers (Bondareff, 1985). This hypothesis gains some support in that extensive loss of locus coeruleus cells and reduced norepinephrine levels have been reported in AD (Adolfsson et al., 1979; Bondareff et al., 1982).

It is apparent that significant age-related deficits in presynaptic activities of the noradrenergic system are confined to losses in norepinephrine cells of origin in the locus coeruleus and that this loss may be exacerbated in AD. The norepinephrine system may have greater losses postsynaptically than presynaptically. There are consistent losses in postsynaptic norepinephrine receptors and membranes (Rogers & Bloom, 1985). As reported by McGeer (1978), loss of beta-adrenergic receptors over the life span, particularly in the cerebellum, occurs in both rodent (30 percent) and human (50 percent) brain.

The substantial loss of cerebellar Purkinje cells in normal aging was mentioned previously. The significance of this finding is that cerebellar Purkinje cells contain beta-adrenergic receptors. Thus, a reduction in the amount of postsynaptic membranes available, coupled with a loss in the number of possible receptor binding sites, would result in a dysfunction of the system regardless of the amount of norepinephrine available.

A study designed to test dysfunction in the cerebellar norepinephrine system was conducted by Marwaha et al. (1981). A measure of the sensitivity of cerebellar Purkinje neurons to locally applied norepinephrine was assessed in both young and old rats. The pathway of norepinephrine fibers to their target membranes in the cerebellum was described by Freedman et al. (1977). Essentially, norepinephrine fibers arising from the locus coeruleus ascend through the superior cerebellar peduncle and synapse on cerebellar Purkinje neurons. Activation of this input inhibits spontaneous discharge of the cerebellar Purkinje neurons. The amount of norepinephrine required to inhibit Purkinje cells increased with age. Although an increase in beta-adrenergic receptors in the cerebellum during aging has been demonstrated (Pittman et al., 1980), this compensatory mechanism was apparently insufficient in the Marwaha et al. study.

These studies, in conjunction with the data on senescent changes in cerebellar Purkinje cells, suggest a postsynaptic change in noradrenergic transmission. A study by Bickford-Wimer et al. (1988) demonstrated that dysfunction of norepinephrine modulation occurs in senescent cerebellum, and the consequences are more than simple disinhibition. There appears to be a reduction in norepinephrine's ability to differentially modulate the actions of target cells (Rogers & Ashton-Jones, 1988).

Norepinephrine may have an essential role in retention rather than acquisition of a novel task, so that manipulations of norepinephrine after training may produce more dramatic results (Zornetzer et al., 1978). Decker and McGaugh (1989) demonstrated that norepinephrine-depleted mice exhibit no disruption in the acquisition of a place-learning task, but they show accelerated forgetting.

This result suggests a possible interaction between norepinephrine and other neurotransmitter substances involved in learning and memory. Several researchers have studied the interaction of norepinephrine and acetylcholine. The concurrent manipulation of the two substances has been examined, as has the direct effect of norepinephrine on isolated acetylcholine-rich cerebral cortical slices. Vizi (1980), using an isolated cerebral cortex slice preparation, reported that removal of noradrenergic input via lesion of the locus coeruleus resulted in an enhanced rate of acetylcholine release. Vizi interpreted this result to demonstrate the modulatory role of norepinephrine on acetylcholine release.

In a related study, Sara (1989) demonstrated that lesions of the septo-hippocampal cholinergic pathway led to an enhancement of noradrenergic activity. This resulted in an inhibition of the spared cholinergic neurons. Results demonstrating interactions between neurotransmitter systems may have implications for the study of AD. There are major losses of cholinergic and noradrenergic cells of origin in AD. Many of the cells of origin for acetylcholine in the brain are located in the nucleus basalis of Myenert. Cells of origin for norepinephrine are located in the locus coeruleus. Cell loss in AD is extensive in both nucleus basalis and the locus coeruleus.

The exact role of the noradrenergic system in learning and memory is less defined than that of the cholinergic system. As noted by Whitehouse (1988), manipulations of the noradrenergic system by experimental lesions of locus coeruleus in animals do not produce consistent memory impairments as compared to analogous procedures in the cholinergic projection system. Nevertheless, it is clear that the loss in locus coeruleus cells has negative implications for memory capacity in later life. Loss of cells in the locus coeruleus results in a drop in norepinephrine in normal aging, along with a decline in the postsynaptic responsiveness to norepinephrine.

One technique which has been successful in increasing brain norepinephrine level and improving memory performance in older rats is the transplantation of fetal locus coeruleus neurons into the older rats' brains (Collier et al., 1985). Techniques such as pharmacological interventions and brain transplants are of demonstrated usefulness in ameliorating learning and memory in animal models.

Serotonin.   Cell bodies of origin for serotonin lie in nine clusters in or near the raphe region of the pons and upper brainstem. There are six distinct pathways through which raphe nuclei project. These pathways connect to a variety of forebrain structures. Both the dorsal raphe nucleus and the median raphe nucleus project to the neocortex, especially to layer IV of the visual cortex.

The serotoninergic system may play a highly selective role in the processes underlying learning and memory. It has been suggested that serotonin may be involved in the ability of an animal to acquire or express novel behaviors (Altman & Normile, 1988). Age-related cell loss in the raphe nucleus has been observed, but age changes in the serotoninergic system appear to be more discrete than age changes in the noradrenergic system. Most changes are confined to losses in receptor density.

One consistent finding in normal aging is a decrease in the density of serotonin binding sites (e.g., Wenk et al., 1987). In a study using PET, Wong et al. (1984) found a linear decline of serotonin receptor binding with age. This type of *in vivo* preparation suggests a correlation between receptor binding and the density of receptor sites. Marcusson et al. (1984) reported an age-related decrease in serotonin receptors.

Several studies have been undertaken in an effort to determine the role of the serotoninergic system in the processes underlying learning and memory. Pharmacological manipulations of serotonin uptake have produced contradictory results. Altman (1985) found significant interference in a one-trial inhibitory avoidance paradigm, when postsynaptic serotonin receptors were blocked with pirenperone. In a subsequent study the effects appear to be dose- and time-dependent (Altman & Normile, 1987). The results suggest a differential role of the serotoninergic system in learning and memory, with reduction in serotonin levels administered prior to training producing an impairment in performance. Post-training administration produces a facilitative effect (see also Normile & Altman, 1988).

Synaptic plasticity and molecular changes

Over the past several years, many researchers have redirected the target of their investigation from neurotransmitter systems to actions at the molecular level within cells. Among the sub-cellular phenomena which are being investigated are changes in extracellular or intracellular calcium levels, decrements in the function of excitatory amino acid receptors, and changes in electrophysiological measures of neural response to external stimulation such as frequency potentiation (FP) and long-term potentiation (LTP). Although these aspects of neuronal function appear to be diverse, it can be shown that these elements interact. Changes in any one measure can affect the others.

Calcium has been shown to have actions at both the cellular and molecular levels. Evidence suggests that neurotransmitter release is directed by voltage-sensitive calcium conductance. Calcium homeostasis must be preserved for the efficient release of neurotransmitters. Moreover, calcium-dependent potassium channels respond to an influx of calcium into the neuron during the course of an action potential. Thus calcium plays a role in regulating the outflow of potassium from the neuron and the resultant hyperpolarization of the neuron. Any disruption or alteration in the calcium balance or regulatory actions poses an immediate threat to the integrity of the neuron. Too much intracellular calcium can result in dysfunction or cell death (Schanne et al., 1979). Some cognition-enhancing drugs ameliorate calcium balance and thus improve cognition (Disterhoft et al., 1993; Nabeshima, 1994).

The calcium channel hypothesis of aging was presented by Khachaturian (1984, 1989). It was proposed that the aging brain loses the ability to regulate intracellular calcium homeostatically. This impairment results in a cascade of problems, depending on the type of neuron involved and the amount of disregulation. Among the consequences of cellular impairment resulting from intracellular calcium regulating are chronic changes in neurotransmitter release at the synapse and neuronal death (Feig & Lipton, 1990).

One of the mechanisms hypothesized to contribute to an increase of intracellular calcium is overstimulation of a subtype of excitatory amino acid receptor (Azmitia et al., 1988). The most widely studied excitatory amino acid receptor is *N*-methyl-D-aspartate (NMDA). Significant age-related changes occur in NMDA receptors. Magnusson and Cotman (1993) reported a decrease in NMDA receptor binding sites in old mice in regions of the cerebral cortex and hippocampus. NMDA receptors appear to be selectively vulnerable to processes of aging throughout much of the cerebral cortex and hippocampus.

Summary

Aging in the nervous system cannot be described as occurring in systematic and predictable phases such as is the case for development in the nervous system. Instead, a number of structures change in the nervous system with age, and the rate and magnitude of these changes vary among individuals. One of the most generalized findings in the literature on aging in the nervous system is the observation of fewer cells in older brains. However, this result is presently receiving serious challenge. The loss of cells that has been reported is not random, but occurs in selected regions of the brain and in specific types of cells. Furthermore, although some cell loss likely occurs in normal aging, it is not necessarily accurate to associate all cell loss with inevitable age-related loss in behavioral capacity. Plasticity in the aging brain is retained throughout adulthood and old age.

Two brain regions significant for cognition, in which cellular changes and behavioral capacity are likely associated, are the frontal lobes and the hippocampus. There is a convergence of evidence from morphological studies carried out post-mortem and imaging studies of neuroanatomical (MRI) and physiological (PET) function in the frontal lobes in aging. The portion of the frontal lobe most associated with executive function in patients with frontal lobe lesions, the prefrontal cortex, is smaller in volume and less activated during cognitive tasks in older adults. Many of the age-related deficits in cognition can be interpreted to occur as a consequence of the observed deficits in the older frontal lobe.

The functional organization of the hippocampus involves a unidirectional system of hippocampal subdivisions in which information flows from the dentate gyrus to the subiculum. Earlier studies reported loss of pyramidal cells in the CA1 pyramidal region of hippocampus, but more recent studies using techniques now regarded as more valid identify a reduction in the number of cells in the hilus and subiculum of the human hippocampus. Memory impairment would be the consequence of any disruption of the unidirectional flow of information in the system of fiber connections within the hippocampus. Thus, whether it is CA1 pyramidal cells that are lost or neurons in the hilus and subiculum, the net result is to impair the major circuit that translates recent sensory and perceptual experiences into long-term memories.

More direct association between atrophy in the hippocampus and impairment in memory was provided in an imaging study in which brain scan data and memory test performance in the same individuals were assessed. Visual inspection of MRI or CT scan data from these participants indicated reduced volume in the hippocampus in one-third of them. The prevalence of hippocampal atrophy increased significantly with age and was more common in male than female participants. Declarative memory was significantly impaired in the participants who had hippocampal atrophy.

Purkinje cell loss in cerebellar cortex has been observed in many sub-human species as well as in humans. In rabbits this cell loss was highly associated with the rate of associative learning. It is not possible to assess Purkinje cell number *in vivo*, but MRI investigations of the cerebellum corroborate the post-mortem studies indicating that there is tissue loss in human cerebellar cortex. Because the cerebellum is increasingly thought to play a role in human cognition, the fact that the "highest" regions of cerebellar cortex show age-related impairment has significance in the neuropsychology of aging.

The loss of neurons is one of the most significant age changes in the nervous system. There are a number of other changes as well, including changes in some of the components comprising the neuron such as the membrane and nucleus, a build-up in all parts of the neuron interior of a substance called lipofuscin, and an increase in the number and density of support cells (glial cells). Non-neural tissue shows age-related effects as well.

Arteries throughout the body lose elasticity and become more rigid and narrow in older adults. This change begins in the decade of the 30s and is a part of normal aging. The elastin tissue in the arteries is replaced by collagen which is a stiffer, more rigid fiber. This constricts the arteries and often results in an increase in blood pressure as well as a decrease in blood flow. The process is exacerbated in the case of arteriosclerosis. When neurons receive less oxygen supply from blood they function less efficiently and will die if the oxygen reduction is significant.

Neurotransmitters are the chemicals stored at axon terminals and released when neurons fire. Brain neurotransmitter systems typically have their cells of origin located in nuclei in the brain stem. Axons from these nuclei project to designated regions activating specific postsynaptic structures. Neurotransmitter systems interact with one another rather than functioning independently. There are age-related changes in neurotransmitter systems producing acetylcholine, dopamine, norepinephrine, and serotonin that may affect learning, memory, attention, executive function, and other behavioral processes.

In addition to investigations of brain neurotransmitters, sub-cellular phenomena such as changes in extracellular or intracellular calcium levels, decrements in the function of excitatory amino acid receptors, and changes in electrophysiological measures of neural response to external stimulation are being investigated. Although these aspects of neuronal function appear to be diverse, it can be shown that these elements interact. Calcium has been shown to have actions at both the cellular and molecular level. Evidence suggests that neurotransmitter release is directed by voltage-sensitive calcium conductance. Calcium homeostasis must be preserved for the efficient release of neurotransmitters. The calcium channel hypothesis of aging suggests that the aging brain loses the ability to regulate intracellular calcium homeostatically. This impairment results in a cascade of problems, depending on the type of neuron involved and the amount of disregulation.

Further Reading

Golomb, J., de Leon, M. J., Kluger, A., George, A. E., Tarshish, C., & Ferris S. H. (1993). Hippocampal atrophy in normal aging. *Archives of Neurology, 50,* 967–973.
This unique study reports neuropsychological test data on memory in relation to brain imaging data for a large group of older adults.

West, M. J. (1993). New stereological methods for counting neurons. *Neurobiology of Aging, 14,* 275–285. Reprinted in Vol. 17 (1996) of *Neurobiology of Aging.*
The new standards for assessing differences in brain tissue are described in this article – a must for any reader who needs to understand state-of-the art cell counting techniques.

West, M. J. (1993). Regionally specific loss of neurons in the aging human hippocampus. *Neurobiology of Aging, 14,* 287–293.
An application of the new standard stereological methods to human brain tissue over the adult life span.

Mesulam, M.-M. (1988). Involutional and developmental implications of age-related neuronal changes: In search of an engram for wisdom. *Neurobiology of Aging, 8,* 581–583.
A commentary on the fact that age-related loss of neural cells need not be interpreted simply in terms of a biological decremental aging model.

Disterhoft, J. F., Moyer, J. R., Jr., & Thompson, L. T. (1994). The calcium rationale in aging and Alzheimer's disease. In J. F. Disterhoft, W. H. Gispen, J. Traber, & Z. S. Khachaturian (Eds.), *Calcium hypothesis of aging and dementia* (Vol. 747, Annals of the New York Academy of Sciences; pp. 382–406). New York: New York Academy of Sciences.
This article presents an overview of the calcium hypothesis of cellular impairment in aging and presents an animal model to test the hypothesis.

6

Neuropathological
Brain Aging

Dementia is undoubtedly the most feared outcome in old age, although depression, a topic addressed in chapter 7, is probably the most common emotional problem of the elderly. Older adults hope to avoid becoming a burden to their families and experience unjustified anxiety at the mildest sign of cognitive impairment. When a young person misplaces the keys, little concern is experienced. It is quite a natural thing to forget where you put something you use every day. However, when an old person misplaces something, he or she wonders if this is the beginning of senility. There is a tremendous fear among the elderly that they are going to "lose their mind." A common symptom of depression in the aged is memory loss. Conversely, severe depression often occurs as an individual realizes that his or her memory is failing significantly. Devastating, progressive degeneration of cognitive and eventually physical capacity occurs in Alzheimer's disease (AD). Other diseases causing dementia in older adults include cerebrovascular dementia (CVD), and Huntington's disease (HD). The dementia observed in about 30 percent of the patients with Parkinson's disease (PD) is now attributed to a relatively low level of co-existing AD pathology that is sufficient to burden the already compromised brain and lead to dementia (E. Braak & H. Braak, 1996).

A brief history of dementia and Alzheimer's disease (AD)

Dementia is a state of mind in which extreme memory loss, confusion, and lack of orientation in location and time prevail. The word was first used as the adjective "demented," dated to 1644 by the *Oxford English Dictionary* and having ancient origins stemming from the Latin *demens* ("without mind";

Berrios, 1994). The idea that dementia had a vascular origin is over 100 years old, and at the turn of the twentieth century virtually all cases of dementia were associated with arteriosclerosis. Although earlier neuropathologists had associated non-vascular pathology with clinical signs of dementia, the association of dementia with vascular pathology prevailed. It was Alois Alzheimer's key findings in a single case, reported in 1906, that separated the concepts of dementia and aging and established Alzheimer's disease as a distinct illness apart from cerebrovascular dementia (figure 6.1).

Interestingly, like many cases that confront us in the clinical neuropsychology of aging, the first patient diagnosed with AD was not a pure case. A contemporary diagnosis would be mixed AD and CVD. Alois Alzheimer's

Figure 6.1 Photograph of Professor Alois Alzheimer
Source: *The News*, Hoechst AG; reproduced by permission of National Library of Medicine/ Science Photo Library, London

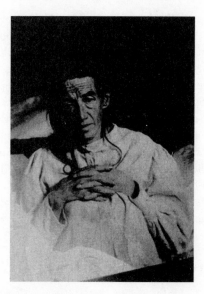

Figure 6.2 Photograph of the first case diagnosed with Alzheimer's disease, a 51-year-old woman named Auguste D.
Source: O'Brien, C. (1996). Auguste D. and Alzheimer's disease. *Science, 273,* 28

patient was a 51-year-old woman called Auguste D. who came under his care in 1901 at Frankfurt's Hospital for the Mentally Ill and Epileptics (figure 6.2). She remained there until her death in 1906. Her file, with many notes in Alzheimer's handwriting, was recently found and contained transcripts of conversations that revealed her confusion (O'Brien, 1996). Alzheimer wrote that she sat on her bed with a helpless expression, and when he asked her name, she said, "Auguste." Then he asked for her last name, and she replied, "Auguste." Finally, he asked her what her husband's name was. "Auguste, I think," was her reply (O'Brien, 1996, p. 28). Samples of her handwriting included in the file indicate that she was unable to write her own name without being reminded of what she was doing. Alzheimer tested her and interviewed her over a 5-day period and concluded that she suffered from senile dementia at an early age. When she died four and a half years later, he autopsied her brain and discovered the characteristic neurofibrillary tangles and senile plaques that characterize AD. What his notes also revealed was his observation of occlusions in the smaller cerebral blood vessels, a pathology that would rule out pure AD in contemporary diagnoses.

Alois Alzheimer described the symptoms of this patient at a meeting of psychiatrists in Tübingen, Germany, in 1906 and published the results in 1907, but it was Emil Kraepelin, a co-worker and close intellectual collaborator of Alzheimer's, who really named the disease. Kraepelin published an influential psychiatry textbook in 1910, mentioning "this Alzheimer's disease" (O'Brien, 1996). It was from 1910 that the diagnosis of AD was occasionally applied to non-vascular dementia, even though part of Auguste D.'s dementia may have been cerebrovascular as well. Until the last two decades, AD was considered to be extremely rare, and it is only with recent developments in diagnostic techniques that recognition of the prevalence of AD has occurred.

AD accounts for a major portion of the senility in older people. Robert Katzman (1984), an authority on neuropathology in aging and AD, estimated that if he were to carry out 1,000 autopsies of individuals who had been demented in late life, 53 percent would be diagnosed as having AD, 23 percent would have had CVD, 14 percent would have had mixed CVD and AD, and 10 percent would have had various other pathologies. Thus, the majority of dementia cases are caused by AD.

Late-life onset (sporadic) AD

AD is not the outcome of normal aging. It is not a disease to which we will all succumb if only we live long enough. Rather it is a disease affecting a relatively small proportion of the older population at any given time. Mortimer (1983) estimated that after the age of 65 about 1 percent of the aged per year will suffer the onset of AD. This estimate indicated that the cumulative risk to individuals surviving to 85 years of age was 20 percent (Mortimer et al., 1981). More recent estimates of the incidence of AD are higher. Katzman and Kawas (1994) estimated that 2 percent of the population aged between 65 and 70 would have AD, 4 percent between the ages of 71 and 75, 8 percent between the ages of 76 and 80, and 16 percent over the age of 80. Evans et al. (1989) projected an even steeper rate of increase in the incidence of AD with advancing age. The projection for the age categories of 65–74 was 3 percent; for the ages of 75–84, the projection was 18.7 percent; and for individuals over the age of 85, the incidence in the population was projected to be 47.2 percent.

Most estimates of the prevalence of AD make it appear to be a relatively rare disease, but because there is an increasing percentage of older people in the population, especially in the over 85 age group that has the highest incidence of AD, the numbers of AD patients are high. It is difficult to count accurately the number of victims of AD because accurate pre-mortem diagnosis requires extensive testing, often including brain imaging. Many elderly demented patients are not tested thoroughly because presently there is little additional treatment available when AD is diagnosed.

Various estimates of the number of victims of AD exist. United States government statistics published by the National Institute on Aging in the early 1980s estimated that two million people suffered from AD. At present, that figure has been doubled to 4 million. It has been projected that the number of Americans over the age of 65 in the year 2020 will reach 43 million. If the prevalence of AD remains similar to what it is at the present time, there could be 10 million victims of this devastating disease. Significant resources have been committed to research on AD since the mid-1970s. To diagnose, treat, and prevent the occurrence of AD in future cohorts of elderly, the National Institutes of Health have increased support of research on dementia by more than 800 percent.

Diagnosis of AD

Impaired learning and memory ability are the behavioral hallmarks of AD. AD is a progressive dementia characterized neuropathologically by extensive loss of neurons and the presence of amyloid-containing senile plaques (SPs) as well as neurofibrillary tangles (NFTs; Price et al., 1989). Alzheimer-like neuropathology has been observed in the brains of virtually all adults with DS autopsied over the age of 35 years (Mann & Esiri, 1989). It has been proposed that the progressive accumulation of amyloid fibrils in the extracellular space of the AD and DS/AD brain is a central event in the pathogenesis of the disease (Hardy & Allsop, 1991), and many scientists maintain that the initiation of the cascade of events resulting in AD begins with genetic triggering of excess production of β-amyloid (Selkoe, 1996). The relationship between β-amyloid deposits, neuronal function, and behavioral impairment observed in AD and DS/AD is unclear. It has not been demonstrated that amyloid plaques disrupt neural functioning, although many investigators assume that the accumulation of β-amyloid deposits is deleterious (Beyreuther et al., 1991; Selkoe, 1993). The pathology that does correlate with cognitive impairment is the accumulation of NFTs, and other prominent scientists investigating AD maintain that the earliest manifestation of the disease is the accumulation of NFTs in the entorhinal cortex region (H. Braak & E. Braak, 1996).

It is not possible to assign the diagnosis of AD to a living individual because there are no pre-morbid tests that detect AD. It is only at autopsy that the pathological brain changes characterizing AD can be observed. The most accurate pre-morbid diagnosis that can be given is "probable AD." The diagnosis of probable AD is given when the person is showing slowly progressing cognitive impairment and when medical tests identify no other cause of the impairment. The American Academy of Neurology (1994) provided guidelines for a diagnostic work-up that included neurologic history and examination including mental status examination (see chapter 2 for examples such as the MMSE and the Blessed IMC). It is recommended that careful attention be paid to the existence of focal abnormalities, extrapyramidal signs (e.g., tremor), and gait disorders. Diagnostic tests are also necessary in the differential diagnosis of dementia to rule out metabolic and structural causes. It is recommended that the following tests be carried out: complete blood cell count, serum electrolytes (including calcium), glucose, BUN/creatinine, liver function tests, thyroid function tests, serum vitamin B_{12}, level, and syphilis serology. Additional tests that are options but are not recommended as routine studies include: sedimentation rate, serum folate level, HIV testing, chest X-ray, urinalysis, 24-hr urine collection for heavy metals, toxicology screen, neuro-imaging study (computerized tomography or magnetic resonance imaging), neuropsychological testing, lumbar puncture, electroencephalography, positron emission tomography (PET) or single-photon emission computerized tomography (SPECT).

Neuro-imaging was deemed essential for the diagnosis of probable AD in the initial guidelines developed by neurologists, called the National Institute of Neurological and Communicative Disorders and Stroke (NINCDS) and Alzheimer's Disease and Related Disorders Association (ADRDA) guidelines (McKhann et al., 1984). MRI or CT scans were carried out to rule out causes of dementia *other* than AD. For example, tumors, subdural hematomas, hydrocephalus, and strokes are identifiable with imaging and are potentially treatable conditions. In the current American Academy of Neurology (1994) guidelines, neuro-imaging should be considered in every patient but not necessarily carried out.

Neuroimaging should be considered in every patient with dementia based on the clinical representation and may facilitate identification of potentially treatable conditions that can otherwise be missed, such as tumors, subdural hematomas, hydrocephalus, and strokes. However, these conditions are uncommon when not anticipated clinically, particularly when clinical evaluations are performed by experienced examiners. In particular, there is no consensus on the need for such studies in the evaluation of patients with the insidious onset of dementia after age 60 without focal signs or symptoms, seizures, or gait disturbances (American Academy of Neurology, 1994, p. 2204).

It is important to emphasize some of the limitations of our knowledge about AD. A major problem is that even at a histopathological level during post-mortem examination of the brain, diagnosis of AD is based on elimination of other neuropathologies. Furthermore, we use quantitative analysis of SPs and NFTs to identify the disease. Matsuyama (1983) demonstrated that all of the pathological brain changes characteristic of AD occur in normal aging in individuals who show no signs of senility. Nevertheless, a close correlation exists between the extent of NFTs and the dementia in AD (Arriagada et al., 1992; Dickson et al., 1991; McKee et al., 1991). What is different in AD is the incidence of SPs and NFTs. There is a higher number of plaques and tangles per field of brain tissue. There is no unique identifying neuroanatomical feature of AD known at present, so post-mortem diagnosis is quantitative rather than qualitative.

Consensus criteria for the diagnosis of AD were established by the National Institute on Aging (Khachaturian, 1985). The minimum criteria are based on the examination of tissue sections from nine neural regions: three regions of neocortex (e.g., frontal, temporal, parietal), amygdala, hippocampus, basal ganglia, substantia nigra, cerebellar cortex, and spinal cord. Age of the person at death is also considered in the diagnosis, with fewer SPs or NFTs per mm^2 of tissue required at younger ages. The diagnosis of AD is given to a 50-year-old brain if there are more than five SPs or NFTs per $1 mm^2$ field. In the age range of 50–65, eight SPs or NFTs per field are required. Ten SPs or NFTs per field are required for a diagnosis of AD in a brain aged 66–75 years. At age 75 and older, more than 15 SPs or NFTs per field are required for the AD diagnosis. It should be emphasized that a relatively small percentage of older adults have a post-mortem brain autopsy. The majority of demented individuals die with a diagnosis of probable AD that is not confirmed by autopsy.

Behavioral signs of AD

Neuropsychology plays an important role in the diagnosis of AD because the most significant presenting symptoms are cognitive and behavioral. AD begins with mild impairment in memory and semantic knowledge capacities. The patient is conscious of his or her difficulties and attempts to compensate. Notes are written as reminders. Indeed, the homes of some AD patients in the early stages of the disease are littered with little pieces of paper with indecipherable notes. One of the tragedies of the disease is that its onset is so gradual that the patient becomes aware that he or she is losing cognitive capacities such as memory, spatial abilities, and perhaps some language function. Indeed, the unprovoked spontaneous sobbing frequently observed after AD has progressed has been interpreted as a conscious or unconscious mourning by the victim for the loss of his or her intellect (Reisberg, 1983).

Barry Reisberg (1983) presented a seven-stage categorization of the behavioral progression of AD which he developed with colleagues Steven Ferris and Thomas Crook. Others have pointed out that not all cases of AD present the seven stages, and patients have remissions, moving back and forth between stages rather than deteriorating in a consistent progression. For these reasons, a three-stage categorization is usually adequate for treatment. Here we will describe seven stages for descriptive purposes rather than to prescribe an unvarying trajectory of the progression of the disease.

Stage 1 is normal functioning with no cognitive decline. Very mild cognitive decline characterizes *Stage 2*, and this stage is difficult to distinguish from normal aging or from overload in a younger adult. The patient is forgetful of where familiar things have been placed and of the names of well-known people or places.

Stage 3 marks the onset of confusion, and clear-cut deficits begin to appear. Co-workers notice a decline in performance; the patient forgets what he or she has just read; the patient may lose or misplace an object of value. Also, at this point the patient may start to deny the cognitive losses. In *Stage 4*, denial becomes more apparent. When asked, "Who is the President of the United States?" a patient might answer, "I don't follow politics very closely." Patients at this stage manifest decreased knowledge of current and recent events, they begin to forget their own personal history, they can no longer carry out such tasks as serial subtractions, and they find difficulty with traveling, handling their personal finances, and their daily affairs. At this point they begin to withdraw from challenging situations.

Stage 5 is called the early dementia stage, and the patient can no longer survive without some assistance. Things as familiar as their long-time address or telephone number cannot be recalled, nor can the names of their grandchildren. They become disoriented with respect to time or place. However, they still know their own name, and the name of their spouse and children. They can eat, but they may have difficulty dressing themselves.

By *Stage 6* severe cognitive decline is apparent to the point that they may forget the name of the spouse or child upon whom they are totally dependent. They cannot remember recent events, and they can only partly remember past experiences. They are unaware of time or place and may have difficulty counting to ten. They may become incontinent, and to the consternation of caretakers, they may fail to discriminate between day and night.

Finally, at *Stage 7* involving very severe cognitive decline, verbal abilities are lost. There may be no speech – only grunting. Assistance with feeding and toileting is required. Even the ability to walk is lost. The brain no longer controls the body, and the patient eventually dies in this extremely deteriorated state.

Death ensues usually about 5–7 years after the first symptoms, but survival time can be as long as two decades after diagnosis. At the present time there is no cure and little in the way of effective treatment for the alleviation of symptoms. The first drug approved for the treatment of cognitive decline is tacrine (Cognex®), a cholinesterase inhibitor. Tacrine works by preventing acetylcholinesterase (AChE) from breaking down acetylcholine in the synaptic gap and thus prolongs the effect of acetylcholine on the postsynaptic receptors (see figure 6.3). Tacrine has mild to moderate efficacy in some probable AD patients, but this drug also has serious side effects including the impairment of liver function. A second cholinesterase inhibitor called Aricept® was approved by the Food and Drug Administration on November 25, 1996 to treat memory loss in AD. Aricept® has several advantages over Cognex including the fact that it selectively targets brain acetylcholine rather than affecting the peripheral nervous system, it has fewer side effects, and it is taken only once a day instead of four times daily. Nevertheless, neither drug actually slows the progression of the disease. Rather, they ease mild to moderate symptoms of memory loss by inhibiting the breakdown of acetylcholine at the synapse. Experts on AD recognize that in the last 6–7 years we

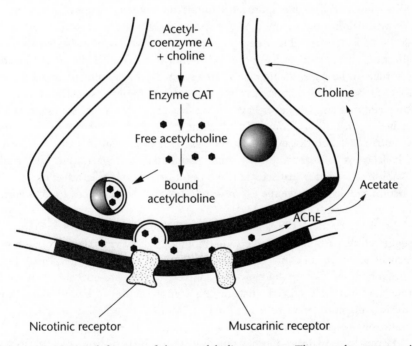

Figure 6.3 Essential features of the acetylcholine synapse. The acetyl-coenzyme A is supplied by glucose and is combined with choline by the enzyme choline acetyltransferase (CAT) to form free acetylcholine. Free acetylcholine is bound in synaptic vesicles, preventing its destruction by acetylcholinesterase (AChE). Acetylcholine is released into the synaptic cleft by exocytosis, where it binds with one of the two types of cholinergic receptors, nicotinic or muscarinic. Acetylcholine molecules are then quickly dissociated from the receptor and inactivated by AChE

have made remarkable advances in our understanding of the disease, but our ability to treat the disease is still extremely limited.

Hypotheses about causes of AD

The causes of AD are unknown, but there are a number of hypotheses about its origin. The diversity of these hypotheses dramatizes the degree to which our knowledge about AD is at a rudimentary stage. It has also been suggested that it may be less important to understand the ultimate cause(s) of AD than to address the neuropathology, itself. The formation of SPs and NFTs may be the point at which causes of AD converge and then lead to the dysfunction and death of central nervous system neurons, and dementia (Trojanowski & Lee, 1994). Treatment for AD may lie in targeting the lesions, even if they have different originating causes.

Slow virus studies. One approach to understanding the cause of AD continues with studies on central nervous system diseases believed to be caused by slow-acting transmissible viruses. Scrapie is a central nervous system disease affecting sheep, and it has provided a model for the study of dementing disorders in humans, including AD. It is difficult to identify an animal model for AD because dementia involves the loss of cognitive capacities such as language that animals never have in the first place. Nonetheless, scientists are actively pursuing an animal or other model. Scrapie is similar to kuru and Creutzfeldt–Jakob disease. The latter two diseases are rare diseases in humans which cause progressive, irreversible dementia. This fact, plus the well-established evidence that scrapie is the result of a slow-acting infectious agent, encouraged a new avenue of research on the possible causes of central nervous diseases in humans.

Stanley Prusiner (1982) at the University of California at San Francisco suggested that AD may involve something like a slow virus. He proposed that a small proteinaceous infectious particle, which he calls a "prion," may be a component of the amyloid plaques in AD. At the present time Prusiner's research tentatively suggests that the SPs seen in victims of Creutzfeldt–Jakob disease and kuru, may be composed of prions. SPs are also present in the brains of the victims of AD.

Prions have many properties which distinguish them from typical viruses. Although viruses contain nucleic acids which carry all of the information necessary for the virus to multiply and spread infection, prions may or may not contain a nucleic acid. Since nucleic acids are necessary for proteins to replicate, molecular biologists are challenged by the puzzle of how prions transmit their effect.

Using transgenic mice, Hsiao and Prusiner (1990) genetically modeled a dominantly inherited, neurodegenerative process similar to a human disease. The disease (Gerstman–Straussler–Scheinker syndrome, GSS), that is an autosomal, dominantly inherited, human neurodegenerative disease, can sometimes be transmitted to nonhuman primates and rodents through intracerebral inoculation of brain homogenates from patients. Because of this potential for disease transmission, and because of its association with the human prion protein, it was suggested that GSS may be a neurodegenerative disease that has a human familial prion origin (Hsiao et al., 1991).

Trace metal studies. Daniel Perl and his associates (1982) at the University of Vermont developed an environmental hypothesis based on the parallels between the high aluminum content in the affected neurons of Alzheimer's patients and the dementia and aluminum content in the brains of Chamorra natives of Guam dying of amylotrophic lateral sclerosis (ALS). The research suggests that aluminum may contribute to the development of AD and ALS.

In AD patients the neurons affected by the disease have accumulations of aluminum within them, along with neurofibrillary tangles. In a collaborative study, Perl and a group of other scientists reported high accumulations of aluminum, iron, and calcium in the brains of Chamorra natives of Guam who had died of ALS or of Parkinsonism–dementia (Perl et al., 1982). This population is adversely affected by these two chronic disorders, both of which were previously suspected to be transmitted by a slow-acting virus.

Researchers in the field of aging have carefully observed the studies in Guam because of the similarities between the Parkinsonism–dementia syndrome and AD. In both disorders, there is an excessive accumulation of neurofibrillary tangles in the brains of victims that is associated with severe dementia and death.

More recent research demonstrated a dramatic tendency for the accumulation of aluminum in NFTs among neurons of cortical regions associated with the olfactory system (Perl & Good, 1991). The olfactory system is the only portion of the central nervous system with exposure to the external environment. Thus, the olfactory system is uniquely capable of uptake and transneuronal spread of exogenous substances. Perl and Good (1991) argued that aluminum is not employed in any physiological process, and thus the deposits must arise from exogenous sources. Using the Parkinsonism–dementia complex of Guam as a model, Perl and Good (1991) presented data suggesting that the olfactory system is particularly vulnerable to damage and is affected very early in the disease. They pointed out that the cause of AD may be environmental and airborne in nature, and may enter the central nervous system via the olfactory pathways.

Future studies in this area will determine whether accumulations of metals in the brain are a primary cause of AD or if other factors or circumstances might combine with environmental factors to trigger the onset of chronic, but ultimately fatal, diseases of the nervous system. At the present time, we simply do not know whether the accumulation of trace metals results as a consequence of the breakdown of the central nervous system in AD or whether exposure to excessive levels of these metals initiates the disease process.

Genetic studies. For several decades there have been hints that AD in either its early onset form or senile form might be hereditary. Researchers have found an increased incidence of some form of dementia among parents and siblings of AD victims. Some studies show a slight increase; others show a considerable increase over the occurrence of dementia in the general population. Early onset AD apparently poses a greater risk to relatives than the late onset form of the disease. The studies show a clustering of the incidence of dementia cases in some families of AD victims, but there is no single abnormal gene that is common to every family. Rather, there appear to be different genes on different chromosomes causing dementia in different families. Studies of the molecular genetics of familial and sporadic AD implicate genes on three different chromosomes (i.e., 14, 19, and 21), and the apolipoprotein E (ApoE) 4 allele is a risk factor for both familial and sporadic AD (Hardy, 1993; Mullan & Crawford, 1993; Price et al., 1993; Saunders et al., 1993). Genetic research may eventually indicate whether there is one disease or more than one in the pre-senile and senile forms of AD. Studies may also provide a way to diagnose dementia accurately using a "marker" for the disease.

Having at least one ApoE 4 allele is a risk factor for AD, but Roses et al. (1996) cautioned that the utility of considering ApoE 4 as a risk factor should be limited to patients who are showing signs of cognitive loss. Screening the adult population for the ApoE 4 allele would not identify all potential future AD patients. Of the three forms of the ApoE allele (2, 3, and 4), combinations of both the ApoE 3 and ApoE 4 alleles have been found in patients with AD. Reporting on three independent samples of brains autopsied for AD, Roses et al. (1996) noted that among the patients that had been diagnosed pre-morbidly with probable AD, the positive predictive value of an ApoE 4 allele in the diagnosis was 100 percent. The absence of the ApoE 4 allele does not rule out AD, as AD cases are found with two ApoE 3 alleles. Nevertheless, when the patient has cognitive decline, no other neurological conditions, and at least one ApoE 4 allele, it is likely that the patient has probable AD. All patients in Roses et al.'s (1996) sample who were diagnosed with probable AD but did not have the AD diagnosis on autopsy did not have an ApoE 4 allele.

Research has identified a central role for the ApoE protein in the brain's response to injury. The coordinated expression of ApoE includes the production of new dendrites, intracellular cholesterol release, choline metabolism, and thus acetylcholine production (Poirier, 1996). ApoE is a key regulator of plasticity in the central nervous system. A double-blind study with probable AD patients using the Alzheimer's Disease Assessment Scale (ADAS) was carried out to evaluate responsivity to treatment in probable AD patients of various ApoE allele types. Most probable AD patients with at least one ApoE 4 allele were not responsive to therapy with the cholinesterase inhibitor, tacrine, whereas 80 percent of ApoE 4 negative probable AD patients exhibited marked improvement (Poirier, 1996). These results support the concept that ApoE 4 plays a crucial role in the cholinergic dysfunction associated with AD. Cholinesterase inhibitors may not have therapeutic value in probable AD patients with an ApoE 4 allele.

Brain neurotransmitters. Since the first reports in the mid-1970s, research scientists have been studying evidence of a significant and progressive decrease in the activity of the enzyme choline acetyltransferase (CAT) in the brain tissue of AD patients. CAT is a crucial ingredient in the chemical process which produces acetylcholine, a neurotransmitter involved in learning and memory (see figure 6.3). One of the most interesting results indicated a link between a change in levels of acetylcholine in the brain and changes in cognition (e.g., memory loss and disorientation) and in the neuroanatomy in brains of patients with AD. The number of SPs was higher when CAT and acetylcholine concentrations were decreased. In order to explore further the relationship between CAT and AD, scientists are using techniques such as those employing monoclonal antibodies to help map areas of the brain where CAT is present.

In studying the brains of AD victims, researchers found a marked loss of nerve cells in a part of the base of the brain called the nucleus basalis (Coyle et al., 1983). Some patients with classical AD have been shown to lose as much as 90 percent of these cells. There is likely to be a link between the loss of cells in the nucleus basalis and the decrease in cholinergic activity. The nucleus basalis produces acetylcholine and utilizes this neurotransmitter and its enzymes in communicating with the brain's cortex via connecting pathways. In AD, cholinergic cells are lost at a much higher rate than most other types of cells. Between 75 and 95 percent of cholinergic cells are lost in AD patients, and the loss of acetylcholine is detrimental to these patients in that profound memory impairment ensues.

Describing the history of the cholinergic hypothesis of AD, Geula and Mesulam (1994) noted that experiments in the early 1970s demonstrated that cholinergic blockade with scopolamine (a drug that blocks the muscarinic cholinergic receptors shown in figure 6.3) caused memory loss in young human subjects resembling the memory loss seen in early AD. Subsequently, two laboratories independently reported a major depletion of cortical cholinergic innervation in AD (Bowen et al., 1976; Davies & Maloney, 1976). The cholinergic theory of memory loss in AD was based on these observations (Coyle et al., 1983). Subsequent research demonstrated that losses in many neurotransmitter systems occur in the brains of patients diagnosed with AD, and that SPs, NFTs, and neuronal loss have their concentration in the limbic system, a part of the brain clearly involved in learning and memory. Whereas impaired cholinergic neurotransmission is likely not the single cause of memory impairment in AD, disruption of the cholinergic system impairs memory, and this system has received major attention in the study of AD. As mentioned previously, the only drug therapy presently available to treat probable AD patients are the cholinesterase inhibitors Cognex and Aricept.

Neuropsychology and AD

AD is significant for neuropsychology because the main presenting symptom is cognitive. Severe memory impairment that has worsened at a slow rate is a hallmark of AD. This cognitive decline must have occurred in at least two behavioral domains (e.g., memory, language, visual spatial abilities) to meet a NINCDS–ADRDA diagnostic criterion for probable AD (McKhann et al., 1984).

One of the goals that must be met to ensure effective treatment is to develop a differential diagnosis positive to AD. It would be of great utility to find pathology unique to AD and qualitatively different from normal aging and other neuropathological diseases. At present we diagnose the disease only by exclusion of other dementing diseases, such as CVD and tumors, and by quantitatively greater neuropathology than is seen in normal aging. It has been pointed out that data accumulating from various lines of research support the notion that AD is a heterogeneous disorder (Trojanowski & Lee, 1994). The evolving perspective is that AD represents a group of neurodegenerative conditions that appear similar behaviorally and medically. Trojanowski and Lee (1994) suggested that the unfortunate consequence of the heterogeneity of AD may be that we have to "solve" the riddle of AD multiple times in order to prevent or block the progression of each variant of this late-life dementia.

It is most important to develop behavioral indices which more precisely differentiate normal aging from AD. Early and accurate diagnosis of AD can have a major impact on the progression of the disease. One of the problems in treating the disease is that it is often diagnosed in its late stages, so that the few interventions that exist are no longer effective. As mentioned previously, the cognition-enhancing drugs, Cognex and Aricept, are the only drugs that have been approved by the FDA to treat cognitive impairment in AD. These drugs are not effective in all AD patients and Cognex causes liver dysfunction in many. These drugs show efficacy in ameliorating memory loss in AD in some patients, but they are most effective in the early stages of the disease. Drugs which improve memory must be administered before the cells that can use them are lost.

Zaven Khachaturian (1985) has pointed out that the only practical way to screen for AD in the aged population as a whole would be to use short, easily-administered measures. We need to discover a reliable neuropsychological "marker" which would differentiate between a patient in the early stages of AD and an individual showing normal cognitive aging. To develop such a measure we need to undertake longitudinal studies on large samples of middle-aged and aged individuals so that we can identify behavioral profiles of those who eventually develop AD. The discovery of such a profile would revolutionize the care and treatment of AD by allowing us to begin care early. Early diagnosis might also speed up the identification of the causes.

Tests for the early detection of AD

Composite criteria for the identification of individuals at risk for AD are required for clinical trials to test new drug therapies and for the eventual treatment and prevention of the disease. It is entirely feasible that the course of AD can be altered with early detection and treatment of individuals at risk (Khachaturian, 1996). At present, tests that are relatively inexpensive and selectively sensitive to AD early in its course are not available. Yet as treatments for AD become available, tests for the early detection of the disease become critical for the success of therapeutic measures.

Early detection of AD is critical to preserve mental and physical capacity in the patient, yet few available tests have utility in identifying AD early. It is only with a fairly extensive testing regimen that early AD patients are identified.

The neuropsychological test used most frequently in clinical trials to identify AD and to test change as a function of drug administration is the ADAS. The ADAS has proved to be more sensitive to AD-related changes than a variety of mental status tests including the Blessed IMC (Christensen et al., 1991). However, there is a "ceiling effect" on the ADAS for very early AD patients who make only a few errors on this test (Zec et al., 1994). Stern et al. (1994) reported that very mild AD patients with low error scores display only a very modest decline on the total ADAS score over a period of 24 months. To enhance the ability of the ADAS to detect early AD, seven additional subtests and two modifications were made to create the extended

ADAS (Zec et al., 1994). Error score is increased from 70 to 170, and the subtests enhanced the ability of the test to measure cognitive deficits in early AD patients. Total test time for the extended ADAS is 50 min. However, most investigators use the ADAS without the extended subtests.

A number of tests for the early detection of AD are in experimental stages. Only two of them will be mentioned here. The two tests that have initially been shown to be sensitive for the NINCDS–ADRDA diagnosis of probable AD are eyeblink classical conditioning (EBCC; Ferrante & Woodruff-Pak, 1995; Woodruff-Pak et al., 1990) and the pupil dilation response (PDR; Scinto et al., 1994). It is disruption of the brain cholinergic neurotransmitter system in AD that links this dementing disease to the model system of EBCC in rabbits and humans. Hypersensitivity to an acetylcholine receptor antagonist in the peripheral nervous system is the characteristic of AD patients that is thought to be significant for the PDR test.

EBCC had a sensitivity of 95 percent for AD and a specificity of 65 percent (Woodruff-Pak et al., 1990). Solomon et al. (1991) reported disruption of EBCC in patients with a diagnosis of probable AD who had a mean age in the early 70s; thus a decade younger than the Woodruff-Pak et al. (1990) sample. Results from the Solomon et al. (1991) study were similar to the Woodruff-Pak et al. (1990) results. EBCC was seriously impaired in AD.

Longitudinal results suggest that EBCC may have utility in the *early* detection of dementia. A 3-year longitudinal study of non-demented adults tested on EBCC revealed that three of the seven normal subjects testing in the AD range (below 25 percent CRs) at Time 1 became demented within 2 or 3 years (Ferrante & Woodruff-Pak, 1995). A fourth "normal" subject who scored just above criterion (26 percent CRs) also developed dementia within 2 years of the initial testing. A fifth subject in this group died within a year of the initial testing. Thus, of eight non-demented subjects age-matched to probable AD patients who scored on EBCC in the AD range, only three were cognitively normal at the end of a 3-year period. Age-matched non-demented subjects scoring above criterion remained cognitively intact during the period of the longitudinal investigation. These 3-year longitudinal data on elderly subjects suggest that the specificity of EBCC for the detection of true normals may have been better than we initially concluded (Woodruff-Pak et al., 1990). Of the eight "normal" elderly producing 26 percent CRs or less, a 3-year follow up finds five (62.5 percent) demented or dead, and only three who are cognitively normal.

Similarities between neuropathology in AD and DS led Scinto and his colleagues to explore common responses present in DS/AD and AD (Scinto et al., 1994). One of the known responses in DS is a hypersensitivity to compounds acting as antagonists to acetylcholine neurotransmission. Hypersensitivity of the heart rate of young adults with DS to atropine administration was demonstrated using a 12-lead electrocardiogram (Harris & Goodman, 1968). Berg et al. (1959) demonstrated that one drop of 1 percent atropine maximally dilated the pupils of children with DS, using a three-point scale to indicate slight to maximal dilation of the pupil. Sacks and Smith (1989) used a photographic method developed by Smith and Dewhirst (1986) and took Polaroid photographs of subjects' pupils and demonstrated that 0.01 percent tropicamide dilates the pupils of adults with DS significantly more than the pupils of normal subjects. It was the data on hypersensitivity to cholinergic antagonists in subjects with DS that led Scinto, Potter, and their colleagues to assess pupil size in probable AD patients in response to the cholinergic receptor antagonist tropicamide (Scinto et al., 1994).

The EBCC and PDR tests can be administered simultaneously within a 1-hr session (Woodruff-Pak et al., 1996). Comparing pupil dilation in the five probable AD and 17 normal subjects we observed a statistically significant difference between the groups, with greater dilation in the probable AD patients. Among the normal elderly subjects, eight were normal conditioners and nine were poor conditioners (less than 25 percent conditioned responses [CRs]). Poor conditioners were at risk of dementia within 3 years after testing (Ferrante & Woodruff-Pak, 1995). There also were statistically significant differences in EBCC between the groups of subjects. Combining the results of the two tests, all five probable AD subjects fell within the predicted range, making the sensitivity of the combined tests 100 percent (figure 6.4). Five normal elderly subjects performed in the normal range for both EBCC and the PDR. Five poor conditioners in the AD range for EBCC also fell in the AD range for the PDR. Thus, 15/22 subjects (68 percent) were consistent in their performances on both tests. Only longitudinal data will reveal whether normal elderly in the AD range on both the PDR and EBCC are more likely to develop AD than the subjects in the AD range only on EBCC ($n = 4$) or the PDR ($n = 3$). It was concluded that in very demented probable AD patients in whom the disease has progressed, pupil dilation to a solution of 0.01 percent tropicamide was dramatic (75 percent). Pupil dilation to 0.01 percent tropicamide was minimal (19 percent) in normal elderly who scored in the normal range on the Blessed IMC test and who tested in the normal range on EBCC. Elderly adults testing in the normal range on the Blessed IMC test but in the poor conditioner range on EBCC (>25 percent CRs) showed more pupil dilation (24 percent) than normal conditioners. These preliminary results indicate that there is potential utility in combining EBCC and the PDR in an attempt to detect AD early in its course. It is in the early-detected probable AD patients that cognition-enhancing and neuroprotective drugs have the greatest potential to ameliorate memory loss and prevent neuronal death.

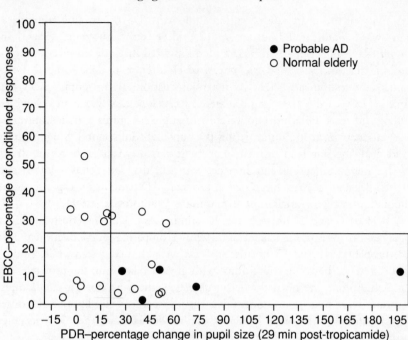

Figure 6.4 Predicted normal range of pupil dilation response (PDR) and eyeblink classical conditioning (EBCC) scores for probable Alzheimer's disease (AD) patients and elderly control participants and actual scores on the two tests for 22 participants tested on both. Participants in the normal range have a PDR of 20 percent or less at the 29 min point and have more than 25 percent conditioned responses (CRs) on EBCC. Participants in the AD range have a PDR greater than 20 percent at the 29 min point and 25 percent CRs or less on EBCC. Probable AD patients are filled circles and elderly control participants are open circles

Source: Woodruff-Pak, D. S., Romano, S. J., & Hinchliffe, R. M. (1995). Detection of Alzheimer's disease with eyeblink classical conditioning and the pupil dilation response. *Society for Neuroscience Abstracts, 21,* 482

Dementia resulting from single gene defects

On the 46 human chromosomes, it is estimated that there are approximately 100,000 genes. Surprisingly, one out of 100,000 genes can make a dramatic difference in physical or mental health. Unfortunately, in the case of single gene effects, that one gene can have tragic consequences. Single gene effects have profoundly deleterious consequences for development if they are left untreated. For HD and familial AD, there is no treatment.

Huntington's disease

Most single genes share several features in common: (a) they involve a recessive allele; and (b) the disease is expressed early in life. HD is a single gene disorder different from the others on both counts. HD involves a lethal *dominant* allele, and it is expressed later in life. Indeed, a lethal dominant allele could not continue to be carried in the gene pool if it did not express itself late in development after the individual carrier had children. Until recently, HD patients had no knowledge of whether they were carriers of a fatal, dominant gene until the symptoms began at the age of 35–45 years old. DNA testing can now identify the existence of the lethal HD gene. However, not all people who had a parent with HD want to know. This knowledge is imperative if offspring with a parent who has HD plan to have children. If they have children, the children have a 50 percent chance of having the disorder.

HD is a degenerative disease of the nervous system. Once this deterioration begins, it is progressive, irreversible, and inevitably lethal. There is currently no way that the disease can be diagnosed before the onset of symptoms. However, some progress is being made at mapping the Huntington's gene. The gene is believed to lie near the tip of human chromosome 4. Mapping genes at the tip of chromosomes is particularly difficult because the DNA that constitutes the tips of the chromosomes is hard to identify. Thus, molecular biologists have worked for years to map the Huntington's gene. Identification of the gene resulted in the development of tests to identify those carrying it. However, as in the case of lethal genetic diseases such as Tay Sachs, knowledge of who has the gene does not provide a cure. On the other hand, information about the gene provides one additional step in the direction of prevention and treatment.

Familial AD

A very late-onset, lethal genetic disease is Familial AD. The average age of onset for this disease is in the decade of the 50s, although there is a wide range of ages from 30 to 90 years when the disease can appear. This disease is similar to sporadic AD and involves a progressive deterioration of the brain with the earliest presenting symptoms being impairment of learning and memory. Gradually the patient loses more and more mental capacity until he or she requires full-time care. Eventually, the individual loses the capacity to speak or perform normal bodily functions. Death ensues, on average, 7 years after onset of the disease with the patient in a grossly deteriorated state.

There is such variety in the age of onset, the behavioral symptoms, and the brain pathology of patients with Familial AD that investigators have suggested that more than one gene may be involved. In a study representing the largest collection of families with pathologically documented Familial AD compared by a single group of investigators, the data supported heterogeneity (Bird et al., 1989). Different families had unique features of AD consistent within the family but different from AD in other families. For example, one group of families had early onset of the disease, typically in the decade of the 40s. Another group of families had generally late onset, typically in the decades of the 60s and 70s. One family had an unusually long disease duration, and the onset of the disease often appeared to be more like schizophrenia which then progressed into AD. Because there are all these different configurations to the disease, investigators speculated and eventually demonstrated that more than one gene was involved.

While progress in understanding the genetic basis of Familial AD contin-ues to make inroads, the impetus for exploring a genetic basis of AD originated in part from research on chromosomal aberrations. The focus of genetic research on AD was initially on the 21st chromosome. This is the chromosome affected in Down's syndrome (DS), and it is the changes in the brain occurring in 35–40-year-old patients with DS that directed research on the genetic basis of Familial AD to chromosome 21.

Chromosomal aberrations and dementia

In the discussion of single gene effects, we have been considering the physical and behavioral consequences of alterations in one gene or approximately 1/100,000 of the genetic material. Alterations in one chromosome involve a much larger amount of genetic material. Alterations in a chromosome en-compass 1/46 of the human genetic potential. Hundreds, and in some cases thousands, of genes reside on one chromosome. The effect of adding or deleting an entire chromosome has the potential to alter a large number of traits in the organism. The most common chromosomal abnormality is Trisomy 21 or DS. This disorder has neuropsychological consequences for adults with Down's syndrome over the age of 35.

Down's syndrome

A DS baby has an extra 21st chromosome. This syndrome is also called Trisomy 21 to indicate the third or extra 21st chromosome. The name that used to be applied to this syndrome is Mongolism. Because the child has a round face and a fold of skin on the eyes making them appear almond-shaped, it was thought that there was a resemblance to the Mongoloid racial division.

DS is one of the most serious forms of chromosomal aberration. Approximately one out of every 600 children born have DS, and the incidence of the syndrome is related to the age of the parents. One of 1,925 births to 20-year-old mothers results in DS, but one of 12 births to 50-year-old mothers yields a baby with the syndrome.

Until fairly recently, children with DS did not survive beyond adolescence. With medical advances, many of these individuals now live to their 50s and 60s. By the age of 35–40, virtually all adults with DS suffer from profound dementia characteristic of AD. Autopsy examinations of the brains of 40-year-old patients with DS reveal pathology identical to the pathology of AD. As mentioned previously, it was the observation of similarities between the brains of DS and AD patients that led investigators to examine the 21st chromosome for clues to a genetic basis for AD. It is a virtual certainty that AD-like neuropathology will be found in the brains of all adults with DS who die after the age of 35 (Thase, 1988; Wisniewski et al., 1985). Adults with DS develop neuropathology that is remarkably similar to the neuropathology apparent in AD. Thus, adults with DS over the age of 35 are frequently referred to as DS/AD patients. Cholinergic deficits comparable in the brains of adults with DS and patients diagnosed with AD have also been observed (Yates et al., 1980, 1981).

Summary

Dementia, a state of mind involving extreme memory loss, confusion, and lack of orientation in location, is a greatly feared outcome of old age. The vast majority of older adults never become demented, but because there are so many elderly in society, the number of demented patients is great. The disease that accounts for the majority of dementia patients is Alzheimer's disease, named early in the twentieth century after Alois Alzheimer who first diagnosed it. Ironically, the first case diagnosed with AD probably had dementia from cerebrovascular impairment as well as AD. It has been estimated that in the United States there are 4 million individuals suffering from AD.

Impaired learning and memory ability are the behavioral hallmarks of AD, and cognitive deterioration is progressive. The neuropathology is characterized by extensive loss of cortical and sub-cortical neurons and the presence of amyloid-containing senile plaques as well as neurofibrillary tangles. Confirmation of the diagnosis of AD can only come at autopsy. Although the disease does not always progress sequentially through seven stages, these stages are described to characterize the disease which begins as normal, age-related memory loss and progresses through severe cognitive decline to the degree that all language abilities are lost.

The causes of AD are unknown, but hypotheses about its origin include slow viruses, trace metal particles, genetic determination, and brain neurotransmitter loss resulting from unknown causes. Tests for the early detection of the disease are being researched, but at present knowledge about the cause, treatment, or even the early diagnosis of the disease is not available. Two tests in the research stage for the early detection of AD, the pupil dilation response and eyeblink classical conditioning, are described. The Alzheimer's Disease Assessment Scale (ADAS) is the most widely used test in clinical trials, but it has a ceiling effect in early AD patients.

AD is the most prevalent diagnosis among demented patients, but dementia can also have other causes including HD and CVD. HD involves a lethal dominant allele that is expressed later in life, usually in the late 30s or early 40s. The locus of the gene has been identified, and tests are available to identify carriers of the disease. However, there is no treatment at present. Adults with DS inevitably develop Alzheimer-like neuropathology. It was the observation of similarities between the brains of adults with DS and AD that led investigators to examine chromosome 21 for a role in AD.

Further Reading

Berrios, G. E. (1994). Dementia and ageing since the nineteenth century. In F. A. Hippert et al. (Eds.), *Dementia and normal ageing*. Cambridge, UK: Cambridge University Press.
An interesting history of study and treatment of dementia.

Geula, C., & Mesulam, M. (1994). Cholinergic systems and related neuropathological predilection in Alzheimer's disease. In R. D. Terry, R. Katzman, & K. L. Bick (Eds.), *Alzheimer's disease* (pp. 263–291). New York: Raven Press.
An overview of the cholinergic hypothesis in Alzheimer's disease.

Giacobini, E., & Becker, R. (Eds.). (1994). *Alzheimer's disease: Therapeutic strategies*. Boston: Birkhauser.
This book has an excellent variety of articles addressing contemporary issues in the diagnosis and treatment of Alzheimer's disease.

Gauthier, S. (Ed.). (1996). *Clinical diagnosis and management of Alzheimer's disease*. London: Martin Dunitz.
Accessible to working clinicians and research workers alike is this multidisciplinary collection on Alzheimer's disease.

7

Emotion, Aging, and Brain Function

A small segment of the aging population experiences maladjustment and/or brain pathology only in late life. They have been adjusted throughout the major part of their adult lives, but they experience the onset of psychopathology in late life. They may break down when they have difficulties with the social and psychological phenomena accompanying aging, they may be suffering from organic neurological syndromes that interfere with normal mental processes, or they may have a combination of environmental stressors and organic deficits. They may develop a major depression in old age.

There are relatively fewer psychopathologies which have their onset in later life. If an individual has adjusted throughout adulthood to the various psychosocial crises and non-normative life events causing unusual stress, it is likely that he or she will adjust to old age. Clearly, the incidence in psychopathology is no greater in aged individuals. However, the type of psychopathology which begins in late life may be different. The most common form of psychopathology with first onset in late life is depression. This does not necessarily mean that the incidence of depression increases with age, although there is a debate in the literature on the psychopathology of aging about this issue. It means that of those individuals who have mental health problems late in life, a majority are depressed. There are other late life psychopathologies such as paranoia and hypochondriasis, but they are less prevalent than depression.

The incidence of organic pathology as a cause of psychological distress increases in old age. Strokes and brain tumors result in behavioral impairment which may or may not be reversible. Late life onset diseases such as Parkinson's disease can result in dementia, although this probably results from co-occurring Alzheimer's disease pathology (Braak & Braak, 1996). However, severe memory impairment to the degree that the individual must be institutionalized is relatively rare in old age. As discussed in chapter 6, the most common cause of dementia in late life is Alzheimer's disease (AD).

The prognosis for depression is significantly better than the prognosis for AD. Old people who are depressed often get over their sadness, but victims of AD lose their memory, lose control of their normal bodily functions, and eventually die. Interventions are being designed and tested for both depression and AD, and in the case of depression, the interventions are often successful.

Depression is the most common form of emotional disruption in old age, but there are other forms. Agitation is common in elderly demented patients. Age-related impairment in the frontal lobes, the major cortical center for affect, has consequences for the expression of emotion in older adults.

Depression in the elderly population

Popular belief has it that depression has a higher prevalence among the elderly. This belief is probably in error. Epidemiological surveys of the incidence of depression in the adult population indicate that the aged are not any more prone to depression than younger adults (Blazer, 1982b, 1994; Boyd & Weissman, 1982; Craig & Van Natta, 1979; Hirschfeld & Cross, 1982). Depression is not as widely prevalent among older adults as is commonly believed. In community dwelling samples of older adults, the prevalence of depression is around 8–15 percent (Blazer, 1994).

Some would argue that estimates of the prevalence of depression are underestimates, especially in samples of older adults (e.g., Cappeliez, 1993). There may be factors masking depression in older adults, such as the fact that older respondents present somatic symptoms rather than admitting that they suffer from depression. Older adults' unwillingness to admit to being depressed may lead to an underestimation of the prevalence of depression in late adulthood. Furthermore, among institutionalized elderly adults, the prevalence of depression may be as high as 20–30 percent (Blazer, 1994; Parmelee et al., 1989).

Definitions of depression

To present a specific definition of depression for which there would be general agreement among psychologists, psychiatrists, psychiatric nurses, and other mental health specialists is simply not feasible. Beck (1967) dramatized this contemporary dilemma by pointing out that the condition that we label today as depression is not new to humankind. It has been described by ancient writers for centuries under the classification of "melancholia."

The first clinical description of melancholia was made by Hippocrates in the fourth century BC. Aretaeus, a second century AD physician, described the melancholic patient as "sad, dismayed, sleepless. . . . They become thin by their agitation and loss of refreshing sleep. . . . At a more advanced stage, they complain of a thousand futilities and desire death" (Beck, 1967, p. 4). Although we have acknowledged the existence of depression in human behavior since at least the fourth century BC, we still cannot agree as to exactly what defines this affective disorder. Unfortunately, defining depression in old age is even more problematic than defining it in younger adulthood.

There is no general agreement about a definition of depression. However, most mental health professionals would agree to the following attributes of the disorder as presented by Beck (1967, p. 6):

1 A specific alteration in mood: sadness, loneliness, apathy.
2 A negative self-concept associated with self-reproaches and self-blame.
3 Regressive and self-punitive wishes: desires to escape, hide, or die.
4 Vegetative changes: anorexia, insomnia, loss of libido.
5 Change in activity level: retardation or agitation.

Young and middle adulthood are the most common periods for depression to manifest itself, even though depression is one of the most common psychopathologies in later adulthood. The reason for this seeming paradox is that if individuals maintain mental health throughout their life span and have a break down only in late life, the most likely form it will take is depression. The incidence of depression does not increase in old age. Depression is simply one of the few forms of psychopathology which appear for the first time in late life.

The lifetime risk for developing a major depression is between 6 and 18 percent (Boyd & Weissman, 1981). The reason that this figure is presented as a range of 12 percentage points rather than a more precise estimate is that the actual incidence of depression is extremely difficult to pinpoint. For one thing, depression is a heterogeneous disorder (or set of disorders), rather than a clearly defined disorder. Variability is introduced in population estimates due to the definition of depression that is adopted, the assessment instruments used, and the sample populations selected.

Age differences in depression were assessed by self-report on the Center for Epidemiological Studies Depression scale, which has recently become a prominent measure of depression. A total of 1,330 male and female respondents aged 20–100 years completed the scale. The group in the aged range of 55–69 actually had significantly *lower* depression scores than the youngest and oldest groups. Adults over the age of 70 scored no higher on the depression scale than subjects aged 20–54 years (Gatz et al., 1986). The researchers concluded that, overall, older adults were not more depressed. However, on items asking whether the person had a hopeful outlook, old adults were more likely to respond that they lacked such positive feelings.

In a cross-national study carried out in the United States and Great Britain, only 5 percent of the patients over the age of 65 were diagnosed as depressed by psychiatrists participating in the study (Gurland, 1976). Boyd and Weissman (1981) estimated the prevalence at one point in time for nonbipolar depression diagnosed with current techniques to be about 3.7–4.3 percent in the adult population. A comparison of the cross-national study data on the incidence of depression in the elderly with the Boyd and Weissman estimates for the total adult population suggests about the same rate of depression for older adults as for the adult population in general. However, Gurland (1976) pointed out that apart from the psychiatrists' diagnosis in the cross-national study, many more older patients gave them- selves high depression ratings on a symptom checklist. Gurland concluded that psychiatrists may diagnose older adults as clinically depressed less fre- quently because the older adults may be subject to a higher incidence of transient depressive episodes which are frequently precipitated by external events. For example, the aged are more likely to experience grief reactions resulting from the death of a spouse, relative, or friend. Grief reactions mimic the symptoms of depression, but they are not enduring.

Although the incidence of depression is no greater in community residing older adults, and although older adults do not score higher on self-report scales of depression, the most common psychiatric disorder among the elderly is depression (Blazer, 1982b; Butler, 1975; Storandt et al., 1978; Zung, 1967, 1973). Depression takes a high toll among older adults. In particular, the suicide rate among elderly men is extraordinarily high (Manton et al., 1987). Older adult Caucasian men, more than any other group in the population, are more likely to take their own lives.

Suicide and depression

The incidence of suicide increases with age and reaches the highest rate in the group aged 75–84 years (National Center for Health Statistics, 1986). Adolescent suicide gets more media coverage, perhaps leading us to believe that the suicide rate is highest in that period of life. The suicide rate in the group aged 17–24 years is 12.5 per 100,000, while the rate for the 75–84 age group is 22 per 100,000. Compared to adolescents, older adults are almost twice as likely to take their own lives. Also, since death is a more likely event for old people, the suicide rate in late life may be underestimated. Older adults are likely to have one or two chronic diseases that are life threatening, but adolescents typically enjoy excellent health. Thus, it is easier to cover up a suicide in late life to make it appear to be naturally caused than it is in a healthy adolescent.

Suicide is a relatively common occurrence in contemporary society. Of the 15 leading causes of death, suicide ranks eighth. Men are far more likely than women to succeed at suicide. The age-adjusted death rate for suicide was 3.6 times higher for men than for women in the most recently available health statistics (National Center for Health Statistics, 1986). In the United States the most likely individual to commit suicide is an older white male. By the 35–44 age period, the suicide rate for white men exceeds the rate for all other groups, and it surges dramatically until it is over three times the rate for other racial groups and women in the 75–83 age group.

Failing health may be the primary reason that older men take their own lives. Losses they have experienced in old age may be another cause. Social and economic losses felt as a result of retirement, and the loss of identity from the work role may be felt especially strongly by older white males who previously had experienced a position of power and prestige in their community. When older men decide to commit suicide, they usually succeed. In their case, suicide is not a cry for help, and they do not choose a means such as an overdose of sleeping pills from which there is a chance for rescue. It is essential to recognize the symptoms of depression and diagnose and treat it in these elderly individuals before it is too late.

Symptoms and diagnosis of depression

The most common symptoms of clinical depression in the aged include helplessness, despair, feelings of worthlessness, apathy, pessimism, suicidal thoughts, and less frequently, guilt over real or imagined past failures (Salzman & Shader, 1979). Problematic in the diagnosis of depression in the elderly are physical complaints. Whereas scales assessing depression include somatic complaints as symptoms of depression, many of the typical somatic symptoms of depression in younger adults (such as disturbances of sleep and appetite) may be the result of normal processes of aging, other diseases common in the elderly, or a number of medications commonly prescribed for older adults. This leads some mental health professionals to argue that self-rating scales for depression, such as the Zung Self-Rating Depression Scale (Zung, 1965), identify more elderly as depressed than are actually clinically depressed (Gallagher et al., 1980). Similar problems arise with the Beck Depression Inventory (Zemore & Eames, 1979) and the MMPI Depression scale (Harmatz & Shader, 1975).

Ratings provided by a professional external observer may provide more accurate diagnosis of depression in the elderly. An observer rating scale which has been used in a number of studies involving older patients is the Hamilton

Psychiatric Rating Scale (Hamilton, 1967). Gallagher et al. (1980) endorse the structured interview technique provided by the Schedule for Affective Disorders and Schizophrenia (SADS) as promising in the reliable assessment of depression in the elderly. Whatever assessment technique is used, it is important to supplement the measure with screening measures for organic dysfunction and health function so that the older individual's depressive symptoms can be evaluated from a realistic perspective of physiological health status and perceived physical health.

Neuropsychological assessment of depression in the aging

Memory loss and poor concentration are typical complaints of depressed patients. Using neuropsychological tests, it is typical to find evidence of cognitive impairment (e.g., Caine, 1986; Marcopulos, 1989). In most cases of depression the cognitive impairment is mild to moderate. However, in severely depressed elderly patients, about 20 percent experience severe cognitive loss (La Rue, 1992). These cases have been called "depressive pseudodementia" or "dementia syndrome of depression."

Mild to moderate depression. Comparisons of normal aged, probable AD patients, and depressed elderly patients who were matched with respect to age and education on neuropsychological tests emphasized the cognitive similarities between normal aged and depressed patients and differences between these two groups and probable AD patients (La Rue et al., 1986a). Depressed patients were diagnosed with the DSM-III (American Psychiatric Association, 1980) as having a unipolar major depression, and they had relatively severe levels of depressive symptoms. However, none had pseudodementia. On the MMSE, a mental status test, depressed patients and normal aged performed similarly (means = 26.6 and 27.4, respectively). MMSE scores (mean = 13.3) and general intellectual level (Full-scale WAIS IQ mean = 80.9) were much lower in the probable AD patients. Both the normal aged and depressed patients had mean WAIS IQ scores above 100.

Although the depressed patients in the La Rue et al. (1986a) study were diagnosed as having a major depression, they had only a slight general lowering of performance on the neuropsychological test battery. The clearest areas of difference for depressed patients and normal aged were on certain tests of learning and recall (Object Memory Evaluation and Visual Retention Test) and visuospatial processing (WAIS Performance Subtests and Coloured Progressive Matrices).

A neuropsychological profile for depression summarizing expected behaviors and outcomes has been provided by La Rue (1992). Table 7.1 provides

Table 7.1 Summary of neuropsychological testing findings in geriatric depression[a]

I *Typical presentation:*
Depressed mood or pervasive loss of interest, accompanied by:
   A. Mild memory deficit.
   B. Mild to moderate visuospatial impairment.
   C. Reduced abstraction and cognitive flexibility.

II *Behavior during testing:*
Self-critical of performance; may underestimate ability or reject positive comments from the examiner.
Complaints of fatigue or physical distress, often accompanied by an objective loss of stamina.
Complaints of poor concentration, but usually can attend to tasks if encouraged.

III *Most informative tests:*
   A. List-learning tests:
      1. Storage, recognition, and rate of forgetting close to normal.
      2. Mild to moderate impairments in recall.
      3. Low rate of intrusion errors.
      4. Benefit from cuing and encoding enhancement.
   B. Intelligence testing:
      1. WAIS Verbal IQ close to normal levels.
      2. WAIS Digit Span $\leq$ other verbal subtests.
      3. Mild to moderate impairment on WAIS Performance subtests, due primarily to slowing, carelessness, or refusal to complete the test.

IV *Findings that raise a question about the diagnosis:*
Depressive symptoms mild or questionable.
Problems in language comprehension.
Severe memory deficit.

V *Cautions:*
Cognitive loss may be linked more closely to global dysfunction than to severity of depresion *per se.*
Depression often coexists with organic brain disorder.
10% to 20% of patients have cognitive problems that are hard to distinguish from AD or other organic dementias.

---

[a]From La Rue (1992, p. 655); adapted by permission.

a summary of this profile. It is also emphasized that the neuropsychologist must gain insights about the patient from the testing situation, as well. Obvious indications of depressed mood and/or anxiety are typically apparent during the testing session. The patient may actively insist that he or she is incapable of performing the tests, or the patient may passively withdraw from the demands of the testing environment. Withdrawal may take the form of limited speech, quitting on tasks when they become difficult, or daydreaming and failing to pay attention. In the case of depressed patients, they can often be prodded and encouraged to continue, and their subsequent performance yields additional correct answers. In the case of demented patients, prodding yields confabulation or erroneous answers. When the neuropsychologist provides helpful strategies or cues to improve performance, the depressed patient is likely to take advantage of these prompts whereas the demented patient cannot.

To reduce the risk of diagnosing dementia in a patient who is suffering from severe depression, it is essential to used age-adjusted tests. It is also useful to retest the patient several months after the initial testing when therapy has been able to impact the depression.

Pseudodementia.　Heterogeneity characterizes the group of depressed patients that have severe cognitive impairment. This group of elderly comprises about 20 percent of the depressed population. Some may be at the very early stages of organic brain disease such as AD. Whether pseudodementia is a unique subtype of depression or whether individuals in this group are simply at the lowest end of depressed elderly in the cognitive domain is unclear.

Elderly with low levels of education or those who scored low on intelligence tests throughout their lives are the most likely individuals to be diagnosed as suffering from pseudodementia (La Rue, Spar, & Hill, 1986b; Post, 1966). Patients who are delusional or agitated, or those who have experienced lengthy physical illness are also more likely to fall in this category. Treatment for depression is effective with pseudodementia, although the treatment regimen may need to be longer and more aggressive. When the mood disorder is effectively treated, the cognitive impairment subsides.

The ability of neuropsychological tests to differentiate pseudodementia from the early onset of AD or other organic dementia is limited. There is overlap in the cognitive profile of pseudodementia and mild organic dementia. It is especially important to differentiate pseudodementia from organic dementia because the depression causing the pseudodementia is treatable.

Causes of depression in the elderly

At both a biochemical level and an environmental level the elderly may be predisposed toward depression. Losses initiated in the external environment – loss of income, loss of employment through retirement – along with psychological losses – such as the loss of loved ones due to death, loss of physical health – are tangible factors causing older individuals to feel depressed. Losses in physical capacity and energy level also undoubtedly play a role. Additionally, some evidence suggests that on a biochemical level, production of certain neurotransmitters in the aging brain may be altered. This may also predispose old people to feel depressed. Thus, the aged may be in a state of double jeopardy. Whether biological changes are caused by these environmental stresses, whether the biological and physiological changes are completely independent, or whether they exacerbate one another has not clearly been determined.

Perhaps we will find that biologically older organisms are more predisposed toward depression without any environmental stresses. This is clearly the view of Dan Blazer who stated, "Any attempt to understand and explain the phenomenon of depression that excludes biologic factors is severely limited" (Blazer, 1982a, p. 55). The loss of physical vigor and health is extremely depressing to many older people, and this loss is thought to account, in part, for the steep increase in suicide rate in elderly white men. The decline in physical health which accompanies aging may be the most severe stressor the elderly experience (Lieberman, 1982).

Neurobiological aspects of depression

Age-related changes in brain neurotransmitter systems possibly predispose older adults to depression, although some investigators argue that there is insufficient evidence to make this conclusion (Veith & Raskind, 1988). The classic catecholamine theory of depression posits that decreased activity of the neurotransmitter norepinephrine is responsible for depression (Mann et al., 1989). Although this theory is probably overly simplistic, there is supportive evidence. The action of antidepressant drugs such as monoamine oxidase inhibitors and tricyclic antidepressants affect the norepinephrine neurotransmitter system. These drugs prevent the breakdown of norepinephrine and also alleviate depressive symptoms. The fact that they take a couple weeks to become effective and that amino acid precursors of norepinephrine such as L-dopa do not relieve depression, are results that are not explained by the classic catecholamine theory of depression. It has also been suggested that the neurotransmitters serotonin and acetylcholine interact with norepinephrine to create depressive mood and symptoms. As discussed in chapter 5, all three of these neurotransmitter systems are affected by processes of aging.

The neurotransmitter serotonin probably interacts with norepinephrine to create depressive mood and symptoms. Second-generation antidepressants such as Prozac are also called serotonin reuptake blockers. The mechanism is the same as monoamine oxidase inhibitors and tricyclic drugs, but the effect is more selective, acting primarily on serotonin. Serotonin is also involved in the regulation of sleep cycles. One of the effects of antidepressant drugs is to regulate sleep and restore the 24-hour sleep–wake cycle.

Surveying research related to the issue of the neurobiology of aging and depression, Veith and Raskind (1988) concluded that there was insufficient evidence to support the proposition that neurobiological aging changes predispose older adults to depression. The possibility of a neurobiological predisposal to depression in old age is not ruled out. However, more investigations are required to conclusively link neurobiological aging with depression. In part, the lack of conclusion results from technical obstacles. The problem is complex, involving more than one neurotransmitter system. In humans, it is methodologically difficult to assess one brain neurotransmitter level, let alone more than one. Neurotransmitters act differently in the peripheral and central nervous systems. Most easily accessible measures of neurotransmitter level use blood and urine samples that are contaminated by peripheral nervous system neurotransmitter levels. The assessment of depression is not comparable across studies, so that inclusion criteria for samples of depressed patients vary.

Psychological and social causes of depression in the elderly

Some of the major psychological and social causes of depression in the aged are:

1 Physical illness and sensory loss.
2 Bereavement and loss of significant others.
3 Economic deprivation and poor living conditions.
4 Retirement and the loss of social roles.

Retirement and the loss of social roles is the only cause limited to older adulthood. Nevertheless, the first three causes of depression listed above are also more likely to affect the elderly than other age groups of individuals.

With hypotheses about the cause of depression in old age including explanations ranging for biological to social-environmental, it is clear that gerontologists have no precise understanding of the causes of depression in the aged. Furthermore, it appears that there are some myths about depression in aging. Exploration of the literature on aging and depression revealed several false premises held about depression in the elderly (Hybels, 1986).

First, it is assumed that geriatric depression is of a different character from that found in younger people. Reviewers of the objective data, including the American Psychiatric Association Task Force on Nomenclature and Statistics which designed the DSM-III diagnostic system, have reached the conclusion that no clinical justification exists for retaining a separate category of depression based on old age. There are some differences in presentation of symptoms. Old people are more willing to present physical symptoms than they are to discuss sadness and psychological problems. However, the substance of the depression is similar to depression in younger individuals.

Second, it is often assumed that the prevalence of geriatric depression is greater than for younger groups. This myth has been challenged previously in this chapter. The number of identifiable symptoms of depression may be greater in older populations, but it is incorrect to interpret this as meaning that the prevalence of depression is greater. Symptoms of actual physical illness and of grief reactions must be excluded before a diagnosis of clinical depression in the elderly is accurate. When physical illness and grief reaction symptoms are excluded, the prevalence of clinical depression in the aged is roughly the same or even less than in the younger adult age groups.

Given the numerous potential causes for depression in the elderly, it is indeed remarkable that only 5 percent of the aged suffer a clinical depression late in life. It is as important to ask why 95 percent of the individuals over the age of 65 *do not* get clinically depressed as to dwell on the causes for depression in old age.

Psychotherapeutic treatments for depression in late life

It has already been pointed out that depression is the most common psychiatric complaint among the elderly, and it is essential to treat depressive symptoms in older adults. Depression is treatable in old age, and the alternative to treatment is tragic because a common outcome of depression in the elderly is suicide. The actual number of suicides in the over-65 age group, including those not reported, may exceed 10,000 annually according to Miller (1979).

Two aspects of depression making it particularly troublesome to treat were pointed out by Gatz et al. (1980). The first is that loss is a central aspect of old age, and there are clear reasons why the older people should be feeling depressed. As we have mentioned previously, when the actual number of depressive *symptoms* is counted, older people have more. However, when the prevalence of depressive *disorders* as diagnosed by psychiatrists is examined, the rate is highest between the ages of 25 and 65. The other problematic aspect of depression in the elderly is that family and friends find it difficult to be around the depressed individual. Elderly people typically have fewer living relatives and friends, and when they alienate these few potential helpers with the dependent and demanding behaviors characteristic of depressed individuals, they become isolated. Gatz et al. (1980) suggested that the families and caretakers need assistance, and interventions to maximize the helpers' effectiveness are required, as well as interventions for the elderly depressed themselves.

Several relatively long-term follow-up studies have been conducted to examine the effectiveness of various treatments for elderly depressives. Evidence to date indicates that several forms of individual psychotherapy and some forms of group therapy are effective in helping the elderly overcome their depression. It is only very recently that such a positive picture for the efficacy of treatment of depression in the aged has been presented.

Gallagher et al. (1986) reported 1-year follow-up results on three modalities of individual psychotherapy: behavioral, cognitive, or psychodynamic. The investigators had selected 120 older people over the age of 60 who had evidence of a major depressive disorder as assessed by Research Diagnostic Criteria (Spitzer et al., 1978). On average, participants had been depressed for 2 years before participating in the study. The program lasted for 4 months, with weekly sessions in one of the three types of psychotherapy.

Among the common ingredients in the three types of individual psychotherapy used in the study were (a) a strong therapeutic alliance between the therapist and elderly client. This alliance was equivalent in all of the three therapy modalities. (b) A clear focus on mutually defined goals. The therapist and client had a contract. (c) All the therapies were brief, lasting 4 months, and the client and therapist were aware of the need to use the time effectively. There was structure to the sessions. (d) There were individual difference variables which predicted success in the various therapies. While the patients were randomly assigned to treatment in the study, data from it can be used to assign individuals to the most effective therapy for them in future treatment programs.

Of the 91 participants who completed the study, 52 percent had complete remission of their depression, 18 percent had reduced the level of depression to minor, and 30 percent were still as depressed as in the beginning of the study. This post-treatment assessment of depression was based on the SADS assessment. There was no difference in the outcome as a function of the type of individual psychotherapy. All three treatments were equally effective. A year after the treatment, 82 of the patients were assessed again, and at this point 57 percent were still not depressed. Thirteen percent had experienced minor depression with brief episodes of depression. Major depression existed in 27 percent of the subjects, and 3 percent had other diagnoses at the time of the 1-year follow-up. Thus, a clear majority of older depressed patients were successfully treated in 4 months and maintained their improved mental health status for 1 year.

Beutler and his associates (1986) described a study of older depressed patients in which they compared the effects of cognitive group therapy and the drug Alprazolam in the treatment of depression. Alprazolam is commonly prescribed for depression in older adults. Fifty-six older adults carefully screened for depression were randomly assigned to one of four groups: drug, placebo, cognitive group therapy and drug, cognitive group therapy and placebo. Therapy lasted 10 weeks, and there was a 3-week follow-up assessment. Sleep efficiency was also assessed in these patients for four nights. Sleep disorders are a common problem in depression.

Assessment with the Beck Depression Inventory indicated that there was some improvement in the cognitive therapy group. Sleep efficiency improved about 5 percent in this group, while sleep efficiency in the groups not receiving cognitive group therapy decreased by 12 percent. While cognitive group therapy was somewhat effective in this group of older depressed patients, Alprazolam was not effective. Beutler et al. (1986) found no evidence that prescription of this drug is indicated in the case of elderly depressed patients.

Beutler suggested that the individual psychotherapy intervention used by Gallagher and associates was probably more effective than the cognitive group therapy he used. That treatment results in these studies was not an outcome due to spontaneous remission is indicated in several different ways. In the Gallagher study, patients on the waiting list who were tested for depression but not accepted for several months for treatment did not show improved scores on depression until after treatment. Beutler's study had non-treatment control groups, and these individuals showed no improvement. Age of onset of depression also did not predict improvement in either study. Thus, regardless of how old an individual is when depression occurs, he or she can still be treated and show improvement.

Depression is frequently seen in older adults in the early stages of AD. Indeed, who would not be depressed to find one's mental capacities gradually failing? Teri et al. (1986) have undertaken the treatment of depression in AD, both for the caregivers and the patients. In this behavioral approach, the patient as well as the caregiver are involved. Teri and her associates pointed out that all too often patients are left sitting outside in the hall while the family discusses the patient with the doctors and mental health personnel. Even if the patient has deteriorated cognitively, he or she still has an emotional reaction to being literally left out in the hall. It is Teri's recommendation that the patient always be included in these conferences, regardless of his or her capacity to understand what is being discussed.

One of the therapies used by this group is to get the patient involved in activities similar to things that used to give the patient pleasure. For example, if the patient used to enjoy crossword puzzles, find easier crossword puzzles, including large crossword puzzles for children, that the patient can still master. When the patient can no longer undertake those puzzles, find simple word rhymes and games. If the patient used to enjoy sewing, introduce sewing cards. While it is important never to infantilize older adults, in the case of AD mental capacities do regress severely, and simple children's activities relating to the patient's past interests do not insult the individual at this point.

In a typical 7-week treatment program, Teri's group would first interview the patient and caregivers and identify pleasant activities the caregivers can introduce for the patient. In the first 2 weeks of the program these pleasant activities involving things the patient used to enjoy are introduced, and caregivers are encouraged to use these activities and identify other pleasant activities for the patient throughout the time they are providing care. In the third week of the program, relaxation training for the caregiver is introduced, and in the fourth week problem-solving with the caregiver is undertaken by the mental health professionals. Relaxation training and problem-solving continue with the caregivers until the end of the treatment program. Finally, in the seventh week a review of the entire period is carried out. The effect on patients' moods of working at a pleasant activity, such as the kind identified by Teri's group, can be dramatic. Although patients with AD regress in their cognitive capacity, their emotions can be positively affected with sensitive interventions.

The frontal lobes and emotion

Practicing neuropsychologists call it the frontal-lobe syndrome, and it is likely the most common neuropsychological symptom cluster in the neurological population (Ogden, 1996). The syndrome is common after closed-head injury, but more relevant to aging is the fact that it occurs in people with damage to the frontal lobes caused by stroke, tumor, or prolonged alcoholism. Sufferers of Korsakoff's syndrome and people with various forms of dementia such as AD and Huntington's disease often show signs of frontal-lobe syndrome. Parkinson's disease also disrupts frontal-lobe function by impairing the large number of frontal lobe neurons that use the neurotransmitter dopamine.

Emotional as well as cognitive deficits are associated with damage to the prefrontal cortex. Mild frontal-lobe dysfunction is often associated with subtle impairments such as irritability, poor motivation, and a quick loss of temper. More severe frontal-lobe impairment can result in a complete loss of social inhibition and a total change in personality.

The classic case of frontal-lobe syndrome was observed and treated by Harlow (1868), and more recently revived by Damasio et al. (1994). It is the tragic case of Phineas Gage. Gage was a responsible and respected member of the community who worked as a foreman to a railroad construction crew in

New England. As some of his workers were arranging the explosive powder in a hole to remove some boulders from the pathway where they were building a track, Gage was momentarily distracted and began tamping directly over the powder before it had been covered with sand. The resulting explosion hurled the tamping iron, that was over an inch in diameter and three and half feet long, into the orbit of his eye and through the top of his skull (see figure 7.1). The blast was so powerful that the tamping iron passed completely through Gage's skull and brain, landing yards away on the ground. Miraculously, Gage never lost consciousness. A physician stated that he could touch his fingers when inserted in the two ends of the hole created by the tamping iron. That Phineas Gage was a strong man is attested by the fact that he survived this lobotomy-producing accident, but he was dramatically changed as a human being. Gage's physician, J. M. Harlow, described him in what is a prototype of the frontal-lobe syndrome.

> He is fitful, irreverent, indulging at times in the grossest profanity (which was not previously his custom), manifesting but little deference to his fellows, impatient of restraint or advice when it conflicts with his desires, at times pertinaciously obstinate yet capricious and vacillating, devising many plans for future operations which no sooner are arranged than they are abandoned in turn for others appearing more feasible. His mind was radically changed so that his friends and acquaintances said he was no longer Gage (Harlow, 1868, p. 336).

A behavioral symptom that is typical of the frontal-lobe syndrome is the inability to inhibit inappropriate behaviors (called disinhibition). Gage exhibited this symptom by using excessive profane language. Before his accident he had been an exceedingly proper man who simply would not use such language in public. A very mild form of disinhibition is seen in the garrulousness of old age. Older adults frequently tell and retell in extensive detail stories that their relatives have heard before. Less restraint in speaking up and speaking out is somewhat typical of the elderly. This pattern of verbal behavior is not inappropriate, but it may result as a consequence of very mild frontal-lobe syndrome in older adults.

More severe behavioral consequences of frontal-lobe damage observed in patients with dementia, patients with Korsakoff's or Parkinson's disease, or individuals who suffered from tumors or strokes affecting the frontal lobe, include lack of insight into one's problems and an inability to learn from mistakes. Frontal-lobe syndrome is associated with a diminished sense of responsibility, impulsiveness, mild euphoria, and a tendency to made inappropriate and childish jokes. Another capacity that apparently resides in the frontal lobes and that is impaired in frontal-lobe syndrome is the ability to

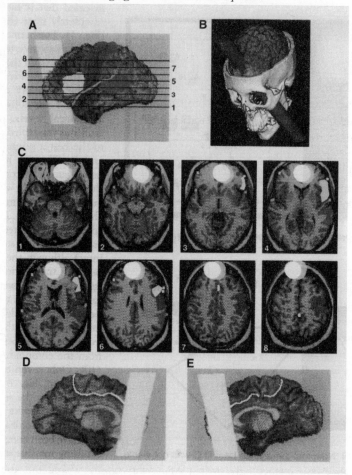

Figure 7.1 Hypothetical trajectories of five different angles with the best-fitting rod highlighted in solid white in (a), (d), and (e). The reason it is possible to identify the best-fitting rod is that Phineas Gage's skull was available to be measured. (a) Lateral view of a standard brain with numbered black lines showing the levels of brain section shown in (c). (b) The actual skull of Phineas Gage shown with a rod drawn at the angle the tamping iron must have passed through the brain. (c) Coronal sections showing lesion from tamping iron in white. (d) and (e) Medical view of left and right hemispheres, respectively, with the rod shown in white

Source: Damasio, H., Grabowski, T., Frank, R., Galaburda, A. M., & Damasio, A. R. (1994). The return of Phineas Gage: Clues about the brain from the skull of a famous patient. *Science, 264,* 1102–1105. Copyright © 1994, American Association for the Advancement of Science

initiate activities or to act spontaneously. Kolb and Whishaw (1995) characterized frontal lobe patients as appearing lethargic or lazy. These neuropsychologists described a patient who was a prominent lawyer who suffered a midline meningioma in the frontal lobe in late middle age. The tumor was removed surgically leaving bilateral damage to prefrontal lobes. Although his memory for legal matters was unimpaired, and his IQ remained superior (over 140), he was unable to return to his profession. He preferred to stay in bed late and to watch television rather than to go to work. When his wife forced him to go to the office, he was disruptive to his co-workers who could not tolerate him in the office. They preferred to consult with him on the telephone when they had legal questions, but his frontal-lobe syndrome behavior was impossible for them to deal with face to face.

Brain lateralization and emotion

Asymmetries recorded in the EEG from anterior temporal and prefrontal scalp sites are associated with important features of emotional reactivity and affective style (Davidson, 1995). Lesions of the left and right hemispheres appear to have different effects on emotions. On the one hand, the initial suggestions that normal aging might affect the right and left cerebral hemispheres differently have not received empirical support (Hellige, 1993; Libon et al., 1994). Thus, a discussion of hemispheric differences in emotion addresses those older patients with lesions to the left or right hemisphere resulting from tumors or stroke.

In an overview of the research on brain lateralization and emotion, Kolb and Whishaw (1995) concluded first that the frontal lobes and the right hemisphere appear more involved in the mediation of emotion than the left hemisphere. However, they pointed out that not all neuropsychologists share their view. In a thoughtful review, Tucker (1981) concluded that the right hemisphere had a special role in mediating negative emotions, whereas the left hemisphere was more engaged in positive emotions.

Patients with lesions in the right prefrontal lobe typically make poor jokes and puns and tell pointless stories. Their sense of humor seems altered, and they are also more likely to use profane language. The patient is often so amused by his or her own stories that they persist in telling them even when listeners are obviously not engaged. Patients with lesions of the right temporal or parietal lobes have very different patterns of speech. They talk about their personal life and express excessive concern for their own shortcomings. Furthermore, they ignore the fact that they are boring to others. In contrast to the increased volume of speech in patients with right cortical lesions, the volume of speech is decreased in patients with left cortical lesions. The patients in these studies that have left lesions are not aphasic. However, they talk less.

Facial expression is another way to assess emotions. Individuals with lesions to anterior portions of the brain seem to reduce their facial expression compared to those with lesions to posterior brain areas (Kolb & Milner, 1981). Some studies have also indicated that facial expression is reduced more in right than in left cortical lesions, but the evidence is weaker than for the anterior versus posterior lesion effect on facial expression.

Summary

The emotional state of the older adult is significant for the neuropsychologist, as affect has an impact on neuropsychological assessment and evaluation. In particular, depression, the most common psychopathology of old age, can make an older adult appear to have impaired cognitive function and even dementia.

Although popular belief is that depression increases with age, epidemiological surveys of the incidence of depression in the adult population indicate that the aged are no more prone to depression than are younger adults. Young and middle adulthood are the most common periods for depression to manifest itself, although the most likely form of break down in old age is depression. Depression is one of the few forms of psychopathology that appear for the first time in old age.

Memory loss and poor concentration are typical complaints of depressed patients, and depression can result in mild to moderate cognitive impairment as assessed by neuropsychological tests. To reduce the risk of diagnosing dementia in a patient who is suffering from severe depression, it is essential to used age-adjusted neuropsychological tests and norms. Following up the patient after treatment also has utility in differentiating dementia from depression, as depression can be alleviated whereas dementia is typically progressive.

Hypotheses about the cause of depression in old age include explanations ranging from biological to social-environmental. There is some evidence that age-related changes in monoamine brain neurotransmitters such as norepinephrine and serotonin predispose older adults to be more depressed. There is no complete biochemical theory of depression, but converging evidence implicates these two neurotransmitters in affective disorders. In chapter 5 age-related losses in these two monoamine neurotransmitter systems was discussed. In particular, cells of origin in the locus coeruleus that supply norepinephrine to the brain are lost in normal aging. AD exacerbates this loss. Social and psychological losses that increase in incidence with age also place an emotional burden on the elderly that may make them depressed. Age-related changes in physical health status are so devastating to some older adults, especially elderly men, that they attempt suicide.

Therapy for depression in old age is often successful in ameliorating the condition. Among features of individual psychotherapy that made it effective were a strong therapeutic alliance between the therapist and elderly client, a clear focus on mutually defined goals, and relative brevity of therapy so that it lasted several months, making the client and therapist aware of the need to use the time effectively. Depression is not a typical emotional status in old age, and when it is experienced, it can be treated successfully.

The cortical region associated with emotion and affect is the prefrontal region, and frontal-lobe syndrome occurs in adults with damage to the frontal lobes from trauma more common in old age, such as stroke or tumor. Frontal-lobe syndrome is also seen in patients with Korsakoff's syndrome or Parkinson's disease and in dementia resulting from AD and Huntington's disease. Mild frontal-lobe dysfunction can be associated with irritability, poor motivation, and quick loss of temper. Severe frontal-lobe impairment results in total loss of social inhibition and significant change in personality. The classic case of Phineas Gage who experienced severe frontal lobe damage in a construction accident was the first recorded illustration of the dramatic personality changes caused by damage to the frontal lobes. Gage became irreverent and capricious, lost respect for social convention, and offended all those who heard his abundant profanity. The inability of frontal-lobe patients to initiate activities and act spontaneously makes them appear lethargic and lazy. This aspect of the syndrome was characterized by a patient who was a successful attorney before suffering from a large frontal-lobe tumor. After the tumor was removed, he could not return to his office even though his memory and intelligence were intact. His distractibility and irritability at work coupled with his preference to be in bed at home watching television led his co-workers to persuade his wife to keep him at home and to let them consult with him over the phone.

Brain lateralization has been associated with emotion in that lesions of the left and right hemispheres have different effects. The frontal lobes and the right cerebral hemisphere appear move involved with emotion than the left hemisphere. Some evidence exists for a special role for the right hemisphere in mediating negative emotions, with the left hemisphere being more engaged in positive emotions. Using facial expression to assess emotion, it has been observed that patients with right hemisphere lesions reduce expression more than patients with left hemisphere lesions. There is not a differential aging effect on the left or right cerebral cortex, making brain lateralization of emotion relevant to aging only in the case of brain damage cause by trauma with a higher incidence in old age (e.g., strokes, tumors).

Further Reading

Levinson, R. W., Carstensen, L. L., Friesen, W. V., & Ekman, P. (1991). Emotion, physiology, and expression in old age. *Psychology and Aging, 6,* 28–35.
Exploration of the relationship between neurobiological and health factors in emotion in the elderly.

Lawton, M. P., Van Haitsma, K., & Klapper, J. (1996). Observed affect in nursing home residents with Alzheimer's disease. *Journal of Gerontology: Psychological Sciences, 51B,* P3–14.
A method for assessing affect states in AD using facial expression, along with results from the assessment are described in this article.

Parmelee, P. A., Katz, I. R., & Lawton, M. P. (1989). Depression among institutionalized aged: Assessment and prevalence estimation. *Journal of Gerontology: Medical Sciences, 44,* M22–29.
This article gives a perspective on the extent and impact of depression in institutionalized elderly.

Damasio, H., Grabowski, T., Frank, R., Galaburda, A. M., & Damasio, A. R. (1994). The return of Phineas Gage: Clues about the brain from the skull of a famous patient. *Science, 264,* 1102–1105.
A fascinating account of the application of modern neuro-imaging methodology to a landmark case in neuropsychology.

Hellige, J. B. (1993). *Hemispheric asymmetry: What's right and what's left.* Cambridge, MA: Harvard University Press.
A thorough overview of the research and clinical literature on hemispheric asymmetry and its effect on cognition and emotion.

Part III

Human Behavior:
A Neuropsychological
Perspective

8

Arousal and Sleep

The levels of consciousness encompassed by arousal and sleep reflect opposite ends of the continuum of awareness. Arousal and sleep are considered together in this chapter because they may be regulated by common neurophysiological and neurochemical mechanisms. The observed age changes in arousal in the waking state may be related to age changes in sleep patterns. Conversely, arousal level changes during the waking state in older adults may alter requirements for sleep. Neuropsychologists do not traditionally assess arousal level or sleep patterns, but performance on neuropsychological tests can clearly be affected by these states of consciousness. Arousal level and the quality of an elderly client's sleep are aspects that are of significance to the neuropsychology of aging.

A typical measure of states of arousal and stages of sleep is brain electrical activity, discussed in chapter 3. Brain electrical activity is the measure of primary discussion in this chapter. The electroencephalogram (EEG) and event related potentials (ERPs) have been useful in elucidating age differences in arousal and sleep in the central nervous system. Particularly in the arousal literature, a component of the peripheral nervous system, the autonomic nervous system has also received a great deal of attention. In our discussion of the peripheral nervous system in chapter 4, we presented a discussion of aging and arousal describing biochemical measures such as free fatty acid level and bioelectric measures such as galvanic skin response (GSR) and heart rate.

In dealing with neuropsychological variables it is not unusual to assume that differences between young and old groups represent age changes rather than simply differences between cohort groups. Schaie (1965) and Baltes (1968) have pointed out that this is not a reasonable assumption, and we discussed some general concerns about the proper interpretation of longitudinal and cross-sectional data in chapter 1, and the issue was discussed again with regard to neuron counts in human brains in chapter 5. However, there are few studies in the neuropsychological literature which are longitudinal. Age changes in the EEG observed in cross-sectional studies have been replicated longitudinally, but the ERP and sleep studies are almost exclusively cross-sectional. Thus, in this chapter the age functions will be referred to as age differences unless longitudinal data are available. It is likely that many of the cross-sectional results will be replicated in longitudinal designs because cross-sectional studies have been carried out on ERPs and on sleep over several cohorts of older adults. Nevertheless, it is important to keep in mind that the research represents comparisons of different individuals born at different times and tested at one point in time when they are different ages.

In attempting to understand brain mechanisms in arousal, sleep and aging, there are a number of related concepts and models along with empirical research apart from neuropsychological correlates of arousal and sleep which are important to consider. One area of significance is excitability and inhibition in the nervous system. Researchers have recognized that changes in the aging brain may involve changes in excitation and inhibition since the early twentieth century when Ivan Pavlov articulated these points. Contemporary neuropsychological research supports with elaboration Pavlov's initial assertion that inhibitory processes decline in aging (e.g., Arbuckle, & Gold, 1993; Hartley & Kieley, 1995; Hasher et al., 1991; Kramer et al., 1994). What is less clear is the relationship between decreasing inhibitory processes and arousal. It is possible that a decline in inhibition signifies more excitability and hence overarousal for the elderly. However, many possibly independent changes occur in the nervous system with age which might lead to over-arousal in one system and underarousal in another. Furthermore, compensatory mechanisms occur which may result in organization at a new functioning level.

Bondareff (1980) termed the loss of axosomatic synapses in the dentate gyrus of the senescent as "compensatory." He argued that a reorganization of the dentate gyrus occurs in senescent rats, including a 27 percent loss of axodendritic synapses in the molecular layer, and a coincident loss of 15 percent of the axosomatic synapses. Axodendritic synapses are excitatory, whereas axosomatic synapses are inhibitory. Bondareff suggested that a compensatory loss of synapses may result in the aging animal's ability to maintain a reasonably adaptive level of function in spite of neuronal loss.

Another related model developed from the behavioral literature on aging and perception involves stimulus persistence. This could be conceived as an excitability model which stipulates that the older nervous system responds in a prolonged fashion to stimuli. A given visual or auditory stimulus persists longer in the older nervous system, implicating greater excitability, and perhaps less inhibition. This phenomenon might be viewed as another form of overarousal in the older nervous system, particularly if arousal is conceptualized in phasic as well as tonic terms.

The empirical literature on neuroanatomical and electrophysiological changes in the aging brain is significant to this chapter as it suggests a common origin for observed changes in arousal and sleep. A predominant and oft-cited change is the loss of cortical neurons and dendritic branching in the frontal lobes (Scheibel & Scheibel, 1976) which probably underlies the observed electrophysiological changes over the frontal cortex (Michalewski et al., 1980; Pfefferbaum et al., 1979; Tecce et al., 1980). It was emphasized in chapter 5 that the frontal lobes show significant age-related deficits. The inhibitory function of frontal cortex on the ascending reticular arousal system (ARAS) is documented (e.g., Fuster, 1989; Scheibel & Scheibel, 1966; Skinner & Yingling, 1977). The frontal cortex has also been implicated in the regulation of sleep (Fuster, 1989; Prinz, 1976). Thus, age changes in the frontal lobes may account in part for alterations in arousal and sleep. At the same time, other changes in the aging brain including cell loss in various areas in addition to the anterior cortex, declines in blood flow, and alterations in neurotransmitters and synaptic mechanisms are undoubtedly involved in age changes in sleep and arousal states. Thus, the observed age differences in sleep and arousal may involve common mechanisms, and they probably also involve independent causes.

The focus of this chapter is on electrophysiological measures, and neurophysiological and neuroanatomical processes of aging. However, it should not be overlooked that social and behavioral phenomena are also causally involved in age differences in sleep and arousal. Retirement is a socially imposed milestone that has profound implications for sleep and wakefulness. The demands of work affect sleep patterns, energy level, attention, motivation, and arousal. The abrupt change in the work cycle caused by retirement leads to alterations in sleep, including altered demands for sleep which in turn can affect psychophysiological measures of these activities. A behavioral phenomenon frequently observed in aging which may profoundly affect sleep and wakefulness is depression, discussed in chapter 7 on emotions and aging. Social and psychological events involving loss predispose the elderly toward depression which in turn can alter sleep patterns and levels of arousal. These social and behavioral phenomena reinforce the point that most data on sleep, arousal, and aging are cross-sectional and reflect differences between groups. The age differences are not necessarily a function of ontogeny or biological aging. They may reflect different environmental demands or circumstances of the aging population as well as age changes in the brain.

Sleep

The EEG is the measure that makes it possible to detect stages of sleep. In chapter 3 we discussed age-related changes in the waking EEG. The greatest EEG changes with age occur during sleep.

Sleep stages

Sleep is divided into five stages, four of which reflect a progression to deeper sleep (non-rapid eye movement [NREM] sleep which includes stages I–IV) and one called paradoxical or rapid eye movement (REM) sleep (see figure 8.1). The NREM sleep states involve the absence of eye movements and

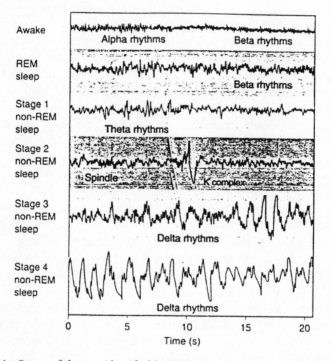

Figure 8.1 Stages of sleep as identified by EEG. Rapid eye movement (REM) sleep is characterized by an EEG that looks similar to the awake EEG, and REM sleep is thus sometimes called paradoxical sleep. The lightest stage of sleep (Stage 1) is characterized by theta waves (4–7 c.p.s.). Stage 2 sleep contains sleep spindles (rhythmic 14 c.p.s. activity) and K-complexes. Delta waves (1–3 c.p.s.) emerge in Stage 3 sleep and comprise less than 50 percent of the EEG record. Stage 4 sleep is characterized by a predomination of delta waves (>50 percent)

moderately reduced muscle tonus. In stage I the EEG pattern is of low amplitude, irregular, fast frequency activity. Stage II includes synchronous waves of 12–16 c.p.s. (spindles) which occur against a background of low amplitude, fast frequency activity. High amplitude (75 μV or more) slow waves (0.5–2.5 c.p.s.), also called delta waves, characterize stage III sleep and comprise 20–50 percent of the EEG record during this stage. When these slow waves comprise 50 percent or more of the EEG record, stage IV sleep is achieved. REM sleep is characterized by low amplitude, fast frequency EEG activity, similar to the EEG during wakefulness. The phenomenon which gives this stage its name is the presence of bursts of rapid eye movements. Just at the onset of a REM sleep period, muscle tonus undergoes a marked decrease which is sustained throughout most of the REM period.

The most prominent EEG sign of adult aging is the steady decrease in delta wave amplitude during slow wave sleep (SWS; Miles & Dement, 1980). The delta waves that characterize stages III and IV are greatly attenuated in amplitude. For example, Prinz (1976) reported in a study of 12 healthy subjects between the ages of 75 and 92 whose EEGs were recorded while they slept in their homes, the largest slow wave amplitudes rarely exceeded 150 μV, while 200 μV or greater waves are commonly seen in young adults. There is an overall decrease in the amount of delta wave activity in the all-night EEG record. In addition, there is a decline in the growth hormone secretion that usually passively follows the occurrence of SWS.

The age change in delta activity may have several causes. The enzyme monoamine oxidase increases in the brain stem with age, and such increased activity could impair the function of the neurotransmitter, serotonin. This neurotransmitter appears to be involved in the induction or maintenance of NREM sleep. Another possible cause of the decline in delta waves during sleep in the aged may be the loss of the oblique-horizontal dendrite systems of pyramidal cells in cortical layers 2, 3 and 5. The horizontal networks may facilitate cooperative or synchronous neural behavior.

Another age change in sleep EEG is the change in spindle activity. Senescent sleep spindles are often poorly formed and of lower amplitude, resulting in an infrequent occurrence of typical spindling activity (Feinberg et al., 1967). Spindle frequencies are often slower in older adults as well (Feinberg et al., 1967; Kales et al., 1967). Feinberg (1974) pointed out that these changes are analogous to the changes in alpha activity, which also decreases in frequency, amplitude, and overall amount in senescence. Similarly, the changes in sleep-related EEG slow waves with advanced age also decrease in both amplitude and overall amount.

In addition to the altered EEG characteristics during sleep, there are also age changes in the amounts and patterning of the various sleep stages. Most likely as a result of the reduced amplitude of sleep-related EEG slow waves characterizing stage IV sleep, this stage is greatly reduced or absent in senescence (Feinberg et al., 1967; Foret & Webb, 1980; Kahn & Fisher, 1969; Kales et al., 1967; Prinz, 1976). Webb (1981) reported that after two nights of sleep deprivation subjects in their early 20s and in their 40s showed sharply reduced latencies to SWS and increased stage IV sleep. The proportionate distribution of stage amounts and numbers was not different in the two age groups, but the younger group entered SWS more quickly.

Several of the hypotheses reported by Miles and Dement (1980) to explain the decline in stage IV sleep in the elderly involve a reduced need for deep sleep in a more sedentary population. When need is altered by sleep loss, stage IV is achieved and maintained equally well in older (though only middle-aged) subjects. These observations have led sleep experts such as Donald Bliwise and Mary Carskadon to recommend that older adults get out of bed and read, watch television, or pursue some other activity rather than lying in bed awake.

Older people tend to spend more time in bed (10–12 hr) and more time awake in bed. Carskadon (1982) suggested that if older people would spend only 6 hr a night in bed, the quality of their sleep, including time spent in deep sleep, might improve. When the need for sleep is increased by sleep loss, Stage IV sleep is achieved in old subjects for a time period approaching the time adolescents spend in Stage IV.

An age change which received major emphasis is the increased number of awakenings and time spent awake in bed in the elderly. Miles and Dement (1980) reported an almost linear increase in waking after sleep onset with age, which is paralleled by a very marked increase in the occurrence of brief (10 s or less) arousals which are not perceived or remembered and may not cause actual wakefulness. The most prominent subjective symptom is the complaint of increased number and duration of sleep disruptions. This complaint often parallels the objective finding of increased wakings after sleep onset.

Taken as a whole, the changes observed in the sleep characteristics of elderly subjects are used as evidence that sleep is impaired in the aged. The changes are similar in men and women, but impairment may be greater in men. Increased wakefulness and decreased SWS are subjectively experienced as less-sound sleep. These phenomena may account for more frequent complaints of poor sleep and greater usage of drugs to promote sleep among elderly individuals. To compensate for impaired sleep, the elderly may also take more frequent daytime naps.

Sleep pattern variables in elderly groups parallel mental function test scores. Among aged men selected for good health, Feinberg et al. (1967) found a correlation between time spent in REM sleep and WAIS performance and Wechsler Memory scores. This result has been replicated (Kahn & Fisher, 1969; Prinz, 1977).

Sleep apnea

Sleep apnea is the name given to the cessation of airflow in breathing for 10 s or longer during sleep. The cessation of breathing during sleep may have life threatening consequences for individuals at the early and late portions of the life span. Respiratory disturbances are a major cause of impaired sleep and frequent awakenings in the elderly (Ancoli-Israel et al., 1981; Bliwise et al., 1983). These respiratory disturbances are a health risk in themselves. However, more alarming is the evidence that sleeping pills and alcohol increase the incidence and length of these episodes (Guilleminault & Dement, 1978).

The occurrence of apnea or several other kinds of abnormal respiratory events at a rate of more than five per hour is considered pathological. Some elderly have hundreds of these events during the night. The incidence of respiratory problems in the sleep of the elderly has been variously reported at 32–63 percent (e.g., Ancoli-Israel et al., 1981; Bliwise et al., 1983). Longitudinal data collected by Bliwise et al. (1984) suggest that increases in respiratory disturbances during sleep may occur primarily during the fourth and fifth decades and remain high in subsequent years.

Taken as a whole, the age differences observed in sleep characteristics serve as evidence that the pattern of sleep is altered in the normal aged. The age differences are similar in men and women, but impairment may be greater in men (Miles & Dement, 1980). Increased wakefulness and decreased SWS are subjectively experienced as less sound sleep. However, it is the fragmentation of sleep most frequently caused by disturbed night-time breathing which has been shown to be most closely related to sleepiness and reduced daytime well-being in the aged.

It is evident that there is a higher incidence of complaints of poor sleep and a greater usage of drugs to promote sleep among elderly individuals. It has been reported that in the United States, those 60 and older consume 33 percent of all prescriptions for sleeping pills such as secobarbital and diazepam (Institute of Medicine, 1979). Advances in knowledge of respiratory disturbances associated with sleep in the aged indicate that these drugs may increase the incidence of apnea and associated cardiac arrythmia. Another behavior common in the elderly is to compensate for inadequate night-time sleep by napping during the day. Like sleeping pills, napping may be inappropriate for the sleepless aged. Sleep deprivation studies have demonstrated that sleep loss actually improves the quality of sleep by increasing the time spent in deep sleep the next night. Thus, by avoiding sleeping pills and staying in bed at night for shorter rather than longer intervals, older adults might improve the quality of their sleep.

Arousal

Arousal theory received its major impetus with the discovery of the ascending reticular arousal system (ARAS) in a series of ingeneous experiments (e.g., Lindsley et al., 1950; Moruzzi & Magoun, 1949). Moruzzi and Magoun observed the relationship between direct electrical stimulation from electrodes implanted in the reticular formation and behavioral arousal. Furthermore, Lindsley et al. (1950) observed that lesions to the midline reticular formation resulted in a permanent sleeping state in the animal, but that the animal could be aroused by stimulation higher in the brain than the lesion (see figure 8.2). These discoveries led to the generation of a large body of research, and Lindsley (1952, 1960) reviewed much of this literature and organized it into a general theory of arousal.

For over 45 years, it has been known that electrical brain stimulation has an alerting function in animals when it involves the midbrain reticular formation or the thalamic intralaminar nuclei upon which reticular formation axons synapse. However, cases had been observed in which lesion of these reticular or thalamic regions failed to impair arousal and vigilance, making the role of the ARAS controversial. A recent study using positron emission tomography (PET) in humans showed activation in the midbrain reticular formation and thalamic intralaminar nuclei when human participants went from a relaxed awake state to an attention-demanding reaction time task (Kinomura et al., 1996). These results confirm the role of the ARAS and thalamic intralaminar nuclei in arousal and vigilance.

The main dependent measure in research on arousal and behavior before the advent of PET was the EEG, and in Lindsley's theory, various EEG frequency bandwidths were associated with stages of arousal ranging from deep sleep to alert problem solving. In its simplest form, the theory associates very slow EEG frequencies called delta waves (1–3 c.p.s.) with deep sleep, a bandwidth ranging from 4–7 c.p.s. and called theta waves with light sleep, and the transition between sleep and wakefulness, the 8–13 c.p.s. range called alpha frequency, with alert wakefulness, and the faster frequencies of 14–40 c.p.s. or more, called beta, with thinking and problem solving.

The precise origin and mechanism for the generation of rhythmic brain activity is still not fully understood, but it is generally agreed that the EEG generators reside in the cortex. However, the maintenance and regulation of all of the rhythmic activity is probably not cortical, but rather originates in

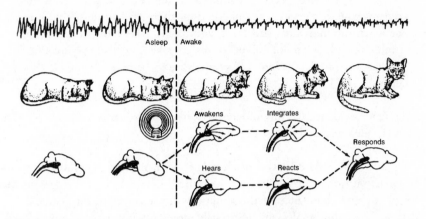

Figure 8.2 Schematic drawing of the EEG, brain, and behavior of a cat as it passes through the arousal stages from deep sleep to waking alertness. In the first frame, the cat is in deep sleep. In the second frame, the ringing bell rouses the cat. Collaterals from the primary auditory pathway provide input to the reticular formation. The cat awakens and integrates in the third and fourth frames and responds in the fifth frame. Coincidentally, in the third frame, the ARAS acts (black arrows) to awaken the cortex so that it can "hear" signals arriving in the auditory area. The EEG changes from a pattern of sleep to one of wakefulness at the end of the second frame. The ARAS then integrates brain activity so that the brain can react as a whole. The cat finally responds in the fifth frame with a motor impulse. The entire process takes place in a matter of a few seconds
Source: French, J. D. (1957). The reticular formation. *Scientific American*, May, 54–60

subcortical pacemakers. The ARAS inputs to the nonspecific nuclei of the thalamus, thus affecting the frequency of the EEG. EEG desynchronization and fast activity are related to cortical "activation," while slowing of the EEG frequency is an index of low arousal. The fluctuations in arousal are attributed to activity of the brainstem and thalamic reticular systems that also appear to regulate behavioral arousal and responsivity.

Underarousal

Birren (1960) first articulated the underarousal hypothesis when he stated:

There is the possibility that the well-established psychomotor slowing of advancing age is a consequence of reduced physiological activation. This agrees with what limited literature exists on age differences in activity and drive levels. Assuming a less energized or activated organism with age, in any unit of time there will be less interaction between the individual and his environment. This reduces the opportunity for all psychological processes to take place, e.g., perception, acquisition, manipulation of symbols, and storage (Birren, 1960, pp. 326–327).

The major evidence for the underarousal hypothesis was provided by studies of brain electrical activity in the aged.

EEG and aging. As discussed in chapter 3, four major changes in the brain-wave activity of older adults were identified. These include changes in the frequency and abundance of the alpha rhythm, changes in the incidence of beta activity, diffuse slowing (especially noted in institutionalized elderly), and focal slowing and abnormal activity in the temporal lobes (for reviews, see Marsh & Thompson, 1977; Obrist & Busse, 1965; Thompson & Marsh, 1973; Woodruff, 1978). The most reliable age change in EEG activity is the slowing of the dominant frequency, the alpha rhythm. Since slower EEG frequencies are associated with lower states of arousal, the slowing in the aged was assumed to signify a lowered state of arousal in that population.

As early as 1931, the scientist who discovered the human EEG, Hans Berger, noticed that patients with senile dementia had slower alpha rhythms than normal young individuals, but he assumed that the slowing was related to the patients' illness. Davis (1941) was the first to demonstrate that the alpha rhythm was slower in aged samples, and her work has been upheld in subsequent research. Most of these studies have also reported a decrease in the percentage of time older subjects produce alpha rhythm, which is reported as a decrease in alpha abundance. In young adulthood the frequency of the alpha rhythm reaches its maximum, which is 10.0–10.5 c.p.s. (Brazier & Finesinger, 1944; Eeg-Olofsson, 1971). The average frequency for healthy adults in their 60s is around 9 c.p.s., and for adults beyond 80, it is further decreased to 8–8.5 c.p.s. (Obrist, 1954, 1965; Obrist & Busse, 1965). In a group of ten healthy centenarians, the average alpha frequency was 8.62 c.p.s. (Hubbard et al., 1976).

The mechanisms underlying this change, as well as the clinical significance, remain unclear at the present time, at least in healthy, community residing older adults. The association between measures of vascular function and EEG slowing in patient groups has raised the question of whether alpha slowing reflects cerebral metabolic changes. Reliable relationships between slowing of alpha frequency and cognitive impairment have been obtained in samples of elderly patients, which suggests that alpha frequency may be associated in some way with efficiency of information processing. However, attempts to find similar relationships between alpha frequency and cognition in healthy older adults have not been successful. Alpha frequency and cognition relationships may be an example of Birren's (1963) discontinuity hypothesis that states that behavior correlates with a physiological measure (in this case, alpha frequency), only when the physiological measure is in an abnormal range.

ERPs and aging. A variety of brain electrical responses exhibit stable temporal relationships to a definable external event, and these can be elicited in any of the sense modalities. The name for all of these signals is ERPs. The ERP and aging literature addresses a number of issues beyond the scope of arousal theory. The sub-group of ERP studies that has been most typically related to arousal are studies of sensory evoked potentials. The sensory evoked potential data which support the underarousal hypothesis are based on the manner in which researchers have interpreted the significance of various evoked potential components. In sensory evoked potential research in which the subject is required to attend passively while stimuli are presented, two major types of cortically generated components have been observed and related to two different brain systems. The primary response comprising the early components is associated with the primary sensory pathways and cortical projection centers, and the secondary response is representative of more diffusely projecting pathways involving the reticular formation.

The post–primary response comprises any evoked activity occurring after the primary response components and recorded up to 500–1,000 ms after the stimulus. The amplitude of this activity is considerably greater than that of the primary response. The post–primary responses of relevance to arousal are the ones that are not topographically associated with the primary response and are eliminated by either anesthesia or brain stem transection. It is widely accepted that these components are determined to a great extent by neural impulses conducted via the reticular formation. These post–primary responses are considered to be polysensory in nature and are seen at a latency of 100 ms or more in recordings from most association areas, as well as in the post–100 ms portions of ERPs recorded from primary areas. Since the post–primary components are affected by conditions related to attention, consciousness, and anesthesia, it is assumed that they are related to nerve impulses conducted via the reticular formation and the unspecific midline nuclei of the thalamus.

As discussed in chapter 3, the largest input to sensory evoked potential data over the life span has come from the Salt Lake City, Utah, laboratories of Edward Beck, Robert Dustman and their associates. Some of the data collected by Schenkenberg (1970) in the Salt Lake City laboratory of

Dustman and Beck were shown in figure 3.2, and here these data are considered as they pertain to underarousal. Eight age groups of human subjects comprised of ten males and ten females in each group over the age range of 4–86 years were tested on visual, auditory, and somatosensory sensory evoked potentials. Post-primary activity showed age differences at several points in the life span. Amplitude of later evoked response activity between 80 and 200 ms increased during childhood. Peak delays of the post-primary components became consistently shorter from early childhood to adolescence for all three types of evoked responses. Myelination of non-specific pathways and the development of collaterals to the reticular formation continues throughout childhood (Yakovlev & Lecours, 1967). Hence, the electrophysiological and neuroanatomical data were consistent. A pattern of reduced amplitude of the post-primary components was observed in the data of middle-aged and older subjects. Peak delays of visually evoked responses (VERs) and somatosensory evoked responses (SERs) occurred in middle age and increased in senescence. Auditory evoked response (AER) peak delays did not show age differences beyond adolescence. Schenkenberg (1970) concluded that the fact that in all modalities there was reduced amplitude of post-primary components and peak delays in two of the three modalities suggested that the alerting, activating functions of the reticular system, which has been implicated as the possible source of this activity, become less effective with advancing years. This subcortical explanation is supported by the observations of Yakovlev and Lecours (1967), who noted that the reticular formations shrink and contain fewer myelinated fibers in the brains of older individuals.

Inhibition

A decrease in inhibition in the central nervous system with age has been advanced as a hypothesis to explain behavioral aging phenomena since Pavlov interpreted age-related deficits in classical conditioning in older dogs in terms of a deficit in inhibitory processes. Following from the older dogs' impaired ability to acquire conditioned responses was the generalization to older humans. It was hypothesized that older adults showed a reduction in inhibitory control over behavior (Jerome, 1959). This was the explanation first used in studies of eyeblink classical conditioning (EBCC) in humans, a behavior that is performed much less efficiently in old age (Braun & Geiselhart, 1959; Kimble & Pennypacker, 1963). Jerome's (1959) description of the Russian study carried out by Gakkel and Zinina in 1953 of eyeblink conditioning differentiation and word-association was:

Failure to obtain even the gross differentiation between the sounds of the buzzer and the bell was accepted as indicative of a serious impairment of the process of inhibition, and a high frequency of garrulous responses in the word-association test was regarded as supporting this conclusion (Jerome, 1959, p. 670).

It has been more than three decades since Jerome published his interpretation of the classical conditioning and aging results in humans, and during that period the neural circuitry for the conditioned eyeblink response has been almost completely identified. It is reasonably clear now that age-related effects in subcortical structures (in particular in the cerebellum) are likely responsible for aging effects on classical conditioning (e.g., Daum & Schugens, 1996; Woodruff-Pak, 1997).

The issue of inhibition and aging has not been abandoned, however, as research attention has focused on the hypothesis that age-related changes in behavior result from loss of inhibitory capacity from at least two different levels of analysis. The neurophysiological approach has been to assess behavior in conjunction with ERPs in an effort to directly assess inhibitory processes in the central nervous system (Prinz et al., 1990). The cognitive approach has been to develop theories about inhibition and aging and test these theories with behavioral studies (Hasher & Zacks, 1988). Both approaches have supported the position that age-related deficits in inhibition affect cognitive performance in older adults.

A neurophysiological approach to inhibition and aging

A review of the evidence for failure of inhibitory processes in the elderly appeared in an article on ERP research in adult aging by Smith et al. (1980). They pointed out that the enhancement of ERP waveforms which results from nonspecific cerebral lesions has been attributed to reduced inhibitory control of afferent stimulation. On this basis, high amplitude ERP components observed in some neurological conditions have been interpreted as arising from deficits in central inhibition (Callner et al., 1978). It had been reported that one or more ERP components in the middle-latency range were significantly larger in older than in young individuals. Straumanis et al. (1965) interpreted this difference as due to a reduction in inhibitory activity, and subsequent research was also interpreted in this manner (Dustman & Beck, 1969; Schenkenberg, 1970).

ERP data provide evidence for a decline in inhibitory function, at least in the visual system of the aging (Dustman & Snyder, 1981; Dustman et al., 1981). In one study (Dustman & Snyder, 1981), the augmenting–

reducing phenomenon was investigated in 220 male subjects aged 4–90. A predisposition towards augmenting or reducing is related to level of inhibitory functioning (e.g., Knorring & Perris, 1981). Individuals who reduce their ERP responses to intense stimuli have relatively strong inhibitory functions while those who are augmenters are less able to dampen their responses.

Individuals with Down's syndrome (DS) who are described as having cortical inhibitory deficits have abnormally large visual ERPs, especially in recordings from frontal and central scalp. Individuals with DS also have ERPs which augment substantially more in reaction to increased flash intensity in comparison to normal control subjects (e.g., Galbraith et al., 1970; Gliddon et al., 1975). Dustman and Snyder (1981) reported that the amplitude of ERP's to flashes was greater in central scalp recording sites at waveform latencies of 90–110, 110–150, and 150–200 ms in very young (4–15 years) and older (50–90 years) individuals. The very young and old subjects were also greater augmenters. Brighter flashes were accompanied by larger increases in ERP amplitude in these two age groups as compared to subjects of intermediate ages (figure 8.3).

The ERPs of those with DS, believed to have inhibitory deficits, are strikingly similar to the ERPs of children and older adults (Dustman & Snyder, 1981). The predominant action of monoamines is thought to be inhibitory, and monoamine levels are low during childhood and old age. Additionally, anterior cortical areas which exert inhibitory control over the ascending reticular formation are immature during early development and suffer cell loss in old age. This developmental course parallels the findings of Dustman and Snyder (1981). They suggested that the chemical and structural deficiencies in aging are reflected by a relative inability to suppress brain potentials elicited by repetitive and relatively meaningless stimuli.

Dustman et al. (1981) examined VERs elicited by patterned and unpatterned flashes in the same 220 healthy males tested in Dustman and Snyder (1981). Dustman et al. (1981) reasoned that inhibition in the visual system is essential for optimal detection of edges and contours. Thus, reduced inhibitory function should result in a less differentiated VER to patterns. In other words, VERs to patterns and to diffuse flashes should be relatively similar, and correlations between the patterned and unpatterned conditions should be higher in those individuals having less inhibitory function. Correlating the digital values comprising the two waveforms, Dustman et al. (1981) found that correlations followed a U-shaped curve over the life span. Patterned and unpatterned flash VERs were most alike for the youngest and oldest subjects. The age effect was localized to scalp areas overlying the visual cortex, where cortical tissue is organized to maximize the detection of lines and edges. The effects were much stronger for the earlier VER epochs which

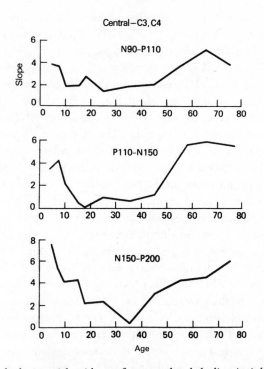

Figure 8.3 Evoked potential evidence for age-related decline in inhibition. Participants who show less response after intense visual simulation are called "reducers" and have demonstrably stronger inhibitory capacity. The figure shows composite amplitude slope data at three latencies after intense visual stimulation for 220 male subjects in the age range between 4 and 90 years. Age differences are smallest in the top tracing representing the early evoked potential wave occurring between 90 and 110 ms, and the effect of age is largest in the two later waves occurring at 110–150 and 150–200 ms. At all three latencies, older adults have large responses to repeated visual stimulation suggesting less inhibition. Young children whose frontal inhibitory systems have not fully developed show similar patterns of high amplitude evoked potential response to repeated visual stimulation especially in the longer latency waveforms

Source: Dustman, R. E., & Snyder, E. W. (1981). Life-span changes in visually evoked potentials at central scalp. *Neurobiology of Aging, 2,* 303–308

encompass waveforms known to be associated with checkerboard stimulation. These results are compatible with a concept of reduced inhibitory functioning within the visual systems of the very young and the old. Dustman et al. (1981) suggested that the reduced inhibition may have been related to reduced catecholaminergic activity, although biochemical measures were not made in this study.

Another line of evidence implicating decreased inhibition in the elderly has been presented by Drechsler (1977, 1978). Studying somatosensory and visual ERPs in 65 healthy elderly subjects aged 62–91, and 48 young normals aged 18–38, Drechsler (1977) reported that the amplitudes of both the somatosensory and visual ERPs were significantly higher in the aged sample. The evidence Drechsler used to suggest that inhibitory capacity was diminished in the aged was the increase in amplitude of the ERPs in the elderly and the fact that in the young the somatosensory potentials were confined to the centro-parietal region, but in the aged these potentials spread over the whole hemisphere. Drechsler (1978) attributed this phenomenon in the aged to loss of inhibitory processes producing a spread of cortical excitability that encompassed the whole hemisphere.

Additional evidence was presented by Dustman, Emmerson, and Shearer (1996) to support the position that electrophysiological measures show age-related deficits in inhibition. In older adults there is a greater incidence of EEG alpha rhythm in anterior cortical areas, and there is also a reduction in the heterogeneity of EEG and ERP activity across recording sites. These findings suggest a relative weakening of central inhibition in old age and a loss of functional independence of cortical centers. Recent research suggests that the magnitude of inhibitory loss in old age may be related to cardiovascular health. Older men who frequently participated in vigorous physical activity demonstrated greater electrophysiological indices of inhibition than did their age-matched peers who seldom exercised.

It has been stated several times in this chapter that it is believed that the frontal cortex exerts an inhibitory control over the reticular formation. Recent behavioral and electrophysiological data corroborate the neuroanatomical evidence that the frontal cortex may be an area of particular vulnerability in aging. Albert and Kaplan (1980) reviewed the neuropsychological evidence which suggested that many behavioral deficiencies which are apparent in the elderly resemble behavioral deficits in patients with frontal-lobe lesions. Scheibel and Scheibel (1976) identified losses of dendritic masses in pre-frontal and temporal areas of aging brains in histological studies.

The electrophysiological measure which has implicated selective aging in the anterior cortex is the contingent negative variation (CNV). The term CNV denotes a class of negative slow potential shifts lasting in the order of seconds (as compared to the milliseconds of duration of most other ERPs) which occur in conjunction with certain sensory, motor, and cognitive activities. Donchin et al. (1978) described the CNV as a cortical change that occurs when an individual's behavior is directed toward a planned action in response to a sequence of two or more events. The action referred to can be an overt motor response, the inhibition of a motor response, or a decision. The optimal situation first demonstrated by Walter and his colleagues (1964) for the production of the CNV is a simple reaction time task in which the first stimulus (S1) serves as a ready signal for a second stimulus (S2) to which an operant motor response is made. Walter (1968) suggested that a massive depolarization of the dendrites in the frontal cortex was likely to be involved in the generation of the CNV. This waveform has been of interest to gerontologists because it has been conceived as a measure of attention and arousal (Tecce, 1972).

Initial studies of the CNV in aging yielded no age differences in CNV amplitude in scalp locations over central motor areas (Marsh & Thompson, 1973; Thompson & Nowlin, 1973). However, Loveless and Sanford (1974) found age differences in the shape of the CNV in long S1–S2 intervals, and they suggested that the aged failed to modulate arousal as efficiently as the young. CNV studies involving a wider array of electrode recording sites and more complex tasks have found significant age differences.

Tecce (1979) identified a CNV rebound effect occurring when a short-term memory task, demanded of subjects on half of the CNV trials, was absent. A normal CNV developed in a control condition when the typical S1–S2 reaction time paradigm was used, but when three letters were presented between the S1 and S2 which the subject later had to remember, CNV amplitude was diminished. On half of the trials in the short-term memory condition, the letters were not present. This is when the CNV rebound effect occurred. CNV amplitude was greater than in the control condition or when letters were present. Reaction time to S2 was also faster when the letters were not present. Young subjects verbalized a strategy of recognizing after a certain time-interval past S1 that the letters would not appear. Then they concentrated solely on responding to S2. The supranormal increase in CNV amplitude was interpreted as reflecting a switching of attention from the divided attention-set intrinsic to letters trials to an undivided attention-set in no-letters trials. Tecce et al. (1980) tried this task in older subjects and found that the CNV rebound effect was diminished in fronto-central brain areas. None of the older subjects verbalized the strategy of realizing that no letters were coming and hence preparing only for S2, and their CNV indicated that they did not use this strategy. The older subjects also made significantly more perseverative responses than young subjects on the Wisconsin Card Sorting Test, a finding associated with frontal-lobe patients (Milner, 1963). Tecce and his colleagues concluded that the diminution of CNV rebound in the older group appeared to indicate a perseverative attention set which was mediated significantly by fronto-central brain areas and which interfered with the switching of attention. Using a task similar to the task employed by Tecce (1979), Michalewski et al. (1980) independently produced the same result. Frontal CNVs for the older subjects were reduced in every condition compared to the young group. In a group of extraordinarily healthy and active old women, researchers noted a marked reduction in frontal recording sites in a wave they called the late sustained potential (SP; Pfefferbaum et al., 1979). The investigators suggested that the diminished SP might result from a loss in dendritic mass in frontal areas in the elderly.

Three independent laboratories have reported diminished electrophysiological activity at frontal recording sites in brains of normal elderly subjects. The generators of these CNV and SP waveforms are thought to be dendritic layers in the frontal lobes. In two of the laboratories the diminished frontal activity occurred as a correlate of diminished capacity to switch attention. These data, coupled with behavioral and histological evidence, begin to point to a selective aging of the frontal lobes which impairs the capacity of the elderly to modulate attention. This frontal lobe impairment might result in decreased inhibitory control of the ARAS.

A cognitive approach to inhibition and aging

A theoretical framework developed by Hasher and Zacks (1988) has postulated that the performance of cognitive tasks, especially those involving language comprehension, require the limited-capacity operations of working memory. Of course, working memory is a behavioral construct that has been firmly tied to the frontal lobes (Goldman-Rakic, 1992). Thus, although the framework devised by Hasher and Zacks is cognitive, it is directly relevant to a neuropsychological approach.

According to Hasher and Zacks' (1988) perspective, fundamental to the limited-capacity operations of working memory is the use of inhibitory mechanisms that prevent irrelevant information from entering working memory. Examples of irrelevant information are contextually inappropriate interpretations of words or phrases that would interfere with the comprehension of and memory for a particular message. Results from several types of studies of text comprehension are consistent with the postulation of an age-related decline in inhibitory function (e.g., Carlson et al., 1995; Connelly et al., 1991; Gerard et al., 1991).

An age-related decline in the selective aspect of attention, specifically in the ability to inhibit the distracting effect of irrelevant information, has been used to support the cognitive perspective of inhibitory decline with aging. Experiments involving visual information processing at a more perceptual level have also suggested an age-related decline in inhibition. For example, the negative priming phenomenon, in which an irrelevant item that was inhibited on a previous trial interferes with the selection of this item as the target on a subsequent trial, is less pronounced in older adults (Hasher et al., 1991). Similar results were reported by McDowd and Oseas-Kreger (1991) using a letter-reading paradigm. In this study the age-related decline in the efficiency of inhibition resulted in a reduction in the subsequent effects of irrelevant items (less negative priming) and also to an increase in the immediate effects of the items (greater distraction).

Psychophysiological techniques have also been used in the investigation of the cognitive hypothesis of aging and inhibition. The investigation was based on the premise that inhibition would be demonstrated when participants showed habituation to stimuli that were not relevant to the task. That is, when the responding of participants diminished to irrelevant stimuli, inhibition would be demonstrated. Measuring autonomic nervous system reactivity during cognitive processing by using surface electrodes on the skin to assess skin conductance, McDowd and Filion (1992) observed significant habituation to tones in young adults when the tones were defined as irrelevant. However, there was less habituation to irrelevant tones in the older participants. Here again is evidence for the lowered ability of older adults to inhibit responding to irrelevant material.

Distractibility, or lack of inhibition of response to irrelevant stimuli, has long been identified as a deficit in older adults (e.g., Rabbitt, 1965). It was pointed out by Madden and Plude (1993) that the more recent findings suggesting an age-related decline in inhibitory processing are consistent with the previous work and have the positive feature of defining relevant and irrelevant information on the basis of a specific stimulus dimension. This advantage was not often the case in the earlier studies.

Summary

Although arousal and sleep are seemingly states of consciousness that are at opposite ends of the continuum, these states are likely regulated by common neurobiological mechanisms. The observed age changes in arousal in the waking state may be related to age changes in sleep patterns. Conversely, arousal-level changes during the waking state in older adults may alter requirements for sleep. Performance on neuropsychological tests can clearly be affected by alterations in arousal and sleep, and thus age-related disruptions in these states of consciousness have relevance for the neuropsychology of aging.

Brain structures implicated in arousal and sleep include structures in the brain stem including the ARAS and the frontal lobes. The inhibitory role of the frontal lobes on the ARAS is significant, and because significant age-related changes in the frontal lobes occur, inhibition is another major topic of this chapter. Both neurophysiological and cognitive approaches to inhibition and aging were covered.

Of the five stages of sleep indexed by the EEG, the greatest age-related change is in deep sleep or stage IV SWS that occurs for a shorter period of time in older adults. This is a major cause of the feeling of older adults that they are less refreshed from sleep. Older adults also awaken more frequently during the night and are more likely to experience sleep apnea, the cessation of breathing for 10 s or longer during sleep.

Data from EEG and ERP studies indicate that older adults are in a state of lowered arousal. The ARAS appears less reactive and capable of arousing the older cortex. ERP data also suggest a decline in the inhibitory capacity of the older brain. Diminished electrophysiological activity at frontal recording sites in the brains of normal elderly participants has been observed in several laboratories, suggesting diminished frontal inhibitory activity. The diminished frontal activity occurred as a correlate of diminished capacity to switch attention. These data, coupled with behavioral and histological evidence, indicate selective aging of the frontal lobes impairing the capacity of the elderly to modulate attention. This frontal lobe impairment might result in decreased inhibitory control of the ARAS.

An age-related decline in the selective aspect of attention, specifically in the ability to inhibit the distracting effect of irrelevant information, has been used to support the cognitive theory about inhibitory decline with aging. Distractibility has long been identified as a deficit in older adults. The more recent findings suggesting an age-related decline in inhibitory processing are consistent with the previous work and have the positive feature of defining relevant and irrelevant information on the basis of a specific stimulus dimension. Thus, as investigators continue to document a deficit in inhibitory processes in normal aging, they also continue to refine methodology and characterize the phenomenon more precisely.

Further Reading

Prinz, P. N., Dustman, R. E., & Emmerson, R. (1990). Electrophysiology and aging. In J. E. Birren & K. W. Schaie (Eds.), *Handbook of the psychology of aging* (3rd ed., pp. 135–149). San Diego, CA: Academic Press.
An excellent overview of research on sleep and arousal in aging is presented in this chapter.

Hasher, L., & Zacks, R. T. (1988). Working memory, comprehension, and aging: A review and a new view. In G. H. Bower (Ed.), *The psychology of learning and motivation* (Vol. 22, pp. 193–225). Orlando, FL: Academic Press.
This chapter that advances a theory about aging and inhibition has generated controversy and a great deal of research interest.

Madden, D. J., & Plude, D. J. (1993). Selective preservation of selective attention. In J. Cerella, J. Rybash, W. Hoyer, & M. L. Commons (Eds.), *Adult information processing: Limits on loss* (pp. 273–300). San Diego, CA: Academic Press.

Aspects of attention that are spared as well as age-related deficits in arousal and inhibition are discussed.

9

Response Speed and Timing in Behavior

The slowing of response speed with age is likely the most pervasive of all age changes (Birren & Fisher, 1995). Reaction time slowing occurs in other species as well as humans, and is observed even in the healthiest of individuals (Birren et al., 1963; Szafran, 1968). Moreover, age changes in speed and timing do not appear to be limited to changes in one or two sensory modalities, or to a limited number of tasks. The slowing of psychomotor speed with age is general and invariant. If an individual lives long enough, it is inevitable that his or her reaction time will slow. Psychomotor slowing is a primary aging factor (Birren, 1965).

Longitudinal studies of reaction time in adults support the claim that slowing is age-related. In a 5-year longitudinal study of reaction time on a card sorting task, participants were an average of age 70 on the first testing, and they were 75 at the retest (Botwinick & Birren, 1965). There was a statistically significant slowing in reaction time over the 5-year period. Follow-up data on the volunteers who participated in a study of optimally healthy older men (Birren et al., 1963) found slower reaction times for subjects at the 11-year retest (Granick & Patterson, 1971). Data from a longitudinal study conducted at the National Institute on Aging Intramural Research Branch also indicate that reaction time slows as the participants age (Arenberg, 1982).

Age-related effects on neuropsychological tests of working memory, for example, may result more as a function of central nervous system slowing than from other causes (Salthouse, 1994). If we examine the brief neuropsychological test battery for assessment of older adults described in table 2.2, it is apparent that response speed is a significant factor. Of the 11 tests in that battery, at a minimum six are timed and/or significantly affected by response speed (Digit Span, Block Design, Digit Symbol, Logical Memory, Visual Reproduction, Trail Making Test). The slowing of response time with age is an important phenomenon in the neuropsychology of aging and one that must be considered and addressed by neuropsychologists who assess older adults.

Simple reaction time

Simple reaction time is the time it takes to perceive a stimulus and respond. The reason the term "simple reaction time" is applied is that there is no decision involved. An example of a simple auditory reaction time task would be that a loud buzzer would sound and the participant would press a switch with his or her index finger. Instructions would be, "You will hear a loud buzzer. When the buzzer sounds, press the switch with your index finger as fast as you can." It would be common for the experimenter to add, "Stay alert and be sure to press the switch just as rapidly as you can." The goal is to motivate the participant to respond as quickly as possible.

The underlying assumption in this and other reaction time tasks is the idea that the time taken to perform the task represents a series of operations known as information processing. The time taken to depress the switch is assumed to be the end result of the processing that has been carried out in real time at various levels of the nervous system (Johnson & Rybash, 1993). By manipulating the task requirements and observing the effect on response speed, the various stages of information processing are assessed.

Assessment of the various components affecting reaction time over the life span has been ongoing throughout the twentieth century. Inferences about the impact of sensory processes on response speed were made by Koga and Morant (1923). Using reaction times collected by Sir Francis Galton in 1884 at the International Health Exhibition in London, they analyzed data from more than 9,300 male and female subjects ranging in age from 5 to 80. Koga and Morant found that simple reaction time increased with age to both visual and auditory stimuli in adulthood, independent of age differences in sensory acuity. Whereas mean auditory reaction time was 154 ms and mean visual reaction time was 182 ms for subjects aged 18–20, subjects in the 70s had mean reaction times of 174 and 205 ms for auditory and visual reaction time, respectively. The data demonstrated that both auditory and visual reaction time increased by about 20 ms (13 percent) between the ages of 18 and 70. Even so, these data probably underestimate the magnitude of age-related slowing, inasmuch as Galton's sample was probably not representative of the older adult population in general. In the first place, those individuals who were able to attend the Exhibition were presumably the most affluent, healthy, and ambulatory older adults. Moreover, because individuals actually paid to be tested on Galton's 17 measures, they were most likely confident that they were "well preserved."

Koga and Morant's (1923) results have been supported by subsequent studies in visual and auditory reaction time. Moreover, this work has been extended by studies showing age changes in simple reaction time to tactile stimuli (e.g., Hugin et al., 1960). Invariably, older individuals have been found to be slower than younger individuals. Over the adult age span from roughly 20 to 70 years, simple reaction time slows anywhere from 11 percent to 102 percent, depending on the type of stimulus, the stimulus modality, and the complexity of the task (Hicks & Birren, 1970).

Slowing with age may be ameliorated by at least three factors (Salthouse, 1985). One factor is physical health and fitness. Age differences in reaction time disappear when healthy older adults are compared to younger, but less healthy adults (e.g., Abrahams & Birren, 1973; Hertzog et al., 1978; Light, 1978). Physically fit older adults also have faster reaction times than age-matched sedentary adults (Botwinick & Thompson, 1968; Spirduso, 1975, 1980; Spirduso & Clifford, 1978). Simply engaging in aerobic exercise for 4 months has been shown to statistically improve reaction time of older adults across a number of measures (Dustman et al., 1984).

Physiological reversals – that is, improvement in physiological functioning in the aged – occurs as a result of moderate exercise (DeVries, 1983). It is not age alone which causes individuals to decline physiologically. Other factors, some of which it may be possible to alter, are associated with declining physiological capacity in the aged. DeVries demonstrated that one of the factors associated with physiological decline is disuse, the lack of exercise in contemporary sedentary life styles. With a modified exercise program, even very old individuals can regain some of the physiological efficiency they had lost with advancing years. Indeed, Dustman and Ruhling (1986) demonstrated that even brain function as assessed by the P300 wave of the ERP was more efficient in a group of older runners compared to a control group of sedentary older adults.

A second factor that can influence reaction time is the nature of the response required by a given task. Age differences in reaction time are minimized when a vocal response is used. For example, oral versions of the digit-symbol task show smaller age differences than the written versions (Kaufmann, 1968). The digit-symbol task appears on the Wechsler Adult Intelligence Scale (WAIS) and is one of the tasks most susceptible to slowing as a function of age. The task requires an individual to correctly associate ten different symbols with their preassigned numbers (0–9). In the written version the individual is presented with rows of the various symbols and must fill in the blank underneath each symbol with the correct number. In the oral version, the person must say the number. The test is timed, and the score is the number of correctly filled in or spoken numbers. Although Salthouse (1985) cautions that the presently available evidence is not sufficient to determine if vocal response is an exception to the trend of slowing with aging, in many of the studies carried out thus far, age differences in vocal reaction time are minimal.

The third factor that may influence reaction time in older adults is practice. Several investigations have indicated that reaction time can be improved with practice, regardless of age. In one study, Murrell (1970) sampled 12,500–16,200 reaction time trials with three subjects aged 17, 18, and 57 years. Although Murrell found initial age differences in reaction time were largely eliminated with practice, the older subject did perform slightly more slowly on two- and eight-choice reaction time tasks and needed up to 300 responses on the complex tasks before showing improvement. More recent studies of the effects of practice on reaction time in older adults have demonstrated that even with extensive practice (50 1-hr sessions), a fairly large residual age difference in reaction time remains (Salthouse & Somberg, 1982). In general, older adults appear to be slower than younger adults even when they have had the opportunity to practice 4–50 hr (Berg et al., 1982; Madden & Nebes, 1980; Plude & Hoyer, 1981).

Choice or complex reaction time

If the time taken to perform a reaction time task is the manifestation of an underlying series of mental operations, then increasing the number of mental operations in the task should increase the reaction time. Choice or complex reaction time tasks require participants to make a decision before they respond. The choice may involve responding with the right finger to some stimuli and with the left to others. It may involve responding to some types of stimuli and withholding a response to other types. It may involve matching stimuli (e.g., capital and small letters that are the same letter) and responding only to matches. Numerous choice or complex reaction time tasks have been used to evaluate age differences in reaction time. The consistent result is that reaction time is disproportionately slowed in older adults when decisions are required.

Increasing the number of choices makes a reaction time task more difficult, and increased task complexity slows older adults to a greater degree than it slows young adults. In a classic study, Goldfarb (1941) found that age differences in reaction time increased as the number of choices increased. Goldfarb compared reaction time between a 20-year-old group and a 60-year-old group on tasks varying in complexity. Whereas the difference between the young and old subjects on a simple reaction time task was 11 ms, the difference on a two-choice task was 57 ms, and on a five-choice task it was 66 ms. This result suggests that the efficiency of information processing decreases with age.

The increased difficulty with choice reaction time tasks demonstrated by older adults indicates a slowing of central, rather than peripheral, activity. The reason that central slowing is implicated is that the input sensory pathway and the output motor pathway are the same in the individual for the simple and for the choice reaction time task. It takes the same amount of time for the stimulus input to reach the brain and the same amount of time for the motor output to leave the brain. Central information processing steps required in making the choice must be the cause of the excessive delay in older adults.

Search for the locus of reaction time slowing

Assuming that the input time for a stimulus and the motor time for a response are comparable in simple and complex reaction time tasks, then the disproportionate slowing observed in older adults performing complex reaction time tasks must represent slowing of central decision-making processes. Investigations have been carried out at all steps in the information processing pathway to determine the locus of the slowing in older adults.

Movement time

One possible source of difference in reaction time between young and old individuals is movement time. However, because movements are usually timed in a decision-making context, it is difficult to differentiate time usage between motor components and decision-making processes. Tapping speed may be a relatively "pure" measure of movement time, inasmuch as tapping speed is a measure of movement time which is probably least involved with decisions. Although the old have been found to move more slowly than the young (Miles, 1931; Pierson & Montoye, 1958; Talland, 1962), Szafran (1951) found no age difference in movement speed when subjects were blindfolded. Szafran explained these results as reflecting older adults' tendency to visually monitor their movements.

Birren (1955) has also argued that movement time alone could not account for the slower reaction time of older adults compared to younger adults. Birren found that reaction time still increased with task difficulty even when movement time was held constant.

Sensory acuity

Although a large number of independent changes occur in the receptors of all sensory modalities (discussed in chapter 4), these age-related changes can account for only a small proportion of the total slowing of reaction time. When we conduct reaction time studies, we use stimuli which are far above the sensory thresholds of the old as well as the young subjects. We make sure that elderly subjects can see visual stimuli clearly and hear auditory stimuli well. Since the work of Koga and Morant (1923) was published, it has been apparent that reaction time had little relation to the acuity of sensory receptors. The correlation between visual reaction time and auditory reaction time was much higher than the correlation between sensory acuity in either of those sensory modalities and reaction time. Koga and Morant's results suggested that a process common to all sensory modalities was related to the age change in psychomotor speed.

Conduction velocity

Since all information from sensory receptors is coded in nerve impulses and travels to the brain in neural sensory pathways, the slowing in nerve conduction velocity with age could lead to the results observed by Koga and Morant (1923). Several groups of investigators have measured conduction velocity in human peripheral nerves and have found decreases in mean conduction velocity from the ages of 30 to 80 to be 3 m/s (Wagman & Lesse, 1952) and 10 m/s (Norris, Shock, & Wagman, 1953). Birren and Wall (1956) found no change in conduction velocity in the sciatic nerve of rats. Norris et al. (1953) pointed out that small age changes in human peripheral nerve conduction velocity could account for only 4 ms in reaction time assuming a 1 m pathway. Since simple reaction time slows by at least 20 ms over the age range of 20–70 years, peripheral nerve conduction velocity slowing accounts for only a fraction of the observed age change in reaction time.

Testing the possible significance of age changes in conduction velocity in another manner, Birren and Botwinick (1955) measured simple auditory reaction time of the foot, finger, and jaw in old and young subjects (figure 9.1). The investigators reasoned that if conduction velocity was a factor in age-related slowing, the difference between the old and young in foot reaction time, which is transmitted over a long peripheral nerve pathway, would be relatively greater than the age difference in jaw reaction time. The age difference in foot, finger, and jaw reaction time was equal, with the old always slower than the young. Birren and Botwinick (1955) concluded that age changes in peripheral conduction velocity could not account for age

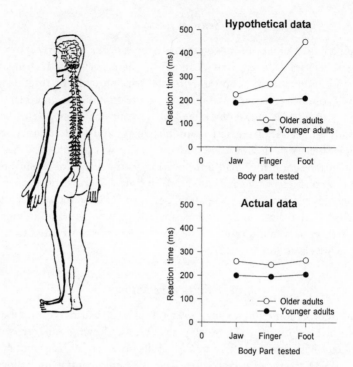

Figure 9.1 Conceptualization of the Birren and Botwinick (1955) jaw, finger, and foot reaction time study, testing the hypothesis that the slowing of peripheral nerve conduction velocity was the cause of reaction time slowing with age. The illustration at left shows the human body and placement of brain and spinal cord demonstrating the different lengths of the pathway from the skin of the jaw, finger, and foot to the brain and back. At right are the data for young and old participants. Although the neural pathway between the foot and the brain is much longer than the pathway between the jaw and brain, older adults were not disproportionately slower on the foot reaction time task. These results indicated that nerve conduction velocity slowing does not account for the slowing of reaction time in older adults
Source: Illustration by Michelle H. Pak

changes in reaction time. Inference led to the conclusion that the slowness of older subjects was a function of the central nervous system rather than of peripheral structures.

Synaptic delay

The synapse is another structure in the nervous system which might change with age, and age changes in synapses could lead to observed age change in reaction time (figure 9.2). There are a number of events in synaptic transmis-

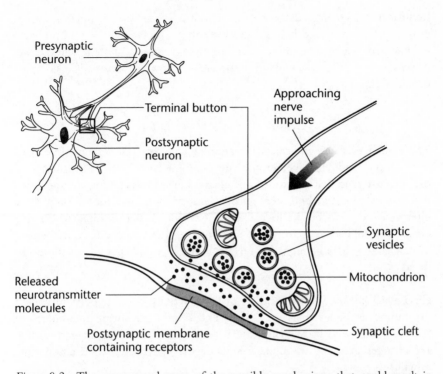

Figure 9.2 The synapse and some of the possible mechanisms that could result in slowing of neural transmission across the synapse. Age-related changes in the pre- or postsynaptic neural membrane could slow or inhibit transmission. An increase in the time it takes to open presynaptic vesicles to release neurotransmitter might be associated with impaired capacity in the neuronal membrane. Other potential causes of slowing at the synapse include a diminished amount of neurotransmitter released, causing it to take longer for the postsynaptic receptors to be activated; slowed spread of neurotransmitter through to synaptic cleft; diminished sensitivity of post-synaptic receptors

sion that could be delayed. Some of the possible synaptic changes that could slow neurotransmission include: an increase in the time it takes to open presynaptic vesicles to release neurotransmitter; a diminished amount of neurotransmitter released, causing it to take longer for the postsynaptic receptors to be activated; slowed spread of neurotransmitter through to synaptic cleft; diminished sensitivity of postsynaptic receptors. Wayner and Emmers (1958) measured synaptic delay in a monosynaptic reflex in rats and found a significant increase in synaptic delay from 0.97 ms in young rats to 1.36 ms in old rats. This represents an increase of 40 percent, suggesting that a large proportion of the slowing of behavior may be accounted for by the summation of synaptic delays in the central nervous system. Since a greater number of neurons and hence a greater number of synapses would probably be involved in a complex rather than a simple reaction time task, age changes in synapses could also account for the greater slowing observed in complex reaction time tasks.

Central nervous system factors

The evidence clearly indicates that peripheral factors (movement time, sensory acuity, conduction velocity) alone cannot account for the magnitude of the age change in reaction time. Age changes in synapses and in the functioning of the brain and brainstem where sensory input and motor output are integrated, seem to be the loci where the major changes leading to slowing occur. It would seem appropriate, therefore, to focus on the measurement of central factors which might be related to the age changes in psychomotor speed.

EEG alpha rhythm. One measure of brain activity that has been related to the timing of behavior is the EEG. The careful measuring techniques of Surwillo (reviewed in Surwillo, 1968) have provided results suggesting that age changes in the EEG alpha frequency may be related to reaction time slowing in the aged.

Consideration of the alpha rhythm as a timing mechanism for behavior began almost with the discovery of the human EEG, and in a review of the early literature, Lindsley (1952) suggested that a cycle of approximately 10 c.p.s., as reflected in the alpha rhythm, is the basic metabolic rhythm of brain cells. A large body of research literature has accumulated to support Lindsley's contention that the alpha frequency is related to excitability in the nervous system.

A proponent of the EEG excitability cycle hypothesis is Surwillo (1968) whose life-span data on EEG and behavior first led him to devise a model in which frequency of the EEG determined the timing of behavior. Subsequently, Surwillo (1975) revised this model into a two-factor model in which speed of information processing is governed by: (a) the time characteristics of the cortical gating signal; and (b) the recovery cycle of the information processing operations which are activated by the gating signals.

Measuring the duration (inverse of frequency) of waves occurring between the onset of an auditory signal and the initiation of the subject's response, Surwillo found a statistically significant rank order correlation of 0.81 between reaction time and alpha period in a group of 13 subjects between the ages of 18 and 72 years. On the basis of these results, Surwillo hypothesized that period of the alpha rhythm, or some multiple of the alpha cycle, serves as the master timing mechanism in behavior. The presence of slow brain potentials appeared to be necessary for the occurrence of slow reaction time in old age, and this fact suggested to Surwillo (1968) that EEG frequency is the factor behind age-associated drops in processing capacity of the brain. He further speculated that the frequency of the EEG may reflect the operation of a "biological clock" within the central nervous system which is a determining factor in how rapidly and effectively information can be processed.

A major criticism of Surwillo's work is that a model predicting causal relationships is based on correlational data. Indirect manipulation of the EEG alpha rhythm leads to changes in the timing of behavior (Creutzfelt et al., 1976; Harter, 1967; O'Hanlon et al., 1974). However, such relationships could be mediated by metabolic factors affecting EEG and behavior independently.

The underarousal hypothesis (presented in chapter 8) could account for the correlations between alpha period and reaction time reported by Surwillo. Participants producing fast alpha activity may have been more aroused and thus had faster reaction time. Reducing arousal level may be associated with production of EEG frequencies bordering on the theta range. Research indicates that reaction time and performance declines when subjects' brain waves verge into theta bandwidths (Davies & Krkovic, 1965; Groll, 1966; Kornfield, 1974; Morrell, 1966; Williams et al., 1962). Increasing the amount of EEG theta activity over the right occipital hemisphere during a long radar watch impaired the efficiency of detection (Beatty et al., 1974). Operant conditioning procedures were used to enable participants to increase EEG theta waves, and this increase in theta activity was associated with a decrease in the efficiency of participants' performance on the radar task. When operant conditioning was used to reduce the amount of theta activity in participants' EEG, performance on the radar task improved.

Brain wave frequency itself may not serve as a biological clock, but it may be correlated with arousal level which does influence behavior. The fact that older individuals have slower modal brain wave frequencies and the fact that slow brain wave activity is associated with lowered states of arousal were used as one of the rationales for suggesting that, compared to young individuals, the aged are in a state of underarousal (Thompson & Marsh, 1973).

Neural noise hypothesis. The neural noise hypothesis stipulates that there is more randomness in the older nervous system and that the signal-to-noise ratio decreases with age (e.g., Crossman & Szafran, 1957; Welford, 1958; 1981). It suggests that the older nervous system is less efficient. Neurons fire more randomly in the older brain, making it more difficult to tell what stimulus is meaningful among the random neuronal activity. The difficulty in distinguishing signal from noise slows information processing. It is the case that dying neurons may fire more sporadically, and the older nervous system does seem to have a greater number of impaired cells. Nevertheless, behavioral researchers have addressed the neural noise hypotheses only infrequently in their investigations.

P300 and the locus of central decision time. The P300 wave of the ERP is prominent only when the stimulus which has elicited the ERP has some meaning or significance for the subject (figure 9.3). The paradigms used to elicit the P300 wave involve decision making. The factor that appears to determine the latency of the P300 component is decision time; more specifically, the time required for the subject to perceive and categorize the stimulus according to a set of rules. When task difficulty is increased, young subjects have prolonged processing times and longer P300 latencies. Thus, the assessment of P300 in young and older adults appears to be a means to assess the central information processing effects of aging.

Current explanations of the significance of P300 latency suggest that the component provides an index of the point in central nervous system processing when stimulus-related events are translated into response-related events. The P300 latency reflects the time taken to evaluate and categorize stimulus events and is relatively independent of the time required to select and execute a response (Bashore, 1993). In the P300, we have a measure with the potential to offer direct evaluation of hypotheses about the nature of slowing with aging.

The brain generators of the P300 have not yet been definitively determined. Depth electrode recordings and magnetic field studies in humans suggest that at least some portion of the P300 is generated in the medial temporal lobe, probably including hippocampus (Halgren et al., 1980; Knight et al., 1989; McCarthy et al., 1989; Pineda et al., 1989). The theoretical interpretation of these data is that the P300 indexes tasks required in the maintenance of working memory (Donchin et al., 1986).

The P300 was first described over three decades ago (Sutton et al., 1965). Research relating the P300 to problems of aging was initiated in the early 1970s (Marsh & Thompson, 1972), and the first large studies of P300 over the adult age span were reported in the late 1970s (e.g., Goodin et al., 1978). Since that period over a dozen studies have been carried out with hundreds of adults having been tested (Bashore, 1993; Polich & Starr, 1984).

The availability of P300 data published in a variety of studies has resulted in attempts to provide overviews of the work using meta-analyses (Bashore, 1993). Meta-analyses of P300 latency data combined with the behavioral reaction time data collected in the P300 paradigm led researchers to conclude that response-related processes show much more age-related slowing than stimulus-related processes (Bashore, 1993, 1994). Age-related slowing does

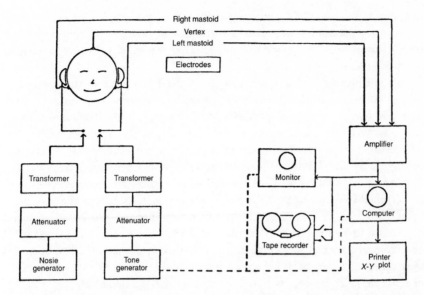

Figure 9.3 Techniques for assessing the P300 and the resulting waveform. On the bottom left a white noise generator inputs a background hissing sound through an attenuator and transformer to eliminate any room noise. A tone generator with the timing of presentations controlled by the computer, presents high and low pitched tones in random order. The participant is instructed at the beginning of the experiment that the task is to count the high pitched tones. Although the participant does not know this, 15 percent of the tones will be high pitched and 85 percent will be low pitched. This ERP paradigm is called the "oddball" paradigm (Sutton et al., 1965). The participant has cup electrodes attached to the top of the head (vertex) and referenced to electrodes at a "neutral" area that is not over any portion of the brain (earlobes or mastoid bones just behind the earlobes). These signals generated by the brain are amplified a million times and input to a computer that digitizes and stores the EEG data occurring just before the tone onset (baseline) and for at least one second after the tone onset. Data can be monitored on an oscilloscope display or polygraph paper and stored on analog tape, but most laboratories simply store the digitized data in the computer or on floppy disk. The computer averages each of the digitized points representing a specific time period before or after the stimulus. Typically, 1,024 points are used to represent the ERP epoch that is around one second long. Thus, each point represents 4 ms. If 200 stimuli were presented, 30 will have been the high pitched tone. These 30 records are analyzed separately from the 170 records representing brain response to low-pitched tones. Comparison of the two waveforms yields much greater positivity in a wave about 300 ms after tone onset in the record for the high-pitched tones. This wave is called the P300

not apparently affect all processing components equally, as would be predicted if synaptic delay were the major source of slowing. Rather, response-related processing components are affected more than stimulus-related components.

In addition to the changes that occur in the P300 wave in normal aging, further effects on this ERP component have been demonstrated in dementia. The P300 wave is exceedingly delayed in dementia and, depending on the study, between 50 to 80 percent of demented patients have P300 latencies more than two standard deviations longer than the latency that would be predicted by the P300 age regression line of nondemented adults (e.g., Gordon et al., 1986). Later ERP waves such as the P300 have been shown to be specifically affected by cortical dementia such as AD. Earlier components with latencies less than 200 ms are more likely to also be affected by subcortical dementia (Goodin & Aminoff, 1986). Changes in mental status in neurological patients, including those with dementia that varied in severity over time, have also been shown to be indexed by the P300 wave (Goodin et al., 1983). These results led Ball et al. (1989) to determine the rate of

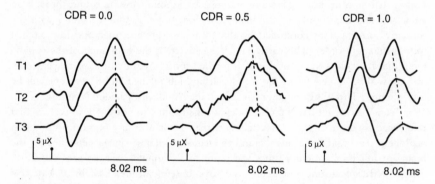

Figure 9.4 Sample ERP traces from one normal control participant (CDR = 0.0) and two patients with probable Alzheimer's disease (CDR = 0.5; CDR = 1.0). Recording were taken at three successive sessions (T1, T2, and T3) a minimum of 1 year apart. Dots represent the midwave point in the P300 used for latency measurement. The dashed line illustrates the change in P300 latency over time. These recordings were from the top of the head (Cz) with a reference electrode at the earlobe. The recording epoch is one second, with the tone onset marked by the arrow at the bottom at 100 ms after the beginning of the recording epoch. The two probable AD patients have longer P300 latencies than the normal control participant at the initial recording, and the change in P300 latency over the longitudinal period is more pronounced in the probable AD patients

Source: Ball, S. S., Marsh, J. T., Schubarth, G., Brown, W. S., & Strandburg, R. (1989). Longitudinal P300 latency changes in Alzheimer's disease. *Journal of Gerontology: Medical Sciences, 44*, M195–200

change of the P300 latency in patients with AD. Eighteen patients with a diagnosis of probable AD and 15 age-matched control participants were tested three times within approximately 3 years. The latency of the P300 in probable AD patients increased over time in relation to control participants (figure 9.4). Early mild AD patients could be distinguished from age-matched control participants on the basis of age-adjusted P300 latency, and the rate of change of P300 latency in AD was significantly greater than in normal elderly participants. The results, coupled with results from a number of other investigations of the P300 in normal aging and dementia, have led investigators to suggest that the auditory ERP has utility as a biological marker of aging that reflects changing cognitive abilities.

Timing in cognition and behavior

The discussion of response speed and aging has addressed peripheral sensory and motor aspects of reaction time tasks, as well as central, presumably cortical, aspects. Other brain structures are also involved in reaction time and also in the precise coordination and timing of cognition and behavior. For example, voluntary commands for movement are initiated in the frontal cortex and proceed to the basal ganglia. The basal ganglia appear to have a primary role in the production of speeded responses (Bashore, 1993).

Another subcortical brain structure essential in movement is the cerebellum. One of the most vigorous areas of research in cognitive neuroscience at present relates to the putative role of the cerebellum in higher-order mental processes (Schmahmann, 1997). The cerebellum was previously thought to be involved exclusively in motor control. However, a number of avenues of research have led to the view that there is substantial contribution of the cerebellum in areas of central nervous system function that extend beyond the motor system.

To investigate whether the cerebellum is involved in timing, Ivry and Keele initiated a study of neurological patients including patients with cerebellar lesions (Ivry & Keele, 1989; Ivry et al., 1988; Keele & Ivry, 1990). All subjects were faced with two tasks that required precise timing, as well as control tasks that did not involve temporal processing. One task involved the production of a regular series of taps with the fingers at a pacing rate of 550 ms. After synchronizing their responses with the pace tone, the tone was terminated, and the subjects continued tapping until they had generated 30 unpaced intervals. A second task was that of perception of duration. Sets of tones were presented with two pairs of tones per set. The task was to judge which pair bounded the longest interval. The tones of the first pair were always separated by 400 ms and the tones of the second pair created an interval that was either shorter or longer. The third task, perception of loudness, was a control task for the perception of duration. The task was included to control for age-related decline in hearing acuity. Sets of tones were presented, but the task of subjects was to judge which pair of tones was the loudest, not which interval was the longest. A threshold (in dB) was calculated for each subject. The loudness task allowed a determination of whether observed deficits on the perceptual duration task were specific to temporal judgments or whether they could be attributed to decreased auditory acuity in general.

The results showed that the patients with cerebellar lesions were selectively impaired on the timing tasks. The patients were more variable in producing periodic intervals on a motor timing task. More surprising, their timing deficit was also evident on a perceptual task in which they had to judge the duration of auditory signals. Thus, the investigators argued that the cerebellar timing system was invoked whenever tasks required the precise representation of temporal information, be it for action, perception, or learning.

Ivry and Keele (1989) also demonstrated age-related increases in variability on the timing tasks in normal adults. To test the relationship between eyeblink conditioning (a task that also engages the cerebellum) and the cerebellar timing tasks, Woodruff-Pak and Jaeger (1997) analyzed data from a sample of 160 adults aged 20–89 using multiple regression with four groups of predictor variables. Age accounted for 30 percent of the variance. The second highest predictor of eyeblink conditioning performance was the cerebellar assessment, Timed Interval Tapping, designed by Ivry and Keele (1989). This component accounted for an additional 8 percent of the variance and was statistically significant. Reaction time and declarative learning and memory measures were not significant predictors of conditioning. These behavioral data are suggestive of age-related impairment in the cerebellum which is likely to be related to observed age-related deficits in eyeblink classical conditioning.

Summary

An age-related change in behavior that will occur to every individual if he or she lives long enough is the slowing of response speed. Slowing of the timing of behavior affects neuropsychological test performance in a number of domains. It has been suggested that some age-related changes, such as the decline in working memory, may in actuality be caused by the slowing of response speed.

Simple reaction time involves no decision about the stimuli but is simply the time it takes to perceive a stimulus and respond. Simple reaction time slows with age, and choice reaction time that includes making a decision about at least two stimuli slows even more than simple reaction time. The locus of the slowing in reaction time is central rather than peripheral. Sensory processes, movement time, and nerve conduction velocity cannot account for the magnitude of the slowing. Alteration at the neural synapse is a likely cause of age-related changes in reaction time.

Age changes in decision time are documented in the P300 wave of the ERP. The latency of the P300 wave is almost 100 ms greater in elderly adults than it is in young adults. This ERP is an index of age-related slowing in central, cortical regions. P300 is significantly longer in patients with dementia than it is in normal control participants. This waveform that indexes central decision time shows fluctuations as the mental status of neurological patients changes, and it shows an increasing latency with the progression of AD.

The slowing of response speed with age has not been associated with a specific locus. The P300 wave is associated with cortical generators, likely including the medial temporal lobe. However, a precise locus is not identified. Reaction time slowing has been associated with underarousal and therefore with age-related changes in the ARAS. Other areas of the brain that are also implicated in the slowing of response speed with age include the basal ganglia and the cerebellum.

Further Reading

Birren, J. E., & Fisher, L. M. (1995). Aging and speed of behavior: Possible consequences for psychological functioning. *Review of Psychology, 46,* 329–353. A contemporary review of the literature on aging and response speed by James Birren, the individual who has been a leading authority on this topic for many decades.

Salthouse, T. A. (1994). The aging of working memory. *Neuropsychology, 8,* 535–543. A perspective about how the slowing of response speed can affect other significant cognitive processes.

Polich, J., Howard, L., & Starr, A. (1985). Effects of age on the P300 component of the event-related potential from auditory stimuli: Peak definition, variation, and measurement. *Journal of Gerontology, 40,* 721–726. One of a number of studies describing P300 techniques and applying them to the investigation of normal aging.

10

Intelligence

In the absence of brain damage, physiological correlates of intelligence are difficult to identify. In this sense, intelligence tests are not neuropsychological tests. Lesions in the frontal lobes do not impair abilities assessed by intelligence tests, and IQ scores after a frontal lobe trauma can even be a few points higher (Kolb & Whishaw, 1995). In previous chapters, it has been emphasized that the frontal lobes are a part of the brain significantly affected by processes of aging. Lesions to the parietal lobe most affect IQ scores, and temporal lobe lesions impair performance on some of the intelligence test subtests. Interestingly, differences in intelligence test scores between young and older adults may be less related to neurobiological aging than to other factors. Nevertheless, neuropsychologists typically assess intelligence, or at a minimum use some subtests from standardized intelligence tests, in an attempt to place their older clients' capabilities in the context of intelligence test performance of other adults.

At present, behavioral assessment of intelligence is the most effective way to measure this predictor of academic performance. The tests were not developed as a neuropsychological assessment. Rather they are useful to neuropsychologists as a measure of global functioning of the older adult. Also, some of the subtests of intelligence tests such as the Wechsler Adult Intelligence Scale (WAIS) are related to brain function (e.g., Block Design on the WAIS and right parietal lobe function) and thus are useful to the neuropsychologist in the evaluation of brain and cognition.

Defining intelligence

Intelligence has been defined in many different ways. The following are four definitions of intelligence from the perspectives of four major scholars on intelligence and its assessment:

1 The ability to carry on abstract thinking (Terman, 1921).
2 The aggregate or global capacity of an individual to act purposefully, to think rationally, and to deal effectively with the environment (Wechsler, 1944).
3 Adaptive thinking or action (Piaget, 1950).
4 Innate, general, cognitive ability (Jensen, 1973).

These definitions refer to intellectual capacity in an individual. However, we must observe behavior in order to evaluate intelligence. Thus inferences about intellectual capacity must be drawn from observable performance on some task, and intelligence tests consist of samples of behavior on a variety of tasks designed to tap whatever the investigators' definition of intelligence may include. The particular tasks that go into each intelligence test vary as widely as do the psychologists' definitions. What constitutes intelligent behavior in one test battery may not even be assessed in another psychometric battery of intelligence.

In defining and evaluating intelligence in late life, it is useful to know if intelligence is consistent over the life span. The data we will explore in this chapter suggest that there is some consistency over the life span in terms of scores achieved on intelligence tests. On the other hand, intelligence test scores can be influenced by a variety of environmental factors. In other words, the structure of cognitive behavior as well as the number, variety, and speed of responses can be evaluated, and these qualitative and quantitative aspects are not always highly related.

The work of Jean Piaget is an example of the qualitative approach to intellectual capacity. Piaget wanted to describe universals in the development of intelligence, and he moved away from the approach of quantitatively measuring individual differences in ability. His approach was to describe patterns of thinking which every human being goes through. The French psychologist Alfred Binet took a quantitative perspective. His work resulted in the development of assessment techniques which are the basis for modern-day tests of intelligence. This quantitative approach was also pursued by well-known psychologists such as Lewis Terman, Charles Spearman, J. P. Guilford, and Raymond Cattell.

Psychometric assessment of intelligence

Some historians credit Sir Francis Galton as initiating the intelligence testing movement with the measures he devised and used at the London Health Exhibition in 1884. Remember from chapter 9 that he used 17 different measures of human ability on over 9,000 people ranging in age from 5 to 80 years. However, Galton felt that sensory abilities determined human intelligence. He used tests such as visual and auditory sensitivity, visual and auditory reaction time, and grip strength, that are quite different from the behaviors measured in tests we now call measures of intelligence. So we might credit Galton with initiating the idea that human mental ability could be measured, but we have to acknowledge Alfred Binet for the creation of the intelligence test that has been used throughout most of the twentieth century to assess human mental capacity.

Modern intelligence testing began in France early in the twentieth century with Binet, who worked with Theodore Simon, a psychiatrist, to identify backward children in the schools of Paris. School authorities sought to separate students who lacked motivation and interest from those who clearly did not have the capacity to perform well in the regular school curriculum. Binet began by carefully observing his own children and the development of their ability to master certain tasks. Binet wanted to devise a metric scale of intelligence. Binet and Simon succeeded in devising an instrument that comprised a set of 30 problems emphasizing judgment, comprehension, and reasoning (Binet & Simon, 1905). Grading was achieved by ordering the tests by level of difficulty, administering them to large numbers of schoolchildren, and noting the average age at which each task could be completed.

In the United States a psychologist, Lewis Terman of Stanford University, translated the Binet scale from French into English and reworked the test considerably. Terman called his test the Stanford–Binet Intelligence Test after the university where he worked and the test's originator. Such tests were quite successful with children, and they were adapted to test adults by 1911 (Anastasi, 1976). One of Terman's greatest legacies was to follow longitudinally from childhood into old age a very large sample of those who scored exceptionally high on the Stanford–Binet Intelligence test (e.g., Oden, 1968; Terman & Oden, 1947). In these individuals, IQ test scores remained stable or showed increments throughout adulthood and into old age.

One of the innovations developed shortly after Binet died was a means to standardize scores across ages. A German psychologist named William Stern observed that with the Binet scoring method, a 5-year-old child with a mental age of 3 and a 12-year-old child with a mental age of 10 would be judged to have equal degrees of retardation – they would each be retarded by 2 years. However, having a mental age of 3 when you are already 5 years old is much more seriously retarded than having a mental age of 10 when you are 12. Being 2 years behind in your development as early as the age of 5 suggests serious and potentially profound retardation. Two years behind out of a lifetime of 12 years is a proportionately smaller retardation. Stern recommended dividing each child's mental age by his or her chronological age to produce a mental quotient. When Terman created an American version of the test, he incorporated Stern's idea of dividing mental age by chronological age. Furthermore, Terman multiplied the quotient by 100 so that he would have no scores less than one. In this manner, the intelligence quotient was created.

Much remains of the legacy of intelligence testing first generated by Binet and Simon. The concept of comparing mental age to chronological age which evolved into the intelligence quotient was originally Binet's idea. Using a wide variety of tasks to assess intelligence is another legacy from Binet, along with the selection of items based on the ability of children of a given age to pass them. At this point in the development of intelligence tests, and for decades to come, there was little attempt to associate performance on IQ tests with brain function. The tests were designed to predict success in school, and they were adapted for adults to predict whether an army recruit had the mental capacity to function in the armed services.

The "G" factor. The variety of questions asked is intended to tap a number of different abilities that were thought to be components of intelligence. Whether all these abilities are related to one general intelligence factor ("G"), or whether intellectual abilities are independent and non-overlapping, is one of the continuing debates concerning intelligence. The notion of a G factor of intelligence implies rather than explicitly states that there is a neurobiological basis for generalized intellectual capacity. The debate about the G factor began early in the history of intelligence testing with Charles Spearman, a prominent American psychologist who became interested in intelligence around 1900.

Spearman was more interested in some of the theoretical issues surrounding the concept of intelligence, in contrast to Binet who took on the more applied task of measuring intelligence. Binet's construction of a test comprised of seemingly unrelated tasks appeared to imply that intelligence consisted of a group of unrelated abilities. But Spearman considered that intelligence might involve a large single, general capacity as well as some specific abilities. He sought answers to questions such as, "Could a person be quite a genius at mathematical problems, a perfect fool at expressing himself in writing, and an average man in handling sensitive social situations?" Such divergence in abilities in one individual seemed improbable to Spearman, who very early and very clearly asked some of the most critical questions about the nature of human intelligence.

Spearman also developed a highly original and effective method for answering questions about the generalizable aspects of intelligence. His technique, known as factor analysis, involves a statistical methodology for observing the relationships among a large number of items (such as the ones found on intelligence tests). With this technique it is possible to observe whether certain types of items tend to be answered in the same way. The analysis determines whether a group of items are related or correlated. Groups of items that are highly inter-correlated are identified as factors. A typical intelligence test is composed of a large number of items that fall into at least several different factors. Factor analytic techniques have not completely resolved whether there are one or many components of intelligence, because the analysis can be carried out in various ways which yield different results. Contemporary views range from the Spearman position that there is one general (G) factor of intelligence, to the perspective first articulated by E. L. Thorndike (1926) that there are a "few big abilities," to the view that originated in Binet's work and was stated more strongly by John B. Watson (1913) and other learning theorists that intelligence is a vast collection of specific acquired competencies.

For geroneuropsychologists, the concept of factors of intelligence raises questions such as: Are intellectual factors the same over the life span, or are there different components of intelligence that are different at different ages? Do some factors remain stable while others change? Does the interrelation among factors and the number of factors remain constant? Thus the emergence of intelligence as a multivariate trait makes the issue of aging of intellectual behavior all the more complicated.

Intelligence tests and the assessment of normal aging

Many of the earliest studies in the psychology of adult development and aging involved intellectual behavior. Quantitative evaluation of adults' intellect is still an important issue in the study of adult development. A great deal of controversy has been generated in the debate about whether intelligence declines with age. To this day, investigators do not agree on mental capacity in later life. They interpret the data from different perspectives and reach conflicting conclusions. Thus, in intellectual behavior, we have a topic which has received intensive study, has involved multiple perspectives, and yet has no general consensus at present.

Perspectives about intelligence in adulthood and old age have gone through four major phases in the twentieth century (Woodruff-Pak, 1989). The phases are roughly chronological, but at the same time, research continues to be undertaken in all categories with the possible exception of the first phase. The term "phase" and a Roman numeral were used to identify each of the four broad perspectives on intelligence in adulthood and old age which have been influential in this century (see figure 10.1). The sequential num-

Phase I
Age-related decline

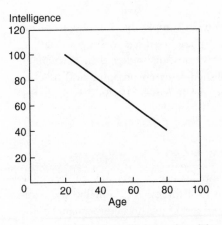

Simple, unidirectional model

Phase II
Stability versus decline

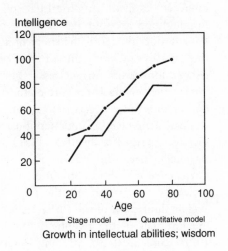

Multiple functions by cohort and ability

Phase III
Manipulation of adult IQ

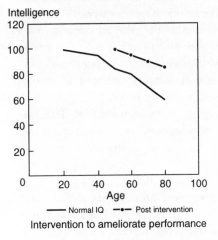

Intervention to ameliorate performance

Phase IV
Growth of adult intellect

Growth in intellectual abilities; wisdom

Figure 10.1   Schematic representation of the four phases of research on aging and intelligence. The Phase I perspective reflected in the research literature between 1920 and the mid- to late-1950s was a unidimensional model of age-related decline. Negative stereotypes of the aged in a period of rapid industrialization coupled with cross-sectional data on intelligence measures designed to predict academic success yielded the Phase I view. Phase II beginning in the 1960s emerged because of the changing social climate, but more important, as a result of longitudinal studies demonstrating stability in intelligence. Multiple age-functional relationships were recognized arising from cohort differences and from differential effects of development and aging on different abilities such as fluid and crystallized measures of intelligence. In the period of the 1970s, interventions to ameliorate intelligence in the age were representative of the Phase III perspective. The Phase IV perspective involved a rejection of traditional psychometric measures of academic success in favor of assessment of competence in the everyday world

Source: Woodruff-Pak, D. S. (1989). Aging and intelligence: Changing perspectives in the twentieth century. *Journal of Aging Studies, 3*, 91–118

bering of each of the perspectives is intended to imply that subsequent phases emerged from previous ones. The term "phase" is used to suggest that the perspective, while pervasive at the time, is transitory rather than permanent. Extensive literature searches of the published research on aging and psychometric intelligence have validated this model (Chapell, 1996; Woodruff-Pak & Finkbiner, 1988).

Causes of changing perspectives

The causes of changing perspectives on intelligence in later life are viewed as emanating from social, cultural, and historical forces. Additionally, the addition of data and the improvement in research methodology changed the perspective on age and intelligence. Changing attitudes about older adults coupled with an evolving and sometimes contradictory database on adult intelligence forced investigators to take new perspectives. The combination of prevailing socio-cultural and historical viewpoints and discontinuities or discrepancies in the empirical data on psychometric measures of intelligence in adulthood and old age caused a progression of perspectives to emerge. Four distinct phases in the study of aging and intelligence are apparent over the last 70 years. Only one of these perspectives, the first, has been more or less abandoned in current research. Investigations into the nature of adult intelligence in the latter part of the twentieth century continue to involve one or more of the perspectives identified as Phases II–IV.

Phase I involves a unidimensional view of age-related decline. This perspective emerged in the 1920s based on cross-sectional studies of psychometric intelligence. This was a period when faith in psychometric measures of intelligence was almost absolute, and the rapid industrialization of American society favored youth and the acquisition of new skills.

The limitations of the Phase I perspective were infrequently articulated in the first half of the twentieth century (e.g., Cattell, 1943; Hollingworth, 1927; Kuhlen, 1940). Its long duration was conclusively challenged only in the 1950s, when longitudinal data on intelligence became available. These data suggested at a minimum that adult intelligence was stable until the age of 50 which was the oldest age for which longitudinal data were available.

Social attitudes toward aging were changing in the 1950s. Life expectancy had increased dramatically, and the percentage of individuals over 65 in the population had more than doubled since the turn of the century. The aged were becoming more visible and more vocal. Legislation to provide social supports for the later years, beginning with the Social Security Act in 1935 and culminating in the Older Americans Act in 1965 reflected a positive change in attitudes toward older adults.

Phase II embraced a more sophisticated view of adult intelligence, with intellect varying by cohort and by specific type of ability. Age functions could be incremental or decremental, and took many forms. From the contradiction between longitudinal and cross-sectional data emerged a new synthesis in Phase II of a more complex perspective of intelligence in later life.

The acknowledgment in Phase II that environmental forces could affect intelligence scores of a given cohort led investigators to consider that manipulation of environmental contingencies might affect intelligence scores within a cohort as well. If experience in the environment could result in differences in IQ scores as a function of when one was born, then within an individual at some point in the life span environmental manipulations might affect performance on intelligence tests. This was one impetus for the Phase III perspective.

The social context for this Phase III perspective was a result of the Great Society programs envisioned during the John F. Kennedy administration and legislated and implemented by the Lyndon B. Johnson administration. In these programs, intervention into many forms of social problems were being attempted. In some ways Project Head Start as an intervention in early development served as a model for the Phase III approach involving attempts to modify older adults' performance on intelligence tests.

While gerontologists found in Phase III that performance on intelligence tests could be manipulated, it became more apparent that training was simply familiarizing older people with abilities which were novel or unused by them. At a time when the context in which intelligence was defined and measured was seen as an increasingly important issue, the relevance of the psychometric tasks to the lives of the aged was questioned, and the search for new age-appropriate tasks was begun.

The Phase IV perspective emerged in the mid-1970s at a time when the growing size and social and economic power of aging adults was being recognized in all segments of society. The Phase IV perspective challenged the validity of existing psychometric measures of intelligence for assessment of older adults and introduced the notion of growth in intellectual ability over the adult years.

The relevance of the phase model to neuropsychology is its fundamental questioning of the validity of intelligence tests for older adults. It should be emphasized that the model does not imply that ideas representative of the four phases emerged exclusively at the beginning of each of the phases. The foundation of the concept of differential age functions for fluid and crystallized measures of intelligence which characterizes Phase II can be traced to data collected at the height of Phase I in the late 1920s. Respect for the wisdom and experience of the aged, which identifies Phase IV, was representative of attitudes toward aging in the period between 1790 and 1864 in the United States (Achenbaum & Kusnerz, 1978).

Social, cultural, and historical phenomena fostering a particular view of intelligence in later adulthood, along with the insights provided by the empirical data, are the two primary factors contributing to the changing perspectives from Phase I to Phase IV. Social and historical impacts on behavior and aging have been elaborated by social scientists such as Havighurst, Neugarten, and Riegel (e.g., Havighurst, 1973; Neugarten & Havighurst, 1976; Riegel, 1977). Hence, in the following sections the emphasis will be on the empirical data on psychometric intelligence over the adult life span and how those data contributed to new perspectives on adult intelligence.

Phase I: misperception of age-related decline

Group tests for adult intelligence were devised for the United States Army in the second decade of the twentieth century. At that time, the United States became involved in World War I, and large numbers of young men had to be inducted into the service. Intelligence tests were used to screen out candidates who simply did not have the mental capacity to perform in the military. The test was called the Army Alpha Examination, and it was administered to thousands of recruits.

One of the major results of this first intelligence testing of large numbers of adults was that it was observed that older adults performed more poorly than younger adults. This was the first indication that investigators had that over the age of 20, there appeared to be a "decline" in intelligence. This was not a comparison of young to very old individuals. It was a comparison ranging over the ages of 18 to a maximum age of 60 years. Nevertheless, the older men in the sample performed more poorly, and even past the age of 25 there appeared to be "decline."

The first of these data were published in 1921 by the National Academy of Sciences (Yerkes, 1921). An analysis of the data on over 1.7 million men tested during World War I was included, although the analysis by age was carried out only on officers. Men between the ages of 18 and 20 scored higher than all other individuals on the examination. Men in the late 20s were already scoring 0.2 of a standard deviation lower than the youngest men, and the difference between the 51–60 year old group and the 18–20 year old group was a whole standard deviation or 15 points on total intelligence score. This sample was not the general group of soldiers, but the actual leaders of the corps – the officers who would be expected to be among the brightest of the group. Yerkes stated:

The most reasonable surmise is that older officers are selected more on the basis of their specific experience or training, professional or military, and less on native intelligence than are younger officers who have as yet little valuable experience (Yerkes, 1921, p. 813).

However, Yerkes recognized that the data were problematical because of the selective bias in cross-sectional samples. He stated:

it is unsafe for us to assert that the apparent relation is not spurious (Yerkes, 1921, p. 813).

In spite of reservations by investigators such as Yerkes (1921), the initial perspective of intelligence in adulthood and old age was one of decline. This initial perspective had a lasting impact on the psychology of aging, and it was the dominant perspective for more than 30 years.

In 1944 David Wechsler standardized his Wechsler–Bellevue Intelligence scales on a sample chosen to be representative of the occupational distribution of the United States census. He found that the Verbal scores in this cross-sectional sample were relatively stable across the age range of 20–60, while the Performance scores were lower in older adults. This result was replicated in the 1955 standardization of the Wechsler Adult Intelligence Scale (WAIS). Wechsler concluded that intelligence declined with age, and he devised standardized scores for his test such that an older adult received an average score of intelligence of 100 for a lower raw score than a young adult.

The perspective of Phase I is one of intellectual decline with adulthood. This was the perspective generated with the initial studies of intelligence in 1920 and apparently confirmed in studies conducted throughout the decades of the 1930s, 1940s, and even into the 1950s. So pervasive was this model that the standardized scores of the WAIS were designed to conform to a "decline" in intelligence with age. It was widely held that intellectual ability peaked between the ages of 15 and 20. Subsequent decline in ability was thought to be inevitable.

The only data that had been available at this period were cross-sectional studies comparing individuals of different age and experience at one point in time. Little consideration was given to the appropriateness of the tests, to the different experiences of the individuals including different levels of education, or to the degree of similarity between the individual's daily experiences and activities and the testing material. The many factors which might bias cross-sectional testing were not clearly apparent to investigators during this period. A number of studies converged to confirm that older people scored lower on intelligence tests, and psychologists and laymen simply accepted the conclusion that intelligence declined with age. It was not until longitudinal data became available and revealed a different pattern of age and intellectual function that a new level of awareness pervaded the interpretation of research on age and intelligence.

Phase II: stability versus decline

The first longitudinal data on adults' performance on psychometric intelligence tests were published by Owens (1953). The study was a 31-year follow-up of 127 young men who had been tested on the Army Alpha Examination in 1919. All of the men had been freshmen entering Iowa State College, and their average age had been 19. Upon retest, they were middle aged, and on the basis of 30 years of cross-sectional data, they would be predicted to show declines in their performance. Instead, the total scores of these individuals showed a gain of over half of a standard deviation. None of the eight subtests showed loss, while four of the subtests (Practical Judgment, Vocabulary, Disarranged Sentences, Information) showed statistically significant improvement. Four other subtests showed no change (Following Directions, Arithmetical Problems, Number Series Completion, Analogies). A subsequent follow-up more than a decade after the first indicated continued stability in intelligence (Owens, 1966). These results were remarkable. The subjects showed gains in IQ scores, and the gains were as large as the supposed losses demonstrated in the previous cross-sectional studies.

Several explanations for Owens' (1953) results were offered by scholars of the period who were still imbued with the notion that intelligence declined with age (Jones, 1959). It was argued that Owens' sample was selected from a group of college students with initially higher ability level. The implication was that intellectual ability at the highest levels shows greater maintenance than ability at average or lower levels. The college freshmen in the sample also received 4 years of additional education. It was argued that if they had been tested 4 years after the initial test (when they were seniors), their ability level would have been even higher than it was in the 1950 retest. Thus, college education was thought to have affected the results.

Another interpretation of Owens' results was that sampling contributed to the outcome. In 1919, 363 freshmen had been tested at Iowa State College, and 162 of the original sample were unlocated or deceased. An additional 63 of the 201 who were located refused to participate. Owens argued that there were zero level correlations between initial scores and gain scores within the retested group and concluded that the sampling bias was unimportant. Jones (1959), on the other hand, speculated that the alumni who had been successful in life were more likely the ones to have been found or to have come forward, and he felt that the bias of the selective sampling produced a more favorable picture of intellectual change with time than would have been found in the sample as a whole.

The perspective developed in Phase II is one of conflict. It arose from the impact between 30 years of replication of cross-sectional results indicating age decline, and the emerging longitudinal results documenting intellectual stability or gain. What was once a simple and relatively straightforward age and behavior relationship became an age-function for which there was no consistent picture. Phase II shifted the interpretation of adult intellectual behavior to a new level of complexity. It was acknowledged that the earlier model simply did not fit all of the data, and never since in the history of the study of adult intelligence has one model been successful in gaining unqualified support.

The controversy engendered in Phase II has never been totally resolved. From the 1950s to the present, investigators have debated the perspectives of stability versus decline. What differentiates Phase II from Phase I is that no simple, unidirectional model prevails.

The period after the appearance of longitudinal data on intelligence was one of puzzlement, with investigators pursuing a number of avenues for interpretation of the discrepant age functions. Articulation of the various biasing factors in cross-sectional and longitudinal designs had began as early as 1940, when Raymond Kuhlen first acknowledged the potential bias in comparing individuals of different age and experience and interpreting the results only in terms of maturational aging effects. Problems with longitudinal and cross-sectional designs were also elaborated by James Birren (1959) when he pointed out that true developmental age-functions could only be viewed with longitudinal data and that cross-sectional designs were flawed by experiential differences between different age groups. It was during the 1960s that the clear inadequacies of cross-sectional and longitudinal designs were fully elaborated, along with proposals for strategies to remedy the weaknesses.

One of the major emphases of the Phase II perspective is the realization of a much more complex picture of adult intellectual performance. The initial perspective of Phase I was that of a univariate measure of intelligence changing with age in one direction – the direction of decline. Phase II evolved from the discrepancy between cross-sectional and longitudinal data. The picture which emerged was more than a simple picture of cross-sectional decline and longitudinal stability.

In addition to the identification of the cohort effect in Phase II, it became clearer that sub-components of intelligence varied differently over time. Some abilities showed stability or increment, while others showed decline. Almost any direction and shape of age function was present when the data were analyzed for individual abilities and individual cohorts. Thus, the notion of generalized age curves of intelligence appeared to be less useful than a perspective which recognized the complexity and individuality of age changes and age differences in intelligence over the life span.

Theory of fluid and crystallized intelligence. During the period when the Phase II perspective was most influential, Cattell's theory of fluid and crystallized intelligence was examined over the life span (Cattell, 1971; Horn, 1968). Cattell and Horn argued that there were two basic and general types of intelligence, and that all measures of intellectual performance could be factor-analyzed into one of the two categories: fluid intelligence (Gf), representing the fluidity of the mind; and crystallized intelligence (Gc), analogous to the "crystals" of knowledge which accumulate with experience.

Horn and Cattell (1967) provided empirical support for their theory in the form of cross-sectional data collected on a highly heterogeneous sample of adults. The age-functions generated from this sample approximated the age-functions generated by the theory. More recently, Horn (1982) presented an overview of a series of studies on fluid and crystallized intelligence in which paid volunteers from the inmate population of a penitentiary served as subjects. Horn argued that losses in capacities for maintaining spontaneous alertness, focused intensive concentration, and awareness of possible organization for otherwise unorganized information, were largely responsible for age differences in fluid intelligence measures.

Research demonstrating the plasticity of older adults' performance on fluid as well as crystallized intelligence measures (Phase III perspective) provided challenges to the theory of fluid and crystallized intelligence. On the other hand, the theory has been widely adopted by gerontologists and serves as a useful framework to organize data on abilities which remain stable, as opposed to abilities which are impacted by age. Indeed, the bulk of Phase II work carried out in the last decade is based on the theory of fluid and crystallized intelligence (Chapell, 1995). An example of the pervasiveness of this theoretical approach is a study by Dai et al. (1993) involving over 2,000 Chinese participants divided into four age groups across the adult life span. The results showed significant age differences in fluid measures of intelligence, with older Chinese adults scoring more poorly. In these same adults, crystallized intelligence was stable or higher in old age.

Phase III: optimizing intelligence in older adults

Contrasting with Phases I and II involving descriptive methodology, Phase III involves experimentation. In its formative decades, the psychology of adult development and aging involved the descriptive identification of the nature of behavior during the adult years. Researchers focussed on the normative aspects of adult development and primarily identified behavioral decline. Kastenbaum (1968) captured the essence of Phase I and Phase II by stating that researchers in gerontology up to the 1960s were largely satisfied with "counting and classifying the wrinkles of aged behavior" (p. 280). This was an important first step in the understanding of processes of aging, but it had limitations. The step taken in Phase III was to move to experimentation. The question of why and how much plasticity in aging generated a new intellectual climate of optimism. The possibility of redesigning the aging process was suggested, and practitioners were given an emerging set of tools for intervention.

The empirical demonstration that cohort differences in intelligence scores were often greater than age changes, contributed to the willingness to attempt to improve intelligence test scores in older adults. The cohort variable could be explained in part by forces operating in the environment. Thus, it was reasoned that if environmental forces such as education led to differences in adults' intelligence test scores, manipulation of these factors should alter the scores. In this sense, Phase III was a direct outcome of one of the models evolving in Phase II.

One of the arguments for moving in a new direction away from the descriptive designs characteristic of Phase II to the experimental designs of Phase III was that a goal of science is to explain, and explanation relies upon experimental demonstration. Enough descriptive data had been accumulated to suggest that different experiences of different cohorts might account for some of the age differences in intelligence scores. Providing that experience in an experimental format would provide a test of the environmental hypothesis. Another rationale for the interventionist approach was humanitarian. If older cohorts had certain experiential deficiencies which led to their poorer performance on intelligence tests, then it was desirable to ameliorate these deficiencies. A third argument for experimental studies was expedience. Longitudinal and sequential research designs required tremendous time and resources to collect data. If age differences could be simulated and manipulated in experimental studies, then a great deal of time and effort could be saved. Knowledge would also advance more quickly with this approach, as experimental studies could be completed sooner than most longitudinal or sequential studies.

Currently, there are almost two decades of research results that have been generated from the Phase III perspective. A literature search covering the years between 1976 and 1985 identified 18 published studies involving training to manipulate intelligence test scores in older adults (Woodruff-Pak & Finkbiner, 1988). Covering the years between 1986–1995, an additional 27 published intervention studies on intelligence and aging were identified (Chapell, 1996).

One of the simplest and yet most effective strategies used to improve

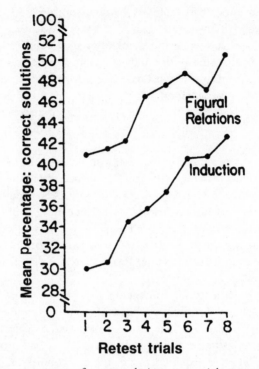

Figure 10.2 Mean percentage of correct solutions across eight retest sessions for older adults aged 60–80 years. The measures used were Figural Relations and Induction
Source: Hofland, B. F., Willis, S. L., & Baltes, P. B. (1981). Fluid intelligence performance in the elderly: Intraindividual variability and conditions of assessment. *Journal of Educational Psychology, 73*, 573–586. Copyright © 1981, American Psychological Association; reprinted by permission

performance on intelligence tests by older adults is practice on the test (see figure 10.2). Indeed, much of the training involved in intervention studies may work simply because it provides familiarization and practice to old people on tasks which had initially been novel to them. Such training has long-term consequences. Longitudinal investigation revealed that fluid ability training facilitated performance in 108 elderly adults 3 years after the initial training (Hayslip et al., 1995). These results are significant for neuropsychologists who may be providing older adults with their first testing experience. Familiarizing the client with the tests, including giving practice tests, is especially important in the case of older adults.

Phase III denies the inevitable deterioration of intellect with aging. From a neuropsychological point of view, it is evident that age differences on intelligence tests are not simply the result of neurobiological deficits. Plasticity in older adult test behavior attests to the non-biological causes of some of the deficits. The empirical work undertaken from this perspective demonstrates that the decrement can be reversed and/or compensated with other skills. This perspective emphasizes the existence of plasticity in behavior in the aged and points out that the decremental age-functions can be altered with training and practice. From this point of view, the number of possible age-functions of intelligence is unknown and unknowable until all possible attempts at manipulation have been made. Intervention research has contributed to a better understanding of theories of adult intelligence. It has also provided practitioners with new tools with which they can help older adults.

Phase IV: intellectual development and wisdom

One of the major limitations of Phases I–III is that all perspectives base information about intellect in older adulthood on tests initially designed for children or, at best, young adults. All three perspectives accept psychometric measures of intelligence as valid measures for the aged. Old people are assessed with the yardstick designed to measure the young, and if they deviate from the young pattern, they are labelled deficient. One of the characteristics of Phase IV is that it re-examines the psychometric approach in an attempt to determine what are the most appropriate tests of intellect in late life. The ecological validity of traditional intelligence tests is questioned in the case of the aged.

The capacity for continued improvement in intellectual ability is an underlying assumption of the Phase IV perspective. Characteristic of Phase IV is the notion that intelligence is dynamic over the adult years and that certain abilities change and even improve with age. Gisela Labouvie-Vief captured the essence of this assumption when she stated:

> Thus, adulthood is no longer to be seen as the cessation of growth and development (and, consequently, as the beginning of aging) but as a life stage programmed for plasticity and further growth (Labouvie-Vief, 1985, p. 501).

A related aspect of Phase IV is the search for qualitative changes in adult intelligence and cognition using the available data and measuring instruments as well as novel methodology. Working in this paradigm are investigators who are applying statistical techniques such as factor analysis to the psychometric intelligence data to determine if the factor structure and hence the organization of adult intelligence would change over time.

The search for ecologically valid adult intelligence tests. The initial attempts to devise age-appropriate tests of intelligence did not represent a break with the psychometric intelligence or cognitive psychology approaches for the most part, but involved instead the attempt to make standard tests more relevant to old people. Older adults are typically very removed from the academic environment which would most likely sustain formal, abstract modes of thinking. Their average educational attainment is much less than the educational achievement of even the middle-aged cohort, and many more years have elapsed since they were in school as compared to the young and middle aged with whom they are evaluated. It is not surprising that the aged perform better on tests tapping practical experience. In this study, older non-college-graduates scored even proportionately higher on the familiar set of materials than any other group. They scored 113 percent higher on the familiar materials than on the formal materials (Sinnott, 1975).

Traditional cognitive tests may alienate older individuals, because the tests seem trivial and fail to tap cognitive operations that occur in daily thinking and problem solving. Hulicka (1967) reported an 80 percent attrition rate of older adults on an attempted memory task. Because older adults may find the tasks presented to them by psychologists displeasing, we must consider the context within which the individuals live, in order to study their cognitive processes.

Change in adult cognition. It may be more appropriate in exploring adult cognition to seek age-appropriate constructs rather than merely altering the content of the tasks. It has been known for decades that tests can be constructed to favor performance in the aged (Demming & Pressey, 1957; Gardner & Monge, 1977). Such tests generally tap experiential, practical skills. It has been demonstrated that over the age range of 20–78, everyday problem solving and crystallized intelligence were greater in older cohorts (Cornelius & Caspi, 1987; Diehl et al., 1995). On the other hand, measures of fluid intelligence in these studies indicated deficits after middle age.

From the period when the Phase I perspective prevailed, it was acknowledged that older adults maintained vocabulary and information scores. It was indicated from the Phase II perspective that these abilities may increase with age, and it continues to be demonstrated that tests which tap memory for general information favor performance by middle-aged and older adults (Diehl et al., 1995). For the most part, however, researchers have been more concerned with the acquisition of new information and new skills, while overlooking the potential for acquired knowledge in facilitating problem solving in aging. The emphasis appears to be gradually changing, as psychologists are coming to study possible forms of progressive cognitive development in adulthood. The Phase IV perspective reflects a shift from analytic to synthetic world views of aging and intelligence (Kramer, 1987), and such patterns of thought have been documented as more common in older thinkers (Kramer et al., 1992).

Cognitive phenomena such as wisdom, ego integrity, and life review have been associated with old age. All of these phenomena involve a greater synthesis of ideas reflecting an integration to a more mature stage of cognition. Schaie (1977–1978) devised a model of the development of adult cognition which had at its final stage a period he called "reintegrative." He contended that in old age cognition is oriented toward integrating one's life experiences in order to make sense of one's life and to find continuity. Such a stage parallels Erikson's (1968) ideal of ego integrity, the final psychosocial adjustment in his eight stages of personality development over the life span.

Consideration has also been given to the concept of wisdom, a quality often associated throughout history with thinking in old age (Clayton & Birren, 1980). Clayton (1982) compared and contrasted wisdom and intelligence and concluded that intelligence focuses on questions of how to accomplish tasks while wisdom involves consideration of whether a particular course of action should be pursued. Wisdom also involves an integration of affect and cognition, and Roodin et al. (1984) suggested that it is precisely the integration between cognition and affect which characterizes adult development.

Summary

Intelligence tests do not really belong in the category of neuropsychological assessments, as the global IQ score is not associated with discrete brain function. Differences in intelligence test scores between young and older adults may be less related to neurobiological aging than to education level, socioeconomic status, and other factors. Nevertheless, neuropsychologists typically assess intelligence, or at a minimum use some subtests from standardized intelligence tests, in an attempt to place their older clients' capabilities in the context of intelligence test performance of other adults.

In defining and evaluating intelligence in late life, it is useful to know if intelligence is consistent over the life span. There is some consistency over the life span in terms of scores achieved on intelligence tests, but intelligence test scores can be influenced by a variety of environmental factors. Research on psychometric measurement of intelligence in adulthood and old age has generated a great deal of debate, and four contrasting perspectives of intelligence in older adults were presented to illustrate the changing ideas.

Phase I involves a unidimensional view of age-related decline. This perspective emerged in the 1920s, based on cross-sectional studies of psychometric intelligence. The limitations of the Phase I perspective were infrequently articulated in the first half of the twentieth century, and its long domination was conclusively challenged only in the 1950s when longitudinal data on intelligence became available. These data suggested at a minimum that adult intelligence was stable until the age of 50.

Phase II embraced a more sophisticated view of adult intelligence, with intellect varying by cohort and by specific type of ability. From the contradiction between longitudinal and cross-sectional data emerged a new synthesis in Phase II of a more complex perspective of intelligence in later life. Age-functions could be incremental or decremental, and took many forms.

The acknowledgment in Phase II that environmental forces could affect intelligence scores of a given cohort led investigators to consider that manipulation of environmental contingencies might affect intelligence scores within a cohort as well. If experience in the environment could result in differences in IQ scores as a function of when one was born, then within an individual at some point in the life span environmental manipulations might affect performance on intelligence tests. This was an impetus for the Phase III perspective of plasticity in adult intelligence. Training studies made it apparent that training simply familiarizes older people with abilities that were novel or unused by them. This is an important observation for neuropsychologists, who typically administer tests to older adults that they have never taken before. Practice tests and time to become familiar with the testing setting are particularly important for accurate evaluations of older adults.

The Phase IV perspective emerged at a time when the growing size and social and economic power of aging adults was being recognized in all segments of society. The Phase IV perspective challenged the validity of existing psychometric measures of intelligence for assessment of older adults and introduced the notion of growth in intellectual ability over the adult years. The relevance of the Phase model to neuropsychology is its fundamental questioning of the validity of intelligence tests for older adults.

Further Reading

Labouvie-Vief, G. (1985). Intelligence and cognition. In J. E. Birren & K. W. Schaie (Eds.), *Handbook of the psychology of aging* (pp. 500–530). New York: Van Nostrand Reinhold.
An overview of the research literature with a re-interpretation of its evaluative nature is presented in this chapter.

Schaie, K. W. (1977–1978). Toward a stage theory of adult cognitive development. *International Journal of Aging and Human Development, 8,* 129–136.
The notion of progression in cognitive capacities is presented.

Baltes, P. B. (1991). The many faces of human ageing: Toward a psychological culture of older age. *Psychological Medicine, 21,* 837–854.
Some conditions for a positive culture fostering wisdom in old age are presented.

11

Learning and Memory

Research on learning, memory and aging has almost as long a history as research on reaction time or intelligence and aging. Since these cognitive capacities have been studied, investigators have documented age-related deficits. Modest deficits in memory are one of the major complaints of older adults. The problem appears, at least in part, to be one of overload. In a brain that has accumulated 70 years of information, new information represents a very small portion of the whole. It is more difficult to assimilate, and it is more difficult to retrieve. Mild memory impairment in older adults is not incapacitating in most cases. It is simply a nuisance.

A decline in the efficiency of learning and memory processes is seen to some degree in all older adults. However, there is a subset of elderly adults who have severe memory impairment. These are the people most likely to be seen by a clinical neuropsychologist. In these affected individuals, the consequences of memory impairment are often severe and prevent efficient functioning in the environment.

The disorders of memory associated with cognitive senescence are generally not recognized as national health problems, in contrast to diseases such as cancer or cardiovascular disorders (Jensen et al., 1980). However, in terms of the number of impaired individuals, cognitive senescence should come to be recognized as a major problem in health care. Therefore, gaining an understanding of the neurobiological processes underlying age-related impairments in learning, memory, and cognitive functioning is an important goal. Effective and rationally based therapies for the disorders of learning and memory associated with advanced age can be developed only with a foundation of knowledge provided by basic research.

Although some of the cognitive dimensions of age-related memory loss were documented, until relatively recently the task of identifying those neurobiological changes that underlie impaired memory in the aged received little attention from cognitive-oriented researchers. This has occurred in part because the neurobiological substrates of learning and memory remain largely unknown for humans or animals of any age. However, the need for data about the physiological and psychological bases of learning and memory loss will become progressively more acute in the coming years as an ever-increasing proportion of the population has exceeded 65 and even 85 years of age.

Brain memory systems

Brain memory systems are defined in terms of: (a) the cognitive processes by which learning and memory occur, and (b) by the neural structures that support those functions. From the cognitive perspective, the subjective awareness of "trying to learn" is typically present on declarative (also called explicit) tasks (Shiffrin & Schneider, 1977). In contrast, nondeclarative (implicit) learning occurs primarily through the performance of a given task. On a nondeclarative task, the individual is not aware that learning is occurring, but when tested subsequently, the person's performance indicates that learning has occurred.

Cognitive neuroscience studies of learning and memory in neurological patients with discrete brain lesions, in normal adults using brain imaging with positron emission tomography (PET), and in animals using stimulating, recording, lesion, and pharmacological studies, have converged to demonstrate that different types of learning and memory are performed by different brain systems. At present, there is evidence for two major forms of memory systems, called declarative and nondeclarative. These memory systems have been classified into forms that rely on medial temporal lobe brain circuitry (declarative) and forms that do not depend on the medial temporal lobe circuitry (nondeclarative; Schacter, 1992; Squire, 1992; Thompson, 1989). Brain substrates of separate memory systems are often physically remote from one another; they are comprised of qualitatively different types of neurons, neurotransmitters, and projections; and they are likely affected differentially by processes of aging.

Declarative learning and memory

The brain memory system associated with age-related deficit is the declarative system (Craik, 1991; Hultsch & Dixon, 1990). Typical memory tests used by neuropsychologists assess this form of learning and memory. The California Verbal Learning Test (CVLT) and the WAIS Paired Associates subtests are two examples of declarative memory measures. These tests are performed

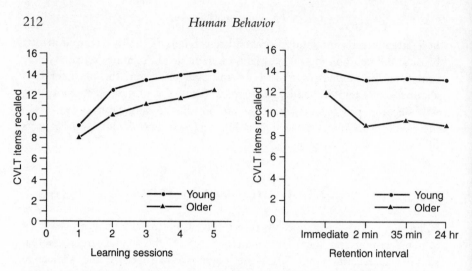

Figure 11.1 Left: Acquisition over five learning trials on the California Verbal Learning Test (CVLT) in young and older adults. *Right:* Retention immediately after five learning trials and at intervals of 2 min, 35 min, and 24 hr on the CVLT in the same young and older adults whose acquisition is shown on the left

Source: from data reported in Woodruff-Pak, D. S., & Finkbiner, R. G. (1995a). Larger nondeclarative than declarative deficits in learning and memory in human aging. *Psychology and Aging, 10,* 416–426. Woodruff-Pak, D. S., & Finkbiner, R. G. (1995b). One-day retention of eyeblink classical conditioning and verbal free recall in young and older adults. *Aging and Cognition, 2,* 108–127

more poorly by adults in their 70s and beyond (figure 11.1; Woodruff-Pak & Finkbiner, 1995a). As discussed in chapter 5, age-related changes in the medial temporal lobe region including the hippocampus are thought to be associated with deficits in declarative learning and memory. In about one-third of the 154 medically healthy and cognitively normal older adults ranging in age from 55 to 88 years, there was evidence from computerized tomography (CT) or magnetic resonance imaging (MRI) scans of hippocampal atrophy (Golomb et al., 1993). It was primarily the participants with hippocampal atrophy who performed more poorly on tests of immediate and delayed recall of prose paragraphs and paired associate words. Frontal-lobe impairment with aging may also contribute to poor performance on some declarative learning and memory tasks, because frontal-lobe function affects attention, motivation, regulation, and self-monitoring which are components of declarative memory tasks.

Declarative learning and memory in the adult years

Often the question is asked, "Is learning or memory affected by aging?" The research evidence suggests that it is neither one nor the other alone that is affected by aging. Both processes show moderate age differences over the adult years.

Forgetting. Attempts to equate young and older adult participants on learning when the aim is to assess retention are typically doomed to failure. The number of trials to attain criterion is greater for the older subjects, so they may overlearn the simpler aspects of the task to a greater degree than the young. Since older subjects are less likely to use mediators, they may learn by rote. This is a qualitatively different way of storing information, and it is less resistant to forgetting. Hence, both quantitatively and qualitatively, what has been learned is different between young and old participants, even in studies in which attempts have been made to equate acquisition.

Laboratory research demonstrated that aging has little effect on the retention of new material that has been learned fairly thoroughly. Similarly, forgetting in real life was found to be minimal for well-learned material. Kausler (1982) suggested that the laboratory studies offered a time-compressed simulation of forgetting in the real world. The course of forgetting over weeks for artificial laboratory material corresponded closely to the course of forgetting over years for material learned outside of the laboratory.

Research on memories for material learned years earlier indicates that whatever is retained 5 years after the material was learned will probably be retained for life. For example, in a study of 1,000 individuals who had learned Spanish in high school or college, Bahrick (1979) found that most of what people forgot was forgotten in the first 3–5 years after finishing the language course. Of the Spanish that remained, little was forgotten for the next 25 years.

A technique to which participants could readily relate was used to assess forgetting over long periods of time (Bahrick et al., 1975). Pictures of high-school classmates were shown to people who had graduated from high school 35–50 years ago. Middle-aged adults could recognize about 90 percent of the names and faces 35 years after graduation. Fifty years after graduation, they could still identify 70–80 percent of them.

A typical stereotype of older adults is that they remember memories from the remote past better than they remember more recent events. In-depth observational studies by memory and aging researcher Irene Hulicka (1982), indicated that older adults remember events from various decades equally well. They may talk about the past memories more because they are involved in the life review process (described later in this chapter) or because they think it will interest a listener more than their comments about more recent events.

Information processing approaches. Information-processing approaches to memory attempt to break down various stages of memory to understand memory processes more completely. The initial perceptual aspect of the stimulus as it is first recorded is called sensory memory. The span of immediate memory, which is the number of items you can hold in memory after just seeing or hearing them, is called primary or short-term memory. What gets remembered for longer periods of time is called secondary or long-term memory.

The age differences that have been identified from an information-processing perspective are greatest in the long-term memory capacity. No clear aging effects which would be significant enough to affect registration of information in later memory states have been found in sensory memory, and age differences in short-term memory capacity are minor and simply involve encoding.

A classic study on long-term memory and aging was carried out by Schonfield and Robertson (1966; figure 11.2). They presented young and older subjects with a list of 24 words. First the subjects were required to recall the words. Then they performed a recognition task in which each of the words on the list was presented embedded among three other non-target words. The subject had to recognize the word from the list. Age differences were observed on the recall task, but there were no age differences in recognition.

Not all subsequent studies have replicated the absence of age differences in recognition, especially when the recognition task is made more difficult. Nevertheless, many studies have indicated much smaller age differences in recognition than in recall tasks (e.g., Craik, 1971; Erber, 1974; Shaps & Nilsson, 1980). These results indicate that although there may be some problem with encoding, diminished proficiency in the search process is also a contributor to age differences in long-term memory proficiency.

Although a large number of studies on aging and memory have been undertaken from the information-processing perspective, some investigators in the forefront of research on memory and aging are critical of this approach. For one thing, the independence and clarity of the separate storage functions hypothesized in information-processing theories have been lost (Craik & Lockhart, 1972). The model does not focus on the qualitative aspects of memory which apparently are most affected by aging. In this regard, Kausler stated:

Moderate deficiencies of long-term memory phenomena for elderly subjects have been reported in numerous studies. Undoubtedly these deficiencies reflect those found in the real world. Our review has implicated both encoding processes and retrieval processes in this over-

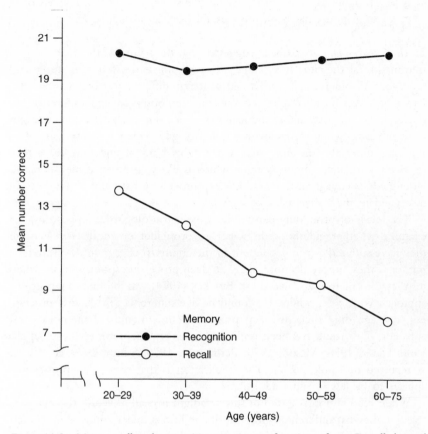

Figure 11.2 Mean recall and recognition scores as a function of age. Recall showed large age differences between the age-decades of the 20s and 60s, but recognition showed no age differences. These data were used to support the position that learning ability was stable in older adults, but the ability to retrieve learned material was impaired

Source: Schonfield, D., & Robertson, B. A. (1966). Memory storage and aging. *Canadian Journal of Psychology, 20,* 228–236. Copyright © 1966, Canadian Psychological Association; reprinted with permission

all age-related decline in the proficiency of long-term memory. It is here that the shortcomings of the dual-store [information processing] model become apparent. Both encoding and retrieval processes are treated rather superficially by proponents of the model. Little effort is made to distinguish between quantitative and qualitative changes in processes. The possibility that age deficits in episodic memory may be due to qualitative changes that may be modified by appropriate training is largely ignored. It is with such qualitative changes that the levels of processing model has been most useful (Kausler, 1982, p. 451).

Levels of processing.   It has been suggested that the nature of the processing of information at the time it is being perceived affects the way it is stored and retrieved. If older adults processed material differently from young, this encoding mechanism might account for the observed age differences in retrieval. To theorists taking the levels-of-processing perspective, encoding is most effective when items are processed deeply. Deep processing involves thinking about the meaning of a word. This kind of encoding leads to a relatively permanent memory trace which is likely to be available for recall. Young adults engage in this kind of deep processing naturally when they are instructed to memorize a list of words.

The levels-of-processing perspective gave gerontologists an opportunity to examine whether elderly adults were less proficient on recall tasks because they have suffered a true decrement in the ability to engage in deep process-ing, or if they simply do not engage in deep processing spontaneously when instructed to memorize a word list. Eysenck (1974) was the first to report this approach with older adults. He found no age differences in shallow process-ing, but age differences in deep processing and intentional memory were apparent. This result has been replicated in several laboratories (Erber et al., 1980; Lauer, 1976; Mason, 1979; Perlmutter, 1979; Smith, 1979; S. White, as reported in Craik, 1977). The implication is that processing proficiency appears to be less in older adults.

When recognition is tested in this paradigm instead of recall, the perspec-tive is somewhat different. Under recall conditions, older adults remembered fewer words, but after the subjects attempted to recall the words, they were given a recognition task (Craik, 1977). In recognition conditions, older subjects performed as well as younger subjects in both the deep and shallow processing conditions. The only age differences were in the control groups instructed simply to memorize the words. Using the purely declarative memory instructions, "remember these words," older adults performed more poorly. Because older adults' recall was not affected by the deep or shallow processing instructions, older adults may not have lost the capacity to process information deeply. It was suggested that they simply do not do so sponta-neously (Craik, 1977). Even when durable memory traces have been built with deep levels of processing, older adults are less able to retrieve memory traces.

Whereas Craik and Simon (1980), Erber et al. (1980), and Perlmutter (1979) replicated White and Craik's results on depth of processing and recognition in the aged, Mason (1979) and Smith and Winograd (1978) did not. In the latter two studies, pronounced age differences in recognition as well as recall occurred. Cued recall has been attempted in some studies as an alternative to recognition in an attempt to separate encoding and retrieval processes. After reviewing the depth-of-processing work, Kausler concluded:

> Our best guess is that there is a modest age deficit in encoding proficiency, and the degree of that deficit has been overestimated in a number of studies. Why the overestimation? Our best guess, here, is that any task involving the recall of a lengthy list of items is viewed suspiciously by many elderly subjects as being trivial and of dubious ecological relevance (Kausler, 1982, p. 459).

Even when very serious attempts have been made to develop and implement memory improvement techniques for older adults, performance of the elderly is seldom brought to the level of the young (e.g., Poon et al., 1980). Nevertheless, older adults can be trained to improve their performance on memory tasks (Poon, 1985). Although processing deficiency may account for some of the age-related differences in performance on memory tasks, it does not account totally for the differences between young and older adult groups.

Declarative memory deficits and the diencephalon

Korsakoff's syndrome results from excessive use of alcohol and a resultant thiamine (vitamin B_1) deficiency. Brain damage involved in this disease includes lesions in the medial thalamus and possibly in the mammillary bodies of the hypothalamus, as well as generalized cerebral atrophy. Severe memory loss is characteristic of the cognitive symptoms of Korsakoff's syndrome, indicating that lesions in the thalamus can produce memory impairment. Because it is long-term abuse of alcohol that leads to Korsakoff's syndrome, patients with this disease are typically in late middle age or old age. They are unable to form new memories (anterograde amnesia), they have extensive impairment of remote memory such that most of their adult life is forgotten (retrograde amnesia), they make up stories about past events rather than admit memory loss (confabulation), their spontaneous conversation is meager, they lack insight about their profound memory impairment, and they tend to show indifference and apathy to ongoing activities (Talland, 1969). The syndrome is progressive and can be arrested with massive doses of vitamin B_1, but the condition cannot be reversed. Prognosis is poor in patients with Korsakoff's disease.

An extensive retrograde amnesia can arise from acute injury to the diencephalon. McCarthy and Hodges (1995) described a patient called PS with a lesion very similar to the principal common site of damage in alcoholic

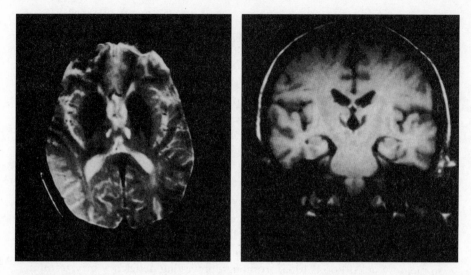

Figure 11.3 MRI scan of the patient PS with a symmetrical bilateral thalamic infarction: horizontal T2 (left) and coronal T1 (right) weighted images at the level of the thalamus showing symmetrical infarction of the dorsomedial nuclei, internal medullary lamina and mammillo-thalamic tract bilaterally

Source: McCarthy, R. A., & Hodges, J. R. (1995). Trapped in time: Profound autobiographical memory loss following a thalamic stroke. In R. Campbell & M. A. Conway (Eds.), *Broken memories: Case studies in memory impairment* (pp. 31–44). Oxford: Blackwell

Korsakoff's syndrome. PS had a symmetrical bilateral thalamic infarction in the region of the paramedian artery (see figure 11.3). Excerpts from his case report were as follows:

PS, a 67-year-old, right-handed garage proprietor was admitted to Addenbrooke's Hospital, Cambridge, on 12 June 1989 in coma. He had retired to bed the night before with his wife as normal, but the following morning was unrousable. There was no evidence of drug overdose. He had been in good general health with no history of prior strokes. Careful questioning of his wife and other family members established that his alcohol consumption was, at most, modest.

Following admission to hospital he remained in coma for less than 24 hours. The diagnosis at this stage was uncertain. . . . Upon recovery of his conscious level, he was noted to be severely confused, disorientated in time and place with marked impairment in new learning capacity. No language or perceptual abnormalities were noted. . . .

He remained in hospital for a month. When discharged in July 1989 he was fully alert but exhibited features of a profound memory disorder which has persisted ever since. His retention of new information remains negligible and he has a extensive retrograde amnesia encompassing the whole of his adult life. There has also been a marked change in his personality; having been a vigorous and successful garage owner and a keen member of various business clubs, he is now apathetic and lethargic. He is content to sit in the house all day watching the television and shows little interest in the family or his business. He lacks insight into his deficits and denies any cognitive impairment. We assume that these frontal features are due to the fact that the thalamic lesion has interrupted pathways essential for normal frontal lobe function. . . .

Clinically, the most striking feature of PS's autobiographical memory was his persistent belief that he was currently in the Navy on active service, but away from his boat on shore leave. He usually stated that he was called up two years previously at the start of the war. Many core details of his naval career (1941–6) appeared to be related accurately (McCarthy & Hodges, 1995, pp. 32–4).

The neuroanatomical locus of the lesion in the thalamus is similar to areas lesioned in Korsakoff's syndrome, and McCarthy and Hodges (1995) pointed out that the qualitative features of PS's retrograde amnesia resemble very closely those described by Oliver Sacks (1987) in his patient with Korsakoff's syndrome who had a similar memory fixation in his wartime Naval service days. The lesion, that is relatively small, probably severed a critical link within an integrated system according to McCarthy and Hodges (1995). They suggested that the lesion produced a disconnection within the cortical–subcortical memory processing system, disrupting links between the frontal and parieto-temporal regions. The frontal and parieto-temporal memory regions are at least partly segregated in PS so that he is trapped in time in his past.

PS's unusual symptoms of memory impairment underscore the concept that there are several regions in the brain involved in memory. The medial temporal lobes and hippocampus form the central core of a system most closely associated with declarative memory. Classic amnesic syndromes limited to anterograde amnesia involve medial temporal lobe lesions. Additional brain centers significant for memory include the frontal lobes and portions of the diencephalon. Patients such as PS with circumscribed diencephalic lesions confirm that the retrograde amnesia observed in patients with Korsakoff's syndrome are probably related to damage in the diencephalon rather than the result of widespread neurotoxic effects of alcohol.

Nondeclarative learning and memory

Different brain circuits support declarative and nondeclarative learning and memory. Furthermore, nondeclarative forms of learning and memory do not comprise a unitary memory system. Tasks operationally defined as nondeclarative include: (a) repetition priming; (b) acquisition and retention of motor, perceptual, or problem solving skills; (c) simple classical conditioning; and (d) non-associative learning (Schacter, 1987; Squire, 1992). The cerebellum is essential for eyeblink classical conditioning (e.g., Thompson, 1986). Motor skill learning engages motor cortex (e.g., Grafton et al., 1992). Repetition priming involves occipital cortex (Buckner et al., 1995; Fleischman et al., 1995; Gabrieli et al., 1995a). These various brain substrates of nondeclarative learning and memory are remote from one another and are completely non-overlapping (figure 11.4).

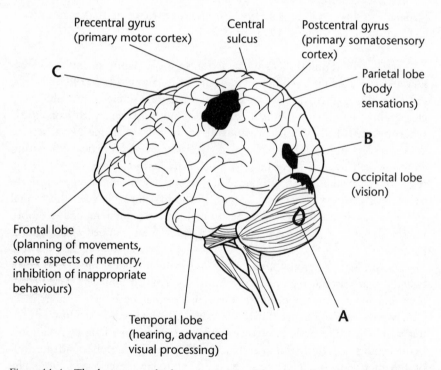

Figure 11.4 The human cerebral cortex and brainstem and the regions essential for various forms of nondeclarative learning and memory. The occipital cortex (A) is essential for repetition priming, the motor cortex is essential for motor skill learning (B), and the cerebellum is essential for simple classical conditioning (C)

Aging affects the brain substrates of declarative and various nondeclarative forms of learning and memory differently; thus, learning and memory show different age functions on the different declarative and nondeclarative measures. Because different types of nondeclarative learning and memory have different brain substrates, it is not surprising that the effects of age vary for the several forms of nondeclarative learning and memory.

Among the rationales used by cognitive theorists for postulating the existence of multiple memory systems is the empirical observation that declarative memory shows age-related deficits, but nondeclarative memory shows stability over adulthood (Graf, 1990; Light & La Voie, 1993). However, this rationale was based on data collected with the nondeclarative measure of repetition priming. Indeed, most studies of nondeclarative memory in aging have tested repetition priming. Although repetition priming is only one of several forms of nondeclarative learning and memory, researchers continue to focus on the early published studies of priming as representative of all nondeclarative learning and memory. The claim continues to be made that nondeclarative forms of learning and memory are stable in old age (e.g., Grady et al., 1995).

Repetition priming. Research suggests that repetition priming with visually presented stimuli has at least two components: a perceptual component mediated by peristriate cortices, and a conceptual component mediated by parieto-temporal cortices (Keane et al., 1991; Marsolek et al., 1992). PET studies were carried out testing young adult participants in two cognitive conditions (declarative – recall; nondeclarative – priming) and three control conditions (baseline, no response, fixation; Buckner et al., 1995). During visual priming there was blood flow reduction in bilateral occipito-temporal regions. Research on aging and priming provides evidence demonstrating that age differences are absent (or minimal) for nondeclarative tasks such as visual repetition priming. Recall and recognition (declarative memory) for the same items are poorer for these adults. In cross-sectional priming studies, age differences were absent (or minimal) for priming tasks such as word-stem completion, identification of degraded words, category exemplar production, or object decision (Chiarello & Hoyer, 1988; Davis et al., 1990; Howard, 1988; Hultsch et al., 1991; Light & Albertson, 1989; Light & Singh, 1987; Light et al., 1986; Mitchell, 1989; Mitchell et al., 1990; Schacter et al., 1992). Studies of aging effects on the brain, discussed in chapter 5, reported relative preservation of much of the occipital cortex, the region essential for perceptual priming (Fleischman et al., 1995; Gabrieli, Fleischman et al., 1995). In contrast, medial temporal regions engaged in the declarative recognition and recall tests are more likely to be impaired in old age (Golomb et al., 1993; West, 1993).

Skill learning. Motor skill learning is assessed by improvement in speed and accuracy across trials on repetitive sensorimotor tasks (e.g., rotary pursuit learning). Grafton et al. (1992) have shown that relative regional cerebral blood flow increases in the primary motor area, supplementary motor area, and the thalamus as subjects learn this nondeclarative task. Subjects with Parkinson's disease and striatal abnormalities are impaired in some non-declarative tasks such as mirror tracing. However, they perform normally on the rotary pursuit task. These results reinforce Grafton et al.'s (1992) observation that rotary pursuit learning activates the motor cortex. Further evidence for the role of the motor cortex in implicit learning was provided by Pascual-Leone et al. (1994). These investigators demonstrated that during a serial reaction time test, subjects developed implicit knowledge of the test sequence as measured by diminishing response times. Motor cortical mapping with transcranial magnetic stimulation revealed that the cortical output maps to the muscles involved in the task became progressively larger until subjects could explicitly state the correct test sequence.

The studies that have examined motor skill learning in normal aging are not consistent in their results. Hashtroudi et al. (1991) pointed out that various studies of skill learning and aging have reported three different kinds of results: superior performance by older adults, equal performance by young and old, and superior performance by young adults. Limiting discussion to the traditional tasks used to assess motor skill learning, rotary pursuit performance, and mirror reading and tracing, the age-related data are still inconsistent. Rotary pursuit performance was reported to be impaired in the elderly by Wright and Payne (1985) and Gutman (1965), but these investigators tested only one single session of acquisition. In Wright and Payne's (1985) data, age differences were minimal in the later stages of training, although early in training young subjects had steeper acquisition curves. Testing young, middle-aged, and older subjects over three daily sessions, Durkin et al. (1993) found greater increases in performance of the middle-aged and older groups than in the young group in the second and third day. Overall, rotary pursuit performance improved similarly in all age groups. Comparing age-matched older adults (mean age of 70.8 years) to patients with a diagnosis of probable AD, Eslinger and Damasio (1986) found non-significant differences in acquisition of a rotary pursuit task, although AD patients were unable to demonstrate declarative memory by learning a series of frequent words and unfamiliar faces.

Mirror tracing and rotary pursuit performance was reported to be impaired in older adults by Ruch (1934). Moscovitch et al. (1986) and Hashtroudi et al. (1991) found age-related deficits on mirror reading. However, Hashtroudi et al. (1991) reported that mirror reading was comparable in young and older subjects when older adults were given a sufficiently long time to view the words. Durkin et al. also reported that skill learning was similar in young and old when subjects had sufficient time to view the stimuli.

Eyeblink Classical Conditioning and normal aging. The standard format for the presentation of stimuli in eyeblink classical conditioning (EBCC) is called the delay paradigm (figure 11.5). A neutral stimulus such as a tone or light is

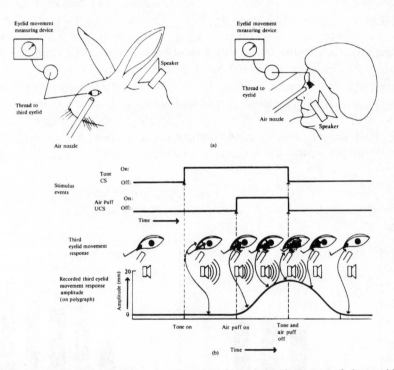

Figure 11.5 Experimental arrangement for classical conditioning of the eyeblink response in rabbits and humans. (a) The rabbit's third eyelid (nictitating membrane, NM) and the human's eyelid are used. A wire is attached to the NM in the rabbit and connected to a transducer and input to a computer for NM/blink measurement. An infrared device is used in humans. Air puffed from a nozzle near the eye serves as the unconditioned stimulus (US). A tone from a speaker is the conditioned stimulus (CS). (b) NM and/or eyelid movement is recorded and displayed by a computer. The example here occurs early in training before learning has occurred. The tone does not elicit an NM or blink response initially, but the airpuff US elicits a blink that is recorded as an upward deflection on the computer. As additional CS and US pairings occur, the organism blinks to the tone CS, before the airpuff US (not shown)

Source: Lindzey, G., Hall, C. S., & Thompson, R. F. (1978). *Psychology* (2nd ed.). New York: Worth

called the conditioned stimulus (CS). It is presented for a duration of around half a second. While it is still on, the unconditioned stimulus (US) is presented, and the CS and US coterminate 50–100 ms later. In humans, the US is a corneal airpuff, usually around 5 p.s.i. in intensity. In rabbits, the US which elicits an eyeblink unconditioned response (UR) is either a shock to the infraorbital region of the eye or a corneal airpuff. What the subject learns (normally without awareness) is that the CS signals the onset of the US. Subjects learn to blink to the CS before US onset. This learned response is called the conditioned response (CR). Timing in the delay paradigm which we have used most often in aging studies with both humans and rabbits involves a 500 ms, 80 dB SPL (sound pressure level) tone CS followed 400 ms after its onset by a 100 ms, 3 p.s.i. corneal airpuff. The CS–US interval is 400 ms. Large age differences in eyeblink conditioning occur in all species that have been tested, including humans and rabbits as shown in figure 11.6.

Early studies of eyeblink conditioning compared young and elderly subjects in the delay paradigm and reported large age differences (e.g., Braun &

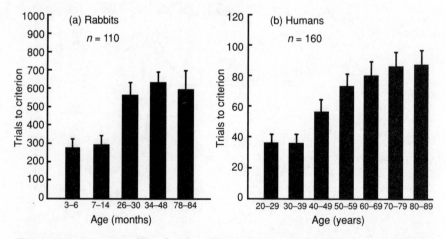

Figure 11.6 Mean number of trials to learning criterion in eyeblink classical conditioning in 110 rabbits over the age range of 3–84 months and 160 humans aged 20–89 years. Trials to criterion is the number of paired tone conditioned stimulus and airpuff unconditioned stimulus trials it took organisms to attain a criterion of eight conditioned responses in nine consecutive trials. (Data collected by D. S. Woodruff Pak)

Geiselhart, 1959; Kimble & Pennypacker, 1963). The main result was the relative inability of the older subjects to acquire CRs. We collected eyeblink conditioning data in the delay paradigm using a 400 ms CS–US interval in over 100 adults ranging in age from 18 to 83 (Woodruff-Pak & Thompson, 1988). Results indicated that age differences in acquisition of conditioning are large. The age differences in EBCC did not appear abruptly in the decade of the 60s. Rather, subjects in the 40s were already demonstrating a lower level of conditioning. Large age differences were observed in the delay classical conditioning paradigm, and they first appeared in the decade of the 40s. These results have been replicated almost exactly (Solomon et al., 1989; Woodruff-Pak & Jaeger, 1997). Durkin et al. (1993) reported age differences in both eyeblink conditioning and heart rate classical conditioning.

The cerebellum and associated circuitry is the brain structure essential for eyeblink conditioning (Thompson, 1986). Extensive evidence has been amassed to implicate the cerebellum in eyeblink conditioning, and data are compelling to indicate that for all mammals, Pavlovian conditioning of a motor response to aversive stimuli is mediated by the cerebellum. Evidence has converged from a variety of sources to suggest that the ipsilateral cerebellum is essential for eyeblink conditioning in animals and humans. For 20 years, scientists have traced the neural pathways involved in and essential for acquisition and retention of eyeblink conditioning in the rabbit, and there has been remarkable success in identifying the brain structures and mechanisms involved in this form of associative learning (for reviews, see Anderson & Steinmetz, 1994; Lavond et al., 1993; Steinmetz & Thompson, 1991; Thompson & Krupa, 1994).

A second line of evidence implicating the cerebellum's essential role in eyeblink conditioning comes from studies of human cerebellar patients (Daum et al., 1993; Topka et al., 1993; Woodruff-Pak et al., 1996). Impairment in eyeblink conditioning is seen in humans with lesions localized to cerebellar regions that are essential for conditioning in rabbits. Studies of normal young adults performing eyeblink conditioning during PET assessment provide yet another line of evidence indicating cerebellar involvement in conditioning. Three PET investigations concur in their reports of changes in the cerebellum during eyeblink conditioning (Blaxton et al., 1996; Logan & Grafton, 1995; Molchan et al., 1994).

Thus, EBCC is a form of learning and memory for which the neural circuitry has been almost entirely identified in animals and humans. This form of learning and memory shows reliable changes associated with normal aging. It is useful in neuropsychology in the elucidation of brain mechanisms affecting memory loss in aging. Cerebellar Purkinje cell number is 25 percent less in elderly adults than in young adults (Hall et al., 1975). Imaging resolution in humans is not fine enough to reveal the presence or absence of individual Purkinje cells. Therefore, investigation of Purkinje cell–eyeblink conditioning relationships in humans is not yet possible. In rabbits, Purkinje cell counts have been carried out using histological techniques after training in EBCC. In these studies the correlations between Purkinje cell number and acquisition of CRs were high (Coffin et al., 1996; Woodruff-Pak et al., 1990), suggesting that Purkinje cell loss may account for much of the age-related difference in eyeblink conditioning.

Purkinje cell loss in the cerebellar cortex is the most observable and documented result of investigations of age differences in the human cerebellum (Flood & Coleman, 1988; Hall et al., 1975). These post-mortem studies are cross-sectional and thus cannot establish a rate of loss, but age differences appear throughout adulthood rather than only in old age. On the other hand, cell loss in the medial temporal lobes, a major brain substrate for declarative learning and memory, may occur later in life (West, 1993). Radiological studies of age differences in the hippocampus identified apparent tissue shrinkage in one-third of elderly participants who also had significantly impaired declarative memory function (Golomb et al., 1993). These patterns of brain aging coupled with behavioral data on age effects in declarative memory measures and EBCC led us to predict that in the same individuals, age differences in EBCC would appear by the age of 50. The hypothesis was supported, with significant age differences in conditioning appearing by the decade of the 40s (Woodruff-Pak & Jaeger, 1997).

EBCC and neurodegenerative disease in old age. Eyeblink conditioning may have significance for neuropsychology in the investigation of learning and memory in neurodegenerative disease, as well as for the study of learning, memory, and normal aging. The medial temporal lobe circuitry that forms the substrate for declarative learning and memory is not essential for simple EBCC. Although the hippocampus is not essential for EBCC, hippocampal function can affect the rate of acquisition of CRs. For this reason the hippocampus is said to play a modulatory role in EBCC (Berger et al., 1986). Disruption of muscarinic receptors in the septo-hippocampal cholinergic system with scopolamine injections impairs acquisition of EBCC in rabbits (Harvey et al., 1983; Moore et al., 1976; Solomon et al., 1983) and humans (Solomon et al., 1993).

Acquisition and retention of EBCC occurred in the well-studied, profoundly amnesic human subject, HM, who had bilateral removal of the medial temporal lobe structures, including most of hippocampus (Woodruff-Pak, 1993). Results with HM suggest that EBCC occurs in humans in spite of the absence of the hippocampus. Other investigators have also reported relatively normal acquisition in the delay paradigm in amnesic patients with medial temporal lobe lesions (Daum et al., 1989; Daum et al., 1991; Gabrieli et al., 1995b; Weiskrantz & Warrington, 1979). These results with humans are consistent with observations in hippocampectomized rabbits in the delay paradigm (Schmaltz & Theios, 1972; Solomon & Moore, 1975; Solomon et al., 1983).

An abnormally functioning hippocampus impairs EBCC, but the absence of a hippocampus does not (Solomon et al., 1983). The memory is not stored in the hippocampus, but the hippocampus can markedly influence the storage process. Woodruff-Pak et al. (1989) pointed out that this modulatory role for the hippocampus may be particularly significant in Alzheimer's disease (AD). In humans, AD appears to profoundly alter hippocampal neuronal function. A major disruption of the brain cholinergic system occurs, impairing cholinergic innervation of cortical and hippocampal neurons. Experimental procedures disrupting hippocampal cholinergic function, such as microinjections of scopolamine to the medial septum (Salvatierra & Berry, 1989) and lesions of the medial septum (Berry & Thompson, 1979), prolong the rate of acquisition of EBCC in rabbits. These data from the animal model led to the prediction that AD patients, having hippocampal dysfunction, would show poorer EBCC than normal adults. That prediction was supported (Woodruff-Pak et al., 1990) and replicated and extended (Woodruff-Pak & Papka, 1996a; Woodruff-Pak et al., 1996), and it has been independently replicated (Solomon et al., 1991).

Adults with Down's syndrome (DS) develop AD-like neuropathology by age 35 and are thus referred to as DS/AD patients. Forty-four adults with DS above and below age 35 were tested to see if EBCC would be sensitive to the presumed AD-like neuropathology in DS/AD (Woodruff-Pak, Papka, & Simon, 1994). Cognitive and behavioral test performance were also assessed. Adults with DS/AD conditioned more poorly than DS adults below age 35, but there were no age differences on cognitive and behavioral measures. In addition, DS/AD subjects performed similarly to AD patients. On the other hand, older adults with fragile X syndrome performed EBCC like normal older adults.

EBCC is severely and consistently impaired in probable AD, presumably due to normal age-related changes in the cerebellum (i.e., Purkinje cell loss) and AD-related hippocampal cholinergic disruption. Less consistent impairment and more variable EBCC performance was expected in patients with cerebrovascular dementia (CVD). It was anticipated that some CVD patients should show impairment in EBCC when their lesions affected the EBCC circuitry, whereas others with lesions in non-critical regions should have normal EBCC. As predicted, variability in EBCC performance was greater in patients with CVD than in probable AD patients (Woodruff-Pak et al.,

1996). Average performance of CVD patients was significantly better than probable AD patients.

On the basis of what is known about the neural circuitry essential for or normally involved in EBCC, the pattern of neurodegeneration in Huntington's disease (HD) would not appear to interfere with this type of learning. HD causes severe atrophy of the basal ganglia and thinning and shrinkage of the cerebral cortex. However, the hippocampus and hippocampal cholinergic system remain relatively intact, as does the cerebellum. It was predicted that HD patients would perform like normal control subjects on EBCC, and the prediction was supported (Woodruff-Pak & Papka, 1996b).

It was anticipated that Parkinson's disease (PD) patients, like HD patients, would perform normally on EBCC because the cerebellum is not lesioned in PD, and the hippocampus is also relatively spared in non-demented PD patients. This prediction was borne out (Daum et al., 1996).

In chapter 2, EBCC was identified as a test that may assist in the early detection of AD. Here we have suggested that EBCC may have utility in differential diagnosis of dementia. Some discrimination between AD and CVD is possible with this test. Patients with HD and PD perform relatively normally in terms of the production of CRs.

Metamemory in older adults

Knowing about remembering – that is, knowing one's own capacities for memory – is what we mean by metamemory. Studies by Lachman et al. (1979) and Perlmutter (1978) suggested that metamemory is stable across the adult age span. Older people appear to know what facts they know or do not know as well as young adults do. Another aspect of metamemory, knowledge of skills needed to store information, may not be equal between young and older adults. Two experiments by Murphy et al. (1981) provided insights about age differences in this type of metamemory and also indicated ways in which the elderly might improve their memory skills. A series of pictures of common objects were given to young and older adult subjects to study. The aim was to recall the names of the objects in serial order. Some of the series were of memory-span length (5–7 items), some were of subspan length (two items less than memory span), and some were of supraspan length (two items more than memory span). Subjects were given as much time with the pictures as they wanted to enable them to study and rehearse the items. Older subjects spent considerably less time (20–30s less) studying both the span and supraspan length series, and their performance was much poorer than the performance of the young. For example, in the supraspan condition, the elderly got 73 percent of the items correct, while the young got 96 percent correct. The older subjects simply did not appreciate the difficulty of the task, and they did not practice enough with the longer lists to succeed. Most research comparing young and old on strategies indicates that the old are more cautious. In the Murphy et al. study, the aged were more careless in their study of items to remember.

Following up on these results, Murphy et al. (1981) performed a second experiment in which they required elderly subjects to spend at least as much time studying the items to be recalled as the young had spent in the first experiment. The older subjects had to increase the time they spent with span-length series to 32 s, and they were made to study supraspan-length series for 59 s. Forced to study in this manner, the older adults recalled as many series without error as did the young subjects in the first experiment.

The Murphy et al. (1981) study has important implications for researchers interested in memory and aging, as well as for the aged in real life. In the Canestrari (1963) study of paired-associate learning, self-pacing helped older adults, but they still performed more poorly than the young. Maybe the older people underestimated the time *needed* to study and learn the lists. Perhaps older individuals overestimate their own competence and fail to give themselves sufficient time to rehearse the items.

In the real world, the elderly may terminate their rehearsal of material they need to learn too soon. With a little more time and effort put into study and practice of the to-be-remembered material, the aged might find that their memory is not failing at all. Maybe it is patience with practicing that declines with age, rather than memory capacity! If the elderly were to recognize that there is only a moderate change in the capacity to learn and remember, they might be willing to make a bit more effort to deeply process and rehearse what they learn. The reward could be memory performance in old age at the level the individual had maintained throughout his or her young adult life.

Memory and life review

From a clinical perspective, it is important to understand the issues that occupy the interest and emotional investment of older adults. Psychiatrist and geriatrician Robert Butler has emphasized the significance of life review for the elderly. The late adulthood years, according to Erik Erikson (1968), are a time when the major psychosocial crisis revolves around the achievement of ego integration versus despair. It is a time when personal adjustment involves the ability to sort through the memories of one's life and pull them together into some kind of a meaningful whole.

Some years ago, Robert Butler (1963) emphasized the need for psychological adjustment in late life through the reminiscing process he called life review. Butler felt that an awareness of the closeness of death led elderly individuals to reminisce about the events of their life. Life review in Butler's conceptualization was less systematic than a chronological autobiography, as the individual might focus on a certain period of life or on certain limited aspects of life in his or her memories. While a preoccupation with one's past could result in depression, bitterness, and even anger, Butler felt that in many cases the insights gained from the life review process could lead to serenity and even wisdom in old age.

Robert Havighurst in his developmental task theory identifies adjustment to the death of a spouse and to one's own death as two of the developmental tasks of late life. Life review, including systematically undertaking one's own autobiography, is a means of adjusting to impending death. Much of what presents itself as late-life depression is really a grief reaction to the loss of loved ones. It is something that an individual experiences intensely for a period of time, but then the pain subsides. In the case of a spouse of many decades, it is a loss which can never be compensated. However, the intensity of the despair is reduced by time. Death is faced by individuals at all points in the life span, but it is associated with old age because that period of life is the natural time to die. Old age is usually the time of life that we are faced most frequently by death – of friends, loved ones, our spouse, and eventually ourselves.

Memory in older adults is remarkable, because events which occurred as long as a century or more ago are remembered so clearly. Consider the memory of a woman who has lived in California since 1949 and who, at the age of 89, typed out some of her early memories for the author. In the following passage, she was reminiscing about her girlhood in New York City in the early 1900s:

New York in the teens of the twentieth century was an exciting place in which to live. Father joined a boat club, and we had a boat on the Hudson. During the summer on in to late October we spent much time living on board and sailing all the waters around New York. We dug clams and picked wild plums on Sandy Hook. We anchored for weeks on the Shrewsbury River, and sitting on the back deck, we netted a pail full of crabs in a short time.

The nearby Carnegie Library was almost my daily haunt. Our school had special days to visit the Museum of Natural History where I learned so much about the peoples of the world and their cultures.

During fall and winter a favorite trip was to take the "L" to the Battery at the south end of Manhattan Island where we could see the magnificent New York harbor, the Statue of Liberty, the aquarium which was housed in Manhattan's first opera house, where the world-famous Lily Langtry had sung. My brother, Bud, and I were especially interested in watching the boat from Ellis Island unload the immigrants who were pouring into our land from all of the European countries. In that day there were no quotas, but there was a strict law that immigrants had to speak and read enough English to apply for citizenship (Woodruff-Pak, 1988, p. 413).

Now at the age of 102 years, this woman continues to reminisce about Christmases in Montclair, New Jersey, and the exciting life she led on the East Coast. She calls herself a "forty-niner" because she moved to California with her husband in 1949 (when she was 56 years old). Although her pleasant memories of her life in California are relatively clear, it is the earlier period of her life lived on the East Coast that she returns to in her memory most often.

People in late life have a particularly vivid imagination and memory for the past (Butler, 1963). They can recall with sudden and remarkable clarity early life events. Think of the detail contained in the autobiography excerpted above. She describes with great intensity sights, sounds, locations, and feelings she had in New York City almost a century ago. According to Butler, who is a psychiatrist, and quite contrary to the beliefs of the original psychoanalyst, Sigmund Freud, in old age during the life review process there is a renewed ability to free-associate and to bring up material from the unconscious.

Individuals realize that their own personal myth of invulnerability and immortality can no longer be maintained (Butler & Lewis, 1982, p. 59).

From the time that he first presented the concept of the life review, Butler (1963) has maintained that the process occurs universally in all persons sometime during the final years. Indeed, in the opening sentence of the original article, Butler wrote,

The universal occurrence of an inner experience or mental process of reviewing one's life in older people is postulated (Butler, 1963, p. 65).

Not all older people are completely aware that they are involved in reminiscence, and some may defend themselves from realizing its presence. Life review is spontaneous, and the memories are not particularly selected by the individual – rather, they emerge into consciousness. While life review is seen in other age groups, particularly during adolescence and middle age, the intensity and emphasis on putting one's life in order are most striking in old age, undoubtedly motivated by the conscious or unconscious awareness of impending death.

Human Behavior

It is common for the life review process to uncover feelings of regret that are increasingly painful. In severe forms reminiscence can yield anxiety, guilt, despair, and depression. In extreme cases, when an individual is unable to resolve the previously experienced problems or to accept them, terror, panic, and even suicide can result. The most tragic life review is that in which a person decides that life was a total waste. Such outcomes do occur. Reichard et al. (1962) identified personality patterns they named the "Angry" and the "Self Hater," which were seen in men who after their retirement expressed feelings of the futility of their lives. The Angry men blamed others for their troubles, while the Self Haters blamed themselves. In his assessments of reminiscence characteristics, Coleman (1974) also observed depression as well as acceptance or satisfaction as outcomes of the life review.

Butler and Lewis (1982) have pointed out some of the positive results of the life review as being a righting of old wrongs, making up with enemies, coming to an acceptance of mortal life, developing a sense of serenity, feeling pride in accomplishment, and gaining a feeling of having done one's best. Reviewing one's life gives individuals the opportunity to decide what to do with the remaining months or years of their lives. They come to a recognition that emotional and material legacies must be worked out. While they are in no hurry to die, they are prepared for death.

Younger people may have the most difficult time with the life review process, when older relatives and friends want and need to discuss their legacies and put their affairs in order. Even listening thoughtfully to the reminiscences of older people may be difficult. However, the life review is a necessary and healthy process which is to be encouraged in older adults. Indeed, attempts are being made to develop life review therapy to aid older adults in undertaking this process (Lewis & Butler, 1974; Merriam, 1980). Life review can also be conducted as part of a group activity. Groups of all kinds such as nursing home residents, senior center participants, social groups, church groups, and therapy groups can engage in the life review to help older individuals re-evaluate their lives (Dietsche, 1979). Several guidebooks to aid groups and individuals in the life review are available (Hendricks, 1979; Daniel, 1980), and Butler and Lewis (1982) urge friends, relatives, and mental health professionals to be supportive and attentive when older adults reminisce, because life review is a necessary and essential aspect of the final stage of life.

Summary

An annoying outcome of advancing years is the decline in the efficiency of learning and memory processes. In most older adults the decline is mild to moderate, but it is severe in a significant subset of the elderly population. It is often as a consequence of memory impairment that older adults are referred to a clinical neuropsychologist.

There is evidence for two major forms of memory systems, called declarative and nondeclarative. These memory systems have been classified into forms that rely on medial temporal lobe brain circuitry (declarative) and forms that do not depend on the medial temporal lobe circuitry (nondeclarative). Age-related deficits are most pronounced in declarative forms of learning and memory. However, some types of nondeclarative learning and memory, such as simple classical conditioning, also show significant age-related deficits.

Even when serious attempts have been made to use memory improvement techniques for older adults, performance of the elderly is seldom brought to the level of young adults. Nevertheless, older adults can be trained to make modest improvements of performance on memory tasks. These improvements do not necessarily translate to real life. Although cognitive processing deficiency may account for some of the age-related differences in performance on memory tasks, it is likely that neurobiological changes that are more resistant to intervention also contribute to the deficits.

In addition to the medial temporal lobe circuitry for declarative learning and memory, there are other structures that can be damaged and result in amnesia. The diencephalon and mammillary bodies are impaired in Korsakoff's syndrome, and assessments of patients with lesions to the medial thalamus from causes other than alcoholism have demonstrated a role for these structures in memory. Profound retrograde amnesia with some anterograde amnesia is observed when there is damage to these diencephalic structures.

Nondeclarative forms of learning and memory do not comprise a unitary memory system. Tasks operationally defined as nondeclarative include repetition priming (occipital cortex substrate), acquisition and retention of motor, perceptual, or problem-solving skills (motor cortex substrate and in some cases basal ganglia), simple classical conditioning (cerebellar substrate), and non-associative learning (substrate in reticular formation and other sensory brain regions). These various brain substrates of nondeclarative learning and memory are non-overlapping and remote from one another and are affected differently by processes of aging.

The occipital cortex is relatively spared in normal aging, and repetition priming is performed about as well by older adults as it is by young adults. Motor cortex and basal ganglia are somewhat spared by aging as well, and motor skill learning is relatively preserved by processes of aging. The cerebellar cortex loses a significant number of Purkinje cells, and this loss may be related to dramatic age differences occurring early in adulthood in the decade of the 40s in eyeblink classical conditioning. Eyeblink conditioning is preserved in HD and PD with damage to basal ganglia and motor cortex. Disruption of the septo-hippocampal system in AD and DS/AD is likely the cause of severe impairment of eyeblink conditioning in patients with these conditions.

Some evidence suggests that older adults' knowledge about their own capacities for memory is stable across the adult age span. Older people appear to know what facts they know or do not know as well as young adults do. Another aspect of metamemory, knowledge of skills needed to store information, may not be equal between young and older adults. Older adults appeared to underestimate the time and effort required to study word lists to successfully remember the words later.

From a clinical perspective, it is important to understand the issues that occupy the interest and emotional investment of older adults. One domain that occupies the thought of many elderly is the people and events that have affected them throughout their lives. In thinking deeply about the past, they are engaging in life review. The late adulthood years are a time when personal adjustment may involve the ability to sort through memories and pull them together into some kind of a meaningful whole. Psychological adjustment in late life for many older adults involves the reminiscing process called life review. Helping the older adult to integrate his or her memories may be a significant contribution that the clinical neuropsychologist can make.

Further Reading

Golomb, J., de Leon, M. J., Kluger, A., George, A. E., Tarshish, C., & Ferris, S. H. (1993). Hippocampal atrophy in normal aging. *Archives of Neurology, 50,* 967–973.

One of the rare and valuable articles in which declarative memory tests and imaging data are presented together.

Bahrick, H. P., Hall, L. K., & Berger, S. A. (1996). Accuracy and distortion in memory for high school grades. *Psychological Science, 7,* 265–271.

New data on the accuracy of very long-term memory.

Craik, F. I. M. (1991). Memory functions in normal aging. In T. Yanigihara & R. C. Peterson (Eds.), *Memory disorders: Research and clinical practice* (pp. 347–367). New York: Marcel Dekker.

A review by a major authority on memory and aging of the age-related effects on declarative memory.

Heindel, W. C., Salmon, D. P., Shults, C. W., Walicke, P. A., & Butters, N. (1988). Neuropsychological evidence for multiple implicit memory systems: A comparison of Alzheimer's, Huntington's, and Parkinson's disease patients. *The Journal of Neuroscience, 9,* 582–587.

One of the early clarifying statements about the dissociation of different tests of nondeclarative memory.

Fleischman, D. A., Gabrieli, J. D., Reminger, S., Rinaldi, J., Morrell, & Wilson, R. (1995). Conceptual priming in perceptual identification for patients with Alzheimer's disease and a patient with right occipital lobectomy. *Neuropsychology, 9,* 187–197.

This article contributes to the identification of the brain locus in occipital lobes for priming and compares impaired performance with an occipital lesion to performance by patients with Alzheimer's disease.

Campbell, R., & Conway, M. A. (Eds.). (1995). *Broken memories: Case studies in memory impairment.* Oxford: Blackwell.

A fascinating series of case studies, some of whom are older adults.

12

Language and Communication

Language is a cognitive capacity unique to humans that is rapidly acquired early in the life span. The extensive research literature on language acquisition focuses primarily on the first 5 years of life. However, knowledge about the neurological substrates of language originated from observations of brain damage in adults. Indeed, the history of the neuropsychology of adulthood and aging can be traced to studies of brain function in language. Insights about the role of brain damage in affecting language capacity gave early neurologists and neuropsychologists their initial perspective on localization of function.

Brain and language: early perspectives

Although he has been discredited for his preoccupation with phrenology (relating bumps on the skull to cognitive and behavioral capacities of individuals, see figure 12.1), it was Franz Josef Gall (1758–1828) who first reported a relationship between damage to the left frontal lobe and language impairment. Gall's insight is documented in his report of a soldier who received a knife wound that penetrated the left frontal hemisphere. The soldier developed aphasia, and Gall related the brain damage to the inability to articulate.

This observation of a localized brain region being associated with a cognitive function languished for 50 years while Gall's notions of localization of function were discredited. The idea was revived in 1825 by Jean Baptiste Bouillaud (1796–1881) when he read a paper to the Royal Academy of Medicine in France based on his clinical work. Bouillaud asserted that language function was localized in the left frontal lobe, and he also suggested that the left cerebral cortex might control the right side of the body. Eleven

Figure 12.1 A nineteenth-century cartoon lampooning the "science" of phrenology which associated complex psychological factors with prominent landmarks on the face and head

Source: Posner, M. I., & Raichle, M. E. (1994). *Images of mind*. New York: Scientific American Library

years later, in 1836, Marc Dax presented a paper in Montpellier, France, reporting his clinical cases consistently demonstrating that speech disorders were associated with left hemisphere damage. This manuscript was published by Dax's son in 1865.

Almost a century had elapsed since Gall first suggested that language was localized in the left cerebral cortex, but the idea had still not received acceptance or even wide recognition. The son-in-law of Jean Bouillaud, Ernest Auburtin, set in motion the events that eventually led to the widespread dissemination of this idea. Auburtin gave a presentation in Paris early in the year 1861 at the Anthropological Society and described several patients with left frontal lobe damage and speech impairment. He challenged the audience in the following manner:

> I saw him [the patient} again recently and his disease has progressed; slight paralysis has appeared but his intelligence is still unimpaired, and speech is wholly abolished. Without a doubt this man will soon die. Based on the symptoms that he presents we have diagnosed softening of

the anterior lobes. If, at autopsy, these lobes are found to be intact, I shall renounce the ideas that I have just expounded to you (Stookey, 1954, p. 563).

Among those attending Auburtin's lecture that night was the founder of the Anthropological Society, the surgeon Paul Broca (1824–1880). Apparently Broca was impressed with Auburtin's ideas, and then a coincidence occurred that had major significance for neuropsychology. Five days after the lecture, a 51-year-old patient named Leborgne came to Broca's attention. This man was paralyzed on the right side and had extremely limited speech. He could only say "tan" and an oath ("Sacre nom de Dieu!"). The patient had spent the last 21 years in a French hospital, so his condition was longstanding. Broca invited Auburtin to see this patient whom they named Tan, and together they predicted that Tan would have a left frontal lesion.

On April 17, 1861 Tan died, and Broca performed the autopsy. Indeed, Tan had an anterior left lesion (and considerably more damage in the left cerebral hemisphere. Tan's brain was preserved, lost, and rediscovered in Paris in recent years). Broca concluded that the aphasia was associated with damage to the third convolution of the left frontal lobe. This region is now called Broca's area. By 1863 Broca had collected and published a report on eight additional cases of speech impairment associated with left frontal lesions. He is credited with describing the behavioral syndrome, called aphasia, that consists of the inability to speak in spite of intact vocal mechanisms and normal comprehension. The notion of brain lateralization and cerebral dominance is also attributed to Paul Broca who stated, "We speak with our left hemisphere."

Because there was a long history of documented insights about the association between the left frontal lobe and speech, it is seemingly inappropriate that Paul Broca should receive the credit for these observations. It has been pointed out that Broca acknowledged the prior contributions of Gall, Bouillaud, Dax, and Auburtin (Kolb & Whishaw, 1995). What Broca did was to lend his considerable prestige to the heretofore discredited notion of localization of function. He also provided many additional detailed clinical case studies and performed the autopsies documenting left anterior cortical involvement. His renown drew the attention of scientists and laypeople to neuropsychology and resulted in us using his name to this day in the syndrome Broca's aphasia, and the brain region Broca's area.

Broca's aphasia

Lesions to the left frontal region can occur from a variety of causes, including penetrating head injuries as described by the aphasic soldier Gall observed who suffered a knife wound in the left eye. From the perspective of aging, vascular disorders and tumors are a likely cause of brain damage. The incidence of both of these causes of brain damage increases dramatically in old age. Thus, age is the single greatest predictor of aphasia (Harasymieu et al., 1981; Obler et al., 1978). If a stroke or cerebral vascular accident affects brain tissue in the left frontal or superior left temporal region, the older adult is likely to become aphasic. The stroke produces an infarct, an area of dead or dying tissue resulting from an obstruction of blood vessels normally supplying the area. A tumor growing in the left hemisphere is another potential cause of aphasia because the adjacent tissue will be compressed and damaged. Removal of the tumor can also damage adjacent tissue. It has been noted that Wernicke's aphasia is more likely to occur in older patients, whereas Broca's aphasia is more likely in younger patients (Harasymieu et al., 1981; Obler et al., 1978). In part this may be due to the greater risk to younger patients of violence and accidents that would damage the frontal lobes, whereas the potential for stroke in the middle cerebral arteries that tends to have a late-life onset would put left middle to posterior cortex more at risk.

Recovery of function occurs, more in the case of Broca's than Wernicke's aphasia (Kolb & Whishaw, 1995). Again, these differences in recovery rate may occur in part due to the age of onset of the trauma. If Broca's area lesions tend to occur more often in younger adults, they would be more likely to experience a better prognosis. Tissue adjacent to the damaged tissue can take over some of the function of dead tissue, or the homologous site on the contralateral hemisphere (in this case the right cortex) can compensate for the loss of neural tissue. The degree of recovery depends on the size and location of the infarct as well as on the patient's motivation and cooperation with the therapist.

Brain damage that is limited to Broca's area results in a syndrome of impaired speech production but relatively normal comprehension. A Broca's area lesion impairs speech production because the patterns for sounds and for the structure of language are blocked from reaching motor cortex (see figure 12.2). This syndrome, Broca's aphasia, causes the patient to talk as little as possible because speech is extremely labored. It is difficult for the patient to articulate words, and sentences are incomplete. In spite of the inability to express themselves, Broca's aphasics understand everything that is said to them.

When neuropsychologists assess aphasia, they use test material such as the well-known "cookie-theft" illustration (Goodglass & Kaplan, 1972; figure 12.3). The limited description that a patient with Broca's aphasia might give to that picture is:

Cookie jar . . . fall over . . . chair . . . water . . . empty (Goodglass & Kaplan, 1983, p. 76).

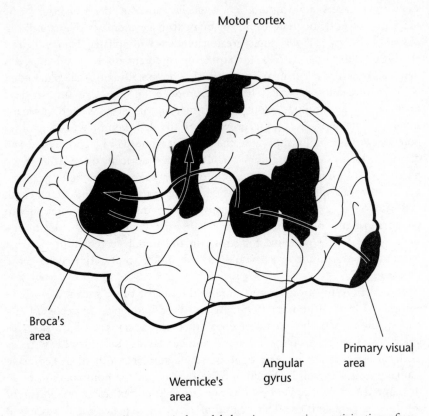

Figure 12.2 Geschwind's anatomical model showing successive participation of several brain areas as a person speaks a written word. The model was based on Wernicke's ideas of brain and language function. To speak a word that is heard, the circuit would involve a starting point at primary auditory cortex (on the superior temporal lobe), and then the information would travel to Wernicke's area, Broca's area, and motor cortex

Broca's aphasia appears to be a disorder in which the essential grammatical components of speech are absent. The patient is reduced to short utterances that tend to lack words describing function (e.g., articles and prepositions) and inflections (e.g., -s, -ed, -ing). When some time has passed so that the brain has recovered from the initial trauma, patients with this form of aphasia may have speech patterns that are telegraphic. The structure of the communication resembles the form of expression in telegrams. Goodglass (1993) gave the following example of telegraphic speech observed in a patient with

Figure 12.3 The "cookie theft" picture used in testing for aphasia
Source: Goodglass, H., & Kaplan, E. (1972). *The assessment of aphasia and related disorders.*
Philadelphia: Lea & Febiger

Broca's aphasia, "Joan and I . . . coffee." The idea is communicated, although
the form is limited.

In addition to difficulty in producing language and telegraphic speech,
patients with Broca's aphasia have difficulty comprehending sentences with
complex syntactic construction. Sentences with embedded clauses are difficult
for these patients to understand. For example, they understand, "The child
was petting the rabbit and fed it a carrot." However, when the clause is
embedded, they become confused: "The child who was petting the rabbit fed
it a carrot." Nevertheless, most sentences are clearly comprehended by
patients with Broca's aphasia, and a clear symptom of this form of brain
damage is superior language comprehension to language production.

Wernicke's aphasia

Broca crystallized localizationist thinking and focused attention on the left
frontal lobe. Within 15 years of Broca's initial report on Tan, Carl Wernicke
(1848–1904) successfully challenged the strict localizationalist view of Broca
and presented a theory of the neuroanatomy of language that has been
revived to contribute to the contemporary perspective of language function.

In 1874, at the age of 26, Wernicke described a type of aphasia that now carries his name, along with a left temporal lobe region for language comprehension that is called Wernicke's area.

The language region identified by Wernicke is located on the superior surface of the left temporal lobe, just posterior to the primary auditory region. Damage to that region results in Wernicke's aphasia, fluid speech that is relatively devoid of meaning. Comprehension but not production of language is impaired in Wernicke's aphasia. The patient responds, but the response is meaningless.

The Wernicke–Geschwind model of brain and language function

By identifying a second language region in the brain, Wernicke elaborated localizationist views. He expanded the localizationist perspective additionally by describing disconnection syndromes. In describing the neural circuitry for language, Wernicke postulated that the posterior comprehension region (Wernicke's area) had to be connected to the anterior production region (Broca's area). This pathway was later identified as the arcuate fasciculus. Norman Geschwind (1974) reintroduced Wernicke's language circuit in the mid-twentieth century, and the Wernicke–Geschwind model of brain and language function is still the basis for contemporary understanding (Kandel et al., 1995). Brain structures involved in the Wernicke–Geschwind model are illustrated in figure 12.2.

The Wernicke–Geschwind model made predictions that are useful clinically. A lesion in Wernicke's area results in impairment in language comprehension. Spoken words that reach the auditory cortex fail to activate Wernicke's area and cannot be comprehended. If the lesion extends posteriorly into the angular gyrus, then the visual input of words cannot be deciphered and the patient cannot read. This feature of the model receives some support from clinical data, but PET data of normal adults reading words and speaking them do not show activation in Wernicke's area or in the angular gyrus region (Petersen et al., 1989). It was suggested that well-known visual words are not necessarily recoded to their phonological representation in Wernicke's area when read aloud. Petersen et al. (1989) speculated that the reading and speaking paradigm used in their study activated a pathway from visual perception (occipital cortex) to speech (motor cortex) that simply bypassed the functions of Wernicke's area. Many cognitive models predict that language processing in the brain can proceed through several parallel pathways, and the PET data can be used to support a parallel processing model (Posner & Raichle, 1994).

Recall the "cookie-theft" illustration shown in figure 12.3. A patient with Wernicke's aphasia had the following response to that picture:

Well this is . . . mother is away here working her work out o' here to get her better, but when she's looking, the two boys looking in the other part. One their small tile into her time here. She's working another time because she's getting to. So two boys work together and one is sneakin' around here, making his work an' his further *funnas* his time he had (Goodglass & Kaplan, 1983, pp. 81–82).

The language of this patient is reasonably fluent, including the use of relatively complex sentence structure. However, the content of the speech is meaningless, to the point that it even also contains a nonsense word. Characteristic of Wernicke's aphasia is normal speech production, but the absence of comprehension.

A common type of cerebrovascular accident in which the blood supply is cut off from a region of the cortex causing ischemia (a loss of oxygen) and eventually resulting in an area of dysfunctional or dead neural tissue (called a stroke or infarction) occurs with relative frequency after the age of 60. These strokes often occur as the result of the gradual buildup of deposited lipids in the arteries providing blood supply to the brain. As part of normal aging, arteries become constricted and the inner walls are enlarged with a lining of lipids. However, this buildup is exacerbated by excessive cholesterol and smoking. The case of Beth, who had Wernicke's aphasia, resulted from this type of stroke. Beth suffered a large left temporo-parietal stroke as the result of a blockage of her left middle cerebral artery. She was a native New Zealander who had lived on a sheep farm for her entire life and was a large consumer of sheep meat as well as rich dairy products. In addition, she had been previously treated for hypertension, and she had been a heavy smoker from the age of 16. She had a number of risk factors for stroke: high cholesterol, high blood pressure, and heavy smoking.

The clinical neuropsychologist who described Beth's case, Jenni A. Ogden (1996), pointed out that Beth's ability to comprehend spoken or written language was severely impaired, but her spoken language was fluent. If a person did not attend carefully to the content of the speech, they might think it was normal. However, anyone attempting to understand Beth's speech quickly realized that her sentences typically made no sense. Beth, herself, did not appear particularly concerned with her receptive language impairment at first, because she was not aware of her impairment. On the other hand, her family was immediately concerned with her loss of ability to communicate with them. As Beth's condition improved she, too, experienced frustration with her inability to communicate.

Ogden described Beth's case of receptive aphasia as follows:

Beth lived an active life in a rural community from the time of her marriage to a farmer at the age of 21 until she awoke one morning confused and muddled in her speech. The previous day she had celebrated her 62nd birthday with her husband and her three adult children and their families. She had retired to bed in the early evening, well before the festivities were over, complaining that she felt very tired. Her husband later recalled that he had noticed that her speech had become a little jumbled after dinner, but he had attributed this to the excitement of the day and her fatigue. In retrospect, Beth may have been suffering from a transient ischemic attack (TIA) caused by spasm and narrowing of her left middle cerebral artery and a decrease in the blood flow and oxygen supply to the posterior part of her left hemisphere. During the night this developed into a full stroke.

In the morning her doctor visited Beth and, after diagnosing a stroke, called an ambulance to transport her the 80 kilometers to Auckland Hospital. A CT scan of her brain some 15 hours or longer after her suspected stroke showed an area of low density in the region of her left temporoparietal cortex, and an angiogram demonstrated a complete blockage of the inferior division of her left middle cerebral artery. She was started on warfarin, a drug that causes thinning of the blood and thus sometimes allows blood to pass through a narrowed vessel, reversing a thrombotic stroke. Unfortunately, the medication did not improve Beth's condition. That area of her cortex had been deprived of oxygen for too long and a nonreversible infarction had resulted.

Beth's speech was fluent and reasonably melodic but often almost incomprehensible. She frequently seemed to have an understanding of the general meaning of what was said to her, although this was sometimes difficult to assess because of her jumbled speech, punctuated with many phonemic paraphasias. She seemed unable to repeat words or sentences, although repetition was difficult to assess properly because of her poor ability to understand instructions. When she was shown a page of writing, she attempted to read it aloud, but again her words often came out as paraphasias, although she occasionally read single words correctly. She was given a paper and pencil and asked to write her name. She managed this, although when she got to the *t* of "Beth," she wrote it four times before writing the *h*.

Beth did not seem particularly upset or frustrated by her difficulties, and she happily chatted to her family whenever there was a gap in their conversation. She almost certainly had a right visual-field defect, given the location of her infarct, although this was difficult to test accurately because of her inability to follow verbal instructions. She had no limb weakness, but she could not feel light touch on her right arm (as a result of damage to her primary sensory cortex).

The following transcript of a conversation I [J. A. Ogden] had with Beth about two weeks following her stroke, provides a good illustration of her fluent but confused oral language and impaired comprehension, typical of jargon or Wernicke's aphasia.

JAO: Do you like to be called Elizabeth or Beth?

Beth: [*Laughing*] Oh no, I've got to be called Beth.

JAO: Do you know where you are now?

Beth: Oh yes, its 200 and just a 150 millibits from where my. . . . Where the hell am I now . . . from down here.

JAO: So where do you live?

Beth: I live away down from up here.

JAO: What is it called, do you remember? Can you say the name of the place?

Beth: This is W-------- . . . and you go up to O-------- . . . and you keep on up to there to W-------- . . . and that's 200 kiraneekers, and that' my plin. [*Beth's pronunciation of the Maori place names was correct or almost correct.*]

JAO: Is it by the sea?

Beth: No, its about, about three minutes from here, and then it comes out. [*Laughs*] Can you fix that one up?

JAO: Can I understand that? Not all of it.

Beth: No.

JAO: Do you know what you're saying inside your head?

Beth: Oh yes, [*laughs*] oh yes, I don't know that alright.

JAO: What does it sound like to you when it comes out?

Beth: Well he's . . . umm . . . well he's never been, you see, you can't, you can't fill the nimbufill [*laughs*] sillo.

JAO: It must be very frustrating.

Beth: I know what I sing, oh yes, I know the truth. The sillo banger. I don't say nothing thats frivo, 'cause I think its impilivariver, and its what you fancy with you can care a little bit of patrinta. You get the next one, and you come and get the ne-e-xt one, and you can't get that one . . .

JAO: And you can't get that word. Oh, it must be really frustrating. . . .

Beth remained in the hospital for three weeks; although she had speech therapy daily, no improvement was noted in either her speech or comprehension. At the end of the second week, she began to demonstrate some frustration at times. . . .

Beth was transferred to a private nursing home, where she remained until her death from a second, much more extensive stroke four years later. During that four years, her speech and comprehension did not improve (Ogden, 1996, pp. 87–89).

One of the values of this case study is to illustrate that there was some comprehension in this patient with Wernieke's aphasia. The theoretical postulates about the damage are seldom exactly met in real life cases.

A prediction initially made by Carl Wernicke and revived by Geschwind was that lesions of Broca's area would not impair comprehension. This is more or less the case, although patients with left anterior lesions in Broca's area have occasional trouble hearing the articles in a stream of speech, and they also have trouble understanding the same word categories that they cannot say – prepositions, conjunctions, and other relational words (Grossman et al., 1986). Frequently, speech is intelligible even without the relational words, but sometimes meaning depends heavily on relational words. In the second sentence in the example given above about the boy and the rabbit, it might be unclear to the patient with Broca's aphasia that the boy was feeding the rabbit a carrot.

Another prediction, made initially by Wernicke, that received empirical support was that lesions of the arcuate fasciculus (causing "disconnection syndromes") disrupt the neural signals initiated at Wernicke's area and prevent them from reaching Broca's area. Both speech sounds and comprehension are intact, but speech is impaired because the person cannot judge the meaning of the words that have been uttered.

One of the contributions of Broca and Wernicke was to identify the aphasias as disturbances of language ability, a cognitive capacity, rather than simply disturbances of mechanical output. Deficits in the muscles controlling the vocal apparatus can dramatically impair speech. In old age, Parkinson's disease causes dysphonia, a disturbance in vocalization. It is a deficit in the muscles controlling the vocal apparatus rather than a deficit of language comprehension or grammatical production. Despite severe speech impairment, non-demented Parkinson's patients retain their language ability. Their cognitive capacity for language is intact, although the speech output is impaired.

The Wernicke–Geschwind model continues to have clinical utility, but recent cognitive and imaging studies have identified several ways in which the model is likely oversimplified. As mentioned previously, in the case of an infarct, tissue surrounding the dead and dying tissue can compensate to some degree for the lost function. Recent studies have found that lesions restricted to the limited areas identified by Broca and Wernicke do not give the full symptoms characteristic of Broca's or Wernicke's aphasia.

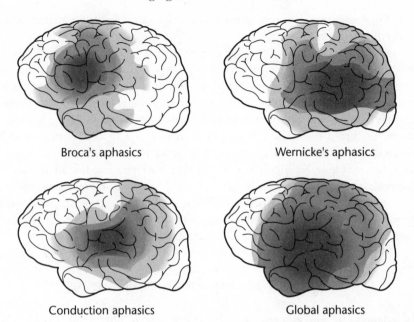

Broca's aphasics Wernicke's aphasics

Conduction aphasics Global aphasics

Figure 12.4 Composite radioisotope brain scan of patients with Broca's, Wernicke's, conduction, and global aphasia. The darker regions indicate areas where the lesions of many individual patients overlap. The isotope scans operate on the principle that the labeled compound can cross the blood-brain barrier in damaged tissue but not in healthy cortical regions

Source: Beatty, J. (1995). *Principles of behavioral neuroscience*. Madison, WI: Brown & Benchmark

For example, Broca's classic case, Tan, had large lesions in the left hemisphere, some of which were posterior and included Wernicke's area. The characteristic symptoms of Wernicke's and Broca's aphasias were associated with lesions much larger than lesions limited to discrete Broca's or Wernicke's areas. Furthermore, lesions in a wide region of cerebral cortex can result in symptoms characteristic of Broca's or Wernicke's aphasia (figure 12.4).

The Wernicke–Geschwind model emphasized cortical regions and subcortical fibers of passage. Evidence has accumulated that subcortical *structures* as well as pathways are involved in language function (Ojemann, 1975). For example, nuclei in the left thalamus and the left caudate nucleus (a nucleus in the basal ganglia) are thought to be involved in integration of auditory (thalamus) and motor (caudate nucleus) processing. The cerebellum is activated in some cases of language production, for example in the generation of verbs (Petersen et al., 1989).

The pathways used for speaking a word that has been read do not follow the route proposed by Wernicke and later by Geschwind. PET data suggest that written words that are processed through the visual system do not travel through Wernicke's area at all. Rather, the signals reach the motor cortex directly from visual association cortex (Posner & Raichle, 1994). In many cases, neither Broca's nor Wernicke's areas are activated during speech reception or production. In part, this may occur because the language stimuli used in the studies are highly over-learned and are processed in an automatic fashion, bypassing centers originally essential for their comprehension and production. On the other hand, PET data suggest the existence of parallel processing and complex involvement of more brain structures than those included in Wernicke's theory elaborated by Geschwind.

Language ability in normal aging

In chapter 10 we pointed out that even during the period when the perspective of unilateral decline of intelligence with aging prevailed, it was acknowledged that vocabulary showed stability or even increment from young to older adulthood. Two early investigations on intelligence and age were carried out with samples of old people in hospitals and nursing homes, and compared them to healthy younger individuals (Beeson, 1920; Foster & Taylor, 1920). In both of these studies, even though the older adults were institutionalized, their performance on the vocabulary subtest was comparable to the performance of young adults.

Longitudinal data on adults' performance on psychometric intelligence tests were first reported by Owens (1953) who retested middle-aged men 31 years after they were initially tested as college freshmen. Four of the subtests, including the vocabulary subtest, showed statistically significant improvement. Two additional longitudinal studies which appeared in the 1950s replicated Owens (1953). The greatest gain was shown in the vocabulary subtest (Bayley & Oden, 1955; Jones, 1959).

Vocabulary is a relatively simple aspect of language ability, and it might still be thought that speech processing should decline with age. However, this is typically not the case. Older adults may complain about many aspects of cognition, in particular their memory, but they rarely complain about problems of understanding language. "The elderly may endure many stereotypes, but an inevitable decline in communicative functioning is generally not among them" (Bayles et al., 1987, p. 133).

Older adults, like their younger counterparts, use the natural context and redundancy of language to understand speech, and older adults sometimes benefit even more than young adults from effective use of context in speech recognition and recall (Tun & Wingfield, 1993). Older adults apparently compensate for age-related sensory deficits (in vision and audition) with an increased use of semantic information available in sentence context.

Our discussion of neuropsychological testing for the elderly in chapter 2 also emphasized the point that language function is typically maintained in older adults. The time and amount of neuropsychological testing set aside for language skills in the elderly is limited, unless there is evident impairment. Nevertheless, when we examine the research literature on language ability in normal aging, it appears that in late life this capacity is not totally preserved.

Age-related decline in selected linguistic functions

If vocabulary is one of the best maintained linguistic abilities, the capacity to access words to name objects is an ability clearly impaired by aging. Problems in accessing words, commonly called "tip-of-the-tongue" phenomena, are experienced at all ages, but in old age such problems increase (Bowles & Poon, 1985). The Boston Naming Test, discussed in chapter 2, provides a direct neuropsychological assessment of the ability to name objects when they are presented in pictures. In adults between the ages of 30 and 50 years naming performance was similar, but adults in the decade of the 60s performed slightly worse and adults over the age of 70 showed clear impairment (Borod et al., 1980). This result has been replicated in different samples of young and older adults (Albert et al., 1988). The famous psychologist B. F. Skinner remarked on the increasing difficulty with naming and word retrieval in reflections on his own aging (Skinner, 1983).

In addition to experiencing an increased incidence of failure to name objects, there are qualitative changes in the nature of naming responses. Four types of qualitative naming errors were reported by La Rue (1992).

1 Circumlocutions – multiword responses providing accurate information (instead of naming with just one word).
2 Nominalizations – words describing the function of the pictured object rather than the object itself (e.g., "ringer" for the clapper of a bell).
3 Perceptual errors – misidentifications of the stimulus (e.g., "ruler" for slide rule).
4 Semantic association errors – responses that name an associate of the pictured object (e.g., "checkers" for chess pieces).

These errors may be an indication that the older respondents possess accurate information about the objects, but they cannot recall the precise name. The observations of neuropsychologists correlate well with what older adults say about naming. They say that they know the item, but that they just cannot think of the name.

Naming is not the only aspect of language that shows age-related deficits. Some aspects of language comprehension are also slightly impaired in older adults. Comprehension of complex sentences was evaluated in older adults by presenting the sentence to the participant and having him or her act out the meaning. There was stability of comprehension through the 60s, but adults aged 70 and older showed marked deficits in comprehension (Feier & Gerstman, 1980). Older adults have more difficulty comprehending, imitating, and producing grammatically complex sentences (Kemper, 1992). The organization, cohesion, quantity, and precision of discourse also show deficits in older adults (Critchley, 1984; Obler, 1989).

The observation of impairment in so many aspects of language function in older adults led investigators to suggest that linguistic functions, themselves, may be impaired by processes of aging (Ulatowska et al., 1985). What is debated at present is whether performance impairment on language tasks reflects changes in neural circuits such as those described in the Wernicke–Geschwind model, or whether the deficits occur as a secondary consequence to nonspecific changes in attention, perceptual acuity, processing speed, memory, and executive function.

Locus of age-related impairment in language

A singularly important factor in the assimilation of language is hearing acuity. Nearly 50 percent of adults aged 65 and older in the United States have some form of hearing impairment (White & Regan, 1987). Hearing impairment affects speech perception and therefore language ability. It has been argued that hearing loss is the major cause of language impairment in older adults (Sheridan, 1976). However, this interpretation is not supported by all of the data (Peach, 1987).

Another age-related phenomenon is the slowing of response speed. Older adults process information more slowly, and this can affect the comprehension of speech. When speech rate is increased, comprehension in older adults decreases (Konkle et al., 1977). In studies of more complex language abilities, it has been difficult to determine the extent to which the age-related deficits were due to the pervasive effects of hearing loss and slowing, and the extent to which the deficit resulted from impairments in language capacity itself. Assessing language processing, working memory, inhibitory efficiency, and processing speed in younger and older adults, it was found that language performance was best predicted by processing speed and inhibitory efficiency (Kwong See & Ryan, 1995).

Other investigations have also provided support for the hypothesis that age-related impairment in language function results from changes in nonlinguistic cognitive processes. The locus for age-related impairment in language does not appear to involve focal alterations in left hemisphere perisylvian structures that are known to be specialized for language processing. Rather, changes in language performance appear to result from impairments in attention, perception, speed, memory, and executive function (Glosser & Deser, 1992). Microlinguistic abilities that depend on the integrity of function in specialized neural systems in the left cerebral hemisphere were compared to macrolinguistic abilities that depend on nonfocal, bilateral neural systems in middle-aged and older adults. The microlinguistic structure of discourse was equivalent in middle-aged and older adults, but there was disruption of macrolinguistic abilities in older adults (Glosser & Deser, 1992). This pattern of results was most compatible with the interpretation that changes in linguistic performances observed in older adults were secondary to disruptions in diffusely represented, nonlinguistic cognitive processes.

Two samples of discourse exemplifying global incoherence in elderly adults are presented in table 12.1. Glosser and Deser (1992) pointed out that in both examples the internal organization of sentences was adequate, and each subsequent utterance was related to the last. However, in both examples, the overall topic of the discussion (family in the first example, work in the second example) is totally abandoned. Furthermore, the speakers never returned to the topic at hand. Rather, they failed to maintain a coherent reference to the general topic. These limitations suggest impairment of executive and inhibitory processes controlled by the frontal lobes, the topic of the next chapter.

Summary

Insights about the role of brain damage in affecting language capacity gave nineteenth-century neurologists their initial perspective on localization of function. Language is a cognitive ability that remains relatively stable in adulthood and old age. For neuropsychologists, language impairment in later life is more often the result of brain injury than it is the result of normal aging. This is the case because tumors and strokes that are the most frequent cause of language impairment are more common in old age.

It was Paul Broca who articulated and popularized the notion that language impairment was associated with the left cerebral hemisphere. Broca concluded that the aphasia was associated with damage to the third convolution of the left frontal lobe. This region is now called Broca's area. Carl Wernicke found Broca's strict localizationist ideas to be limiting in terms of the brain's role in language, and Wernicke identified a more posterior

Table 12.1 Samples of discourse illustrating disruption of macrolinguistic abilities

Coherence rating[a]		Verbalizations	Weighted index of subordination
Global	Local		

Example 1: Discourse about her family by a 78-year-old retired social worker

Global	Local	Verbalizations	Weighted
5	3	And my daughter lives up the street.	0
5	5	She's an artist.	0
2	3	And her friends come quite often.	0
1	4	And most of them are artists, I would say.	1
1	5	They keep journals.	0
1	5	And they write poetry.	0
1	3	And so we have a lot of fun.	0
1	3	And I write poetry too.	0
1	5	It's a kind of a hobby.	0

Example 2: Discourse about her previous work by a 77-year-old high-school graduate

Global	Local	Verbalizations	Weighted
3	5	I worked with a Greek man in the market.	0
2	5	He was an importer and wholesale grocer.	0
5	3	And I worked for him many many years until he retired, but then I was not ready to retire so I got another position which was in the similar field but a little different.	2
5	4	And I worked there for probably ten years.	0
1	1	Then my mother was quite elderly.	0
1	5	She was 96 when she died.	1
1	5	And even though her mentalities were perfect when she got older she began to break down physically.	3
1	5	The only problem she ever had was vascular.	1
1	4	And we used to go to a Dr E.O. who was a vascular doctor.	1
1	5	He was known in Boston probably as the best.	0
1	5	His office was on Beacon Street.	0

[a] A higher rating indicates greater coherence (range 1–5).
Source: Glosser & Deser, 1992, p. P272.

language center that came to bear his name. Wernicke also identified disconnection syndromes, language impairments associated with damage to the fibers of passage connecting Wernicke's to Broca's regions of the left hemisphere. Although clinical cases seldom reflect "pure" Broca's or Wernicke's aphasia symptoms, and although PET data indicate that in normal adults the classic brain centers associated with language are not all activated in speech processing, the model initiated by Wernicke in the nineteenth century and revived by Geschwind just after the mid-twentieth century still guides contemporary neuropsychological research and treatment of language disorders.

Vocabulary is one cognitive ability that increases with age. Language skills, more than most other aspects of cognition, remain relatively intact in the elderly. Older adults use the natural context and redundancy of language to understand speech and may benefit even more than young adults from effective use of context in speech recognition and recall. Age-related sensory deficits in hearing spoken language are compensated with an increased used of semantic information available in sentence context.

If vocabulary is one of the best-maintained linguistic abilities, the capacity to access words and to name objects is an ability impaired by aging. Problems in accessing words, commonly called "tip-of-the-tongue" phenomena, are experienced at all ages, but in old age such problems increase. In addition to experiencing an increased incidence of failures to name objects, there are qualitative changes in the nature of naming responses. Four qualitative changes in naming identified in older adults are: using several words instead of the appropriate one in naming; describing the function of the word rather than its name; misidentifying the word; and naming an associate of the object rather than the object itself. These observations of neuropsychologists about naming difficulties in older adults correlate well with what older adults say themselves. They say that they know the item, but that they just cannot think of the name.

In addition to problems with naming, older adults have more difficulty comprehending, imitating, and producing grammatically complex sentences. The organization, cohesion, quantity, and precision of discourse also show deficits in older adults. These deficits are not apparent in late-middle age. They typically appear in individuals only after they have passed, at a minimum, their 70th birthday. Performance impairment on language tasks may not reflect changes in neural circuits such as those described to comprise the Wernicke–Geschwind model. It is more likely that the deficits occur as a secondary consequence to nonspecific changes in attention, perceptual acuity, processing speed, memory, and executive function.

Hearing impairment affects speech perception and therefore language ability. It has been argued that hearing loss is the major cause of language impairment in older adults, but this interpretation is not supported by all of the data. In addition to hearing impairment, there are other factors affecting language and communication in older adults. One age-related phenomenon that possibly affects language comprehension is the slowing of response speed. Older adults process information more slowly, and this can affect the comprehension of speech. When speech rate is increased, comprehension in older adults decreases. In addition to sensory and speed factors, age-related impairment in language function also results from changes in nonlinguistic cognitive processes. The locus for age-related impairment in language does not appear to involve focal alterations in left hemisphere structures that are known to be specialized for language processing. Rather, the limited changes in language comprehension and performance that exist in older adults appear to result from impairments in attention, perception, speed, memory, and executive function.

Further Reading

Bayles, K. A., Kaszniak, A. W., & Tomoeda, C. K. (1987). *Communication and cognition in normal aging and dementia.* Boston: Little, Brown.
This book, written by experts in neuropsychology and aging, covers a wide range of topics on language ability in normal aging and dementia.

Glosser, G., & Deser, T. (1992). A comparison of changes in macrolinguistic and microlinguistic aspects of discourse production in normal aging. *Journal of Gerontology: Psychological Sciences, 47,* P266–272.
The sophisticated methods required of neuropsychologists to understand causes of age-related language deficits are presented.

Kwong See, S. T., & Ryan, E. B. (1995). Cognitive mediation of adult age differences in language performance. *Psychology and Aging, 10,* 458–468.
Another article illustrating the complexities of aging effects on language ability.

Goodglass, H. (1993). *Understanding aphasia.* San Diego, CA: Academic Press.
This book, written by the 1996 winner of the American Psychological Association Gold Metal Award for Life Achievement in the Application of Psychology, is already a classic.

13

Executive Function, Attention, and Working Memory

Throughout this book we have addressed the fact that frontal lobe function is affected dramatically by processes of aging. In chapter 2 some important measures of frontal lobe function were described, and in chapters 5 and 6 on normal and neuropathological brain aging, changes in the frontal lobe were detailed. Chapter 7 on emotion, aging, and brain function contained the case study of Phineas Gage, the first extensively described case study of the widespread effects of frontal lobe lesions. Frontal-lobe function was relevant to the topics of arousal and sleep in chapter 8, response speed and timing in chapter 9, and learning and memory in chapter 11. It cannot be overemphasized that frontal-lobe functions are central to the understanding of the neuropsychology of aging. Thus, the fact that this chapter on capacities engaging the frontal lobes, such as executive function, attention, and working memory, is relatively short might seem inconsistent with the significance of frontal-lobe function in normal and pathological aging. The fact is that frontal-lobe function has been addressed in many chapters of this book. Rather than repeat previously presented material, we will limit discussion to domains of frontal-lobe function that have yet to be described.

"Executive function" is one term that has been used to encompass the cognitive components controlled in the frontal lobes. Among these components are planning, organizing, thinking divergently, inhibiting, and self-monitoring. Attention and working memory are terms used for meta-cognitive processes controlled in the frontal lobes and affecting aspects of most cognitive behavior. There is overlap in the cognitive functions assessed using the terms executive function, attention, and working memory. However, the research encompassed under these three semi-overlapping terms has been carried out from somewhat different theoretical perspectives.

The term "executive function" is used primarily in neuropsychological studies in which assessment is carried out of frontal-lobe function in normal adults, adults with brain lesions, or normal older adults. Studies of working memory rely heavily on animal research in which direct assessment of neurophysiological function is made. Attention is a function studied in the domain of cognitive psychology, another discipline that has made significant contributions to the neuropsychology of aging. Executive function, working memory, and some aspects of attention have their neural substrate in portions of the frontal lobes of the cerebral cortex. In chapter 5, evidence was presented that the frontal lobes, perhaps more than any region of the brain, are impaired by processes of aging.

Role of the frontal lobes

The frontal lobes of the cerebral cortex comprise the largest mass of neocortex, subserving a number of diverse, higher-order functions. The frontal lobes are at the top of a hierarchy of brain organization. Indeed, it is the frontal lobes, more than any other part of the brain, that distinguish humans from other species. We have already addressed frontal-lobe syndrome in chapter 7 by presenting the case study of Phineas Gage. In Gage is an example of the profound role played by the frontal lobes in emotion, personality, and social behavior. A previously outstanding employee with outstanding prospects became unreliable, temperamental, disrespectful, profane, and lacking in social skills. He lost his job and his social standing in the community. He was "No longer Gage." In this chapter the focus is more on the variety of cognitive aspects affected by frontal lobe function.

John Hughlings-Jackson (1835–1911), the founder of modern neurology, was the originator of the concept of hierarchical organization in the nervous system. The ideas of Hughlings-Jackson were so modern that they are receiving more serious consideration in the present day than they did when he originated them a century ago (Kolb & Whishaw, 1995). He argued that the nervous system was organized into a number of layers arranged in a functional hierarchy.

The frontal lobes of the human cerebral cortex are the last region to develop. The size of the frontal lobes increases dramatically from birth to the second year, and growth continues in childhood. The slow maturation rate of the frontal lobes has been associated with the relatively late development of some human abilities (Diamond & Doar, 1989; Goldman-Rakic, 1987). One of the fundamental principles articulated by Hughlings-Jackson (1931) was that neural structures and their associated abilities laid down earliest should be the most permanent and lasting, and the latest developing structures and functions should be the most vulnerable to processes of aging. Neuropsychological, neuroanatomical, and radiological evidence continues to mount that the frontal lobes are the part of the brain affected earliest and hardest by normal aging (Albert & Kaplan, 1980; Anderson et al., 1983; Coffey et al., 1992; Dempster, 1992; Henderson et al., 1980; Scheibel & Scheibel, 1976; Shimamura, 1990). Capacities subserved by the frontal lobes show age-related impairment.

Executive function

Executive function includes abilities responsible for concurrent manipulation of information (e.g., cognitive flexibility), concept formation, and cue-directed behavior. The frontal lobe as the executive is involved in the planning and initiation of thought and action. The following case study illustrates the degree to which frontal-lobe damage impairs initiation and spontaneity:

> At the age of 46, a successful salesman sustained a compound depressed fracture of the left frontal bone in a traffic accident. Treatment included debridement [surgical removal] and amputation of the left frontal pole. Recovery was slow, and 9 months after the injury he was referred for long-term custodial management. By this time, he had recovered motor function with only a minimal limp and slight hyperreflexia on the right side, had normal sensation, no evidence of aphasia, and normal memory and cognitive ability (IQ 118). Nonetheless, he remained under hospital care because of marked changes in personal habits.
>
> Prior to the accident, the patient had been garrulous, enjoyed people, had many friends and talked freely. He was active in community affairs, including Little League, church activities, men's clubs, and so forth. It was stated by one acquaintance that the patient had a true charisma, "whenever he entered a room there was a change in the atmosphere, everything became more animated, happy and friendly."
>
> Following the head injury, he was quiet and remote. He would speak when spoken to and make sensible replies but would then lapse into silence. He made no friends on the ward, spent most of his time sitting alone smoking. . . . He could discuss many subjects intelligently, but was never known to initiate either a conversation or a request. . . . Formerly a warm and loving father, he did not seem to care about his family. Eventually, the family ceased visiting because of his indifference and unconcern (Blumer & Benson, 1975, pp. 156–157).

Assessment of executive function

A classic measure of cognitive flexibility is seen in the Wisconsin Card Sorting Task (WCST; figure 13.1; Heaton, 1981). This is a task in which

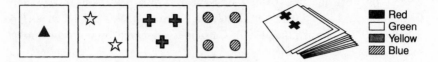

Figure 13.1 The Wisconsin Card Sorting Task (WCST) is of demonstrated utility in the assessment of frontal lobe integrity. Participants are shown four cards that serve as model patterns. These cards differ in color, form of objects, and number of objects presented, and they remain in view throughout the test. The participant is given a pack of similar cards and asked to match them to the models. However, the participant is not given information about whether sorting is to occur on the basis of color, form, or number. After each card is placed by a model, the neuropsychologist says "correct" or "wrong." Cards are sorted first by color, and when seven cards are sorted correctly, without telling the participant, the neuropsychologist switches reinforcing with "correct" to form. After seven correct form matches, reinforcement is switched to number. Normal participants are able to switch their rules for sorting after the first or second "wrong" when the rule changes, but patients with frontal lobe lesions perseverate with their initial rule and have great difficulty switching to a different rule even though they know that the first rule is incorrect

participants are asked to sort stimulus cards on the basis of one principle (e.g., color) for a period of time and then the card-sorting principle is changed (e.g., to form). The WCST is considered to be the best available test of dorsolateral frontal cortex function (Kolb & Whishaw, 1995). *Reactive* flexibility is assessed by the WCST. The participant is presented with cards and asked to react to changes in the rules for sorting them.

In a classic study using the WCST, Brenda Milner (1963) tested patients who had recovered from neurosurgery to treat their intractable epilepsy. She separated patients into two groups: (a) dorsolateral frontal lobe lesions; and (b) lesions in other lobes of the brain. The subgroup with dorsolateral frontal lesions had great difficulty in switching to a second category on the WCST. Their errors were perseverations of the previously correct rule.

Parallel (less severe) deficits have been observed in normal older adults throughout almost five decades of investigation using the WCST (Berg, 1948; Haaland et al., 1987; Heaton, 1981; Libon et al., 1994; Loranger & Misiak, 1960; Parkin, 1996; Wheilihan & Lesher, 1985). Limiting comparisons to older adults of various ages, investigators have reported greater impairment in WCST performance in the oldest participants. Using a wide variety of tests of executive function, including the WCST, it was found that healthy young-old adults (mean age of 67 years) performed significantly better than old-old adults (mean age of 78 years; Wheilihan & Lesher, 1985). In a group of 75 older adults selected for optimal health, Haaland et al. (1987) found WCST performance to be impaired in participants aged 80–87 in that they attained fewer categories and had more errors than participants aged 64–69. Comparisons of older participants of a mean age of 68 years to participants of a mean age of 81 years indicated significantly more perseverative responses on the WCST for old-old participants and a nonsignificant trend toward making fewer sorts (Libon et al., 1994).

Executive function and aging

Some investigators have attempted to determine with neuropsychological tests just what brain and cognitive processes are most impaired in normal aging. Using tests associated with left and right frontal, parietal, and temporal lobe function in a sample of community-residing adults ranging in age from 20 to 75 years, it was reported that frontal lobe tests were the best predictors of age (Mittenberg et al., 1989). Age-related deficits were greatest in neuropsychological tests assessing components of frontal lobe function such as the WCST, the Trail Making Test, word generation, and the Stroop Color–Word Interference Test.

Frontal dysfunction and the neuropsychology of age-related memory loss has been addressed systematically by Alan Parkin (1996). As a result of the significant age-related neurobiological impairment in the frontal lobes, Parkin suggested the idea that normal age-related memory loss might, in part at least, be related to loss of memory abilities specifically associated with the frontal lobes. However, the complexity of behavioral effects of the frontal lobes led Parkin to emphasize that frontal function is fractionated into tests of reactive and spontaneous fluency, with both attributes being considered as components of executive function. Parkin and his co-workers have explored this issue on a purely behavioral basis by examining relationships between performance on several types of memory tasks dependent on frontal-lobe function and participants' ability on standard frontal tasks assessing different aspects of frontal-lobe function.

Planning, organization, and self-monitoring are other aspects of executive function apart from flexibility. The term "prospective memory" has been used to identify the former three forms of executive function (Shimamura, 1990). The prospective memory system differs from the declarative memory system discussed in chapter 11 in that it functions to manipulate and organize memory rather than to acquire and store information. Just because there is a deficit in declarative memory, it does not mean that there is a deficit in prospective memory. For example, patients with medial temporal lobe lesions suffering from amnesia can perform prospective memory functions such as categorizing or organizing information. On the other hand, impairment in prospective memory can impair performance on declarative memory tasks because organizational and retrieval strategies may be underutilized. This seems to be the case in the performance of older adults who fail to use cues for retrieval spontaneously (Hulicka & Grossman, 1967).

Prospective memory includes the processes and strategies used to remember to perform future actions. Remembering to take pills at a certain time, to turn off the lights and lock the door before leaving the house, to make and keep appointments, and to remember birthdays, anniversaries, and other significant dates requires prospective memory. Keeping track of what information has been told to whom is another attribute of prospective memory that falls into the category of self-monitoring. Although everyone repeats the same story twice to a friend or a relative, the frequency of repeating the same story seems to increase with age.

Remembering to perform future actions is done more poorly by older adults in experimental tests of this ability (Dobbs & Rule, 1987; West, 1988). However, in real life situations, older adults may compensate for this declining ability to plan and organize by using external cues such as notes and reminders on the calendar to help them manage. Older subjects were actually more accurate than younger subjects in making telephone calls to the experimenter at scheduled times (Moscovitch, 1982). When left to their own coping strategies, older adults apparently mitigate their difficulties with remembering to perform future actions.

Remembering the source of the information received is yet another aspect of prospective memory. Memory for the source is the ability to remember who told you something or where you read a piece of information. Prospective memory functions are linked to frontal-lobe integrity, and they show age-related impairment. An aspect of source amnesia, the inability to correctly remember the source of knowledge, was assessed by Parkin and Walter (1992) using a technique they called the recognition and consciousness awareness paradigm. Participants in several age groups were shown stimuli and presented later with a larger group of stimuli including foils and asked to specify yes or no regarding whether they had seen the objects before. They were also asked to classify each recognized stimulus on a subjective basis: had they specific recollection of the target's prior occurrence (e.g., an image of the target) or was recognition based simply on familiarity with the object. The effect of age on the distribution of subjective responses was dramatic. There were substantially higher numbers of familiar responses in older adults, and increased numbers of familiar responses were associated with a greater number of errors on the WCST. Even in subgroups of older adults who performed the recognition task as well as younger adults, there were higher numbers of familiar responses over actual recollections. Older adults were less able to remember an image of the target that they had seen during the experiment.

An important function carried out in the frontal cortex is the organization of incoming information in sequence. The temporal ordering of events is a function impaired in patients with lesions localized to the frontal cortex (Milner et al., 1985; Petrides, 1991). Spatio-temporal organization is dependent on contextual memory, and the ability to remember the source of information is linked to the contextual components of the memory. The list discrimination paradigm measures both recognition and the ability to recollect the temporal and context information about a target's prior presentation (Squire et al., 1981). Participants are asked when a target was presented in relation to other targets. They must also specify which list the target was in and if the target was presented to their left or right. Comparing young and older participants on this task, Parkin et al. (1995) observed no age differences in recognition of the targets, but older adults were impaired in their memory for temporal context. Several dimensions of frontal-lobe function were assessed in this study, including reactive flexibility (WCST) and spontaneous flexibility. Spontaneous flexibility involves the ready flow of ideas and answers in response to a question, and it was assessed with word fluency measures. In the case of word generation in which initiation of the response is left totally up to the individual, *spontaneous* flexibility is measured. An illustration of word-list generation was presented in figure 2.4. The degree to which older participants were impaired was correlated with deficits in spontaneous flexibility but not with reactive flexibility. Different memory functions were associated with different components of frontal function, and temporal memory was associated with spontaneous flexibility that is one of several aspects of frontal-lobe function impaired in normal aging.

Parkin and Lawrence (1994) demonstrated impaired spontaneous and reactive flexibility in older adults, and they showed that these two aspects of frontal-lobe function were related to impairments in different types of memory. One memory task was release from proactive interference, and this measure correlated with measures of spontaneous flexibility but not reactive flexibility. A second task assessed recall difficulty relative to recognition, and this task correlated with reactive flexibility but not spontaneous flexibility. Age-related impairment in frontal-lobe function has multiple dimensions that, in turn, are related to qualitatively different kinds of cognitive impairment.

Because the ability to temporally organize information relies on the frontal lobes, it was expected that the ability to remember the source of information would be dependent on intact frontal-lobe function. Tests of source memory depend on presenting information during the experimental session, and providing some sort of context for that memory. For example, McIntyre and Craik (1987) presented fictitious facts such as "Bob Hope's father was a fireman." These "facts" were presented either by male or female speakers. At a later time, participants were asked to recall the "fact" with prompts such as

"What did Bob Hope's father do for a living?" Participants were also asked which of two speakers presented the facts. The latter question queries source memory. Recognition and recall of the "facts" such as Bob Hope's father's occupation are measures of declarative memory involving medial temporal lobe brain circuitry.

When tested for source memory, patients with frontal-lobe lesions were impaired in their ability to remember the source of the information. In spite of this deficit in source memory, they had normal recognition and recall of facts or normal declarative memory (Janowsky et al., 1989; Parkin et al., 1988). The well-documented deficits of older adults on neuropsychological tests assessing frontal-lobe function led investigators to explore older adult's ability to recognize the source of information.

It was observed that older adults were particularly impaired in source memory in that they forgot whether the fact was presented by the male or female voice (McIntyre & Craik, 1987). In another study, memory for source was tested in adults who also were administered the WCST (Craik et al., 1990). Source recognition and source recall were correlated with one another, but neither assessment was correlated with the declarative memory measure of fact recall. Both source measures were significantly correlated with WCST performance. Craik et al. (1990) concluded that source amnesia was not reflective of a general memory impairment in the aged. Rather, normal aging is associated with impairment in frontal-lobe functioning which, in turn, impairs memory for the source of information.

Shimamura (1990) suggested that source memory deficits could contribute to problems that older adults sometimes have in output monitoring, such as the problem of telling the same story more than once. Failure to remember the last spatial–temporal context in which a behavior was enacted could lead to the repetition of that behavior at inappropriate times. Impaired source monitoring was also associated with impaired reality monitoring. Older adults sometimes have difficulty in remembering whether a stimulus was generated externally by someone else or internally from memory. This phenomenon was demonstrated in a study in which younger and older adults read sentences and also generated words to complete a sentence (Mitchell et al., 1986). Older adults were less accurate than younger adults in remembering whether a word had been presented within the sentence or had been generated from memory.

Working memory

The prefrontal cortex in conjunction with the hippocampus subserves working memory which involves the temporary use of knowledge to guide behavior (Milner & Petrides, 1984). Working memory enables humans to plan for the future and to string together thought and ideas. Working memory has been called "the blackboard of the mind" (Goldman-Rakic, 1992). A major deficit in patients with prefrontal cortex lesions is reduced performance in problem-solving tasks that require flexibility in response strategies and are assumed to tax working memory.

Aging and working memory in nonhuman primates

Working memory is most developed in humans, but some elements of working memory exist in other animals, especially in other primates. If their prefrontal cortices are damaged, these animals develop symptoms much like the ones seen in humans with frontal-lobe lesions, and also to a lesser degree in elderly humans. Neuroscientists have therefore turned to monkeys in their efforts to explore basic neurobiological mechanisms of working memory (Goldman-Rakic, 1992).

A brain structure affected by aging processes in humans that is likely to be involved in loss of efficiency in working memory in aged monkeys is the prefrontal cortex (Arnstein & Goldman-Rakic, 1985b). Goldman-Rakic (1987) described the basic neural circuitry underlying delayed-response function in nonhuman primates and has suggested that the developmental increase in synaptic density in the principal sulcus of the frontal lobe coincided with the development of the ability to perform the delayed response task at short delays. Arnstein and Goldman-Rakic (1985a) demonstrated that age-related changes in the prefrontal cortex of older monkeys were likely to be responsible for the difficulties these animals have on delayed response tasks.

In the delayed response task, one of two wells is baited while the animal watches. Then the wells are covered with identical cardboard plaques and a screen is lowered to remove them from the animal's view. After a prescribed delay, the screen is raised and the animal is allowed to choose one of the two wells. Delayed alternation is a variation of this task in which the animal does not see the wells baited. Instead it must remember which side it chose correctly on the last trial and alternate the response.

The neurotransmitter, dopamine, is found in the highest levels in the monkey cortex in the prefrontal region. Most areas of the frontal lobe are innervated in a dense manner with norepinephrine, as well (Levitt et al., 1984). The presence of these neurotransmitters, particularly dopamine, appears to be essential for the prefrontal cortex to function properly (Brozoski et al., 1979). Biochemical analysis of neurotransmitter levels in the brains of "young-old" rhesus monkeys (aged 10–18 years) revealed substantial depletions in cortical catecholamine levels (Goldman-Rakic & Brown, 1981). Of the many regions studied, only the prefrontal and temporal cortices showed large depletions of dopamine of 50 percent or more. The older the animal, the greater were the dopamine depletions.

In those 18–30-year-old rhesus monkeys who were impaired on spatial delayed alternation and delayed response, there was improvement in performance with treatment with the dopamine-enhancing drug, clonidine (Arnstein & Goldman-Rakic, 1985a, 1985b). Robust improvements in delayed response performance were observed in a dose-related manner. At the most effective dose level, a majority of the monkeys were able to achieve near perfect performance. While the neurochemical mechanisms underlying the ability of the drug to ameliorate performance are not understood, the dose–response curves are consonant with clonidine having actions at postsynaptic receptors.

The animal model of nonhuman primates for working memory loss in aging meets all of the criteria for developing animal behavioral models described by Bartus et al. (1983). The working memory deficit occurs naturally, and it parallels extremely well the working memory deficit observed in normal aging and exacerbated in Alzheimer's disease (AD). Parkinson's disease (PD) is another neurological disease of increasing incidence in older adulthood that affects the neurotransmitter dopamine as well as executive function (e.g., Bondi et al., 1993). Neurobiological changes occurring in aging nonhuman primates resemble human neurobiological aging phenomena more closely than any non-primate animal models. This is an excellent animal model for human aging, and it is limited only by expense, by the long life spans of nonhuman primates, and by the scarcity of aged nonhuman primates.

Aging and working memory in humans

The working memory space is used for holding problem statements, performing computing operations, storing intermediate solutions, and so forth. Reducing the storage capacity in working memory introduces delays that affect complex tasks to a greater degree than simple tasks. The effect of aging on working memory has been described as a reduction in storage capacity (Salthouse et al., 1989). The fact that older adults tend to perform more poorly as the complexity of the task is increased is interpreted as an indicator of limited processing resources. Presenting young older adults with number manipulation tasks of increasing complexity from simple digit span forward to a difficult randomized span task, Wiegersma and Meertse (1990) found that age differences increased with the difficulty of the tasks as would be predicted if working memory was impaired in older adults. There were no age differences on tasks that place low demands on reorganization of material such as digit span forward. Tasks requiring frequent exchanges of information, and thus drawing upon the smaller working memory of older adults, were impaired in these individuals.

Attention

Attention is not a unitary construct but has several components. Selective attention refers to an ability to restrict awareness to a limited number of stimuli while ignoring other stimuli. Divided attention involves the ability to engage in concurrent tasks. Sustained attention represents a subjective state in which the observer maintains attentional effort over time. Sustained attention has also been called vigilance, and this aspect of attention was discussed in the context of under- and overarousal in chapters 4 and 8. Selective and divided attention will be discussed in this chapter in relation to executive function, working memory and the frontal lobes.

Selective attention and aging

The predominant paradigm for studying selective attention is the visual search task. In this task the participant judges whether or not a designated target is present in a given stimulus display. Parameters of interest include duration of stimulus presentation, interstimulus interval, number of items in the stimulus display, relation of the target to foils, and learning history in the paradigm (e.g., consistency of targets and foils over trials). This paradigm has been used to investigate facilitatory and inhibitory priming, practice effects, and retention of stimulus-specific and task-specific visual search skills.

Self-report data collected from 415 adults ranging in age from 18 to 100 years indicated that older adults have a number of visual problems, a major one of which is visual search (Kosnik et al., 1988). Questions about difficulty with reading moving signs, reading signs amid other signs, and locating signs amid other signs loaded highly on a factor identified as Visual Problems of Aging. These self-report results are consistent with experimental studies of visual search in older adults (Carlson et al., 1995). Even when older adults are performing visual search tasks in domains in which they have developed years of expertise, they are more distractable. For example, poor visual search in older experts has been reported in the domains of aviation (Morrow et al., 1992; Szafran, 1968), chess (Charness, 1985), miniature golf (Molander & Backman, 1994), and reading (Connelly et al., 1991). This does not mean that older adults cannot compensate for their attention deficiencies. In the domain of chess playing, it has been demonstrated that old expert chess players show strategically superior performance in various components of chess performance, despite losses in visual search speed.

Traditionally research on selective attention has focused on excitatory mechanisms through which selected information enters awareness. Increasingly, however, inhibitory mechanisms responsible for actively suppressing unselected stimuli are coming under scrutiny. There is growing evidence that inhibitory processing plays a crucial role in selective attention (Tipper & Cranston, 1985). It has been suggested since the time of Pavlov that older organisms generally exhibit reduced effectiveness in inhibitory processes (see chapter 8). Research on selective attention suggests that inhibitory processing may be particularly vulnerable to the effects of aging (e.g., Hasher et al., 1991; Kane et al., 1994). A number of studies comparing attentional inhibition in young and older adults converged in reporting that older adults are less able to suppress distracting information (Hasher et al., 1991; Kane et al., 1994; McDowd & Oseas-Kreger, 1991; Stoltzfus et al., 1993). Relative failure of inhibitory function in older compared to young adult participants is interpreted to reflect impaired function in frontal lobes.

Divided attention

One of the critical issues in research examining age-related effects on divided attention concerns the relation between performance on individual tasks carried out independently and carried out concurrently. Age-related effects associated with complex task performance may reflect a difficulty specific to the performance of the complex tasks, or may be an extension of any general decline in processing ability associated with component tasks.

Early work investigating age-related effects on the ability to divide attention between tasks has consistently demonstrated that older adults are at a disadvantage when compared to younger adults (Broadbent & Gregory, 1965; Broadbent & Heron, 1962; Inglis & Caird, 1963; Kirchner, 1958; Welford, 1958). The decline in the ability to divide attention is one of the most predictable age effects (Craik, 1977).

There have been several accounts devised to explain the causes of age differences in divided attention. One explanation is that older adults are more vulnerable to interference between tasks because of decreased "functional distance" between the brain areas required to perform the two tasks (Kinsbourne, 1980). Less space or capacity in the brain (frontal cortex) is proposed to account for the cognitive interference. A second explanation for age differences in divided attention focuses on the information processing ability of older adults. It is the decreased working memory hypothesis. Processing resources are viewed as inadequate in older adults to both control the division of attention and to perform the required tasks.

Summary

Frontal-lobe function plays a significant role in the age-related changes in cognitive processes that have been reported. Age-related changes in emotion, arousal and sleep, response speed and timing, and some forms of memory are associated with neurobiological changes in the frontal lobes along with age-related changes in executive function, working memory, and attention. Planning, organizing, thinking divergently, inhibiting, and self-monitoring are involved in executive function. The function of an executive organizer in programming and regulating behavior is a role attributed to the frontal lobes. Many assessments of this function indicate that it is deleteriously affected by processes of aging. The WCST is considered to be the best available test of dorsolateral frontal cortex function. The WCST assesses individuals' ability to switch mental sets by following changing rules. This ability has been called reactive flexibility. Older adults make more perseverative errors on the WCST, and performance on this test is especially impaired in very old age.

Spontaneous flexibility is another aspect of executive function impaired in old age. The ability to generate ideas is one quality of spontaneous flexibility. It is typically measured with word-generation tasks. The participant is asked to generate as many words as possible, starting with a given letter in a fixed time period. In some cases, additional constraints are added such as specification of the number of letters that must be in the words (e.g., five-letter words beginning with the letter "s"). Release from proactive interference and temporal memory were both associated with spontaneous (but not reactive) flexibility, whereas recall difficulty relative to recognition correlated with reactive flexibility but not spontaneous flexibility.

Planning, organization, and self-monitoring are other aspects of executive function apart from flexibility. The term "prospective memory" has been used to identify the former three forms of executive function. The prospective memory system functions to manipulate and organize memory. Prospective memory includes the processes and strategies used to remember to perform future actions. Remembering the source of the information received is yet another aspect of prospective memory. Older adults' deficits in source memory could contribute to problems that older adults sometimes have in output monitoring, such as the problem of telling the same story more than once.

The prefrontal cortex in conjunction with the hippocampus subserves working memory which involves the temporary use of knowledge to guide behavior. Working-memory deficits occur in nonhuman primates as well as in humans, and the deficit in animals parallels extremely well the working memory deficit observed in normal aging and exacerbated in AD and PD. Changes in the prefrontal lobe, including a decline in dopamine levels, have been associated with working memory deficits in monkeys and humans. Performance on tasks assessing working memory was improved by treatment with the dopamine-enhancing drug clonidine.

Attention is not a unitary construct but has several components. Selective attention refers to an ability to restrict awareness to a limited number of stimuli while ignoring other stimuli. Divided attention involves the ability to engage in concurrent tasks. Even when older adults are performing visual search tasks in domains in which they have developed years of expertise, they are more distractable. There is growing evidence that inhibitory processing plays a crucial role in selective attention. Research on selective attention suggests that inhibitory processing may be particularly vulnerable to the effects of aging. Relative failure of inhibitory function in older compared to young adult participants is interpreted to reflect impaired function in frontal lobes.

There have been several accounts devised to explain the causes of age differences in divided attention. One explanation is that there is less space or capacity in the brain (frontal cortex), and this results in cognitive interference between tasks dividing the attention. The decreased working memory hypothesis views processing resources as inadequate in older adults both to control the division of attention and to perform the required tasks. Both accounts require additional investigation, but the feature common to them is acknowledgement that the neurobiological structures essential for optimal function of attention, the prefrontal lobes, are impaired in older adults.

Further Reading

Coffey, C. E., Wilkinson, W. E., Parashos, I. A., Soady, S. A. R., Sullivan, R. J., Patterson, L. J., Figiel, G. S., Webb, M. C., Spritzer, C. E., & Djang, W. T. (1992). Quantitative cerebral anatomy of the aging human brain: A cross-sectional study using magnetic resonance imaging. *Neurology, 42,* 527–536.
Application of modern neuro-imaging techniques to assess frontal lobes over the adult life span.

Bondi, M. W., Kaszniak, A. W., Bayles, K. A., & Vance, K. T. (1993). Contributions of frontal system dysfunction to memory and perceptual abilities in Parkinson's disease. *Neuropsychology, 7,* 89–102.
This article represents a neuropsychological approach to frontal lobe function in neuropathological aging.

Mittenberg, W., Seidenberg, M., O'Leary, D. S., & DiGiulio, D. V. (1989). Changes in cerebral functioning associated with normal aging. *Journal of Clinical and Experimental Neuropsychology, 11,* 918–932.
A variety of tests of frontal lobe function were used to assess elderly adults in this study, making it instructive both from the viewpoint of assessment technique and neuropsychological aging.

Arnstein, A. F. T., & Goldman-Rakic, P. S. (1985). Catecholamines and cognitive decline in aged nonhuman primates. *Annals of the New York Academy of Science, 444,* 218–234.
One of the first experiments to associate working memory deficits with an age-related decline in dopamine in older monkey brains.

Part IV

The Future

Prospects in the
Neuropsychology of Aging

As we approach the twenty-first century, rapid advances in basic technologies and understanding of neurobiological phenomena provide us with the opportunity to apply some of the knowledge on which the neuropsychology of aging has been building. Some fundamental aspects of neurobiological aging still elude our understanding, but we are at a point where we can apply what we know and have an impact on the lives of many older adults. In this chapter, we discuss how advances in the neuropsychology of aging can lead to new intervention and treatment.

Some implications for
new neurobiological knowledge

Molecular genetics

The Human Genome Project has as its goal the determination of the exact sequence of the three billion bases that make up the human genome. Molecular biologists are unveiling the human genetic code. The team led by Thomas Hudson, Lincoln Stein, and Eric Lander described a new physical map of the human genome (Hudson et al., 1995). This map contains more than 15,000 specific sequence markers distributed over all the human chromosomes which is about half the goal of 30,000 markers set by the Human Genome Project for a physical map. With relevance to the neuropsychology of aging is knowledge of some aspects of that code. For example, identification of the gene (or genes) that speed up the production of β-amyloid in late life might enable scientists to understand and prevent the cascade of dysfunctional events resulting in brain damage caused in Alzheimer's disease (AD). Prevention of deleterious processes in AD for 5–10 years in later adulthood would likely enable most elderly adults to die of other causes with relatively intact brains and cognition.

Research on the molecular genetics of familial and sporadic AD implicates genes on three different chromosomes (i.e., 14, 19, and 21; Hardy, 1993; Mullan & Crawford, 1993; Price et al., 1993). It has also been demonstrated that the apolipoprotein E (ApoE) 4 allele is a risk factor for both familial and sporadic AD (Saunders et al., 1993). At present, it is not clear whether AD is one disease or a constellation of diseases (Trojanowski & Lee, 1994). Molecular genetic research may eventually indicate whether AD is a heterogeneous disorder and may also provide a way to diagnose premorbid AD accurately using a "marker" for the disease.

Tissue transplantation

Perfecting tissue transplants may lead to treatment of pathological, physical, and behavioral conditions in the elderly. In Parkinson's disease (PD), there has been some success with neuronal tissue transplants in alleviating the behavioral symptoms (Langston & Palfreman, 1995). Tissue transplants may also have implications for the profound memory loss accompanying AD. Nerve growth factor, a substance discovered in fetuses by developmental neurobiologists, or related trophic agents may also be useful in helping older neurons to be maintained and even to regenerate.

Tissue transplantation in the brain is at a far earlier stage than is organ transplantation. In many cases, brain tissue transplantation involves two major periods of the life span; the fetal period and late life. It is the cells from the fetus that are the most adaptable to transplantation. Later life is the period when degenerative diseases of the nervous system such as PD and AD have their onset.

In chapter 6 we discussed some of the neurodegenerative effects in AD and PD. PD results when neurons in the region called the substantia nigra degenerate. The substantia nigra is the part of the brain that produces the neurotransmitter dopamine, and it is close to totally destroyed in PD. The behavioral symptoms are tremors and muscular rigidity that can eventually bring voluntary movements to a halt. In the early stages the disease can be treated by giving patients the amino acid L-dopa, which is transported into the brain and converted to dopamine. This treatment makes up for what the brain is incapable of producing. However, after a few years the treatment loses its effectiveness. In part, this is due to continued neural degeneration, but the remaining tissue also becomes less responsive to dopamine and the dopamine precursor. Patients begin experiencing periodic "off" times when their symptoms abruptly return.

A development in the treatment of PD was brain surgery in which tissue from the adrenal medulla cortex of the patient was surgically removed and implanted in the basal ganglia brain region. Adrenal medulla tissue also produces dopamine. Sometimes the tissue functioned when transplanted to the brain, but few patients who experienced this surgery showed long-term improvement. Complications from the abdominal surgery to harvest the adrenal medulla tissue, coupled with the stress of brain surgery to implant that tissue proved to be severe. Furthermore, the adrenal medulla tissue did not appear to survive in the brain. Thus, the long-term prognosis for these patients has not been good, and this treatment has been abandoned. Of the 180 patients with PD in the United States and Canada who received adrenal medulla transplants into the brain, only modest benefits were observed and the benefits may not have outweighed the costs. Pneumonia and bladder infections occurred frequently as a consequence of the adrenal medulla surgery (Marx, 1990a). Neurosurgeons looked for other sources of dopamine–producing neurons to implant into the brains of patients with PD, and they also developed new surgical lesion techniques that have proved effective (Delong, 1995).

One approach avoiding the use of the patient's adrenal medulla tissue is to implant fetal brain tissue into patients with PD. This procedure worked with young adult drug addicts who had severely damaged their substantia nigra and developed full-blown symptoms of PD (Langston & Palfreman, 1995). Fetal tissue has proved to be optimal for transplantation because the implanted neuroblasts divide and differentiate, integrating themselves into the brain where they have been grafted. Swedish researchers reported that transplanting fetal nerve tissue into the brain of a man with severe PD produced a clinically significant improvement in the patient's condition (Lindvall et al., 1990). PET scans used to image the patient's brain demonstrated that the grafted neurons had survived. However, older adults tolerate the surgery less well, and the disease also continues to progress, making fetal transplant therapy less efficacious.

Neuroscience is on the frontier of brain implant surgery. Attempts have been made to implant fetal animal tissue into older animals' hippocampus with some success. The eventual implications of these studies are that there is the potential to replace damaged brain tissue with functioning tissue. If AD devastates hippocampal circuitry, eliminating the ability to store recent memories, it may be possible to augment that part of the hippocampus with more viable tissue. Since memory storage probably does not reside in the hippocampus, personality and long-term memory would not be affected by such surgery. Only the ability to acquire new memories would be affected. This is the ability that appears to be most affected in AD.

Neurotrophic agents

Neurotrophic agents are substances (including chemicals or drugs) that sustain neurons and prolong neuronal life. It is the death of neurons or supporting tissue for neurons, such as myelin, that leads to neuropathology and dementia. Maintaining those neurons maintains cognitive function. A different approach from actually implanting new neural tissue is to bathe the damaged area in substances which would maintain the neurons that remain. The use of nerve growth factor (NGF) in this manner is successful in maintaining neurons in animals with brain lesions. The use of NGF in clinical trials with patients with AD has been seriously contemplated (Marx, 1990b). However, there has been concern about whether the introduction of NGF into the brain of patients with AD would cause more harm than good. The concern of neuroscientists has been that NGF may stimulate abnormal cell growth seen in the brains of patients with AD along with maintaining the remaining, normal neural tissue.

Cognition-enhancing agents

Drugs have been identified that enhance the plasticity for learning in the older mammalian brain. Some cognition-enhancing drugs also have neurotrophic properties, that is they prolong the life of the remaining neurons. Research involving the synthesis and testing of cognition-enhancing drugs for the treatment of dementia is moving at a rapid pace. Nevertheless, the availability of cognition-enhancing drugs is extremely limited because of the long (usually 10 years) process required to ensure drug safety and efficacy for human use. At present, only two drugs, the cholinergic agonists Cognex® and Aricept®, are approved by the FDA for the treatment of cognitive dysfunction in AD. Cognex® ameliorates learning and memory in some patients with probable AD (Knapp et al., 1994; Manning, 1994; Wagstaff & McTavish, 1994). However, this drug is effective only in a minority of AD patients. Furthermore, the utility of Cognex® is limited by adverse reactions including hepatotoxicity.

The long process of evaluating a drug for human use begins with preclinical (animal) research. In my rabbit laboratory, several drugs have been tested as potential cognition-enhancing agents in older (and, in some cases, young) animals. Biochemically diverse drugs significantly facilitated learning in older rabbits, indicating that a number of mechanisms may work to improve cognition in older adults and demented patients.

Nootropic agent. The term nootropic was proposed by Giurgia (1980) with reference to the compound piracetam. The word nootropic is derived from *nos* (mind) and *tropin* (toward). Nootropic agents were designed to have physiological and behavioral effects in experimental animals without disruptive side effects such as those accompanying hypnotics, sedatives, neuroleptics, or antidepressants. Nootropics, such as piracetam, reverse learning and memory deficits induced by cholinergic antagonists such as scopolamine (Piercey et al., 1987). Piracetam has been shown in animal models to enhance learning and retention (Means et al., 1990).

Nootropic agents typically are pyrrolidinone derivatives. The prototypic nootropic, piracetam, a substituted pyrrolidinone, is an analog of gamma aminobutyric acid (GABA) and has clear effects on brain metabolism. Research has demonstrated that similar pharmacophores, including substituted pyrrolidinones such as the acetams, modulate hippocampal synaptic transmission and long-term potentiation (LTP) *in vitro* (Olpe & Lynch, 1982; Satoh et al., 1986).

Nefiracetam is a nootropic drug developed to improve impaired cognitive functioning in old age. This drug has demonstrated efficacy in facilitating learning and memory in laboratory animals (Sarter et al., 1992). Nefiracetam stimulates release of acetylcholine via the GABAergic system, at least in rat cortex (Watabe et al., 1993). Following oxygen and glucose deprivation, nefiracetam protected membrane dysfunction in hippocampal CA1 neurons (Nakamura et al., 1991). Because older rabbits show impaired learning and hippocampal responding in the conditioned response period (Woodruff-Pak et al., 1987), it was anticipated that nefiracetam would enhance acquisition of learning in older rabbits.

In two experiments using retired breeder rabbits, nefiracetam at some doses had a facilitatory effect on acquisition in eyeblink classical conditioning (EBCC) (Woodruff-Pak & Li, 1994). All dependent measures indicated significantly better conditioning in rabbits treated with 10 mg/kg nefiracetam, but this dose did not elevate motor responding. EBCC is performed poorly by older humans and is seriously impaired in AD. These preclinical data – in an animal model with clear parallels in humans – suggest that nefiracetam may prove effective as a cognition enhancer in clinical trials.

Nicotinic cholinergic agonists and antagonists. Nicotinic receptors are significantly reduced in cerebral cortex and hippocampal regions of the brain in AD (e. g., Araujo et al., 1988; Whitehouse et al., 1986). Preliminary investigations using acute administration of nicotine suggest that stimulation of remaining nicotinic receptors alleviates some cognitive deficits in AD (Jones et al., 1992; Newhouse et al., 1993; Sahakian et al., 1989). Chronic nicotine administration may be more effective as a cognition-enhancing agent for age-related impairment in attention and memory and for attention and memory disorders associated with AD. We wanted to determine if nicotinic as well as muscarinic cholinergic receptors were involved in EBCC in rabbits. Our results would determine whether the rabbit EBCC model could be used for preclinical tests of nicotinic agonists to treat memory dysfunction in AD.

First, Woodruff-Pak et al. (1994) tested the effect of the nicotinic receptor antagonist, mecamylamine, on EBCC in young rabbits. A dose of 0.5 mg/kg of mecamylamine was injected subcutaneously daily 15 min before EBCC. Rabbits receiving mecamylamine were slow to acquire conditioned responses (CRs), and they had a learning profile strikingly similar to the learning profile of older rabbits. They took an average of 780 trials to reach learning criterion. Saline-treated rabbits learned almost twice as rapidly and to a higher level of conditioned responding than did mecamylamine-treated rabbits. Control animals given mecamylamine and presented with tones and airpuffs unpaired did not show nonspecific effects of the drug. Motor responses of all animals as measured by the response to the airpuff (the unconditioned response, UR) were comparable, indicating that mecamylamine affected associative learning, rather than nonassociative aspects of performance.

Administration of nicotine or compounds that activate nicotinic cholinergic receptors facilitates acquisition of CRs in older rabbits. We tested the nicotinic agonist GTS-21 using eyeblink classical conditioning (Woodruff-Pak et al., 1994). Older rabbits were administered three different doses of GTS-21, and then they were compared with vehicle-treated rabbits. At two of the three dose levels, GTS-21 ameliorated learning deficits in older rabbits. We concluded that the nicotinic agonist, GTS-21, served as a cognition-enhancing agent in older rabbits on EBCC – a task that is seriously impaired in AD. Given that nicotinic cholinergic receptors are significantly reduced in AD brains, and that acute nicotine administration facilitates cognition in AD, we suspect that chronic administration of nicotinic agonists will significantly improve several dimensions of cognition in AD, including EBCC. We also suspect that nondemented elderly adults aged-matched to patients diagnosed with probable AD will show cognition-enhancing effects from chronic administration of nicotinic agonists; this assumption is based on our observations of older rabbits.

With aging, there is a decline in some aspects of neuronal metabolism and information transfer that, among other things, affects learning and memory. To compensate for these losses, cognition-enhancing compounds are under development to facilitate learning and memory. Many of these compounds are of demonstrated utility in animal models, and they have the potential to ameliorate dysfunction in brain memory systems.

Neuropsychology of aging in the twenty-first century

Estimates of the size of the aging population in the twenty-first century continue to be revised upward (Zopf, 1986). Projections based on data from the United States Bureau of the Census anticipated that by 2030 the population over the age of 65 would number about 65 million and comprise 21.2 percent of the general population (*A Profile of Older Americans*, 1986). Demographers have made these projections on the basis of health and longevity in the present decade. If medical breakthroughs dramatically affect mortality rates for diseases such as heart disease, cancer, and stroke, people aged 65 and older may number 74 million and comprise 23 percent of the population by 2025 (Gordon, 1979). Thus, in the next century, old people in the population will be even more commonplace than they are at present. The large numbers of older adults in society will undoubtedly affect its social, economic, and political structure.

Health and longevity

Major increases in human life expectancy have been achieved in the twentieth century. Not only do we live longer, our health is more optimal throughout our years. These facts have led Fries and Crapo (1981) to predict that life expectancy in the future will become a rectangular curve. The rectangular curve is the survival curve. It depicts the age of death. A rectangular curve means that the whole birth cohort survives to a given age, and then they all die within a period of a few years.

Typical survival curves for wild animals and humans in hostile environments approximate a simple exponential decay. For civilized human populations, the shape of the survival curve begins to bend upward to the right. This indicates that most deaths occur at increasingly advanced ages. The curve has become more and more rectangular as we have eliminated the causes of death in the early years. As we improve health in old age, the curve will become even more rectangular. Fries and Crapo (1981) predicted that given present trends in mortality in the United States, we are on the verge of becoming a "rectangular society" in which nearly all people survive to old age and then die rather abruptly over a narrow age range centering about age 85. Other researchers argue that current trends do not fit the rectangular curve prediction. Rather the whole curve is being shifted upward. Eighty-five years may not be an accurate endpoint for human life expectancy. There is agreement that life expectancy is increasing and that health in old age is improving.

The future health and longevity of individuals in developed countries in the world depends on three major categories of biomedical research (Zopf, 1986). These are: (a) efforts to prevent, diagnose, and treat more effectively the three major causes of death which are heart disease, cancer, and stroke; (b) research designed to describe and manipulate social conditions that affect aging and death; and (c) research directed to the processes of aging including the understanding of the genetic limits on life span.

The rectangular curve described by Fries and Crapo (1981) will be more readily achieved as advances in research on cardiovascular disease and cancer provide insights about how to treat and eliminate these diseases. It is very reasonable to assume that we will continue to reduce mortality due to cardiovascular disease, because the death rate from heart disease has fallen steadily since 1960. Research on the genetic antecedents of cancer is very promising, and it is likely that cancer, too, will be brought under control. Even if these major diseases are more or less eliminated, our biological potential for life averages around 85 years. By eliminating major diseases, we will maximize human life expectancy so that children born in the twenty-first century will have a life expectancy of 85 years. However, to exceed a life expectancy of 85 years, it may be necessary to alter genes that affect the human life span.

The prospect of affecting the human life span is still remote. Nevertheless, interventions into the processes of aging might include efforts to alter the ways that cells, organs, and physiological systems age. It might also involve the regeneration of tissue. These advances are more futuristic than advances in the cure and prevention of known disease processes. However, with the current rate of advances in molecular genetics, it is no longer in the realm of science fiction to state that extension of the human life span is possible.

In mammals, there is one known means of extending the life span. To extend the life span of mice and rats, dietary restriction has been used (Cutler, 1981; Schneider & Reid, 1985; Weindruch, 1984). Underfeeding young mice and rats by reducing food intake by 25–60 percent below what they normally would consume causes them to live almost twice as long as their normally fed littermates and results in lower incidence and later onset of senescence-associated diseases (Barrows & Kokkonen, 1984; Masoro, 1984). Dietary restriction also benefits learning and motor performance in aged mice (Ingram et al., 1987). This intervention may have implications for the human life span; however, the critical experiments to test this intervention will never be undertaken directly. Nevertheless, it is likely that whatever means we attempt to extend the life span in humans will have to be undertaken early in life.

Cognitive aging

Diversity is the hallmark of old age. There is more individual difference at the endpoint of life than during any other period. However, in spite of the diversity, it is possible to make some predictions based on the average. Here we are venturing some guesses about individual behavior in old age based on what research in the neuropsychology of aging has told us about behavioral aging processes.

Response speed. The most pervasive and apparent behavioral change with aging is slowing. This is a primary aging change, occurring in every organism if it lives long enough. It is unlikely that this fundamental aspect of aging will be altered in the future. However, amelioration and prevention of major psychomotor slowing is possible.

The best way to maintain response speed is to remain active. A number of studies have shown that physical exercise facilitates response speed. Older adults who have remained physically active throughout their lives as well as older adults who begin an exercise program in late life have more rapid reaction time than sedentary adults (Dustman, Emmerson, & Shearer, 1994). Many more members of contemporary young and middle-aged cohorts have been socialized to exercise than had contemporary older adults. Thus, for aging and the future, the prospect of maintenance of response speed, or at least a smaller magnitude of slowing, is a reality.

A training study is also showing how new strategies can effectively speed behavior in older adults. Clark et al. (1987) exposed a group of older adults to several video games and allowed them to play the games at least 2 hr per week for 7 weeks. The older adults who played video games were faster on several difficulty levels of a choice reaction time task than were older adults not exposed to the video games. Here again, activity, in the form of playing a video game, increased the speed of performance. The aged in the future, even more than the aged of the present, will likely be able to compensate for the tendency in aging organisms for response speed to be slower. They will be in better health, and they will probably be more physically active. Both of these factors minimize slowing.

Sensation and perception. Impairments in hearing and vision are relatively common in the elderly. Estimates of hearing impairment range from 30 to 50 percent of those 65 and older, and 10 percent of this population had visual impairments (National Center for Health Statistics, 1985). In another survey, depending on age, from 30 to 58 percent of men and from 18 to 44 percent of women reported presence of deafness or other hearing problems (National Center for Health Statistics, 1986). In this sample, visual impairment was reported by 9.5–26.8 percent of respondents, depending on age.

Projections about the incidence of sensory loss in future cohorts of aged are difficult to make. As more is learned about the etiology of impairments of vision and audition, some sensory loss might be prevented or slowed. On the other hand, future cohorts of elderly may suffer similar or greater levels of hearing impairment as a result of hearing loss due to high intensity sounds. Large numbers of teenagers and young adults continue to expose their ears to highly amplified sounds at concerts and clubs. Thus, there is no evidence that the aged in the future will experience any less hearing loss than contemporary older adults.

Research breakthroughs in vision, which could prevent glaucoma and macular degeneration, have the potential to save the eyesight of many future elderly adults. Cataract surgery has become a relatively simple outpatient procedure and now prevents blindness in large numbers of the elderly. Continuing improvements in prosthetic devices for vision and hearing including contact lenses, eyeglasses, and hearing aids also promise to make sensory loss less of a problem for future cohorts of older adults.

Learning and memory. Age changes in the speed of behavior may be the most pervasive age change, but age changes in learning and memory are the most troubling. An almost universal complaint among older adults is the feeling that one's ability to remember and to retrieve information is not as good as it used to be. Research on learning, memory, and aging has already provided insights about what older adults must do to learn and remember better. By unlocking the secrets of the neurobiology of learning and memory, we will understand how learning occurs and how memories are formed. With this knowledge we can design facilitators for these functions. Many cognition-enhancing drugs are in an experimental stage, but some are already available for treatment. Cognex® and Aricept® are used in the United States for AD, and nefiracetam will soon be available in Japan for treatment of cerebrovascular dementia. The aged of the future may carefully monitor their diet and take pills that will maintain and even enhance their ability to learn and remember.

In the case of memory loss due to disease such as AD, aging in the future may also be different. It is possible that the incidence of dementia will become less as treatments and cures for cardiovascular disease are developed and strokes are prevented. If measures to prevent dementia and neural degeneration associated with AD for 5–10 years are discovered, a much larger percentage of the elderly population will be enabled to care for themselves almost until they die. However, with treatments and cures for AD yet to be discovered, we may be faced with as many as 10 million older adults with AD for whom 24-hr nursing care must be provided. The cost in human suffering and in health care dollars for this burden from AD would be enormous.

Intellectual capacity. What is lost in terms of performance on speeded tasks is often more than compensated for by taking the bigger picture and integrating the information into a larger whole. With aging, individuals may lose efficiency on the things they no longer do, but they may maintain or improve competence on the tasks they continue to perform in occupations and in everyday lives (Baltes, 1993). What was called the Phase IV perspective in research on intelligence in chapter 10 emphasizes continued development of cognitive faculties in later life. New and expanded views of mature cognition are needed that take account of age-related changes in processing, thinking, and knowing (Rybash et al., 1986). With the increasing visibility of older adults in society, and with our increasing need for their skills to be used rather than retired, it seems desirable that future attitudes about cognitive capacity in old age become more positive.

Further Reading

Langston, J. W., & Palfreman, J. (1995). *The case of the frozen addicts*. New York: Pantheon.

This exciting nonfiction account of the discovery of cases of poisoning dopamine in drug addicts provides a number of insights about the scientific study of neurotransmitters and Parkinson's disease.

Baltes, P. B. (1993). The aging mind: Potentials and limits. *Gerontologist, 33,* 580–594.

An account of the cognitive strengths and losses in older adults by an expert who has assessed them throughout his career.

Manning, F. (1994). Tacrine therapy for the dementia of Alzheimer's disease. *American Family Physician, 50,* 819–826.

Description of one of the existing therapies for cognitive impairment in AD.

References

Chapter 1   Neuropsychological Approaches to Processes of Aging

Beach, F. A., Hebb, D. O., Morgan, C. T., & Nissen, H. W. (1960). *The neuropsychology of Lashley.* New York: McGraw-Hill.

Bengtson, V. L., & Haber, D. (1983). Sociological perspectives on aging. In D. S. Woodruff & J. E. Birren (Eds.), *Aging: Scientific perspectives and social issues* (2nd ed., pp. 72–93). Monterey, CA: Brooks/Cole.

Birren, J. E. (1969). Age and decision strategies. In A. T. Welford & J. E. Birren (Eds.), *Decision making and age.* Basel, Switzerland: S. Karger.

Birren, J. E., & Woodruff, D. S. (1983). Aging: Past and future. In D. S. Woodruff & J. E. Birren (Eds.), *Aging: Scientific perspectives and social issues* (2nd ed., pp. 1–15). Monterey, CA: Brooks/Cole.

Bruce, D. (1985). The origin of the term "Neuropsychology." *Neuropsychologia, 28,* 813–814.

Cheng, H., Cao, Y., & Olson, L. (1996). Spinal cord repair in adult paraplegic rats: Partial restoration of hind limb function. *Science, 273,* 510–513.

Diamond, M. C., Johnson, R. E., Protti, A. M., Ott, C., & Kajisa, L. (1985). Plasticity in 904-day-old male rat cerebral cortex. *Experimental Neurology, 87,* 309–317.

Diamond, M. C., Linder, B., Johnson, R., Bennett, E. L., & Rosenzweig, M. R. (1975). Differences in occipital cortical synapses from environmentally enriched, impoverished, and standard colony rats. *Journal of Neuroscience Research, 1,* 109–119.

Dustman, R. E., Ruhling, R. O., Russell, E. M., Shearer, D. E., Bonekat, W., Shigeoka, J. W., Wood, J. S., & Bradford, D. C. (1984). Aerobic exercise training and improved neuropsychological function of older individuals. *Neurobiology of Aging, 5,* 35–42.

Floeter, M. K., & Greenough, W. T. (1979). Cerebellar plasticity: Modification of Purkinje cell structure by differential rearing in monkeys. *Science, 206,* 227–229.

Green, E. J., Greenough, W. T., & Schlumpf, B. E. (1983). Effects of complex or isolated environments on cortical dendrites of middle-aged rats. *Brain Research, 264*, 233–240.

Hebb. D. O. (1949). *The organization of behaviour: A neuropsychological theory.* New York: Wiley.

Holden, C. (1996). New populations of old add to poor nations' burdens. *Science, 273*, 46–48.

Kolb, B. (1995). *Brain plasticity and behavior.* Mahwah, NJ: Lawrence Erlbaum Associates.

Kolb, B., & Whishaw, I. Q. (1995). *Fundamentals of human neuropsychology* (4th ed.). New York: W. H. Freeman.

Merzenich, M. M., & Jenkins, W. M. (1993). Reorganization of cortical representations of the hand following alterations of skin inputs induced by nerve injury, skin island transfers, and experience. *Journal of Hand Therapy, 6*, 89–104.

Ogden, J. A. (1996). *Fractured minds: A case-study approach to clinical neuropsychology.* New York: Oxford University Press.

Quinn, J. F. (1996, August). Entitlements and the Federal budget: A summary. *Gerontology News*, pp. 2–3.

Roush, W. (1996). Live long and prosper? *Science, 273*, 42–46.

Schaie, K. W. (1965). A general model for the study of developmental problems. *Psychological Bulletin, 64*, 92–107.

Singer, W. (1992). Adult visual cortex – Adaptation and reorganization. In L. R. Squire (Ed.), *Encyclopedia of learning and memory* (pp. 453–454). New York: Macmillan.

Thompson, R. F., Donegan, N., & Lavond, D. G. (1985). The psychobiology of learning and memory. In R. C. Atkinson, R. J. Herrinstein, G. Lindzey, & R. D. Luce (Eds.), *Stevens' handbook of experimental psychology* (2nd ed., pp. 245–351). New York: Wiley.

Turner, A. M., & Greenough, W. T. (1985). Differential rearing effects on rat visual cortex synapses. I. Synaptic and neuronal density and synapses per neuron. *Brain Research, 329*, 195–203.

Woodruff, D. S., & Birren, J. E. (1972). Age changes and cohort differences in personality. *Developmental Psychology, 6*, 252–259.

Woodruff-Pak, D. S. (1990). Mammalian models of learning, memory, and aging. In J. E. Birren & K. W. Schaie (Eds.), *Handbook of the psychology of aging* (3rd ed., pp. 235–257). New York: Academic Press.

Woodruff-Pak, D. S. (1995). Evaluation of cognition-enhancing drugs: Utility of the model system of eyeblink classical conditioning. *CNS Drug Reviews, 1*, 107–128.

Woodruff-Pak, D. S., & Hanson, C. (1995). Neuronal plasticity, brain compensation, and brain memory systems. In R. Dixon & L. Backman (Eds.), *Psychological compensation: Managing losses and promoting gains* (pp. 191–217). Hillsdale, NJ: Erlbaum.

Young, W. (1996). Spinal cord regeneration. *Science, 273*, 451.

Chapter 2   Neuropsychological Assessment in Adulthood and Aging

Ammons, R. B., & Ammons, C. H. (1962). *The Quick Test (QT)*. Missoula, MT: Psychological Test Specialists.

Balota, D. A., & Ferraro, F. R. (1993). A dissociation of frequency and regularity effects in pronunciation performance across young adults, older adults, and individuals with senile dementia of the Alzheimer type. *Journal of Memory and Language, 32,* 573–592.

Baltes, P. B. (1993). The aging mind: Potentials and limits. *Gerontologist, 33,* 580–594.

Baltes, P. B., Dittmann-Kohli, F., & Dixon, R. A. (1984). New perspectives on the development of intelligence in adulthood: Toward a dual-process conception and a model of selective optimization with compensation. In P. B. Baltes & O. G. Brim, Jr. (Eds.), *Life-span development and behavior* (Vol. 6, pp. 33–76). New York: Academic Press.

Berg, C. A., & Sternberg, R. J. (1985). A triarchic theory of intellectual development during adulthood. *Developmental Review, 5,* 334–370.

Birren, J. E. (1959). Principles of research on aging. In J. E. Birren (Ed.), *Handbook of aging and the individual* (pp. 3–42). Chicago: University of Chicago Press.

Blessed, G., Tomlinson, B. E., & Roth, M. (1968). The association between quantitative measures of dementia and of senile change in the cerebral gray matter of elderly subjects. *British Journal of Psychiatry, 114,* 797–811.

Botwinick, J. (1984). *Aging and behavior* (3rd ed.). New York: Springer.

Cerella, J., Hoyer, W., Rybash, J., & Commons, M. L. (Eds.). (1994). *Adult information processing: Limits on loss.* New York: Academic Press.

Christensen, H., Hadzi-Pavlovic, D., & Jacomb, P. (1991). The psychometric differentiation of dementia from normal aging: A meta-analysis. *Journal of Consulting and Clinical Psychology, 3,* 147–155.

Coslett, H. B., & Saffran, E. M. (1992). Visual information processing disorders in clinical practice. In D. Margolin (Ed.), *Cognitive neuropsychology in clinical practice.* New York: Oxford University Press.

Delis, D. C., Kramer, J. H., Kaplan, E., & Ober, B. A. (1983). *California Verbal Learning Test: Research Edition.* San Antonio, TX: Psychological Corporation.

Dixon, R. A., & Backman, L. (Eds.). (1995). *Compensating for psychological deficits and declines: Managing losses and promoting gains* (pp. 35–79). Mahwah, NJ: Erlbaum.

Ferrante, L. S., & Woodruff-Pak, D. S. (1995). Longitudinal investigation of eyeblink classical conditioning in the old-old. *Journal of Gerontology: Psychological Science, 50B,* P42–50.

Folstein, M. F., Anthony, J. C., Parhad, I., Duffy, B., & Gruenberg, E. M. (1985). The meaning of cognitive impairment in the elderly. *Journal of the American Geriatrics Society, 33,* 228–235.

Folstein, M. F., Folstein, S. E., & McHugh, P. R. (1975). "Mini-Mental State": A practical method of grading the cognitive state of patients for the clinician. *Journal of Psychiatric Research, 12,* 189–198.

Giambra, L. M., Arenberg, D., Zonderman, A. B., Kawas, C., & Costa, P. T. (1995). Adult life span changes in immediate visual memory and verbal intelligence. *Psychology and Aging, 10,* 123–139.

Golden, J. C. (1978). *Stroop color and word test.* Chicago: Stoelting.

Goodglass, H., & Kaplan, E. (1972). *Assessment of aphasia and related disorders.* Philadelphia: Lea & Febiger.

Hamilton, M. (1967). Development of a rating scale for primary depressive illness. *British Journal of Social and Clinical Psychiatry, 6,* 278–296.

Konkle, D. F., Beasley, D. S., & Bess, F. H. (1977). Intelligibility of time-altered speech in relation to chronological aging. *Journal of Speech and Hearing Research, 20,* 108–115.

Kuhlen, R. G. (1940). Social change: A neglected factor in psychological studies of the life span. *School and Society, 52,* 14–16.

Labouvie-Vief, G. (1985). Intelligence and cognition. In J. E. Birren & K. W. Schaie (Eds.), *Handbook of the psychology of aging* (pp. 500–530). New York: Van Nostrand Reinhold.

La Rue, A. (1992). *Aging and neuropsychological assessment.* New York: Plenum Press.

Marsiske, M., Lang, F. R., Baltes, P. B., & Baltes, M. M. (1995). Selective optimization with compensation: Life-span perspectives on successful human development. In R. A. Dixon & L. Backman (Eds.), *Compensating for psychological deficits and declines: Managing losses and promoting gains* (pp. 35–79). Mahwah, NJ: Erlbaum.

Murphy, M. D., Sanders, R. E., Gabriesheski, A. S., & Schmitt, F. A. (1981). Metamemory in the aged. *Journal of Gerontology, 36,* 185–193.

Peach, R. K. (1987). Language functioning. In H. G. Mueller & V. C. Geoffrey (Eds.), *Communication disorders in aging* (pp. 238–270). Washington, DC: Gallaudet University Press.

Radloff, L. S. (1977). The CES-D scale: A self-report depression scale for research in the general population. *Applied Psychological Measurement, 1,* 385–401.

Roca, R. P. (1987). Bedside cognitive examination. *Psychosomatics, 28,* 71–76.

Rosen, W. G., Mohs, R. C., & Davis, K. L. (1984). A new rating scale for Alzheimer's disease. *American Journal of Psychiatry, 141,* 1356–1364.

Salthouse, T. A. (1984). Effects of age and skill in typing. *Journal of Experimental Psychology: General, 113,* 345–371.

Schaie, K. W. (1978). External validity in the assessment of intellectual development in adulthood. *Journal of Gerontology, 33,* 695–701.

Schaie, K. W. (1990). Intellectual development in adulthood. In J. E. Birren & K. W. Schaie (Eds.), *Handbook of the psychology of aging* (3rd ed., pp. 291–310). San Diego, CA: Academic Press.

Schaie, K. W. (1994). The course of adult intellectual development. *American Psychologist, 49,* 304–313.

Sheridan, J. (1976). Restoring speech and language skills. *Geriatrics, 31,* 83–86.

Spreen, O., & Strauss, E. (1991). *A compendium of neuropsychological tests: Administration, norms, and commentary.* New York: Oxford University Press.

Stankov, L. (1988). Aging, attention, and intelligence. *Psychology and Aging, 3,* 59–74.

Stern, R. G., Mohs, R. C., Davidson, M., Schmeidler, J., Silverman, J., Kramer-Ginsberg, E., Searcey, T., Bierer, L., & Davis, K. L. (1994). A longitudinal study of Alzheimer's disease: Measurement, rate, and predictors of cognitive deterioration. *American Journal of Psychiatry, 151,* 390–396.

Sternberg, R. J. (1985). *Beyond IQ: A triarchic theory of human intelligence.* Cambridge, UK: Cambridge University Press.

Stroop, J. R. (1935). Studies of interference in serial verbal reaction. *Journal of Experimental Psychology, 18,* 643–662.

Tuokko, H., Hadjustavropoulos, T., Miller, J., & Beattie, B. (1992). The Clock Test: A sensitive measure to differentiate normal elderly from those with Alzheimer's disease. *Journal of the American Geriatrics Society, 40,* 579–584.

Watson, Y., Arfken, C., & Birge, S. (1993). Clock completion: An objective screening test for dementia. *Journal of the American Geriatrics Society, 41,* 1235–1240.

Wolf-Klein, G., Silverstone, F., Levy, A., & Brod, M. (1989). Screening for Alzheimer's disease by clock drawing. *Journal of the American Geriatrics Society, 27,* 730–734.

Woodruff-Pak, D. S. (1989). Age and intelligence: Changing perspectives in the twentieth century. *Journal of Aging Studies, 3,* 91–118.

Woodruff-Pak, D. S., & Finkbiner, R. G. (1995). Larger nondeclarative than declarative deficits in learning and memory in human aging. *Psychology and Aging, 10,* 416–426.

Woodruff-Pak, D. S., Finkbiner, R. G., & Sasse, D. K. (1990). Eyeblink conditioning discriminates Alzheimer's patients from non-demented aged. *NeuroReport, 1,* 45–48.

Woodruff-Pak, D. S., & Jaeger, M. (1997). Predictors of eyeblink classical conditioning over the adult age span. (Submitted.)

Zec, R. F., Landreth, E. S., Bird, E. et al. (1994). Psychometric strengths and weaknesses of the Alzheimer's Disease Assessment Scale in clinical testing: Recommendations for improvements. In E. Giacobini & R. Becker (Eds.), *Alzheimer's disease: Therapeutic strategies* (pp. 444–449). Boston: Birkhauser.

Chapter 3   Methods for Assessing the Aging Brain

Bashore, T. R. (1993). Differential effects of aging on the neurocognitive functions subserving speeded mental processing. In J. Cerella, J. Rybash, W. Hoyer, & M. L. Commons (Eds.), *Adult information processing: Limits on loss* (pp. 37–76). San Diego, CA: Academic Press.

Bashore, T. R. (1994). Some thoughts on neurocognitive slowing. *Acta Psychologica, 86,* 295–325.

Birren, J. E., Butler, R. N., Greenhouse, S. W., Sokoloff, L., & Yarrow, M. R. (Eds.). (1963). *Human aging: A biological and behavioral study.* Washington, DC: US Government Printing Office.

Brazier, M. A. B., & Finesinger, J. E. (1944). Characteristics of the normal electroencephalogram. I. A study of the occipital–cortical potentials in 500 normal adults. *Journal of Clinical Investigation, 23,* 303–311.

Duncan-Johnson, C., & Donchin, E. (1977). On quantifying surprise: The variation of event-related potentials with subjective probability. *Psychophysiology, 14,* 456–467.

Durkin, M., Prescott, L., Furchtgott, E., Cantor, J., & Powell, D. A. (1993). Concomitant eyeblink and heart rate classical conditioning in young, middle-aged, and elderly human subjects. *Psychology and Aging, 8,* 571–581.

Dustman, R. E., & Beck, E. C. (1966). Visually evoked potentials: Amplitude changes with age. *Science, 151,* 1013–1015.

Dustman, R. E., & Beck, E. C. (1969). The effects of maturation and aging on the wave form of visually evoked potentials. *Electroencephalography and Clinical Neurophysiology, 26,* 2–11.

Dustman, R. E., Beck, E. C., & Schenkenberg, T. (1977). Life-span changes in man. In J. E. Desmedt (Ed.), *Cerebral evoked potentials in man: The Brussels International Symposium.* London: Oxford University Press.

Ford, J. M., & Pfefferbaum, A. (1980). The utility of brain potentials in determining age-related changes in central nervous system and cognitive functions. In L. Poon (Ed.), *Aging in the 1980s: Psychological issues* (pp. 115–124). Washington, DC: American Psychological Association.

Fox, J. H., Kaszniak, A. W., & Huckman, M. (1979). Computerized tomographic scanning not very helpful in dementia – nor in craniopharyngioma [Letter]. *New England Journal of Medicine, 300,* 437.

Goodin, D., Squires, K., Henderson, B., & Starr, A. (1978). Age-related variations in evoked potentials to auditory stimuli in normal human subjects. *Electroencephalography and Clinical Neurophysiology, 44,* 447–458.

Grady, C. L., McIntosh, A. R., Horwitz, B., Maisog, J. Ma., Ungerleider, L. G., Mentis, M. J., Pietrini, P., Schapiro, M. B., & Haxby, J. V. (1995). Age-related reductions in human recognition memory due to impaired encoding. *Science, 269,* 218–221.

Growden, J. H., Corkin, S., Buonanno, F., Davis, K., Huff, F. J., Beal, M. F., & Kramer, C. (1986). Diagnostic methods in Alzheimer's disease: Magnetic resonance brain imaging and CSF neurotransmitter markers. In A. Fisher, I. Hanin, & C. Lachman (Eds.), *Alzheimer's and Parkinson's diseases* (pp. 191–204). New York: Plenum.

Harkins, S. W., & Lenhardt, M. (1980). Brainstem auditory evoked potentials in the elderly. In L. Poon (Ed.), *Aging in the 1980s: Psychological issues.* Washington, DC: American Psychological Association.

Huckman, M. S., Fox, J., & Topel, J. (1975). The validity of criteria for the evaluation of cerebral atrophy by computed tomography. *Radiology, 116,* 85–92.

Kaszniak, A. W. (1977). Effects of age and cerebral atrophy upon span of immediate recall and paired associate learning in older adults. *Dissertation Abstracts International, 37* (7-B), 3613–3614.

Kaszniak, A. W., Garron, D. C., Fox, J. H., Bergen, D., & Huckman, M. (1979). Cerebral atrophy, EEG slowing, age, education, and cognitive functioning in suspected dementia. *Neurology, 29,* 1273–1279.

Khachaturian, Z. (1985). Diagnosis of Alzheimer's disease. *Archives of Neurology, 42,* 1097–1105.

Kutas, M., McCarthy, G., & Donchin, E. (1977). Augmenting mental chronometry: The P300 as a measure of stimulus evaluation. *Science, 197,* 792–795.

Li, Y.-T., Woodruff-Pak, D. S., & Trojanowski, J. Q. (1994). Amyloid plaques in cerebellar cortex and the integrity of Purkinje cell dendrites. *Neurobiology of Aging, 15,* 1–9.

Lindsley, D. B. (1960). Attention, consciousness, sleep, and wakefulness. In J. Field (Ed.), *Handbook of physiology* (Vol. 3), New York: American Physiological Society.

Marsh, G., & Thompson, L. W. (1972). Age differences in evoked potentials during an auditory discrimination task. *Gerontologist, 12,* 44.

Marsh, G., & Thompson, L. W. (1977). Psychophysiology of aging. In J. E. Birren & K. W. Schaie (Eds.), *Handbook of the psychology of aging.* New York: Van Nostrand Reinhold.

Obrist, W. D., & Busse, E. W. (1965). The electroencephalogram in old age. In W. P. Wilson (Ed.), *Applications of electroencephalography in psychiatry.* Durham, NC: Duke University Press.

Obrist, W. D., Henry, C. E., & Justiss, W. A. (1961). Longitudinal study of EEG in old age. *Excerpta Medical International Congress.* Serial No. 37, 180–181.

Posner, M. I., & Raichle, M. E. (1994). *Images of mind.* New York: Scientific American Library.

Rowe, M. J. (1978). Normal variability of the brain-stem auditory evoked response in young and old adult subjects. *Electroencephalography and Clinical Neurophysiology, 44,* 459–470.

Schacter, D. L., Savage, C. R., Alpert, N. M., Rauch, S. L., & Albert, M. S. (1996). The role of hippocampus and frontal cortex in age-related memory changes: A PET study. *NeuroReport, 7,* 1165–1169.

Schenkenberg, T. (1970). Visual, auditory, and somatosensory evoked responses of normal subjects from childhood to senescence. Unpublished doctoral dissertation. University of Utah.

Schenkenberg, T., Dustman, R. E., & Beck, E. C. (1971). Changes in evoked responses related to age, hemisphere, and sex. *Electroencephalography and Clinical Neurophysiology, 30,* 163–164.

Schroeder, M. M., Lipton, R. B., & Ritter, W. (1991). Event-related potentials in the study of aging: Sensory and psychological processes. In J. R. Jennings & M. G. H. Coles (Eds.), *Handbook of cognitive psychophysiology: Central and autonomic nervous system approaches* (pp. 691–705). New York: John Wiley & Sons.

Solomon, P. R., Levine, E., Bein, T., & Pendlebury, W. W. (1991). Disruption of classical conditioning in patients with Alzheimer's disease. *Neurobiology of Aging,* *12,* 283–287.

Solomon, P. R., Pomerleau, D., Bennett, L., James, J., & Morse, D. L. (1989). Acquisition of the classically conditioned eyeblink response in humans over the lifespan. *Psychology and Aging, 4,* 34–41.

Thompson, L. W., & Marsh, G. R. (1973). Psychophysiological studies of aging. In C. Eisdorfer & M. P. Lawton (Eds.), *The psychology of adult development and aging.* Washington, DC: American Psychological Association.

Thompson, R. F. (1986). The neurobiology of learning and memory. *Science, 233,* 941–947.

Woodruff, D. S. (1985). Arousal, sleep, and aging. In J. E. Birren & K. W. Schaie (Eds.), *Handbook of the psychology of aging* (pp. 261–295). New York: Van Nostrand Reinhold.

Woodruff-Pak, D. S., Finkbiner, R. G., & Sasse, D. K. (1990). Eyeblink conditioning discriminates Alzheimer's patients from non-demented aged. *NeuroReport, 1,* 45–48.

Woodruff-Pak, D. S., Papka, M., & Simon, E. W. (1994). Down's Syndrome adults 35 and older show eyeblink classical conditioning profiles comparable to Alzheimer's disease patients. *Neuropsychology, 8,* 1–11.

Woodruff-Pak, D. S., & Thompson, R. F. (1988). Classical conditioning of the eyeblink response in the delay paradigm in adults aged 18–83 years. *Psychology and Aging, 3,* 219–229.

Chapter 4   Normal Aging in the Peripheral Nervous System

Anderson, B. (1987). Eye: Clinical issues. In G. L. Maddox (Ed.), *The encyclopedia of aging.* New York: Springer.

Birren, J. E., Bick, M. W., & Fox, C. (1948). Age changes in light threshold of the dark adapted eye. *Journal of Gerontology, 3,* 267–271.

Birren, J. E., Shapiro, H. B., & Miller, J. H. (1950). The effect of salicylate upon pain sensitivity. *Journal of Pharmacology and Experimental Therapy, 100,* 67–71.

Bogdonoff, M. D., Estes, E. H., Jr., Friedberg, S. J., & Klein, R. F. (1961). Fat mobilization in man. *Annals of Internal Medicine, 55,* 328–338.

Bogdonoff, M. D., Estes, E. H., Jr., Harlan, W. R., Trout, D. L., & Kirschner, N. (1960). Metabolic and cardiovascular changes during a state of acute central nervous system arousal. *Journal of Clinical Endocrine Metabolism, 20,* 1333–1340.

Bogdonoff, M. D., Weissler, A. M., & Merritt, F. L. (1960). Effect of autonomic ganglionic blockade upon serum free fatty acid levels in man. *Journal of Clinical Investigation, 39,* 959–965.

Bolton, C. F., Winkelmann, R. K., & Dyck, P. J. (1966). A quantitative study of Meissner's corpuscles in man. *Neurology, 16,* 363–369.

Botwinick, J., & Kornetsky, C. (1960). Age differences in the acquisition and extinction of GSR. *Journal of Gerontology, 15,* 83–84.

Brant, L. J., Wood, J. L., & Fozard, J. L. (1986). Age changes in hearing thresholds. *Gerontologist, 26,* 156.

Byrd, E., & Gertman, S. (1959). Taste sensitivity in aging persons. *Geriatrics, 14,* 381–384.

Cain, W. S., & Stevens, J. C. (1989). Uniformity of olfactory loss in aging. *Annals of the New York Academy of Science, 561,* 29–38.

Cooper, R. M., Bilash, M. A., & Zubek, J. P. (1959). The effect of age on taste sensitivity. *Journal of Gerontology, 14,* 56–58.

Corso, J. F. (1977). Auditory perception and communication. In J. E. Birren & K. W. Schaie (Eds.), *Handbook of the psychology of aging.* New York: Van Nostrand Reinhold.

Corwin, J., Serby, P., Contrad, P., & Rotrosen, J. (1985). Olfactory recognition deficit in Alzheimer's and Parkinsonian dementias. *IRCS Medical Science, 13,* 260.

Doty, R. L. (1990). Aging and age-related neurological disease: Olfaction. In F. Goller & J. Grafman (Eds.), *Handbook of neuropsychology* (pp. 459–462). Amsterdam: Elsevier.

Doty, R. L. (1991). Olfactory capacities in aging and Alzheimer's disease: Psychophysical and anatomic considerations. In J. H. Growdon, S. Corkin, E. Ritter-Walker, & R. J. Wurtman (Eds.), *Aging and Alzheimer's disease: Sensory systems, neuronal growth, and neuronal metabolism* (Vol. 640, pp. 10–27), New York: New York Academy of Sciences.

Doty, R. L., Reyes, P. F., & Gregor, T. (1987). Presence of both odor identification and detection deficits in Alzheimer's disease. *Brain Research Bulletin, 18,* 597–600.

Eisdorfer, C. (1968). Arousal and performance: Experiments in verbal learning and a tentative theory. In G. A. Talland (Ed.), *Human aging and behavior.* New York: Academic Press.

Eisdorfer, C., Nowlin, J. B., & Wilkie, F. (1970). Improvement of learning in the aged by modification of autonomic nervous system activity. *Science, 170,* 1327–1329.

Engen, T. (1977). Taste and smell. In J. E. Birren & K. W. Schaie (Eds.), *Handbook of the psychology of aging.* New York: Van Nostrand-Reinhold.

Fozard, J. L. (1990). Vision and hearing in aging. In J. E. Birren & K. W. Schaie (Eds.), *Handbook of the psychology of aging* (3rd ed., pp. 150–170). San Diego, CA: Academic Press.

Fozard, J. L., Gittings, N. S., & Shock, N. W. (1986). Age changes in visual acuity. *Gerontologist, 26,* 158.

Froehling, S. (1974). Effects of propranolol on behavioral and physiological measures in elderly males. Unpublished doctoral dissertation. University of Miami, Florida.

Granick, S., Kleban, M. H., & Weiss, A. D. (1976). Relationships between hearing loss and cognition in normally hearing aged persons. *Journal of Gerontology, 31,* 434–440.

Grzegorczyk, P. B., Jones, S. W., & Mistretta, C. M. (1979). Age-related differences in salt taste acuity. *Journal of Gerontology, 34,* 834–840.

Harkins, S. W., & Chapman, C. R. (1976). Detection and decision factors in pain perception in young and elderly men. *Pain, 2,* 253–264.

Harkins, S. W., & Chapman, C. R. (1977). The perception of induced dental pain in young and elderly women. *Journal of Gerontology, 32,* 428–435.

Harkins, S. W., Moss, S. F., Thompson, L. W., & Nowlin, J. B. (1976). Relationship between central and autonomic nervous system activity: Correlates of psychomotor performance in elderly men. *Experimental Aging Research, 2,* 409–423.

Hughes, G. (1969). Changes in taste sensitivity with advancing age. *Gerontologica Clinica, 11,* 224–230.

Hyman, B. T., Arriagada, P. V., & Van Hoesen, G. W. (1991). Pathologic changes in the olfactory system in aging and Alzheimer's disease. In J. H. Gorwdon, S. Corkin, E. Ritter-Walker, & R. J. Wurtman (Eds.), *Aging and Alzheimer's disease: Sensory systems, neuronal growth, and neuronal metabolism* (Vol. 640, pp. 14–19), New York: New York Academy of Sciences.

Kosnik, W., Winslow, L., Kline, D., Rasinski, K., & Sekuler, R. (1988). Visual changes in daily life throughout adulthood. *Journal of Gerontology: Psychological Sciences, 43,* P63–P70.

Lindsley, D. B. (1960). Attention, consciousness, sleep, and wakefulness. In J. Field (Ed.), *Handbook of physiology* (Vol. 3, Section 1), New York: American Physiological Society.

Marsh, G. R., & Thompson, L. W. (1977). Psychophysiology of aging. In J. E. Birren & K. W. Schaie (Eds.), *Handbook of the psychology of aging* (pp. 219–248), New York: Van Nostrand Reinhold.

McFarland, R. A. (1968). The sensory and perceptual processes in aging. In K. W. Schaie (Ed.), *Theory and methods of research on aging.* Morgantown, VW: West Virginia University Press.

McFarland, R. A., & Fisher, M. B. (1955). Alterations in dark adaptation as a function of age. *Journal of Gerontology, 10,* 424–428.

Murphy, C. (1988). Taste and smell in the elderly. In H. L. Meiselman & R. S. Rivlin (Eds.), *Clinical measurement of taste and smell* (pp. 343–371). New York: Macmillan.

Murphy, C., Gilmore, M. M., Seery, C. S., Salmon, D. P., & Lasker, B. R. (1990). Olfactory thresholds are associated with degree of dementia in Alzheimer's disease. *Neurobiology of Aging, 11,* 465–469.

Navarro, M. (1996, August 7). Florida is leading the way in a big generational shift. *New York Times, CXLV,* 1.

Powell, A. H., Jr., Eisdorfer, C., & Bogdonoff, M. D. (1964). Physiologic response patterns observed in a learning task. *Archives of General Psychiatry, 10,* 192–195.

Roberts, J. C. (1987). Eye: Structure and function. In G. L. Maddox (Ed.), *The encyclopedia of aging.* New York: Springer.

Ronge, H. (1943). Altersveränderungen des Berührungssinnes: I. druckpunktschwellen und druckpunktfrequenz. *Acta Physiologica Scandinavica, 6,* 343–352.

Rovee, C. K., Cohen, R. Y., & Shlapack, W. (1975). Life-span stability in olfactory sensitivity. *Developmental Psychology, 11,* 311–318.

Schaie, K. W., Baltes, P. B., & Strother, C. R. (1964). A study of auditory sensitivity in advanced age. *Journal of Gerontology, 19,* 453–457.

Schluderman, E., & Zubek, J. P. (1962). Effect of age on pain sensitivity. *Perceptual and Motor Skills, 14,* 295–301.

Schwab, L., & Taylor, H. R. (1985). Cataract and delivery of surgical services in developing nations. In *Clinical ophthalmology* (Vol. 5), New York: Harper & Row.

Surwillo, W. W. (1966). On the relation of latency of alpha attenuation to alpha rhythm frequency and the influence of age. *Electroencephalography and Clinical Neurophysiology, 20,* 129–132.

Surwillo, W. W., & Quilter, R. E. (1965a). The influence of age on latency time of involuntary (galvanic skin reflex) and voluntary responses. *Journal of Gerontology, 20,* 173–176.

Surwillo, W. W., & Quilter, R. E. (1965b). The relation of frequency of spontaneous skin potential responses to vigilance and to age. *Psychophysiology, 1,* 272–276.

Talamo, B. R., Feng, W.-H., Perez-Cruet, M., Adelman, L., Kosik, K. et al. (1991). Pathologic changes in olfactory neurons in Alzheimer's disease. In J. H. Growdon, S. Corkin, E. Ritter-Walker, & R. J. Wurtman (Eds.), *Aging and Alzheimer's disease: Sensory systems, neuronal growth, and neuronal metabolism* (Vol. 640, pp. 1–7), New York: New York Academy of Sciences.

Talamo, B. R., Rudel, R. A., Kosik, K. S., Lee, V. M.-Y., Neff, S., Adelman, L., & Kauer, J. S. (1989). Pathological changes in olfactory neurons in patients with Alzheimer's disease. *Nature, 337,* 736–739.

Thompson, L. W., & Nowlin, J. B. (1973). Relation of increased attention to central and autonomic nervous system states. In L. F. Jarvik, C. Eisdorfer, & J. E. Blum (Eds.), *Intellectual functioning in adults.* New York: Springer.

Thornbury, J., & Mistretta, C. M. (1981). Tactile sensitivity as a function of age. *Journal of Gerontology, 36,* 34–39.

Troyer, W. G., Jr., Eisdorfer, C., Wilkie, F., & Bogdonoff, M. D. (1966). Free fatty acid responses in the aged individual during performance of learning tasks. *Journal of Gerontology, 21,* 415–419.

US Department of Health, Education, and Welfare. (1965). *National health survey: Hearing levels of adults by age and sex, U.S. 1960–1962.* Washington, DC: US Government Printing Office.

Welford, A. T. (1965). Performance, biological mechanisms and age: A theoretical sketch. In A. T. Welford & J. E. Birren (Eds.), *Behavior, aging and the nervous system.* Springfield, IL: Charles C. Thomas.

Woodruff, D. S. (1985). Arousal, sleep, and aging. In J. E. Birren and K. W. Schaie (Eds.), *Handbook of the psychology of aging* (2nd ed., pp. 261–295). New York: Van Nostrand Reinhold.

Wysocki, C. J., & Gilbert, A. N. (1989). National Geographic Smell Survey: Effects of age are heterogeneous. *Annals of the New York Academy of Science, 561,* 12–28.

Chapter 5 Normal Aging of the Brain

Adolfsson, R., Gottfries, C. G., Roos, B. E., & Winblad, B. (1979). Postmortem distribution of dopamine and homovanillac acid in human brain, variations related to age, and a review of the literature. *Journal of Neural Transmission, 45,* 81–105.

Altman, H. J. (1985). Mediation of storage and retrieval with two drugs that selectively modulate serotonergic neurotransmission. *Annals of the New York Academy of Science, 444,* 496–498.

Altman, H. J., & Normile, H. J. (1987). Different temporal effects of serotonergic antagonists on passive avoidance retention. *Pharmacology, Biochemistry and Behavior, 28,* 353–359.

Altman, H. J., & Normile, H. J. (1988). What is the nature of the role of the serotonergic nervous system in learning and memory: Prospects for development of an effective treatment strategy for senile dementia. *Neurobiology of Aging, 9,* 627–638.

Arnsten, A. F. T., & Goldman-Rakic, P. S. (1985). Alpha 2-adrenergic mechanisms in prefrontal cortex associated with cognitive decline in aged nonhuman primates. *Science, 230,* 1273–1276.

Azmitia, E. C., Whitaker-Azmitia, P. M., & Bartus, R. (1988). Use of tissue culture models to study neuronal regulatory trophic and toxic factors in the aged brain. *Neurobiology of Aging, 9,* 743–758.

Barnes, C. A. (1983). The physiology of the senescent hippocampus. In W. Seifert (Ed.), *Neurobiology of the hippocampus* (pp. 87–108). New York: Academic Press.

Barnes, C. A., Foster, T. C., Rao, G., & McNaughton, B. L. (1991). Specificity of functional changes during normal brain aging. In J. H. Growdon, S. Corkin, E. Ritter-Walker, & R. J. Wurtman (Eds.), *Aging and Alzheimer's disease: Sensory systems, neuronal growth, and neuronal metabolism* (Vol. 640, pp. 80–85), New York: New York Academy of Sciences.

Bartus, R. T., Dean, R. T., & Beer, B. (1983). An evaluation of drugs for improving memory in aged monkeys: Implications for clinical trials in humans. *Psychopharmacology Bulletin, 19,* 168–184.

Bartus, R. T., Dean, R. L., & Flicker, C. (1987). Cholinergic psychopharmacology: An integration of human and animal research on memory. In H. L. Meltzer (Ed.), *Psychopharmacology: The third generation of progress* (pp. 219–232). New York: Raven Press.

Bickford-Wimer, P. C., Granholm, A. C., & Gerhardt, G. A. (1988). Cerebellar noradrenergic systems in aging: Studies *in situ* and in *in oculo* grafts. *Neurobiology of Aging, 9,* 591–599.

Bondareff, W. (1980). Compensatory loss of axosomatic synapses in the dentate gyrus of the senescent rat. *Mechanisms of Aging and Development, 12,* 221–229.

Bondareff, W. (1985). The neural basis of aging. In J. E. Birren & K. W. Schaie (Eds.), *Handbook of the psychology of aging* (pp. 95–108). New York: Van Nostrand Reinhold.

Bondareff, W., Mountjoy, C. Q., & Roth, M. (1982). Loss of neurons of origin of the adrenergic projection to cerebral cortex (nucleus locus ceruleus) in senile dementia. *Neurology, 32,* 164–168.

Brody, H. (1955). Organization of the cerebral cortex. III. A study of aging in the human cerebral cortex. *Journal of Comparative Neurology, 102,* 551–556.

Brody, H. (1978). Cell counts in cerebral cortex and brainstem. In R. Katzman, R. D. Terry, & K. L. Bick (Eds.), *Aging*, Vol. 17: *Alzheimer's disease: senile dementia and related disorders* (pp. 345–351). New York: Raven Press.

Brizzee, K. R., & Ordy, J. M. (1979). Age pigments, cell loss and hippocampal function. *Mechanisms of Ageing and Development, 9,* 143–162.

Brizzee, K. R., Ordy, J. M., & Bartus, R. T. (1980). Localization of cellular changes within multimodal sensory regions in aged monkey brain: Possible implications for age-related cognitive loss. *Neurobiology of Aging, 1,* 45–52.

Brozoski, T. J., Brown, R. M., Rosvold, H. E., & Goldman, P. S. (1979). Cognitive deficit caused by regional depletion of dopamine in prefrontal cortex of rhesus monkey. *Science, 205,* 929–932.

Coffey, C. E., Wilkinson, W. E., Parashos, I. A., Soady, S. A. R., Sullivan, R. J., Patterson, L. J., Figiel, G. S., Webb, M. C., Spritzer, C. E., & Djang, W. T. (1992). Quantitative cerebral anatomy of the aging human brain: A cross-sectional study using magnetic resonance imaging. *Neurology, 42,* 527–536.

Coffin, J. M., Trojanowski, J. Q., & Woodruff-Pak, D. S. (1996). Age differences in cerebellum but not hippocampus are related to deficits in conditioning. (Submitted.)

Collier, T. J., Gash, D. M., Bruemmer, V., & Sladek, J. R. (1985). Impaired regulation of arousal in old age and the consequences for learning and memory: Replacement of brain norepinephrine via neuron transplants improves memory in aged F344 rats. In B. B. Davis & W. G. Wood (Eds.), *Homeostatic function and aging* (pp. 99–110). New York: Raven Press.

Coyle, J. T., Price, D. L., & DeLong, M. R. (1983). Alzheimer's disease: A disorder of cortical cholinergic innervation. *Science, 219,* 1184–1190.

Court, J. A., Perry, E. K. Johnson, M., Piggott, M. A., Kerwin, J. A., Perry, R. H., & Ince, P. G. (1993). Regional patterns of cholinergic and glutamate activity in the developing and aging human brain. *Developmental Brain Research, 74,* 73–82.

Dayan, A. D. (1971). Comparative neuropathology of ageing: Studies on the brains of 47 species of vertebrates. *Brain, 94,* 31–42.

Decker, M. W., & McGaugh, J. L. (1989). Effects of concurrent manipulations of the cholinergic and noradrenergic function on learning and retention in mice. *Brain Research, 477,* 29–37.

Disterhoft, J. F., Moyer, J. R., Jr., Thompson, L. T., & Kowalska, M. (1993). Functional aspects of calcium-channel modulation. *Clinical Neuropharmacology, 16* (Suppl 1), S12–24.

Ellis, R. S. (1920). Norms for some structural changes in the human cerebellum from birth to old age. *Journal of Comparative Neurology, 32,* 1–34.

Feig, S., & Lipton, P. (1990). N-methyl-D-aspartate receptor activation and Ca^{2+} account for poor pyramidal cell structure in hippocampal slices. *Journal of Neurochemistry, 55,* 473–483.

Flood, D. G., & Coleman, P. D. (1988). Neuron numbers and sizes in aging brain: Comparisons of human, monkey, and rodent data. *Neurobiology of Aging, 9,* 453–463.

Freedman, R. D., Hoffer, B., Woodward, D., & Puro, D. (1977). Interaction of norepinephrine with cerebellar activity evoked by mossy climbing fibers. *Experimental Neurology, 55,* 269–288.

Geula, C., & Mesulam, M.-M. (1994). Cholinergic systems and related neuropathological predilection in Alzheimer's disease. In R. D. Terry, R. Katzman, & K. L. Bick (Eds.), *Alzheimer's Disease* (pp. 263–291). New York: Raven Press.

Glick, R., & Bondareff, W. (1979). Loss of synapses in the cerebellar cortex of the senescent rat. *Journal of Gerontology, 34,* 818–822.

Gold, P. E., & Zornetzer, S. F. (1983). The mnemon and its juices: Neuromodulation of memory processes. *Behavioral and Neural Biology, 38,* 151–189.

Goldman-Rakic, P. S., & Brown, R. M. (1981). Regional changes of monoamines in cerebral cortex and subcortical structures of aging rhesus monkeys. *Neuroscience, 6,* 177–187.

Golomb, J., de Leon, M. J., Kluger, A., George, A. E., Tarshish, C., & Ferris, S. H. (1993). Hippocampal atrophy in normal aging. *Archives of Neurology, 50,* 967–973.

Grady, C. L., McIntosh, A. R., Horwitz, B., Maisog, J. Ma., Ungerleider, L. G., Mentis, M. J., Pietrini, P., Schapiro, M. B., & Haxby, J. V. (1995). Age-related reductions in human recognition memory due to impaired encoding. *Science, 269,* 218–221.

Hall, T. C., Miller, K. H., & Corsellis, J. A. N. (1975). Variations in the human Purkinje cell population according to age and sex. *Neuropathology and Applied Neurobiology, 1,* 267–292.

Harms, J. W. (1944). Altern und somatod der Zellverbandstiere. *Zeitschrift für Alternsforschung, 5,* 73–126.

Haug, H., Barmwater, U., Egger, R., Fischer, D., Kuhl, S., & Sass, N. L. (1983). Anatomical changes in the aging brain: Morphometric analysis of the human prosencephalon. In J. Cervos-Navarro & H. I. Sarkander (Eds.), *Aging,* Vol. 21: *Brain Aging: Neuropathology and neuropharmacology* (pp. 1–12). New York: Raven Press.

Kesner, R. P. (1988). Reevaluation of the contribution of the basal forebrain cholinergic system to memory. *Neurobiology of Aging, 9,* 609–616.

Khachaturian, Z. S. (1984). Towards theories of brain ageing. In D. W. Kay & G. D. Burrows (Eds.), *Handbook of studies in psychiatry and old age* (pp. 7–30). New York: Elsevier.

Khachaturian, Z. S. (1989). The role of calcium regulation in brain aging: Reexamination of a hypothesis. *Aging, 1,* 17–34.

Kolb, B., & Whishaw, I. Q. (1995). *Fundamentals of human neuropsychology* (4th ed.). New York: W. H. Freeman.

Knox, C. A. (1982). Effects of aging and chronic arterial hypertension of the cell populations in the neocortex and archicortex of the rat. *Acta Neuropathologica (Berlin), 56,* 139–145.

Levitt, P., Rakic, P., & Goldman-Rakic, P. S. (1984). Region-specific distribution of catecholamine afferents in primate cerebral cortex: A fluorescence histochemical analysis. *Journal of Comparative Neurology, 31,* 533–538.

Lippa, A. S., Pelham, R. W., Beer, B., Critchell, D. J., Dean, R. L., & Bartus, R. T. (1980). Brain cholinergic function and memory in aged rats. *Neurobiology of Aging, 1,* 10–16.

Magnusson, K. R., & Cotman, C. W. (1993). Age-related changes in excitatory amino acid receptors in two mouse strains. *Neurobiology of Aging, 14,* 197–206.

Mamo, H., Meric, P., Luft, A., & Seylaz, J. (1983). Hyperfrontal pattern of human cerebral circulation: Variations with age and atherosclerotic state. *Archives of Neurology, 40,* 626–632.

Mani, R. B., Lohr, J. B., & Jeste, D. V. (1986). Hippocampal pyramidal cells and aging in the human: A quantitative study of neuronal loss in sectors CA1 to CA4. *Experimental Neurology, 94,* 29–40.

Mann, D. M. A., Yates, P. O., & Marcyniuk, B. (1985). Some morphometric observations on the cerebral cortex and hippocampus in presenile Alzheimer's disease, senile dementia of Alzheimer type and Down's syndrome in middle age. *Journal of Neurological Science, 69,* 139–159.

Marcusson, J., Finch, C. E., Morgon, D. G., & Winblad, B. (1984). Ageing and serotonin receptors in human brain. *Clinical Neuropharmacology, 7,* 289–298.

Marwaha, J., Hoffer, B., & Freedman, R. (1981). Changes in noradrenergic transmission in rat cerebellum during aging. *Neurobiology of Aging, 2,* 95–98.

Masliah, E., Mallory, M., Hansen, L., DeTeresa, R., & Terry, R. D. (1993). Quantitative synaptic alterations in the human neocortex during normal aging. *Neurology, 43,* 192–197.

McGeer, E. G. (1978). Aging and neurotransmitter metabolism in the brain. In R. Katzman, R. D. Terry, & K. L. Bick (Eds.), *Alzheimer's disease: Senile dementia and related disorders* (pp. 427–440). New York: Raven Press.

Mesulam, M. M. (1988). Involutional and developmental implications of age-related neuronal changes: In search of an engram for wisdom. *Neurobiology of Aging, 8,* 581–583.

Mesulam, M. M., Mufson, E. J., & Rogers, J. (1987). Age-related shrinkage of cortically projecting cholinergic neurons: A selective effect. *Annals of Neurology, 22,* 31–36.

Miller, A. K. H., Alston, R. L., Mountjoy, C. Q., & Corsellis, J. A. N. (1984). Automated differential cell counting on a sector of the normal human hippocampus: The influence of age. *Neuropathology and Applied Neurobiology, 10,* 123–141.

Mouritzen Dam, A. (1979). The density of neurons in the human hippocampus. *Neuropathology and Applied Neurobiology, 5,* 249–264.

Nabeshima, T. (1994). Ameliorating effects of nefiracetam (DM-9384) on brain dysfunction. *Drugs of Today, 30,* 357–379.

Nandy, K. (1981). Morphological changes in the cerebellar cortex of aging *Macaca nemestrina. Neurobiology of Aging, 2,* 61–64.

Normile H. J., & Altman, H. J. (1988). Enhanced passive avoidance retention following posttraining serotonergic receptor antagonist administration in middle-aged and aged rats. *Neurobiology of Aging, 9,* 377–382.

Pittman, R. N., Minneman, K., & Molinoff, P. B. (1980). Alterations in beta1- and beta2-adrenergic receptor density in the cerebellum of aging rats. *Journal of Neurochemistry, 35,* 273–275.

Raz, N., Torres, I. J., Spencer, W. D., & Acker, J. D. (1993). *Psychobiology, 15,* 21–36.

Rogers, J., & Ashton-Jones, G. (1988). The neurophysiology of aging: Insights from new applications of old techniques. *Neurobiology of Aging, 9,* 601–605.

Rogers, J., & Bloom, F. E. (1985). Neurotransmitter metabolism and function in the aging central nervous system. In C. E. Finch & E. L. Schneider (Eds.), *Handbook of the biology of aging* (2nd ed., pp. 645–691). New York: Van Nostrand Reinhold.

Rogers, J., Silver, M. A., Shoemaker, W. J., & Bloom, F. E. (1980). Senescent changes in a neurobiological system: Cerebellar Purkinje cell electrophysiology and correlative anatomy. *Neurobiology of Aging, 1,* 3–11.

Rogers, J., Zornetzer, S. F., Bloom, F. E., & Mervis, R. E. (1984). Senescent microstructural changes in the rat cerebellum. *Brain Research, 292,* 23–32.

Sara, S. J. (1989). Noradrenergic-cholinergic interactions: Its possible role in memory dysfunction associated with senile dementia. *Archives of Gerontology and Geriatrics,* (Suppl 1), 99–108.

Schacter, D. L., Savage, C. R., Alpert, N. M., Rauch, S. L., & Albert, M. S. (1996). The role of hippocampus and frontal cortex in age-related memory changes: A PET study. *NeuroReport, 7,* 1165–1169.

Schanne, F. A., Kane, A. B., Young, E. E., & Farber, J. L. (1979). Calcium dependence of toxic cell death: A final common pathway. *Science, 206,* 700–702.

Scheibel, M. E., Lindsay, R. D., Tomiyasu, U., & Scheibel, A. B. (1976). Progressive dendritic changes in the aging human limbic system. *Experimental Neurology, 53,* 420–430.

Shaw, T. G., Mortel, K. F., Stirling Meyer, J., Rogers, R. L., Hardenberg, J., & Cutaia, M. M. (1984). Cerebral blood flow changes in benign aging and cerebrovascular disease. *Neurology, 34,* 855–862.

Singer, W. (1992). Adult visual cortex – Adaptation and reorganization. In L. R. Squire (Ed.), *Encyclopedia of learning and memory* (pp. 453–454). New York: Macmillan.

Squire, L. R. (1992). Memory and the hippocampus: A synthesis from findings with rats, monkeys, and humans. *Psychological Review, 99,* 195–231.

Tachibana, H., Meyer, J. S., Okayasu, H., & Kandula, P. (1984). Change in topographic patterns of human cerebral flow with age measured by Xenon CT. *American Journal of Roentgenology, 142,* 1027–1034.

Terry, R. D., DeTeresa, R., & Hansen, L. A. (1987). Neocortical cell counts in normal human adult aging. *Annals of Neurology, 21,* 530–539.

Tomlinson, B. E., Irving, D., & Blessed, G. (1981). Cell loss in the locus coeruleus in senile dementia of Alzheimer type. *Journal of Neurological Sciences, 49,* 419–428.

Turner, A. M., & Greenough, W. T. (1985). Differential rearing effects on rat visual cortex synapses. I. Synaptic and neuronal density and synapses per neuron. *Brain Research, 329,* 195–203.

Vijayashankar, N., & Brody, H. (1979). A quantitative study of the pigmented neurons in the nuclei locus coeruleus and subcoeruleus in man as related to aging. *Journal of Neuropathology and Experimental Neurology, 38,* 490–497.

Vizi, E. S. (1980). Modulation of cortical release of acetylcholine by noradrenaline released from nerves arising from the rat locus coeruleus. *Neuroscience, 5,* 2139–2144.

Wenk, G. L., Hughey, D., Boundy, V., Kim, A., Walker, L., & Olton, D. (1987). Neurotransmitters and memory: Role of cholinergic, serotonergic, and noradrenergic systems. *Behavioral Neuroscience, 101,* 325–332.

West, M. J. (1993a). New stereological methods for counting neurons. *Neurobiology of Aging, 14,* 275–285.

West, M. J. (1993b). Regionally specific loss of neurons in the aging human hippocampus. *Neurobiology of Aging, 14,* 287–293.

West, M. J., & Coleman, P. (1996). Editorial. *Neurobiology of Aging, 17,* x.

Whitehouse, P. J. (1988). Specific neurochemical systems and memory. *Neurobiology of Aging, 9,* 639.

Whitehouse, P. J., Martino, A. M., Antuono, P. G., Lowenstein, P. R., Coyle, J. T., Price, D. L., & Kellar, K. J. (1986). Nicotinic acetylcholine binding sites in Alzheimer's disease. *Brain Research, 371,* 146–151.

Wickelgran, I. (1996). For the cortex, neuron loss may be less than thought. *Science, 273,* 48–50.

Wong, D. F., Wagner, H. N., Dannals, R. F., Links, J. M., Frost, J. J., Ravert, H. T., Wilson, A. A., Rosenbaum, A. E., Gjedde, A., Douglass, K. H., Petronis, J. D., Folstein, M. F., Toung, J. K. T., Burns, H. D., & Kuhar, M. J. (1984). Effects of age on dopamine and serotonin receptors measured by positron tomography in the living human brain. *Science, 226,* 1393–1396.

Woodruff-Pak, D. S., Cronholm, J. F., & Sheffield, J. B. (1990). Purkinje cell number related to rate of eyeblink classical conditioning. *NeuroReport, 1,* 165–168.

Woodruff-Pak, D. S., & Hanson, C. (1995). Neuronal plasticity, brain compensation, and brain memory systems. In R. Dixon & L. Backman (Eds.), *Psychological compensation: Managing losses and promoting gains* (pp. 191–217). Hillsdale, NJ: Erlbaum.

Zornetzer, S. F. (1986). Applied aspects of memory research: Aging. In J. L. Martinez & R. P. Kesner (Eds.), *Learning and memory: A biological view* (pp. 203–236). New York: Academic Press.

Zornetzer, S. F., Abraham, W. C., & Appleton, R. (1978). Locus coeruleus and labile memory. *Pharmacology, Biochemistry and Behavior, 9,* 227–234.

Chapter 6   Neuropathological Brain Aging

American Academy of Neurology (1994). Practice parameter for diagnosis and evaluation of dementia (Summary statement). *Neurology, 44,* 2203–2206.

Arriagada, P. E., Growdon, J. H., Hedley-White, E. T., & Hyman, B. T. (1992). Neurofibrillary tangles but not senile plaques parallel duration and severity of Alzheimer's disease. *Neurology, 42,* 631–639.

Berg, J. M., Brandon, M. W., & Kirman, B. H. (1959). Atropine in mongolism. *The Lancet, ii,* 441–442.

Berrios, G. E. (1994). Dementia and ageing since the nineteenth century. In F. A. Hippert et al. (Eds.), *Dementia and normal ageing.* Cambridge, UK: Cambridge University Press.

Beyreuther, K., Bush, A. I., Dyrks, T., Hilbich, C., Konig, G., Moenning, U., Multhaup, G., Prior, R., Rumble, B., Schubert, W., Small, D. H., Weidemann, A., & Masters, C. L. (1991). Mechanisms of amyloid deposition in Alzheimer's disease. In J. H. Growdon, S. Corkin, E. Ritter-Walker, & R. J. Wurtman (Eds.), *Aging and Alzheimer's disease: Sensory systems, neuronal growth, and neuronal metabolism* (Vol. 640, pp. 129–139), New York: New York Academy of Sciences.

Bird, T. D., Sumi, S. M., Nemens, E. J., Nochlin, D., Schellenberg, G., Lampe, T. H., Sadovnick, A., Chui, H., Miner, G. W., & Tinklenbert, J. (1989). Phenotypic beterogeneity in familial Alzheimer's disease: A study of 24 kindreds. *Annals of Neurology, 25,* 12–25.

Bowen, D. M., Smith, C. B., White, P., & Davison, A. N. (1976). Neurotransmitter-related enzymes and indices of hypoxia in senile dementia and other abiotrophies. *Brain, 99,* 459–496.

Braak, E. & Braak, H. (1996). Lesional patterns in Parkinson's and Alzheimer's diseases. *Neurobiology of Aging, 17,* S116–117.

Braak, H. & Braak, E. (1996). Evolution of Alzheimer's disease related intraneuronal changes. *Neurobiology of Aging, 17,* S36–37.

Christensen, H., Hadzi-Pavlovic, D., & Jacomb, P. (1991). The psychometric differentiation of dementia from normal aging: A meta-analysis. *Journal of Consulting and Clinical Psychology, 3,* 147–155.

Coyle, J. T., Price, D. L., & DeLong, M. R. (1983). Alzheimer's disease: A disorder of cortical cholinergic innervation. *Science, 217,* 1053–1055.

Davies, P., & Maloney, A. J. F. (1976). Selective loss of central cholinergic neurons in Alzheimer's disease. *Lancet, ii,* 1403.

Dickson, D. W., Crystal, H. A., Mattiace, L. A., Masur, D. M., Blau, A. D., Davies, P., Yen, S.-H., & Aronson, M. (1991). Identification of normal and pathological aging in prospectively studied nondemented elderly humans. *Neurobiology of Aging, 13,* 179–189.

Evans, D. A., Funkenstein, H. H., Albert, M. S., Scherr, P. A., Cook, N. R., Chown, M. J., Hebert, L. E., Hannekens, C. H., & Taylor, J. O. (1989). Prevalence of Alzheimer's disease in a community population of older persons. *Journal of the American Medical Association, 262,* 2551–2556.

Ferrante, L. S., & Woodruff-Pak, D. S. (1995). Longitudinal investigation of eyeblink classical conditioning in the old-old. *Journal of Gerontology: Psychological Science, 50,* P42–50.

Geula, C., & Mesulam, M.-M. (1994). Cholinergic systems and related neuropathological predilection in Alzheimer's disease. In R. D. Terry, R. Katzman, & K. L. Bick (Eds.), *Alzheimer's disease* (pp. 263–291). New York: Raven Press.

Hardy, J. (1993). Genetic mistakes point the way for Alzheimer's disease. *Journal of NIH Research, 5,* 46–49.

Hardy, J., & Allsop, D. (1991). Amyloid deposition as the central event in the etiology of Alzheimer's disease. *Trends in Pharmacological Science, 12,* 383–388.

Harris, W. S., & Goodman, R. M. (1968). Hyper-reactivity to atropine in Down's Syndrome. *New England Journal of Medicine, 279,* 407–410.

Hsiao, K., & Prusiner, S. B. (1990). Inherited human prion diseases. *Neurology, 40,* 1820–1827.

Hsiao, K., Scott, M., Foster, D., DeArmond, S. J., Groth, D., Servan, H., & Prusiner, S. B. (1991). Spontaneous neurodegeneration in transgenic mice with prion protein codon 101 proline–Leucine substitution. In J. H. Growdon, S. Corkin, E. Ritter-Walker, & R. J. Wurtman (Eds.), *Aging and Alzheimer's disease: Sensory systems, neuronal growth, and neuronal metabolism* (Vol. 640, pp. 166–170). New York: New York Academy of Sciences.

Katzman, R. (1984). *Clinical and pathologic aspects of Alzheimer's disease.* Invited paper presented at the 14th Annual Meeting of the Society for Neuroscience, Anaheim, CA.

Katzman, R., & Kawas, C. (1994). The epidemiology of dementia and Alzheimer's disease. In R. D. Terry, R. Katzman, & K. L. Bick (Eds.), *Alzheimer's disease* (pp. 105–122). New York: Raven.

Khachaturian, Z. S. (1985) Progress of research on Alzheimer's disease: Research opportunities for behavioral scientists. *American Psychologist, 40,* 1251–1255.

Khachaturian, Z. S. (1996). *Harmonization of dementia drug guidelines: Report of the international working groups.* Paper presented at the 5th International Conference on Alzheimer's Disease, Osaka, Japan.

Mann, D. M. A., & Esiri, M. M. (1989). The pattern of acquisition of plaques and tangles in the brains of patients under 50 years of age with Down's syndrome. *Journal of Neurological Science, 89,* 169–179.

Matsuyama, H. (1983). Incidence of neurofibrillary change, senile plaques, and granulovacuolar degeneration in aged individuals. In B. Reisberg (Ed.), *Alzheimer's disease.* New York: Free Press.

McKee, A. C. K., Kosik, S., & Kowall, N. W. (1991). Neuritic pathology and dementia in Alzheimer's disease. *Annals of Neurology, 30,* 156–165.

McKhann, G., Drachman, D., Folstein, M., Katzman, R., Price, D., & Stadlan, E. M. (1984). Clinical diagnosis of Alzheimer's disease. *Neurology, 34,* 939–944.

Mesulam, M.-M. (1988). Involutional and developmental implications of age-related neuronal changes: In search of an engram for wisdom. *Neurobiology of Aging, 8,* 581–583.

Mortimer, J. A. (1983) Alzheimer's disease and senile dementia: Prevalence and incidence. In B. Reisberg (Ed.), *Alzheimer's disease*. New York: Free Press.

Mortimer, J. A., Schuman, L. M., & French, L. R. (1981) Epidemiology of dementing illness. In J. A. Mortimer & L. M. Schuman (Eds.), *The epidemiology of dementia*. New York: Oxford University Press.

Mullan, M., & Crawford, F. (1993). Genetic and molecular advances in Alzheimer's disease. *Trends in Neuroscience, 16*, 398–403.

O'Brien, C. (1996). Auguste D. and Alzheimer's disease. *Science, 273*, 28.

Perl, D. P., Gajdusek, D. C., Garruto, R. M., Yanagihara, R. T., & Gibbs, C. J., Jr. (1982). Intraneuronal aluminum accumulation in amyotrophic lateral sclerosis and parkinsonism–dementia of Guam. *Science, 217*, 1053–1055.

Perl, D. P., & Good, P. F. (1991). Aluminum, Alzheimer's disease, and the olfactory system. In J. H. Growdon, S. Corkin, E. Ritter-Walker, & R. J. Wurtman (Eds.), *Aging and Alzheimer's disease: Sensory systems, neuronal growth, and neuronal metabolism* (Vol. 640, pp. 8–13). New York: New York Academy of Sciences.

Poirier, J. (1996). Neurobiology of apolipoprotein E. *Neurobiology of Aging, 17*, S74.

Price, D. L., Borchelt, D. R., & Sisodia, S. S. (1993). Alzheimer's disease and the prion disorders amyloid β-protein and prion protein amyloidoses. *Proceedings of the National Academy of Science, USA, 90*, 6381–6384.

Price, D. J., Koo, E. H., & Unterbeck, A. (1989). Cellular and molecular biology of Alzheimer's disease. *Bioessays, 10*, 69–74.

Prusiner, S. B. (1982). Novel proteinaceous infectious particles cause scrapie. *Science, 216*, 136–144.

Reisberg, B. (1983) Clinical presentation, diagnosis, and symptomatology of age-associated cognitive decline and Alzheimer's disease. In B. Reisberg (Ed.), *Alzheimer's disease*. New York: Free Press.

Roses, A., Saunders, C., Hulette, K., Welsh, B., Crain, J., Burke, J., Alberts, M., Strittmatter, W., Breitner, J., Earl, N., Clark, C., Heyman, A., Gaskell, P. Jr., & Pericak-Vance, M. A. (1996). Predictive value of APOE genotyping in a consecutive series of autopsied sporadic probable Alzheimer disease patients. *Neurobiology of Aging, 17*, S74.

Sacks, B., & Smith, S. (1989). People with Down's Syndrome can be distinguished on the basis of cholinergic dysfunction. *Journal of Neurology, Neurosurgery, and Psychiatry, 52*, 1294–1295.

Saunders, A. M., Strittmatter, W. J., Schmechel, D., St. George-Hyslop, P. H., Pericak-Vance, M. A., Joo, S. H., Rosi, B. L., Gusella, J. F., Crapper-MacLachlan, D. R., Alberts, M. J., Hulette, C., Crain, B., Goldgaber, D., & Roses, A. D. (1993). Association of apolipoprotein E allele e4 with late-onset familial and sporadic Alzheimer's disease. *Neurology, 43*, 1467–1472.

Scinto, L. F. M., Daffner, K. R., Dressier, D., Ransil, B. I., Rentz, D., Weintraub, S., Mesulam, M.-M & Potter, H. (1994). Potential noninvasive neurobiological test for Alzheimer's disease. *Science, 266*, 1051–1054.

Selkoe, D. J. (1993). Physiological production of the β-amyloid protein and the mechanisms of Alzheimer's disease. *Trends in Neuroscience, 16*, 403–409.

Selkoe, D. J. (1996). Amyloidosis of Aβ42 as the common pathogenetic mechanism of all forms of Alzheimer's disease. *Neurobiology of Aging, 17,* S37.

Smith, S. A., & Dewhirst, R. R. (1986). A simple diagnostic test for pupillary abnormality in diabetic autonomic neuropathy. *Diabetic Medicine, 3,* 38–41.

Solomon, P. R., Levine, E., Bein, T., & Pendlebury, W. W. (1991). Disruption of classical conditioning in patients with Alzheimer's disease. *Neurobiology of Aging, 12,* 283–287.

Stern, R. G., Mohs, R. C., Davidson, M. et al. (1994). A longitudinal study of Alzheimer disease: Measurement, rate, and predictors of cognitive deterioration. *American Journal of Psychiatry, 151,* 390–396.

Thase, M. E. (1988). The relationship between Down syndrome and Alzheimer's disease. In L. Nadel (Ed.), *The psychobiology of Down syndrome* (pp. 345–368). Cambridge, MA: The MIT Press.

Trojanowski, J. Q., & Lee, V. M.-Y. (1994). Phosphorylation of neuronal cytoskeletal proteins in Alzheimer's disease and Lewy body dementias. *Annals of the New York Academy of Science, 747,* 92–109.

Wisniewski, K. E., Wisniewski, H. M., & Wen, G. Y. (1985). Occurrence of neuropathological changes and dementia of Alzheimer's disease in Down's syndrome. *Annals of Neurology, 17,* 278–282.

Woodruff-Pak, D. S., Finkbiner, R. G., & Sasse, D. K. (1990). Eyeblink conditioning discriminates Alzheimer's patients from non-demented aged. *NeuroReport, 1,* 45–48.

Woodruff-Pak, D. S., Romano, S. J., & Hinchliffe, R. M. (1996). Detection of Alzheimer's disease with eyeblink classical conditioning and the pupil dilation response. *Alzheimer's Research, 12,* 173–180.

Yates, C. M., Ritchie, I. M., Simpson, J., Maloney, A. F. J., & Gordon, A. (1981). Noradrenaline in Alzheimer-type dementia and Down's syndrome. *The Lancet, ii,* 39–40.

Yates, C. M., Simpson, J., Maloney, A. F. J., Gordon, A., & Reid, A. H. (1980). Alzheimer-like cholinergic deficiency in Down syndrome. *The Lancet, ii,* 979.

Zec, R. F., Landreth, E. S., Bird, E., Harris, R. B., Robbs, R., Markwell, S. J., & McManus, D. Q. (1994). Psychometric strengths and weaknesses of the Alzheimer's Disease Assessment Scale in clinical testing: Recommendations for improvements. In E. Giacobini & R. Becker (Eds.), *Alzheimer's disease: Therapeutic strategies* (pp. 444–449). Boston: Birkhauser.

Chapter 7   Emotion, Aging, and Brain Function

American Psychiatric Association (1980). *Diagnostic and statistical manual of mental disorders* (3rd ed., *DSM-III*). Washington, DC: American Psychiatric Association.

Beck, A. T. (1967). *Depression: Causes and treatment.* Philadelphia: University of Pennsylvania Press.

Beutler, L., Scogin, F., Meredith, K., Schretlin, D., Hamblin, D., Potter, R., &

Corbishley, A. (1986). Efficacy of cognitive group therapy for depressed older adults. *Gerontologist, 26,* 214.

Blazer, D. G. (1982a). *Depression in late life.* St Louis, MO: Mosby.

Blazer, D. G. (1982b). The epidemiology of late life depression. *Journal of the American Geriatrics Society, 30,* 581–592.

Blazer, D. G. (1994). Epidemiology of late life depression. In L. Sneider et al. (Eds.), *Diagnosis and treatment of depression in late life: Results of the NIH consensus development conference* (pp. 9–21). Washington, DC: American Psychiatric Press.

Boyd, J. H., & Weissman, M. M. (1981). Epidemiology of affective disorders: A reexamination and future directions. *Archives of General Psychiatry, 38,* 1039–1046.

Boyd, J. H., & Weissman, M. M. (1982). Epidemiology. In E. S. Paykel (Ed.), *Handbook of the affective disorders* (pp. 109–125). New York: Guilford.

Braak, E., & Braak, H. (1996). Lesional patterns in Parkinson's and Alzheimer's diseases. *Neurobiology of Aging, 17,* S116–117.

Butler, R. N. (1975). *Why survive? Being old in America.* New York: Harper and Row.

Caine, E. D. (1986). The neuropsychology of depression: The pseudodementia syndrome. In I. Grant & K. M. Adams (Eds.), *Neuropsychological assessment of neuropsychiatric disorders* (pp. 221–243). New York: Oxford University Press.

Cappeliez, P. (1993). Depression in elderly persons: Prevalence, predictors, and psychological intervention. In P. Cappeliez & R. J. Flynn (Eds.), *Depression and the social environment: Research and intervention with neglected populations* (pp. 332–369). Montreal, Canada: McGill-Queen's University Press.

Craig, T. J., & Van Natta, P. A. (1979). Influence of demographic characteristics on two measures of depressive symptoms: The relation of prevalence and persistence of symptoms with sex, age, education, and marital status. *Archives of General Psychiatry, 36,* 149–154.

Damasio, H., Grabowski, T., Frank, R., Galaburda, A. M., & Damasio, A. R. (1994). The return of Phineas Gage: Clues about the brain from the skull of a famous patient, *Science, 264,* 1102–1105.

Davidson, R. J. (1995). Cerebral asymmetry, emotion and affective style. In R. J. Davidson & K. Hughdahl (Eds.), *Brain asymmetry* (pp. 361–387). Cambridge, MA: MIT Press.

Gallagher, D., Thompson, L. W., & Breckenridge, J. S. (1986). Efficacy of three modalities of individual psychotherapy: One year follow-up results. *Gerontologist, 26,* 214.

Gallagher, D., Thompson, L. W., & Levy, S. M. (1980). Clinical psychological assessment in older adults. In L. W. Poon (Ed.), *Aging in the 1980s: Psychological issues* (pp. 19–40). Washington, DC: American Psychological Association.

Gatz, M., Hurwicz, M., & Weicker, W. (1986). *Are old people more depressed? Cross-sectional data on CES-D factors.* Paper presented at the annual meeting of the American Psychological Association, Washington, DC.

Gatz, M., Smyer, M. A., & Lawton, M. P. (1980). The mental health system and the older adult. In L. Poon (Ed.), *Aging in the 1980s: Psychological issues* (pp. 5–18). Washington, DC: American Psychological Association.

Gurland, B. J. (1976). The comparative frequency of depression in various adult age groups. *Journal of Gerontology, 31,* 283–292.

Hamilton, M. (1967). Development of a rating scale for primary depressive illness. *British Journal of Social and Clinical Psychiatry, 6,* 278–296.

Harlow, J. M. (1868). Recovery from the passage of an iron bar through the head. *Publications of the Massachusetts Medical Society (Boston), 2,* 327–346.

Harmatz, J., & Shader, R. (1975). Psychopharmacologic investigations in healthy elderly volunteers: MMPI Depression Scale. *Journal of American Geriatrics Society, 23,* 350–354.

Hellige, J. B. (1993). *Hemispheric asymmetry: What's right and what's left.* Cambridge, MA: Harvard University Press.

Hirschfield, R. M. A., & Cross, C. K. (1982). Epidemiology of affective disorders: Psychological risk factors. *Archives of General Psychiatry, 39,* 35–46.

Hybels, D. C. (1986). *Depression in the elderly: An application of the reformulated learned helplessness model.* Unpublished doctoral dissertation, Temple University.

Kolb, B., & Whishaw, I. Q. (1995). *Fundamentals of human neuropsychology* (4th ed.). New York: W. H. Freeman.

Kolb, B., & Milner, B. (1981). Observations on spontaneous facial expression after focal cerebral excisions and after intracarotid injection of sodium amytal. *Neuropsychologia, 19,* 505–514.

La Rue, A. (1992). *Aging and neuropsychological assessment.* New York: Plenum.

La Rue, A., D'Elia, L. F., Clark, E. O., Spar, J. E., & Jarvik, L. F. (1986a). Clinical tests of memory in dementia, depression and healthy aging. *Psychology and Aging, 1,* 69–77.

La Rue, A., Spar, J. E., & Hill, C. (1986b). Cognitive impairment in late-life depression: Clinical correlates and treatment implication. *Journal of Affective Disorders, 11,* 179–184.

Libon, D. J., Glosser, G., Malamut, B. L., Kaplan, E., Goldberg, E., Swenson, R., & Sands, L. P. (1994). Age, executive functions, and visuospatial functioning in healthy older adults. *Neuropsychology, 8,* 38–43.

Lieberman, M. A. (1982). The effects of social support on responses to stress. In L. Goldberger & S. Breznitz (Eds.), *Handbook of stress: Theoretical and clinical aspects.* New York: Free Press.

Mann, J. J. et al. (1989). Neurobiological models. In J. J. Mann (Ed.), *Psychological, biological and genetic perspectives.* New York: Plenum.

Manton, K. G., Blazer, D. G., & Woodbury, M. A. (1987). Suicide in middle age and later life: Sex and race specific life table and cohort analyses. *Journal of Gerontology, 42,* 219–227.

Marcopulos, B. A. (1989). Pseudodementia, dementia, and depression: Test differentiation. In T. Hunt & C. J. Lindley (Eds.), *Testing older adults* (pp. 70–91). Austin, TX: Pro-ed.

Miller, M. (1979). *Suicide after sixty: The final alternative.* New York: Springer.

National Center for Health Statistics (1986, September 26). Advance report of the final mortality statistics, 1984. *Monthly Vital Statistics Report* (Vol. 35, No. 6, Suppl. 2. DHHS Pub. No. (PHS) 86–1120). Public Health Service, Hyattsville, MD.

Ogden, J. A. (1996). *Fractured minds: A case-study approach to clinical neuropsychology.* New York: Oxford University Press.

Parmelee, P. A., Katz, I. R., & Lawton, M. P. (1989). Depression among institutionalized aged: Assessment and prevalence estimation. *Journal of Gerontology: Medical Sciences, 44,* M22–29.

Post, F. (1966). Somatic and psychic factors in the treatment of elderly psychiatric patients. *Journal of Psychosomatic Research, 10,* 13–19.

Salzman, C., & Shader, R. I. (1979). Clinical evaluation of depression in the elderly. In A. Raskin & L. F. Jarvik (Eds.), *Psychiatric symptoms and cognitive loss in the elderly.* Washington, DC: Hemisphere.

Spitzer, R. L., Endicott, J., & Robins, E. (1978). *Research diagnostic criteria (RDC) for a selected group of functional disorders.* New York: New York State Psychiatric Institute.

Storandt, M., Siegler, I. C., & Elias, M. F. (Eds.). (1978). *Clinical psychology of aging.* New York: Plenum.

Teri, L., Uomoto, J., & Stoffel, C. (1986). Treatment of depression in Alzheimer's disease: Helping caregivers to help themselves and their patients. *Gerontologist, 26,* 214.

Tucker, D. M. (1981). Lateral brain function, emotion, and conceptualization. *Psychological Bulletin, 89,* 19–46.

Veith, R. C., & Raskind, M. A. (1988). The neurobiology of aging: Does it predispose to depression? *Neurobiology of Aging, 9,* 101–117.

Zemore, R., & Eames, N. (1979). Psychic and somatic symptoms of depression among young adults, institutionalized aged and noninstitutionalized aged. *Journal of Gerontology, 34,* 716–722.

Zung, W. W. K. (1965). A self-rating depression scale. *Archives of General Psychiatry, 12,* 63–70.

Zung, W. W. K. (1967). Depression in the normal aged. *Psychosomatics, 8,* 287–291.

Zung, W. W. K. (1973). From art to science: The diagnosis and treatment of depression. *Archives of General Psychiatry, 29,* 328–337.

Chapter 8 Arousal and Sleep

Albert, M. S., & Kaplan, E. F. (1980). Organic implications of neuropsychological deficits in the elderly. In L. W. Poon, J. Fozard, L. Cermak, D. Arenberg, & L. W. Thompson (Eds.), *New directions in memory and aging: Proceedings of the George A. Talland memorial conference.* Hillsdale, NJ: Erlbaum.

Ancoli-Israel, S., Kripke, D. F., Mason, W., & Messin, S. (1981). Sleep apnea and nocturnal myoclonus in a senior population. *Sleep, 4,* 349–358.

Arbuckle, T. Y., & Gold, D. P. (1993). Aging, inhibition and verbosity. *Journal of Gerontology: Psychological Sciences, 48,* 225–232.

Baltes, P. B. (1968). Longitudinal and cross-sectional sequences in the study of age and generation effects. *Human Development, 11,* 145–171.

Birren, J. E. (1960). Behavioral theories of aging. In N. W. Shock (Ed.), *Aging –*

Some social and biological aspects. Washington, DC: American Association for the Advancement of Science.

Birren, J. E. (1963). Psychophysiological relations. In J. E. Birren, R. N. Butler, S. W. Greenhouse, L. Sokoloff, & M. R. Yarrow (Eds.), *Human aging: A biological and behavioral study.* Washington, DC: US Government Printing Office.

Bliwise, D. L., Carey, E., & Dement, W. C. (1983). Nightly variation in sleep-related respiratory disturbance in older adults. *Experimental Aging Research, 9,* 77–81.

Bliwise, D. L., Carskadon, M., Carey, E., & Dement, W. C. (1984). Longitudinal development of sleep-related respiratory disturbance in adult humans. *Journal of Gerontology, 39,* 290–293.

Bondareff, W. (1980). Compensatory loss of axosomatic synapses in the dentate gyrus of the senescent rat. *Mechanisms of Ageing and Development, 12,* 221–229.

Braun, H. W., & Geiselhart, R. (1959). Age differences in the acquisition and extinction of the conditioned eyelid response. *Journal of Experimental Psychology, 57,* 386–388.

Brazier, M. A. B., & Finesinger, J. E. (1944). Characteristics of the normal electroencephalogram. I. A study of the occipital–cortical potentials in 500 normal adults. *Journal of Clinical Investigation, 23,* 303–311.

Callner, D. A., Dustman, R. E., Madsen, J. E., Schenkenberg, T. & Beck, E. C. (1978). Life span changes in the averaged evoked responses of Down's syndrome and nonretarded subjects. *American Journal of Mental Deficiency, 82,* 398–405.

Carlson, M. C., Hasher, L., Connelly, S. L., & Zacks, R. T. (1995). Aging, distraction, and the benefits of predictable location. *Psychology and Aging, 10,* 427–436.

Carskadon, M. A. (1982). Sleep fragmentation, sleep loss, and sleep need in the elderly. *The Gerontologist, 22,* 187.

Connelly, S. L., Hasher, L., & Zacks, R. T. (1991). Age and reading: The impact of distraction. *Psychology and Aging, 6,* 533–541.

Daum, I., & Schugens, M. M. (1996). On the cerebellum and classical conditioning. *Current Directions in Psychological Science, 5,* 58–61.

Davis, P. A. (1941). The electroencephalogram in old age. *Diseases of the nervous system, 2,* 77.

Donchin, E., Ritter, W., & McCallum, W. C. (1978). Cognitive psychophysiology: The endogenous components of the ERP. In E. Callaway, P. Tueting, & S. Koslow (Eds.), *Event-related brain potentials in man.* New York: Academic Press.

Drechsler, F. (1977). Determination of neurophysiological parameters of the aging CNS. I. Evoked potentials. *Aktuel-Gerontology, 7,* 273–283.

Drechsler, F. (1978). Quantitative analysis of neurophysiological processes of the aging CNS. *Journal of Neurology, 218,* 197–213.

Dustman, R. E., & Beck, E. C. (1969). The effects of maturation and aging on the wave form of visually evoked potentials. *Electroencephalography and Clinical Neurophysiology, 26,* 2–11.

Dustman, R. E., Emmerson, R. Y., & Shearer, D. E. (1996). Life span changes in electrophysiological measures of inhibition. *Brain and Cognition, 30,* 109–126.

Dustman, R. E., & Snyder, E. W. (1981). Life-span changes in visually evoked potentials at central scalp. *Neurobiology of Aging, 2,* 303–308.

Dustman, R. E., Snyder, E. W., & Schlehuber, C. J. (1981). Life-span alterations in visually evoked potentials and inhibitory function. *Neurobiology of Aging, 2,* 187–192.

Eeg-Olofsson, O. (1971). The development of the electroencephalogram in normal children and adolescents from the age of 1 through 21 years. *Acta Paediatrica Scandinavica Supplementum, 208,* 1–46.

Feinberg, I. (1974). Changes in sleep cycle patterns with age. *Journal of Psychiatric Research, 10,* 283–306.

Feinberg, I., Koresko, R., & Heller, N. (1967). EEG sleep patterns as a function of normal and pathological aging in man. *Journal of Psychiatric Research, 5,* 107–144.

Foret, J., & Webb, W. B. (1980). Changes in temporal organization of sleep stages in man aged from 20 to 70 years. *Review of Electroencephalography and Neurophysiology Clinica, 10,* 171–176.

Fuster, J. M. (1989). *The prefrontal cortex: Anatomy, physiology, and neuropsychology of the frontal lobe* (2nd ed.). New York: Raven Press.

Galbraith, G. C., Gliddon, J. B., & Busk, J. (1970). Visual evoked responses in mentally retarded and nonretarded subjects. *American Journal of Mental Deficiency, 75,* 341–348.

Gerard, L., Zacks, R. T., Hasher, L., & Radvansky, G. A. (1991). Age deficits in retrieval: The fan effect. *Journal of Gerontology: Psychological Sciences, 46,* P313–136.

Gliddon, J. B., Busk, J., & Galbraith, G. C. (1975). Visual evoked responses as a function of light intensity in Down's syndrome and nonretarded subjects. *Psychophysiology, 12,* 416–422.

Goldman-Rakic, P. S. (1992). Working memory and the mind. *Scientific American, 267,* 111–117.

Guilleminault, C. C., & Dement, W. C. (Eds.). (1978). *Sleep apnea syndromes.* New York: Alan R. Liss.

Hartley, A. A., & Kieley, J. M. (1995). Adult age differences in the inhibition of return to visual attention. *Psychology and Aging, 10,* 670–683.

Hasher, L., Stoltzfus, E. R., Zacks, R. T., & Rypma, B. (1991). Age and inhibition. *Journal of Experimental Psychology: Learning, Memory, and Cognition, 17,* 163–169.

Hasher, L., & Zacks, R. T. (1988). Working memory, comprehension, and aging: A review and a new view. In G. H. Bower (Ed.), *The psychology of learning and motivation* (Vol. 22, pp. 193–225). Orlando, FL: Academic Press.

Hubbard, O., Sunde, D., & Goldensohn, E. S. (1976). The EEG of centenarians. *Electroencephalography and Clinical Neurophysiology, 40,* 407–417.

Institute of Medicine (1979). *Sleeping pills, insomnia, and medical practice.* Washington, DC: National Academy of Science.

Jerome, E. A. (1959). Age and learning – experimental studies. In J. E. Birren (Ed.), *Handbook of aging and the individual.* Chicago: University of Chicago.

Kahn, E., & Fisher, C. (1969). The sleep characteristics of the normal aged male. *Journal of Nervous and Mental Disease, 148,* 477–505.

Kales, A., Wilson, T., Kales, J., Jacobson, A., Paulson, M., Kollar, E., & Walter, R. D. (1967). Measurements of all-night sleep in normal elderly persons: Effects of aging. *Journal of the American Geriatrics Society, 15,* 405–414.

Kimble, G. A., & Pennypacker, H. S. (1963). Eyelid conditioning in young and aged subjects. *The Journal of Genetic Psychology, 103,* 283–289.

Kinomura, S., Larsson, J., Gulyas, B., & Roland, P. E. (1996). Activation by attention of the human reticular formation and thalamic intralaminar nuclei. *Science, 271,* 512–515.

Knorring, L. von, & Perris, C. (1981). Biochemistry of the augmenting–reducing response in visual evoked potentials. *Neuropsychobiology, 7,* 1–8.

Kramer, A. F., Humphrey, D. G., Larish, J. F., Logan, G. D., & Strayer, D. L. (1994). Aging and inhibition: Beyond a unitary view of inhibitory processing in attention. *Psychology and Aging, 9,* 491–512.

Lindsley, D. B. (1952). Physiological phenomena and the electroencephalogram. *Electroencephalography and Clinical Neurophysiology, 4,* 443–456.

Lindsley, D. B. (1960). Attention, consciousness, sleep, and wakefulness. In J. Field (Ed.), *Handbook of physiology* (Section 1, Vol. 3). American Physiological Society.

Lindsley, D. B., Schreiner, L. H., Knowles, W. B., & Magoun, H. W. (1950). Behavioral and EEG changes following chronic brainstem lesions in the cat. *Electroencephalography and Clinical Neurophysiology, 2,* 483–498.

Loveless, N. E., & Sanford, A. J. (1974). Effects of age on the contingent negative variation and preparatory set in a reaction-time task. *Journal of Gerontology, 29,* 52–63.

Madden, D. J., & Plude, D. J. (1993). Selective preservation of selective attention. In J. Cerella, J. Rybash, W. Hoyer, & M. L. Commons (Eds.), *Adult information processing: Limits on loss* (pp. 273–300). San Diego, CA: Academic Press.

Marsh, G. R., & Thompson, L. W. (1973). Effects of age on the contingent negative variation in a pitch discrimination task. *Journal of Gerontology, 28,* 56–62.

Marsh, G. R., & Thompson, L. W. (1977). Psychophysiology of aging. In J. E. Birren & K. W. Schaie (Eds.), *Handbook of the psychology of aging.* New York: Van Nostrand Reinhold.

McDowd, J. M., & Filion, D. L. (1992). Aging, selective attention, and inhibitory processes: A psychophysiological approach. *Psychology and Aging, 7,* 65–71.

McDowd, J. M., & Oseas-Kreger, D. M. (1991). Aging, inhibitory processes, and negative priming. *Journal of Gerontology: Psychological Sciences, 46,* P340–345.

Michalewski, H. J., Thompson, L. W., Smith, D. B. D., Patterson, J. V., Bowman, T. E., Litzelman, D., & Brent, G. (1980). Age differences in the contingent negative variation (CNV): Reduced frontal activity in the elderly. *Journal of Gerontology, 35,* 542–549.

Miles, L. E., & Dement, W. C. (1980). Sleep and aging. *Sleep, 3,* 119–220.

Milner, B. (1963). Effects of different brain lesions on card sorting. *Archives of Neurology, 9,* 90–100.

Moruzzi, G., & Magoun, H. W. (1949). Brain stem reticular formation and activation of the EEG. *Electroencephalography and Clinical Neurophysiology, 1,* 455–473.

Obrist, W. D. (1954). The electroencephalogram of normal aged adults. *Electroencephalography and Clinical Neurophysiology, 6,* 235–244.

Obrist, W. D. (1965). Electroencephalic approach to age changes in response speed. In A. T. Welford & J. E. Birren (Eds.), *Behavior, aging and the nervous system.* Springfield, IL: Charles C. Thomas.

Obrist, W. D., & Busse, E. W. (1965). The electroencephalogram in old age. In W. P. Wilson (Ed.), *Applications of electroencephalography in psychiatry.* Durham, NC: Duke University.

Pfefferbaum, A., Ford, J. M., Roth, W. T., Hopkins, W. F., & Kopell, B. S. (1979). Event-related potential changes in healthy aged females. *Electroencephalography and Clinical Neurophysiology, 46,* 81–86.

Prinz, P. N. (1976). EEG during sleep and waking states. In B. Eleftheriou & M. F. Elias (Eds.), *Annual review of experimental aging research.* Bar Harbor, ME: Experimental Aging Research.

Prinz, P. N. (1977). Sleep patterns in the healthy aged: Relationship with intellectual function. *Journal of Gerontology, 32,* 179–186.

Prinz, P. N., Dustman, R. E., & Emmerson, R. (1990). Electrophysiology and aging. In J. E. Birren & K. W. Schaie (Eds.), *Handbook of the psychology of aging* (3rd ed., pp. 135–149). San Diego, CA: Academic Press.

Rabbitt, P. (1965). An age-decrement in the ability to ignore irrelevant information. *Journal of Gerontology, 20,* 233–238.

Schaie, K. W. (1965). A general model for the study of developmental problems. *Psychological Bulletin, 64,* 92–107.

Scheibel, M. E., & Scheibel, A. B. (1966). The organization of the nucleus reticularis thalami: A Golgi study. *Brain Research, 1,* 43–62.

Scheibel, M. E., & Scheibel, A. B. (1976). Structural changes in the aging brain. In R. D. Terry & S. Gerschon (Eds.), *Neurobiology of aging.* New York: Raven Press.

Schenkenberg, T. (1970). *Visual, auditory, and somatosensory evoked responses of normal subjects from childhood to senescence.* Unpublished doctoral dissertation, University of Utah.

Skinner, J. E., & Yingling, C. D. (1977). Central gating mechanisms that regulate event-related potentials and behavior. A neural model for attention. In J. E. Desmedt (Ed.), *Progress in clinical neurophysiology.* Basel, Switzerland: Karger.

Smith, D. B. D., Michalewski, H. W., Brent, G. A., & Thompson, L. W. (1980). Auditory averaged evoked potentials and aging: Factors of stimulus, task and topography. *Biological Psychology, 11,* 135–151.

Smith, D. B. D., Thompson, L. W., & Michalewski, H. W. (1980). Averaged evoked potential research in adult aging – Status and prospects. In L. W. Poon (Ed.), *Aging in the 1980's: Psychological issues.* Washington, DC: American Psychological Association.

Straumanis, J. J., Shagass, C., & Schwartz, M. (1965). Visually evoked cerebral response changes associated with chronic brain syndromes and aging. *Journal of Gerontology, 20,* 498–506.

Tecce, J. J. (1972). Contingent negative variation (CNV) and psychological processes in man. *Psychological Bulletin, 77,* 73–108.

Tecce, J. J. (1979). A CNV rebound effect. *Electroencephalography and Clinical Neurophysiology, 46,* 546–551.

Tecce, J. J., Rechik, D. A., Meinbresse, D., Dessonville, C. L., & Cole, J. O. (1980). CNV rebound and aging: I. Attention functions. *Progress in Brain Research, 54,* 547–551.

Thompson, L. W., & Marsh, G. R. (1973). Psychophysiological studies of aging. In C. Eisdorfer & M. P. Lawton (Eds.), *The psychology of adult development and aging.* Washington, DC: American Psychological Association.

Thompson, L. W., & Nowlin, J. B. (1973). Relation of increased attention to central and autonomic nervous system states. In L. F. Jarvik, C. Eisdorfer, & J. E. Blum (Eds.), *Intellectual functioning in adults.* New York: Springer.

Walter, W. G. (1968). The contingent negative variation: An electro-cortical sign of sensori-motor reflex association in man. In E. A. Asratyan (Ed.), *Progress in Brain Research* (Vol. 22). *Brain reflexes.* Amsterdam: Elsevier.

Walter, W. G., Cooper, R., Aldridge, V. J., McCallum, W. C., & Winter, A. L. (1964). Contingent negative variation: An electric sign of sensori-motor association and expectancy in the human brain. *Nature (London), 203,* 380–384.

Webb, W. B. (1981). Sleep stage responses of older and younger subjects after sleep deprivation. *Electroencephalography and Clinical Neurophysiology, 52,* 368–371.

Woodruff, D. S. (1978). Brain electrical activity and behavior relationships over the life span. In P. B. Baltes (Ed.), *Life span development and behavior* (pp. 111–179). New York: Academic Press.

Woodruff-Pak, D. S. (1997). Classical conditioning. In J. D. Schmahmann (Ed.), *The cerebellum and cognition. International Review of Neurobiology,* Vol. 41. New York: Academic Press.

Yakovlev, P. V., & Lecours, A. R. (1967). The myelogenetic cycles of regional maturation of the brain. In A. Minkowski (Ed.), *Regional development of the brain in early life.* Philadelphia: Davis.

Chapter 9 Response Speed and Timing in Behavior

Abrahams, J. P., & Birren, J. E. (1973). Reaction time as a function of age and behavioral predispositions to coronary heart disease. *Journal of Gerontology, 28,* 471–478.

Arenberg, D. (1982). Changes with age in problem solving. In F. I. M. Craik & S. Trehub (Eds.), *Aging and cognitive processes.* New York: Plenum.

Ball, S. S., Marsh, J. T., Schubarth, G., Brown, W. S., & Strandburg, R. (1989). Longitudinal P300 latency changes in Alzheimer's disease. *Journal of Gerontology: Medical Sciences, 44,* M195–200.

Bashore, T. R. (1993). Differential effects of aging on the neurocognitive functions subserving speeded mental processing. In J. Cerella, J. Rybash, W. Hoyer, & M. L. Commons (Eds.), *Adult information processing: Limits on loss* (pp. 37–76). San Diego, CA: Academic Press.

Bashore, T. R. (1994). Some thoughts on neurocognitive slowing. *Acta Psychologica,* *86,* 295–325.

Beatty, J., Greenberg, A., Diebler, W. P., & O'Hanlon, J. F. (1974). Operant control of occipital theta rhythm affects performance in a radar monitoring task. *Science,* *183,* 871–873.

Berg, C., Hertzog, C., & Hunt, E. (1982). Age differences in the speed of mental rotation. *Developmental Psychology, 18,* 95–107.

Birren, J. E. (1955). Age changes in speed of response and perception and their significance for complex behavior. In *Old age in the modern world.* London: Livingstone.

Birren, J. E. (1965). Age changes in speed of behavior: Its central nature and physiological correlates. In A. T. Welford & J. E. Birren (Eds.), *Behavior, aging and the nervous system.* Springfield, IL: Charles C. Thomas.

Birren, J. E., & Botwinick, J. (1955). Age differences in finger, jaw, and foot reaction time to auditory stimuli. *Journal of Gerontology, 10,* 429–432.

Birren, J. E., & Fisher, L. M. (1995). Aging and speed of behavior: Possible consequences for psychological functioning. *Review of Psychology, 46,* 329–353.

Birren, J. E., & Wall, P. D. (1956). Age changes in conduction velocity, refractory period, number of fibers, connective tissue space and blood vessels in sciatic nerve of rats. *Journal of Comparative Neurology, 104,* 1–16.

Birren, J. E., Butler, R. N., Greenhouse, S. W., Sokoloff, L., & Yarrow, M. R. (1963). *Human aging.* Washington, DC: US Public Health Service.

Botwinick, J., & Birren, J. E. (1965). A follow-up study of card-sorting performance in elderly men. *Journal of Gerontology, 20,* 208–210.

Botwinick, J., & Thompson, L. W. (1968). Age differences in reaction time: An artifact? *The Gerontologist, 8,* 25–28.

Creutzfelt, O. D., Arnold, P. M., Becker, D., Langenstein, R., Firsch, W., Wilheim, H., & Wuttke, W. (1976). EEG changes during spontaneous and controlled menstrual cycles and their correlation with psychological performance. *Electroencephalography and Clinical Neurophysiology, 40,* 113–131.

Crossman, E. R. F. W., & Szafran, J. (1957). Changes with age in the speed of information intake and discrimination. *Experientia Supplement, 4,* 128–145.

Davies, D. R., & Krkovic, A. (1965). Skin conductance, alpha activity, and vigilance. *American Journal of Psychology, 78,* 304–306.

DeVries, H. A. (1983). Physiology of exercise and aging. In D. S. Woodruff & J. E. Birren (Eds.), *Aging: Scientific perspectives and social issues* (2nd ed.). Monterey, CA: Brooks/Cole.

Donchin, E., Karis, D., Bashore, T. R., Coles, M. G. H., & Gratton, G. (1986). Cognitive psychophysiology and human information processing. In M. G. H. Coles, E. Donchin, & S. W. Porges (Eds.), *Psychophysiology: Systems, processes and applications* (pp. 244–267). New York: Guilford Press.

Dustman, R. W., & Ruhling, R. O. (1986). *Brain function of old and young athletes and nonathletes.* Presented at the 39th Annual Scientific Meeting of the Gerontological Society of America, Chicago.

Dustman, R. W., Ruhling, R. O., Russell, E. M., Shearer, D. E., Bonekat, H. W.,

Shigeoka, J. W., Wood, J. S., & Bradford, D. C. (1984). Aerobic exercise training and improved neuropsychological function of older individuals. *Neurobiology of Aging, 5,* 35–42.

Goldfarb, W. (1941). An investigation of reaction time in older adults and its relationship to certain observed mental test patterns. *Teachers College Contributions to Education* (No. 831). New York: Teachers College Columbia University, Bureau of Publications.

Goodin, D. S., & Aminoff, M. J. (1986). Electrophysiological differences between subtypes of dementia. *Brain, 109,* 11-3–1113.

Goodin, D. S., Squires, K., Henderson, B., & Starr, A. (1978). Age-related variations in evoked potentials to auditory stimuli in normal human subjects. *Electroencephalography and Clinical Neurophysiology, 44,* 447–458.

Goodin, D. S., Starr, A., Chippendale, T., & Squires, K. (1983). Sequential changes in the P3 component of the auditory evoked potential in confusional states and dementing illnesses. *Neurology, 33,* 1215–1218.

Gordon, E., Kraiuhin, C., Stanfield, P., Meares, R., & Howson, A. (1986). The prediction of normal P3 latency and the diagnosis of dementia. *Neuropsychologia, 24,* 823–830.

Granick, S., & Patterson, R. D. (1971). *Human aging II: An eleven-year followup biomedical and behavioral study.* Washington, DC: US Government Printing Office.

Groll, E. (1966). Central nervous system and peripheral activation variables during vigilance performance. *Zeitschrift für Experimentelle und Angewandte Psychologie, 13,* 148–264.

Halgren, E., Squires, N., Wilson, C., Rohrbaugh, J., Bab, T., & Crandall, P. (1980). Endogenous potentials in the human hippocampal formation and amygdala by infrequent events. *Science, 210,* 803–805.

Harter, M. R. (1967). Effects of carbon dioxide on the alpha frequency and reaction time in humans. *Electroencephalography and Clinical Neurophysiology, 23,* 561–563.

Hertzog, C., Schaie, K. W., & Gribbin, K. (1978). Cardiovascular diseases and changes in intellectual functioning from middle to old age. *Journal of Gerontology, 33,* 872–883.

Hicks, L. H., & Birren, J. E. (1970). Aging, brain damage, and psychomotor slowing. *Psychological Bulletin, 74,* 377–396.

Hugin, R., Norris, A. H., & Shock, N. W. (1960). Skin reflex and voluntary reaction times in young and old males. *Journal of Gerontology, 15,* 388–391.

Ivry, R., & Keele, S. W. (1989). Timing functions of the cerebellum. *Cognitive Neuroscience, 1,* 134–150.

Ivry, R., Keele, S. W., & Diener, H. C. (1988). Dissociation of the lateral and medial cerebellum in movement timing and movement execution. *Experimental Brain Research, 73,* 167–180.

Johnson, S. H., & Rybash, J. M. (1993). A cognitive neuroscience perspective on age-related slowing: Developmental changes in the functional architecture. In J. Cerella, J. Rybash, W. Hoyer, & M. L. Commons (Eds.), *Adult information-processing: Limits on loss* (pp. 143–173). San Diego, CA: Academic Press.

Kaufmann, A. (1968). Age and performance in oral and written versions of the substitution test. In S. Chown & K. F. Riegel (Eds.), *Psychological functioning in the normal aging and senile aged*. Basel, Switzerland: S. Karger.

Keele, S. W., & Ivry, R. (1990). Does the cerebellum provide a common computation for diverse tasks: A timing hypothesis. In A. Diamond (Ed.), *The development and neural bases of higher cognitive functions*. New York: New York Academy of Sciences Press.

Knight, R., Scabini, D., Woods, D., & Clayworth, C. (1989). Contributions of temporal–parietal junction to the human auditory P3. *Brain Research, 502,* 109–116.

Koga, Y., & Morant, G. M. (1923). On the degree of association between reaction times in the case of different senses. *Biometrika, 15,* 346–372.

Kornfield, C. M. (1974). *EEG spectra during a prolonged compensatory tracking task.* Unpublished doctoral dissertation, University of California at Los Angeles.

Light, K. C. (1978). Effects of mild cardiovascular and cerebrovascular disorders on serial reaction time performance. *Experimental Aging Research, 4,* 3–22.

Lindsley, D. B. (1952). Psychological phenomena and the electroencephalogram. *Electroencephalography and Clinical Neurophysiology, 4,* 443–456.

McCarthy, G., Wood, C. C., Williamson, P. D., & Spencer, D. D. (1989). Task-dependent field potentials in human hippocampal formation. *Journal of Neuroscience, 9,* 4253–4268.

Madden, D. J., & Nebes, R. D. (1980). Aging and the development of automaticity in visual search. *Developmental Psychology, 16,* 377–384.

Marsh, G., & Thompson, L. W. (1972). Age differences in evoked potentials during an auditory discrimination task. *Gerontologist, 12,* 44.

Miles, W. R. (1931). Measures of certain human abilities throughout the lifespan. *Proceedings of the National Academy of Sciences, 17,* 627–633.

Morrell, L. K. (1966). EEG frequency and reaction time: A sequential analysis. *Neuropsychologica, 4,* 41–48.

Murrell, F. H. (1970). The effect of extensive practice on age differences in reaction time. *Journal of Gerontology, 25,* 268–274.

Norris, A. H., Shock, N. W., & Wagman, I. H. (1953). Age changes in the maximum conduction velocity of motor fibers in human ulnar nerves. *Journal of Applied Physiology, 5,* 589–593.

O'Hanlon, J. F., McGrath, J. J., & McCauley, M. E. (1974). Body temperature and temporal acuity. *Journal of Experimental Psychology, 102,* 788–794.

Pierson, W. R. & Montoye, H. J. (1958). Movement time, reaction time and age. *Journal of Gerontology, 13,* 418–421.

Pineda, J., Foote, S., & Neville, H. (1989). Effects of locus coeruleus lesions on auditory, long-latency, event-related potentials in monkeys. *Journal of Neuroscience, 9,* 81–93.

Polich, J., & Starr, A. (1984). Evoked potentials in aging. In M. L. Albert (Ed.), *Clinical neurology of aging* (pp. 149–177). New York: Oxford University Press.

Plude, D. J., & Hoyer, W. J. (1981). Adult age differences in visual search as a

316   *References*

function of stimulus mapping and processing level. *Journal of Gerontology, 36,* 598–604.

Salthouse, T. A. (1985). Speed of behavior and its implications for cognition. In J. E. Birren & K. W. Schaie (Eds.), *Handbook of the psychology of aging* (2nd ed.). New York: Van Nostrand Reinhold.

Salthouse, T. A. (1994). The aging of working memory. *Neuropsychology, 8,* 535–543.

Salthouse, T. A., & Somberg, B. L. (1982). Skilled performance: The effects of adult age and experience on elementary processes. *Journal of Experimental Psychology: General, 111,* 176–207.

Schmahmann, J. D. (Ed.). (1997). *The cerebellum and cognition. International Review of Neurobiology,* Vol. 41. New York: Academic Press.

Spirduso, W. W. (1975). Reaction and movement time as a function of age and physical activity level. *Journal of Gerontology, 30,* 435–440.

Spirduso, W. W. (1980). Physical fitness, aging and psychomotor speed: A review. *Journal of Gerontology, 35,* 850–865.

Spirduso, W. W., & Clifford, P. (1978). Neuromuscular speed and consistency of performance as a function of age, physical activity level and type of physical activity. *Journal of Gerontology, 33,* 26–30.

Surwillo, W. W. (1968). Timing of behavior in senescence and the role of the central nervous system. In G. A. Talland (Ed.), *Human aging and behavior.* New York: Academic Press.

Surwillo, W. W. (1975). Reaction time variability, periodicities in reaction time distributions, and the EEG gating-signal hypothesis. *Biological Psychology, 3,* 247–261.

Sutton, S., Braren, M., Zubin, J., & John, E. R. (1965). Evoked-potential correlates of stimulus uncertainty. *Science, 150,* 1187–1188.

Szafran, J. (1951). Changes with age and with exclusion of vision in performance at an aiming task. *Quarterly Journal of Experimental Psychology, 3,* 111–118.

Szafran, J. (1968). Psychophysiological studies of aging in pilots. In G. A. Talland (Ed.), *Human aging and behavior.* New York: Academic Press.

Talland, G. A. (1962). The effect of age on speed of simple manual skill. *Journal of Genetic Psychology, 100,* 69–76.

Thompson, L. W., & Marsh, G. R. (1973). Psychophysiological studies of aging. In C. Eisdorfer & M. P. Lawton (Eds.), *The psychology of adult development and aging.* Washington, DC: American Psychological Association.

Wagman, I. H., & Lesse, H. (1952). Maximum conduction velocities of motor fibers of ulnar nerves in human subjects of various ages and sizes. *Journal of Neurophysiology, 15,* 235–244.

Wayner, M. J., & Emmers, R. (1958). Spinal synaptic delay in young and aged rats. *American Journal of Physiology, 194,* 403–405.

Welford, A. T. (1958). *Aging and human skill.* London: Oxford University Press.

Welford, A. T. (1981). Signal, noise, performance, and age. *Human Factors, 23,* 97–109.

Williams, H. L., Granda, A. M., Jones, R. C., Lubin, A., & Armington, D. C.

(1962). EEG frequency and finger pulse volume as predictors of reaction time during sleep loss. *Electroencephalography and Clinical Neurophysiology, 14,* 64–70.

Woodruff-Pak, D. S., & Jaeger, M. (1997). Predictors of eyeblink classical conditioning over the adult age span. (Submitted.)

Chapter 10   Intelligence

Achenbaum, W. A., & Kusnerz, P. A. (1978). *Images of old age in America: 1790 to the present.* Ann Arbor, MI: Institute of Gerontology, University of Michigan.

Anastasi, A. (1976). *Psychological testing* (4th ed.). New York: Macmillan.

Binet, A., & Simon, T. (1905). Methodes nouvelles pour le diagnostic du niveau intellectual des arnormaux. *Annee Psychologique, 11,* 191–244.

Binet, A., & Simon, T. (1905; reprinted 1916). New methods for the diagnosis of the intellectual level of subnormals. In A. Binet and T. Simon, *The development of intelligence in children.* Baltimore: Williams & Wilkins.

Birren, J. E. (1959). Principles of research on aging. In J. E. Birren (Ed.), *Handbook of aging and the individual* (pp. 3–42), Chicago: University of Chicago Press.

Cattell, R. B. (1943). The measurement of adult intelligence. *Psychological Bulletin, 40,* 153–193.

Cattell, R. B. (1971). *Abilities: Their structure, growth, and action.* Boston: Houghton Mifflin.

Chapell, M. S. (1996). Reevaluation of a four-perspective model of aging and intelligence. (Submitted.)

Clayton, V. (1982). Wisdom and intelligence: The nature and function of knowledge in the later years. *International Journal of Aging and Human Development, 15,* 315–321.

Clayton, V., & Birren, J. E. (1980). The development of wisdom across the life span: A reexamination of an ancient logic. In P. B. Baltes & O. G. Brim (Eds.), *Life-span development and behavior* (Vol. 3, pp. 103–135). New York: Academic Press.

Cornelius, S. W., & Caspi, A. (1987). Everyday problem solving in adulthood and old age. *Psychology and Aging, 2,* 144–153.

Dai, X., Xie, Y., & Zheng, L. (1993). Age, education and intelligence declining in adulthood. *Chinese Mental Health Journal, 7,* 215–217.

Demming, J. A., & Pressey, S. L. (1957). Testing "indigenous" to the adult older years. *Journal of Counseling Psychology, 4,* 144–148.

Diehl, M., Willis, S., & Schaie, K. W. (1995). Everyday problem solving in older adults: Observational assessment and cognitive correlates. *Psychology and Aging, 10,* 309–322.

Erikson, E. H. (1968). *Identity and crisis.* New York: W.W. Norton.

Gardner, E. F., & Monge, R. H. (1977). Adult age differences in cognitive abilities and educational background. *Experimental Aging Research, 3,* 337–383.

Havighurst, R. J. (1973). History of developmental psychology: Socialization and personality development through the life span. In P. B. Baltes & K. W. Schaie

(Eds.), *Life-span developmental psychology: Personality and socialization* (pp. 3–52). New York: Academic Press.

Hayslip, B., Maloy, R., & Kohl, R. (1995). Long-term efficacy of fluid ability interventions with older adults. *Journal of Gerontology: Psychological Science, 50B,* P141–149.

Hofland, B. F., Willis, S. L., & Baltes, P. B. (1981). Fluid intelligence performance in the elderly: Intraindividual variability and conditions of assessment. *Journal of Educational Psychology, 73,* 573–586.

Hollingworth, H. L. (1927). *Mental growth and decline: A survey of developmental psychology.* New York: Appleton.

Horn, J. L. (1968). Organization of abilities and the development of intelligence. *Psychological Review, 75,* 242–259.

Horn, J. L. (1982). The theory of fluid and crystallized intelligence in relation to concepts of cognitive psychology and aging in adulthood. In F. I. M. Craik & S. Trehub (Eds.), *Aging and cognitive processes* (pp. 237–278). New York: Plenum Press.

Horn, J. L., & Cattell, R. (1967). Age differences in fluid and crystallized intelligence. *Acta Psychologica, 26,* 107–129.

Hulicka, I. M. (1967). Age changes and age differences in memory functioning. *Gerontologist, 7,* 46–54.

Jensen, A. R. (1973). *Genetics and education.* New York: Harper & Row.

Jones, H. E. (1959). Intelligence and problem-solving. In J. E. Birren (Ed.), *Handbook of aging and the individual* (pp. 700–783). Chicago: University of Chicago Press.

Kastenbaum, R. (1968). Perspectives on the development and modification of behavior in the aged: A developmental-field perspective. *The Gerontologist, 8,* 280–283.

Kolb, B., & Whishaw, I. Q. (1995). *Fundamentals of human neuropsychology* (4th ed.). New York: Wh. H. Freeman.

Kramer, D. A. (1987). Cognition and aging: The emergence of a new tradition. In P. Silverman (Ed.), *Modern pioneers: An interdisciplinary view of the aged.* Bloomington, IN: Indiana University Press.

Kramer, D. A., Kahlbaugh, P. E., & Goldston, R. B. (1992). A measure of paradigm beliefs about the social world. *Journal of Gerontology: Psychological Science, 47,* 180–189.

Kuhlen, R. G. (1940). Social change: A neglected factor in psychological studies of the life span. *School and Society, 52,* 14–16.

Labouvie-Vief, G. (1985). Intelligence and cognition. In J. E. Birren & K. W. Schaie (Eds.), *Handbook of the psychology of aging* (pp. 500–530). New York: Van Nostrand Reinhold.

Neugarten, B. L., & Havighurst, R. J. (Eds.) (1976). *Social policy, social ethics, and the aging society.* Washington, DC: US Government Printing Office.

Oden, M. H. (1968). The fulfillment of promise: 40-year follow-up of the Terman gifted group. *Genetic Psychology Monographs, 77,* 3–93.

Owens, W. A., Jr. (1953). Age and mental abilities: A longitudinal study. *Genetic Psychology Monographs, 48,* 3–54.

Owens, W. A., Jr. (1966). Age and mental abilities. *Journal of Educational Psychology, 57,* 311–325.

Piaget, J. (1950). *The psychology of intelligence.* London: Routledge.

Riegel, K. F. (1977). History of psychological gerontology. In J. E. Birren & K. W. Schaie (Eds.), *Handbook of the psychology of aging.* New York: Van Nostrand Reinhold.

Roodin, P. A., Rybash, J., & Hoyer, W. J. (1984). Affect in adult cognition: A constructivist view of moral thought and action. In C. Z. Malatesta & C. E. Izard (Eds.), *Emotion in adult development* (pp. 297–316). Beverly Hills, CA: Sage.

Schaie, K. W. (1977–1978). Toward a stage theory of adult cognitive development. *International Journal of Aging and Human Development, 8,* 129–136.

Sinnott, J. D. (1975). Everyday thinking and Piagetian operativity in adults. *Human Development, 18,* 430–443.

Terman, L. M. (1921). Intelligence and its measurement. *Journal of Educational Psychology, 12,* 127–133.

Terman, L. M., & Oden, M. H. (1947). *The gifted child grows up: Twenty-five years follow-up of a superior group.* Stanford, CA: Stanford University.

Thorndike, E. L. (1926). *The measurement of intelligence.* New York: Teachers College, Columbia University, Bureau of Publications.

Watson, J. B. (1913). Psychology as the behaviorist views it. *Psychological Review, 20,* 158–177.

Wechsler, D. (1944). *The measurement of adult intelligence* (3rd ed.). Baltimore: Williams & Wilkins.

Woodruff, D. S. (1983). A review of aging and cognitive processes. *Research on Aging, 5,* 139–153.

Woodruff-Pak, D. S. (1989). Aging and intelligence: Changing perspectives in the twentieth century. *Journal of Aging Studies, 3,* 91–118.

Woodruff-Pak, D. S., & Finkbiner, R. G. (1988). Aging and intelligence: Validation of a model. In B. Turek (Ed.), *Aging and information* (pp. 17–26). Jefferson, NC: McFarland.

Yerkes, R. M. (1921). Psychological examining in the United States Army. Washington, DC: National Academy of Science.

Chapter 11   Learning and Memory

Anderson, B. J., & Steinmetz, J. E. (1994). Cerebellar and brainstem circuits involved in classical eyeblink conditioning. *Review of Neuroscience, 5,* 251–273.

Bahrick, H. P. (1979). Maintenance of knowledge: Questions about memory we forgot to ask. *Journal of Experimental Psychology: General, 108,* 296–308.

Bahrick, H. P., Bahrick, P. O., & Wittlinger, R. P. (1975). Fifty years of memory for names and faces: A cross-sectional approach. *Journal of Experimental Psychology: General, 104,* 54–75.

Berger, T. W., Berry, S. D., & Thompson, R. F. (1986). Role of the hippocampus in classical conditioning of aversive and appetitive behaviors. In R. L. Isaacson

& K. H. Pribram (Eds.), *The hippocampus* (Vol. IV, pp. 203–239). New York: Plenum.

Berry, S. D., & Thompson, R. F. (1979). Medial septal lesions retard classical conditioning of the nictitating membrane response in rabbits, *Science, 205,* 209–211.

Blaxton, T. A., Zeffiro, T. A., Gabrieli, J. D. E., Bookheimer, S. Y., Carrillo, M. C., Theodore, H., & Disterhoft, J. F. (1996). Functional mapping of human learning: A PET activation study of eyeblink conditioning. *The Journal of Neuroscience, 16,* 585–601.

Braun, H. W., & Geiselhart, R. (1959). Age differences in the acquisition and extinction of the conditioned eyelid response. *Journal of Experimental Psychology, 57,* 386–388.

Buckner, R. L., Petersen, S. E., Ojemann, J. G., Miezin, F. M., Squire, L. R., & Raichle, M. E. (1995). Functional anatomical studies of explicit and implicit memory retrieval tasks. *Journal of Neuroscience, 15,* 12–29.

Butler, R. N. (1963). The life review: An interpretation of reminiscence in the aged. *Psychiatry, 26,* 65–76.

Butler, R. N., & Lewis, M. I. (1982). *Aging and mental health: Positive psychosocial and biomedical approaches* (3rd ed.). St Louis, MO: Mosby.

Canestrari, R. E., Jr. (1963). Paced and self-paced learning in young and elderly adults. *Journal of Gerontology, 18,* 165–168.

Chiarello, C., & Hoyer, W. J. (1988). Adult age differences in implicit and explicit memory: Time course and encoding effects. *Psychology and Aging, 3,* 358–366.

Coffin, J. M., Trojanowski, J. Q., & Woodruff-Pak, D. S. (1996). Age differences in cerebellum but not hippocampus are related to deficits in conditioning. (Submitted.)

Coleman, P. G. (1974). Measuring reminiscence characteristics from conversation as adaptive features of old age. *International Journal of Aging and Human Development, 5,* 281–294.

Craik, F. I. M. (1971). Age differences in recognition memory. *Quarterly Journal of Experimental Psychology, 23,* 316–323.

Craik, F. I. M. (1977). Age differences in human memory. In J. E. Birren & K. W. Schaie (Eds.), *Handbook of the psychology of aging.* New York: Van Nostrand Reinhold.

Craik, F. I. M. (1991). Memory functions in normal aging. In T. Yanigihara & R. C. Peterson (Eds.), *Memory disorders: Research and clinical practice* (pp. 347–367). New York: Marcel Dekker.

Craik, F. I. M., & Lockhart, R. S. (1972). Levels of processing: A framework for memory research. *Journal of Verbal Learning and Verbal Behavior, 11,* 671–684.

Craik, F. I. M., & Simon, E. (1980). Age differences in memory: the roles of attention and depth of processing. In L. Poon, J. L. Fozard, I. S. Cermak, D. Arenberg, & L. W. Thompson (Eds.), *New directions in memory and aging.* Hillsdale, NJ: Erlbaum.

Daniel, L. (1980). *How to write your own life story: A step by step guide for the non-professional writer.* Chicago: Chicago Review Press.

Daum, I., Channon, S., & Canavan, A. G. M. (1989). Classical conditioning in patients with severe memory problems. *Journal of Neurology, Neurosurgery, and Psychiatry, 52,* 47–51.

Daum, I., Channon, S., Polkey, C. E., & Gray, J. A. (1991). Classical conditioning after temporal lobe lesions in man: Impairment in conditional discrimination. *Behavioral Neuroscience, 105,* 396–408.

Daum, I., Schugens, M. M., Ackermann, H., Lutzenberger, W., Dichgans, J., & Birbaumer, N. (1993). Classical conditioning after cerebellar lesions in humans. *Behavioral Neuroscience, 107,* 748–756.

Daum, I., Schugens, M. M., Breitenstein, C., Topka, H., & Spieker, S. (1996). Classical eyeblink conditioning in Parkinson's disease. *Movement Disorders, 11,* 1025–1032.

Davis, H. P., Cohen, A., Gandy, M., Columbo, P., VanDusseldorp, G., Simolke, N., & Romano, J. (1990). Lexical priming deficits as a function of age. *Behavioral Neuroscience, 104,* 288–297.

Dietsche, L. M. (1979). Facilitating the life review through group reminiscence. *Journal of Gerontological Nursing, 5,* 43–46.

Durkin, M., Prescott, L., Furchtgott, E., Cantor, J., & Powell, D. A. (1993). Concomitant eyeblink and heart rate classical conditioning in young, middle-aged, and elderly human subjects. *Psychology and Aging, 8,* 571–581.

Erber, J. T. (1974). Age differences in recognition memory. *Journal of Gerontology, 29,* 177–181.

Erber, J. T., Herman, T. G., & Botwinick, J. (1980). Age differences in memory as a function of depth of processing. *Experimental Aging Research, 6,* 341–348.

Erikson, E. H. (1968). *Identity and crisis.* New York: W. W. Norton.

Eslinger, P. J., & Damasio, A. R. (1986). Preserved motor learning in Alzheimer's disease: Implications for anatomy and behavior. *Journal of Neuroscience, 6,* 3006–3009.

Eysenck, M. W. (1974). Age differences in incidental learning. *Developmental Psychology, 10,* 936–941.

Fleischman, D. A., Gabrieli, J. D., Reminger, S., Rinaldi, J., Morrell, & Wilson, R. (1995). Conceptual priming in perceptual identification for patients with Alzheimer's disease and a patient with right occipital lobectomy. *Neuropsychology, 9,* 187–197.

Flood, D. G., & Coleman, P. D. (1988). Neurons numbers and sizes in aging brain: Comparisons of human, monkey, and rodent data. *Neurobiology of Aging, 9,* 453–463.

Gabrieli, J. D., Fleischman, D. A., Keane, M. M., Reminger, S. L., & Morrell, F. (1995a). Double dissociation between memory systems underlying explicit and implicit memory in the human brain. *Psychological Science, 6,* 76–82.

Gabrieli, J. D., McGlinchey-Berroth, R., Carrillo, M. C., Gluck, M. A., Cermak, L. S., & Disterhoft, J. F. (1995b). Intact delay-eyeblink classical conditioning in amnesia. *Behavioral Neuroscience, 109,* 819–827.

Golomb, J., de Leon, M. J., Kluger, A., George, A. E., Tarshish, C., & Ferris, S. H. (1993). Hippocampal atrophy in normal aging. *Archives of Neurology, 50,* 967–973.

Grady, C. L., McIntosh, A. R., Horwitz, B., Maisog, J. Ma., Ungerleider, L. G.,

Mentis, M. J., Pietrini, P., Schapiro, M. B., & Haxby, J. V. (1995). Age-related reductions in human recognition memory due to impaired encoding. *Science, 269,* 218–221.

Graf, P. (1990). Life-span changes in implicit and explicit memory. *Bulletin of the Psychonomic Society, 28,* 353–358.

Grafton, S. T., Mazziotta, J. C., Presty, S., Friston, K. J., Frackowiak, R. S. J., & Phelps, M. E. (1992). Functional anatomy of human procedural learning determined with regional cerebral blood flow and PET. *Journal of Neuroscience, 12,* 2542–2548.

Gutman, G. M. (1965). The effects of age and extraversion on pursuit rotor reminiscence. *Journal of Gerontology, 20,* 346–350.

Hall, T. C., Miller, K. H., & Corsellis, J. A. N. (1975). Variations in the human Purkinje cell population according to age and sex. *Neuropathology and Applied Neurobiology, 1,* 267–292.

Harrison, J., & Buchwald, J. (1983). Eyeblink conditioning deficits in the old cat. *Neurobiology of Aging, 4,* 45–51.

Harvey, J. A., Gormezano, I., & Cool-Hauser, V. A. (1983). Effects of scopolamine and methylscopolamine on classical conditioning of the rabbit nictitating membrane response. *Journal of Pharmacology and Experimental Therapeutics, 225,* 42–49.

Hashtroudi, A., Chrosniak, L. S., & Schwartz, B. L. (1991). Effects of aging on priming and skill learning. *Psychology and Aging, 6,* 605–615.

Hendricks, L. (1979). *Personal life history. Writing for older adults. A handbook for teaching personal life history classes.* Tallahassee, FL: Leon County School Board.

Howard, D. V. (1988). Implicit and explicit assessment of cognitive aging. In M. L. Howe & C. J. Brainerd (Eds.), *Cognitive development in adulthood: Progress in cognitive development research* (pp. 3–37). New York: Springer.

Hulicka, I. M. (1982). Memory functioning in late adulthood. In F. I. M. Craik & S. Trehub (Eds.), *Aging and cognitive processes.* New York: Plenum.

Hultsch, D. F., & Dixon, R. A. (1990). Learning and memory in aging. In J. E. Birren & K. W. Schaie (Eds.), *Handbook of the psychology of aging* (pp. 259–274). San Diego, CA: Academic Press.

Hultsch, D. F., Masson, M. E. J., & Small, B. J. (1991). Adult age differences in direct and indirect tests of memory. *Journal of Gerontology, 46,* P22–30.

Jensen, R. A., Messing, R. B., Martinez, J. L., Jr., Vasquez, B. J., & McGaugh, J. L. (1980). Opiate modulation of learning and memory in the rat. In L. W. Poon (Ed.), *Aging in the 1980s: Psychological issues.* Washington, DC: American Psychological Association.

Kausler, D. H. (1982). *Experimental psychology and human aging.* New York: Wiley.

Keane, M. M., Gabrieli, J. D. E., Fennema, A. C., Growdon, J. H., & Corkin, S. (1991). Evidence for a dissociation between perceptual and conceptual priming in Alzheimer's disease. *Behavioral Neuroscience, 105,* 326–342.

Kimble, G. A., & Pennypacker, H. W. (1963). Eyelid conditioning in young and aged subjects. *Journal of Genetic Psychology, 103,* 283–289.

Lachman, J. L., Lachman, R., & Thronesbery, C. (1979). Metamemory through the adult life span. *Developmental Psychology, 15,* 543–551.

Lauer, P. A. (1976). The effects of different types of word processing on memory performance in young and elderly adults. *Dissertation Abstracts International, 36,* 5833-B [University Microfilms No. 76–11, 591].

Lavond, D. G., Kim, J. J., & Thompson, R. F. (1993). Mammalian brain substrates of aversive classical conditioning. *Annual Review of Psychology, 44,* 317–342.

Lewis, M. I., & Butler, R. N. (1974). Life review therapy: Putting memories to work in individual and group psychotherapy. *Geriatrics, 29,* 165–169.

Light, L. L., & Albertson, S. A. (1989). Direct and indirect tests of memory for category exemplars in young and older adults. *Psychology and Aging, 4,* 487–492.

Light, L. L., & La Voie, D. (1993). Direct and indirect measures of memory in old age. In P. Graf & M. E. J. Masson (Eds.), *Implicit memory* (pp. 207–230). Hillsdale, NJ: Erlbaum.

Light, L. L., & Singh, A. (1987). Implicit and explicit memory in young and older adults. *Journal of Experimental Psychology: Learning, Memory, and Cognition, 13,* 531–541.

Light, L. L., Singh, A., & Capps, J. L. (1986). Dissociation of memory and awareness in young and older adults. *Journal of Clinical and Experimental Neuropsychology, 8,* 62–74.

Logan, C. G., & Grafton, S. T. (1995). Functional anatomy of human eyeblink conditioning determined with regional cerebral glucose metabolism and positron emission tomography. *Proceedings of the National Academy of Science, USA, 92,* 7500–7504.

Marsolek, C. J., Kosslyn, S. M., & Squire, L. R. (1992). Form-specific visual priming in the right cerebral hemisphere. *Journal of Experimental Psychology: Learning, Memory, and Cognition, 18,* 492–508.

Mason, S. E. (1979). Effects of orienting tasks on the recall and recognition performance of subjects differing in age. *Developmental Psychology, 15,* 467–469.

McCarthy, R. A., & Hodges, J. R. (1995). Trapped in time: Profound autobiographical memory loss following a thalamic stroke. In R. Campbell & M. A. Conway (Eds.), *Broken memories: Case studies in memory impairment* (pp. 31–44). Oxford: Blackwell.

Merriam, S. (1980). The concept and function of the reminiscence: A review of the research. *The Gerontologist, 20,* 604–609.

Mitchell, D. B. (1989). How many memory systems? Evidence from aging. *Journal of Experimental Psychology, 15,* 31–49.

Mitchell, D. B., Brown, A. S., & Murphy, D. R. (1990). Dissociation between procedural and episodic memory: Effects of time and aging. *Psychology and Aging, 5,* 264–276.

Molchan, S. E., Sunderland, T., McIntosh, A. R., Herscovitch, P., & Schreurs, B. G. (1994). A functional anatomical study of associative learning in humans. *Proceedings of the National Academy of Science, USA, 91,* 8122–8126.

Moore, J. W., Goodell, N. A., & Solomon, P. R. (1976). Central cholinergic blockage by scopolamine and habituation, classical conditioning, and latent inhibition of rabbit's nictitating membrane response. *Physiological Psychology, 4,* 395–399.

Moscovitch, M., Winocur, G., & McLachlan, D. (1986). Memory as assessed by recognition and reading time in normal and memory-impaired people with Alzheimer's disease and other neurological disorders. *Journal of Experimental Psychology: General, 115,* 331–347.

Murphy, M. D., Sanders, R. E., Gabriesheski, A. S., & Schmitt, F. A. (1981). Metamemory in the aged. *Journal of Gerontology, 36,* 185–193.

Pascual-Leone, A., Grafman, J., & Hallett, M. (1994). Modulation of cortical motor output maps during development of implicit and explicit knowledge. *Science, 263,* 1287–1289.

Perlmutter, M. (1978). What is memory the aging of? *Developmental Psychology, 14,* 330–345.

Perlmutter, M. (1979). Age differences in adults' free recall, cued recall, and recognition. *Journal of Gerontology, 34,* 533–539.

Poon, L. W. (1985). Differences in human memory with aging: Nature, causes, and clinical implications. In J. E. Birren & K. W. Schaie (Eds.), *Handbook of the psychology of aging.* New York: Van Nostrand Reinhold.

Poon, L. W., Walsh-Sweeney, L., & Fozard, J. L. (1980). Memory skill training for the elderly: Salient issues on the use of imagery mnemonics. In L. W. Poon, J. L. Fozard, L. S. Cermak, D. Arenberg, & L. W. Thompson (Eds.), *New directions in memory and aging.* Hillsdale, NJ: Erlbaum.

Reichard, S., Livson, F., & Petersen, P. G. (1962). *Aging and personality.* New York: Wiley.

Ruch, F. L. (1934). Differential effects of age on human learning. *Journal of Genetic Psychology, 11,* 261–286.

Sacks, O. (1987). *The man who mistook his wife for a hat.* New York: Harper & Row.

Salvatierra, A. T., & Berry, S. D. (1989). Scopolamine disruption of septo-hippocampal activity and classical conditioning. *Behavioral Neuroscience, 103,* 715–721.

Schacter, D. L. (1987). Implicit memory: History and current status. *Journal of Experimental Psychology: Learning, Memory, and Cognition, 13,* 501–518.

Schacter, D. L. (1992). Understanding implicit memory: A cognitive neuroscience approach. *American Psychologist, 47,* 559–569.

Schacter, D. L., Cooper, L. A., & Valdiserri, M. (1992). Implicit and explicit memory for novel visual objects in older and younger adults. *Psychology and Aging, 7,* 299–308.

Schmaltz, L.W., & Theios, J. (1972). Acquisition and extinction of a classically conditioned response in hippocampectomized rabbits (*Oryctologus cuniculus*). *Journal of Comparative and Physiological Psychology, 79,* 328–333.

Schonfield, D., & Robertson, B. A. (1966). Memory storage and aging. *Canadian Journal of Psychology, 20,* 228–236.

Shaps, L. P., & Nilsson, L. (1980). Encoding and retrieval operations in relation to age. *Developmental Psychology, 16,* 636–643.

Shiffrin, R. M., & Schneider, W. (1977). Controlled and automatic human information processing: II. Perceptual learning, automatic attending, and a general theory. *Psychological Review, 84,* 127–190.

Smith, A. D. (1979). The interaction between age and list length in free recall. *Journal of Gerontology, 34,* 381–387.

Smith, A. D., & Winograd, E. (1978). Adult age differences in remembering faces. *Developmental Psychology, 14,* 443–444.

Solomon, P. R., Groccia-Ellison, M., Flynn, D., Mirak, J., Edwards, K. R., Dunehew, A., & Stanton, M. E. (1993). Disruption of human eyeblink conditioning after central cholinergic blockade with scopolamine. *Behavioral Neuroscience, 107,* 271–279.

Solomon, P. R., Levine, E., Bein, T., & Pendlebury, W. W. (1991). Disruption of classical conditioning in patients with Alzheimer's disease. *Neurobiology of Aging, 12,* 283–287.

Solomon, P. R., & Moore, J. W. (1975). Latent inhibition and stimulus generalization of the classically conditioned nictitating membrane response in rabbits (*Oryctolagus cuniculus*) following dorsal hippocampal ablations. *Journal of Comparative and Physiological Psychology, 89,* 1192–1203.

Solomon, P. R., Pomerleau, D., Bennett, L., James, J., & Morse, D. L. (1989). Acquisition of the classically conditioned eyeblink response in humans over the life span. *Psychology and Aging, 4,* 34–41.

Solomon, P. R., Solomon, S. D., Vander Schaaf, E., & Perry, H. E. (1983). Altered activity in the hippocampus is more detrimental to classical conditioning than removing the structure. *Science, 220,* 329–331.

Squire, L. R. (1992). Memory and the hippocampus: A synthesis from findings with rats, monkeys, and humans. *Psychological Review, 99,* 195–231.

Steinmetz, J. E., & Thompson, R. F. (1991). Brain substrates of aversive classical conditioning. In J. Madden IV (Ed.), *Neurobiology of learning, emotion, and affect* (pp. 97–120). New York: Raven Press.

Talland, G. A. (1969). *The pathology of memory.* New York: Academic Press.

Thompson, R. F. (1986). The neurobiology of learning and memory. *Science, 233,* 941–947.

Thompson, R. F. (1989). A model system approach to memory. In P. R. Solomon, G. R. Goethals, C. M. Kelley, & B. R. Stephens (Eds.), *Memory: Interdisciplinary approaches* (pp. 17–32). New York: Spinger-Verlag.

Thompson, R. F. & Krupa, D. J. (1994). Organization of memory traces in the mammalian brain. *Annual Review of Neuroscience, 17,* 519–549.

Topka, H., Valls-Sole, J., Massaquoi, S. G., & Hallett, M. (1993). Deficit in classical conditioning in patients with cerebellar degeneration. *Brain, 116,* 961–969.

Weiskrantz, L., & Warrington, E. K. (1979). Conditioning in amnesic patients. *Neuropsychologia, 17,* 187–194.

West, M. J. (1993). Regionally specific loss of neurons in the aging human hippocampus. *Neurobiology of Aging, 14,* 287–293.

Woodruff-Pak, D. S. (1988). *Psychology and aging.* Englewood Cliffs, NJ: Prentice Hall.

Woodruff-Pak, D. S. (1993). Eyeblink classical conditioning in H.M.: Delay and trace paradigms. *Behavioral Neuroscience, 107,* 911–925.

Woodruff-Pak, D. S., Cronholm, J. F., & Sheffield, J. B. (1990). Purkinje cell number related to rate of eyeblink classical conditioning. *NeuroReport, 1,* 165–168.

Woodruff-Pak, D. S., & Finkbiner, R. G. (1995). Larger nondeclarative than declarative deficits in learning and memory in human aging. *Psychology and Aging, 10,* 416–426.

Woodruff-Pak, D. S., Finkbiner, R. G., & Katz, I. R. (1989). A model system demonstrating parallels in animal and human aging: Extension to Alzheimer's disease. In E. M. Meyer, J. W. Simpkins, & J. Yamamoto (Eds.), *Novel approaches to the treatment of Alzheimer's disease* (pp. 355–371). New York: Plenum.

Woodruff-Pak, D. S., Finkbiner, R. G., & Sasse, D. K. (1990). Eyeblink conditioning discriminates Alzheimer's patients from non-demented aged. *NeuroReport, 1,* 45–48.

Woodruff-Pak, D. S., & Jaeger, M. (1997). Predictors of eyeblink classical conditioning over the adult age span. (Submitted.)

Woodruff-Pak, D. S., Lavond, D. G., Logan, C. G., & Thompson, R. F. (1987). Classical conditioning in 3-, 30-, and 45-month-old rabbits: Behavioral learning and hippocampal unit activity. *Neurobiology of Aging, 8,* 101–108.

Woodruff-Pak, D. S., & Papka, M. (1996a). Alzheimer's disease and eyeblink classical conditioning: 750 trace vs. 400 ms delay paradigm. *Neurobiology of Aging, 17,* 397–404.

Woodruff-Pak, D. S., & Papka, M. (1996b). Huntington's disease and eyeblink classical conditioning: Normal learning but abnormal timing. *Journal of the International Neuropsychological Society, 2,* 323–334.

Woodruff-Pak, D. S., Papka, M., & Ivry, R. B. (1996). Cerebellar involvement in eyeblink classical conditioning in humans. *Neuropsychology, 10,* 443–458.

Woodruff-Pak, D. S., Papka, M., Romano, S., & Li, Y.-T. (1996). Eyeblink classical conditioning in Alzheimer's disease and cerebrovascula dementia. *Neurobiology of Aging, 17,* 505–512.

Woodruff-Pak, D. S., Papka, M., & Simon, E. W. (1994). Eyeblink classical conditioning in Down's syndrome, fragile X syndrome, and normal adults over and under age 35. *Neuropsychology, 8,* 14–24.

Woodruff-Pak, D. S., & Thompson, R. F. (1988). Classical conditioning of the eyeblink response in the delay paradigm in adults aged 18-83 years. *Psychology and Aging, 3,* 219–229.

Wright, B. M., & Payne, R. B. (1985). Effects of aging on sex differences in psychomotor reminiscence and tracking proficiency. *Journal of Gerontology, 40,* 179–184.

Chapter 12   Language and Communication

Albert, M. S., Heller, H. S., & Milberg, W. (1988). Changes in naming ability with age. *Psychology and Aging, 3,* 173–178.

Bayles, K. A., Kaszniak, A. W., & Tomoeda, C. K. (1987). *Communication and cognition in normal aging and dementia.* Boston: Little, Brown.

Bayley, N., & Oden, M. H. (1955). The maintenance of intellectual ability in gifted adults. *Journal of Gerontology, 10,* 91–107.

Beatty, J. (1995). *Principles of behavioral neuroscience.* Madison, WI: Brown & Benchmark.

Beeson, M. F. (1920). Intelligence at senescence. *Journal of Applied Psychology, 4,* 219–234.

Borod, J. C., Goodglass, H., & Kaplan, E. (1980). Normative data on the Boston Diagnostic Aphasia Examination, Parietal Lobe Battery, and the Boston Naming Test. *Journal of Consulting and Clinical Psychology, 1,* 342–344.

Bowles, N. L., & Poon, L. W. (1985). Aging and retrieval of words in semantic memory. *Journal of Gerontology, 40,* 71–77.

Critchley, M. (1984). And all the daughters of musick shall be brought low. *Archives of Neurology, 41,* 1135–1139.

Feier, C. D., & Gerstman, L. J. (1980). Sentence comprehension abilities throughout the adult life span. *Journal of Gerontology, 35,* 722–728.

Foster, J. C., & Taylor, G. (1920). The applicability of mental tests to persons over fifty years of age. *Journal of Applied Psychology, 4,* 39–58.

Geschwind, N. (1974). *Selected papers on language and brain.* Boston: D. Reidel.

Glosser, G., & Deser, T. (1992). A comparison of changes in macrolinguistic and microlinguistic aspects of discourse production in normal aging. *Journal of Gerontology: Psychological Sciences, 47,* P266–272.

Goodglass, H. (1993). *Understanding aphasia.* San Diego, CA: Academic Press.

Goodglass, H., & Kaplan, E. (1972). *The assessment of aphasia and related disorders.* Philadelphia: Lea & Febiger.

Goodglass, H., & Kaplan, E. (1983). *The Boston diagnostic aphasia examination.* Philadelphia: Lea & Febiger.

Grossman, M., Carey, S., Zurif, E., & Diller, L. (1986). Proper and common nouns: Form class judgements in Broca's aphasia. *Brain and Language, 28,* 114–125.

Harasymieu, S., Halper, A., & Sunderland, B. (1981). Sex, age, and aphasia type. *Brain and Language, 12,* 190–198.

Jones, H. E. (1959). Intelligence and problem-solving. In J. E. Birren (Ed.), *Handbook of aging and the individual* (pp. 700–783). Chicago: University of Chicago, Press.

Kandel, E. R., Schwartz, J. H., & Jessell, T. M. (1995). *Essentials of neural science and behavior.* Norwalk, CN: Appleton & Lange.

Kemper, S. (1992). Language and aging. In F. I. M. Craik & T. Salthouse (Eds.), *The handbook of aging and cognition* (pp. 213–270). Hillsdale, NJ: Erlbaum.

Kolb, B., & Whishaw, I. Q. (1995). *Fundamentals of human neuropsychology* (4th ed.). New York: W. H. Freeman.

Konkle, D. F., Beasley, D. S., & Bess, F. H. (1977). Intelligibility of time-altered speech in relation to chronological aging. *Journal of Speech and Hearing Research, 20,* 108–115.

Kwong See, S. T., & Ryan, E. B. (1995). Cognitive mediation of adult age differences in language performance. *Psychology and Aging, 10,* 458–468.

La Rue, A. (1992). *Aging and neuropsychological assessment.* New York: Plenum Press.

Obler, L. K. (1989). Language beyond childhood. In J. Berko Gleason (Ed.), *The development of language*. Columbus, OH: Merrill.

Obler, L. K., Albert, M., Goodglass, H., & Benson, D. F. (1978). Aphasia type and aging. *Brain and Language, 6,* 318–322.

Ogden, J. A. (1996). *Fractured minds: A case-study approach to clinical neuropsychology*. New York: Oxford University Press.

Ojemann, G. A. (Ed.), (1975). The thalamus and language. *Brain and Language, 2,* 1–120.

Owens, W. A., Jr. (1953). Age and mental abilities: A longitudinal study. *Genetic Psychology Monographs, 48,* 3–54.

Peach, R. K. (1987). Language functioning. In H. G. Mueller & V. C. Geoffrey (Eds.), *Communication disorders in aging* (pp. 238–270). Washington, DC: Gallaudet University Press.

Petersen, S. E., Fox, P. T., Posner, M. I., Mintun, M., & Raichle, M. E. (1989). Positron emission tomographic studies of the processing of single words. *Journal of Cognitive Neuroscience, 1,* 153–170.

Posner, M. I., & Raichle, M. E. (1994). *Images of mind*. New York: Scientific American Library.

Sheridan, J. (1976). Restoring speech and language skills. *Geriatrics, 31,* 83–86.

Skinner, B. F. (1983). Intellectual self-management in old age. *American Psychologist, 39,* 239–244.

Stookey, B. A. (1954). A note on the early history of cerebral localization. *Bulletin of the New York Academy of Medicine, 30,* 559–578.

Tun, P. A., & Wingfield, A. (1993). Is speech special? Perception and recall of spoken language in complex environments. In J. Cerella, J. Rybash, W. Hoyer, & M. L. Commons (Eds.), *Adult information processing: Limits on loss* (pp. 425–457). San Diego, CA: Academic Press.

Ulatowska, H. K., Cannito, M. P., Hayashi, M. M., & Fleming, S. G. (1985). Language abilities in the elderly. In H. K. Ulatowska (Ed.), *The aging brain: Communication in the elderly* (pp. 125–139). San Diego, CA: College-Hill Press.

White, J. D., & Regan, M. M. S. (1987). Otologic considerations. In H. G. Mueller & V. C. Geoffrey (Eds.), *Communication disorders in aging* (pp. 185–213). Washington, DC: Gallaudet University Press.

Chapter 13   Executive Function, Attention, and Working Memory

Albert, M. S., & Kaplan, E. (1980). Organic implications of neuropsychological deficits in the elderly. In L. W. Poon, J. L. Fozard, L. S. Cermak, D. Arenberg, & L. W. Thompson (Eds.), *New directions in memory and aging: Proceedings of the George A. Talland memorial conference* (pp. 403–432). Hillsdale, NJ: Erlbaum.

Anderson, J. M., Hubbard, B. M., Coghill, G. R., & Sidders, W. (1983). The effect of advanced old age on the neuron content of the cerebral cortex. *Journal of the Neurological Sciences, 58,* 233–244.

Arnstein, A. F. T., & Goldman-Rakic, P. S. (1985a). Alpha 2-adrenergic mechanisms in prefrontal cortex associated with cognitive decline in aged nonhuman primates. *Science, 230,* 1273–1276.

Arnstein, A. F. T., & Goldman-Rakic, P. S. (1985b). Catecholamines and cognitive decline in aged nonhuman primates. *Annals of the New York Academy of Science, 444,* 218–234.

Bartus, R. T., Flicker, C., & Dean, R. L. (1983). Logical principles for the development of animal models of age-related memory impairments. In T. Crook, S. Ferris, & R. T. Bartus (Eds.), *Assessment in geriatric psychopharmacology* (pp. 263–300). Madison, CT: Mark Powley Associates.

Berg, E. A. (1948). Simple objective technique for measuring flexibility in thinking. *Journal of General Psychology, 39,* 15–22.

Blumer, D., & Benson, D. F. (1975). Personality changes with frontal and temporal lobe lesions. In D. F. Benson & D. Blumer (Eds.), *Psychiatric aspects of neurologic disease* (pp. 156–157). New York: Grune & Stratton.

Bondi, M. W., Kaszniak, A. W., Bayles, K. A., & Vance, K. T. (1993). Contributions of frontal system dysfunction to memory and perceptual abilities in Parkinson's disease. *Neuropsychology, 7,* 89–102.

Broadbent, D. E., & Gregory, M. (1965). Some confirmatory results on age differences in memory for simultaneous stimulation. *British Journal of Psychology, 56,* 77–80.

Broadbent, D. E., & Heron, A. (1962). Effects of a subsidiary task on performance involving immediate memory in younger and older men. *British Journal of Psychology, 53,* 189–198.

Brozoski, T. J., Brown, R. M., Rosvold, H. E., & Goldman, P. S. (1979). Cognitive deficit caused by depletion of dopamine in prefrontal cortex of rhesus monkey. *Science, 205,* 929–931.

Carlson, M. C., Hasher, L., Connelly, S. L., & Zacks, R. T. (1995). Aging, distraction, and the benefits of predictable location. *Psychology and Aging, 10,* 427–436.

Charness, N. (Ed.). (1985). *Aging and human performance.* Chichester, UK: Wiley.

Coffey, C. E., Wilkinson, W. E., Parashos, I. A., Soady, S. A. R., Sullivan, R. J., Patterson, L. J., Figiel, G. S., Webb, M. C., Spritzer, C. E., & Djang, W. T. (1992). Quantitative cerebral anatomy of the aging human brain: A cross-sectional study using magnetic resonance imaging. *Neurology, 42,* 527–536.

Connelly, S. L., Hasher, L., & Zacks, R. T. (1991). Age and reading: The impact of distraction. *Psychology and Aging, 6,* 533–541.

Craik, F. I. M. (1977). Age differences in human memory. In J. E. Birren & K. W. Schaie (Eds.), *Handbook of the psychology of aging* (pp. 384–420). New York: Van Nostrand Reinhold.

Craik, F. I. M., Morris, L. W., Morris, R. G., & Loewen, E. R. (1990). Relations between source amnesia and frontal lobe functioning in older adults. *Psychology and Aging, 5,* 148–151.

Dempster, F. N. (1992). The rise and fall of the inhibitory mechanism: Toward a unified theory of cognitive development and aging. *Developmental Review, 12,* 45–72.

Diamond, A., & Doar, B. (1989). The performance of human infants on a measure of frontal cortex function, the delayed response task. *Developmental Psychobiology, 22,* 271–294.

Dobbs, A. R., & Rule, B. G. (1987). Prospective memory and self-reports of memory abilities. *Canadian Journal of Psychology, 41,* 209–222.

Goldman-Rakic, P. S. (1987). Development of cortical circuitry and cognitive function. *Child Development, 58,* 601–622.

Goldman-Rakic, P. S. (1992). Working memory and the mind. *Scientific American,* September, 111–117.

Goldman-Rakic, P. S., & Brown, R. M. (1981). Regional changes of monoamines in cerebral cortex and subcortical structures of aging rhesus monkeys. *Neuroscience, 6,* 177–187.

Haaland, K. Y., Vranes, L. F., Goodwin, J. S., & Garry, P. J. (1987). Wisconsin Card Sort Test performance in a healthy elderly population. *Journal of Gerontology, 33,* 345–346.

Hasher, L., Stoltzfus, E. R., Zacks, R. T., & Rypma, B. (1991). Age and inhibition. *Journal of Experimental Psychology: Learning, Memory, and Cognition, 17,* 163–169.

Heaton, R. (1981). *The Wisconsin Card Sorting Test.* Odessa, FL: Psychological Assessment Resources.

Henderson, G., Tomlinson, B. E., & Gibson, P. H. (1980). Cell counts in human cerebral cortex in normal adults throughout life using an image analyzing computer. *Journal of Neurological Sciences, 46,* 113–136.

Hughlings-Jackson, J. (1931). *Selected writings of John Hughlings-Jackson,* J. Taylor (Ed.). Vols. 1 and 2. London: Hodder.

Hulicka, I. M., & Grossman, J. L. (1967). Age-group comparisons for the use of mediators in paired-associate learning. *Journal of Gerontology, 22,* 46–51.

Inglis, J., & Caird, W. K. (1963). Age differences in successive responses to simultaneous stimulation. *Canadian Journal of Psychology, 17,* 98–105.

Janowsky, J. S., Shimamura, A. P., & Squire, L. R. (1989). Source memory impairment in patients with frontal lobe lesions. *Neuropsychologia, 27,* 1043–1056.

Kane, M. J., Hasher, L., Stoltzfus, E. R., Zacks, R. T., & Connelly, S. L. (1994). Inhibitory attentional mechanisms and aging. *Psychology and Aging, 9,* 103–112.

Kinsbourne, M. (1980). Attentional dysfunctions in the elderly: Theoretical models and research perspectives. In L. W. Poon, J. L. Fozard, L. S. Cermak, D. Arenberg, & L. W. Thompson (Eds.), *New directions in memory and aging: Proceedings of the George A. Talland memorial conference.* Hillsdale, NJ: Erlbaum.

Kirchner, W. K. (1958). Age differences in short-term retention of rapidly changing information. *Journal of Experimental Psychology, 55,* 352–358.

Kolb, B., & Whishaw, I. Q. (1995). *Fundamentals of human neuropsychology* (4th ed.). New York: W. H. Freeman.

Kosnik, W., Winslow, L., Rasinski, K., & Sekuler, R. (1988). Visual changes in daily life throughout adulthood. *Journal of Gerontology: Psychological Sciences, 43,* P63–70.

Levitt, P., Rakic, P., & Goldman-Rakic, P. S. (1984). Region-specific distribution of catecholamine afferents in primate cerebral cortex: A florescence histochemical analysis. *Journal of Comparative Neurology, 31,* 533–538.

Libon, D. J., Glosser, G., Malamut, B. L., Kaplan, E., Goldberg, E., Swenson, R., & Sands, L. P. (1994). Age, executive functions, and visuospatial functioning in healthy older adults. *Neuropsychology, 8,* 38–43.

Loranger, A. W., & Misiak, H. (1960). The performance of aged females on five nonlanguage tests of intellectual functions. *Journal of Clinical Psychology, 16,* 189–191.

McDowd, J. M., & Oseas-Kreger, D. M. (1991). Aging, inhibitory processes, and negative priming. *Journal of Gerontology, 46,* 340–345.

McIntyre, J. S., & Craik, F. I. M. (1987). Age differences in memory for item and source information. *Canadian Journal of Psychology, 42,* 175–192.

Milner, B. (1963). Effects of different brain lesions on card-sorting. *Archives of Neurology, 9,* 90–100.

Milner, B., & Petrides, M. (1984). Behavioural effects of frontal-lobe lesions in man. *Trends in Neuroscience, 7,* 403–407.

Milner, B., Petrides, M., & Smith, M. L. (1985). Frontal lobes and the temporal organization of memory. *Human Neurobiology, 4,* 137–142.

Mitchell, D. B., Hunt, R. R., & Schmitt, F. A. (1986). The generation effect and reality monitoring: Evidence from dementia and normal aging. *Journal of Gerontology, 41,* 79–84.

Mittenberg, W., Seidenberg, M., O'Leary, D. S., & DeGiulo, D. V. (1989). Changes in cerebral functioning associated with normal aging. *Journal of Clinical and Experimental Neuropsychology, 11,* 918–932.

Molander, B., & Backman, L. (1994). Attention and performance in miniature golf across the life span. *Journal of Gerontology: Psychological Sciences, 49,* P35–41.

Morrow, D. G., Leirer, V. O., & Altieri, P. A. (1992). Aging, expertise, and narrative processing. *Psychology and Aging, 7,* 376–388.

Moscovitch, M. (1982). A neuropsychological approach to perception and memory in normal and pathological aging. In F. I. M. Craik & S. Trehub (Eds.), *Aging and cognitive processes* (pp. 55–78). New York: Plenum Press.

Parkin, A. J. (1996). *Explorations in cognitive neuropsychology.* Oxford: Blackwell.

Parkin, A. J., & Lawrence, A. (1994). A dissociation in the relation between memory tasks and frontal lobe tests in the normal elderly. *Neuropsychologia, 32,* 1523–1532.

Parkin, A. J., Leng, N. R. C., & Stanhope, N. (1988). Memory impairment following ruptured aneurysm of the anterior communicating artery. *Brain and Cognition, 7,* 231–243.

Parkin, A. J., & Walter, B. M. (1992). Recollective experience, normal aging, and frontal dysfunction. *Psychology and Aging, 7,* 290–298.

Parkin, A. J., Walter, B. M., & Hunkin, N. M. (1995). Relationships between normal aging, frontal lobe function, and memory for temporal and spatial information. *Neuropsychology, 9,* 304–312.

Petrides, M. (1991). Functional specialization within the dorsolateral frontal cortex for serial order memory. *Proceedings of the Royal Society, London, B246,* 299–306.

Salthouse, T. A., Mitchell, D. R. D., Skovronek, E., & Babcock, R. L. (1989). Effects of adult age and working memory on reasoning and spatial abilities. *Journal of Experimental Psychology: Learning, Memory, and Cognition, 15,* 507–516.

Scheibel, M. E., & Scheibel, A. B. (1976). Structural changes in the aging brain. In R. D. Terry & S. Gerschon (Eds.), *Neurobiology of aging.* New York: Raven Press.

Shimamura, A. P. (1990). Aging and memory disorders: A neuropsychological analysis. In M. L. Howe, M. J. Stones, & C. J. Brainerd (Eds.), *Cognitive and behavioral performance factors in atypical aging* (pp. 37–65). New York: Springer.

Squire, L. R., Nadel, L., & Slater, P. C. (1981). Anterograde amnesia and memory for temporal order. *Neuropsychologia, 19,* 141–145.

Stoltzfus, E. R., Hasher, L., Zacks, R. T., Ulivi, M. S., & Goldstein, D. (1993). Investigations of inhibition and interference in younger and older adults. *Journal of Gerontology: Psychological Sciences, 48,* P179–188.

Szafran, J. (1968). Psychophysiological studies of aging in pilots. In G. A. Talland (Ed.), *Human aging and behavior.* New York: Academic Press.

Tipper, S. P., & Cranston, M. (1985). Selective attention and priming: Inhibitory and facilitatory effects of ignored primes. *Quarterly Journal of Experimental Psychology: Human Experimental Psychology, 4,* 591–611.

Welford, A. T. (1958). *Ageing and human skill.* London: Oxford University Press.

West, R. (1988). Prospective memory and aging. In M. M. Gruneberg, P. E. Morris, & R. N. Sykes (Eds.), *Practical aspects of memory: Current research and issues* (Vol. 2, pp. 119–125). New York: John Wiley & Sons.

Wheilihan, W. M., & Lesher, E. L. (1985). Neuropsychological changes in frontal functions with aging. *Developmental Neuropsychology, 1,* 371–380.

Wiegersma, S., & Meertse, K. (1990). Subjective ordering, working memory, and aging. *Experimental Aging Research, 6,* 73–77.

Chapter 14   Prospects in the Neuropsychology of Aging

A Profile of Older Americans (1986). Program Resources Department, American Association of Retired Persons (AARP) and the Administration on Aging (AoA), Washington, DC: US Department of Health and Human Services.

Araujo, D. M., Lapchak, P. A., Robitaille, Y., Ganthier, S., & Quirion, R. (1988). Differential alteration of various cholinergic markers in cortical and subcortical regions of human brain in Alzheimer's disease. *Journal of Neurochemistry, 50,* 1914–1923.

Baltes, P. B. (1993). The aging mind: Potentials and limits. *Gerontologist, 33,* 580–594.

Barrows, C. H., Jr., & Kokkonen, G. C. (1984). Nutrition and aging: Human and animal laboratory studies. In J. M. Ordy, D. Harman, & R. Alfin-Slater (Eds.), *Nutrition in gerontology.* New York: Raven Press.

Clark, J. E., Lanphear, A. K., & Riddick, C. C. (1987). The effects of videogame playing on the response selection processing of elderly adults. *Journal of Gerontology, 42,* 82–85.

Cutler, R. G. (1981). Life-span extension. In J. L. McGaugh & S. B. Kiesler (Eds.), *Aging: Biology and behavior.* New York: Academic Press.

Delong, M. R. (1995, November 12). *The basal ganglia and Parkinson's disease: Lessons from the laboratory and the operating room.* Special lecture presented at the 25th Annual Meeting of the Society for Neuroscience, San Diego, CA.

Dustman, R. E., Emmerson, R., & Shearer, D. (1994). Physical activity, age, and cognitive-neuropsychological function. *Journal of Aging and Physical Activity, 2,* 143–181.

Dustman, R. E., & Ruhling, R. O. (1986, November). *Brain function of old and young athletes and nonathletes.* Paper presented at the 39th Annual Scientific Meeting of the Gerontological Society of America, Chicago.

Fries, J. F., & Crapo, L. M. (1981). *Vitality and aging.* San Francisco, CA: W. H. Freeman.

Giurgia, C. E. (1980). *Fundamentals to a pharmacology of the mind.* Springfield, IL: Charles C. Thomas.

Gordon, T. J. (1979). Prospects for aging in America. In M. W. Riley (Ed.), *Aging from birth to death.* Boulder, CO: Westview Press.

Hardy, J. (1993). Genetic mistakes point the way for Alzheimer's disease. *Journal of NIH Research, 5,* 46–49.

Hudson, T. J., Stein, L. D., Gerety, S. S., Ma, J., Castle, A. B. et al. (1995). An STS-based map of the human genome. *Science, 270,* 1945–1954.

Ingram, D. K., Weindruch, R., Spangler, E. L., Freeman, J. R., & Walford, R. L. (1987). Dietary restriction benefits learning and motor performance of aged mice. *Journal of Gerontology, 42,* 78–81.

Jones, G. M. M., Sahakian, B. J., Levy, R., Warburton, D. M., & Gray, J. A. (1992). Effects of acute subcutaneous nicotine on attention, information processing and short-term memory in Alzheimer's disease. *Psychopharmacology, 108,* 485–494.

Knapp, M., Knopman, D., Solomon, P., Pendlebury, W., Davis, C., & Gracon, S. (1994). A 30-week randomized controlled trial of high-dose Tacrine in patients with Alzheimer's disease. *Journal of the American Medical Association, 271,* 985–991.

Langston, J. W., & Palfreman, J. (1995). *The case of the frozen addicts.* New York: Pantheon.

Lindvall, O., Brundin, P., Widner, H., Rehncrona, S., Gustavii, B., Frackowiak, R., Leenders, K. L., Sawle, G., Rothwell, J. C., Marsden, C. D., & Bjorklund, A. (1990). Grafts of fetal dopamine neurons survive and improve motor function in Parkinson's disease. *Science, 247,* 574–577.

Manning, F. (1994). Tacrine therapy for the dementia of Alzheimer's disease. *American Family Physician, 50,* 819–826.

Marx, J. (1990a). Fetal nerve grafts show promise in Parkinson's. *Science, 247,* 529.

Marx, J. (1990b). NGF and Alzheimer's: Hopes and Fears. *Science, 247,* 407–410.

Masoro, E. J. (1984). Food restriction and the aging process. *Journal of the American Geriatrics Society, 32,* 296–300.

Means, L. W., Comer, T. R., & Moore, R. (1990). Priacetam and BMY 21502 facilitate performance of two-choice win–stay water–escape in normal rats. *Society for Neuroscience Abstracts, 16,* 1331.

Mullan, M., & Crawford, F. (1993). Genetic and molecular advances in Alzheimer's disease. *Trends in Neuroscience, 16,* 398–403.

Nakamura, J., Higashi, H., Nishi, S., & Nakazawa, Y. (1991). DM-9384, a pyrrolidone derivative, protects the membrane dysfunction induced by deprivation of oxygen and glucose in guinea-pig hippocampal neurons in vitro. *Biological Psychiatry, 29,* Abst. P-29–36.

National Center for Health Statistics (1985, September). Current estimates from National Health Interview Survey, United States, 1982. *Vital and Health Statistics.* Series 10, No. 150. DHHS Pub. No. (PHS) 85–1578. Public Health Service. Washington, DC: US Government Printing Office.

National Center for Health Statistics (1986, September 19). R. J. Havlik. Aging in the eighties: Impaired senses for sound and light in persons age 65 years and over. Preliminary data from the Supplement on Aging to the National Health Interview Survey, United States, January–June 1984. *Advance Data from Vital and Health Statistics.* No. 125. DHHS Pub. No. (PHS) 86–1250. Public Health Service. Hyattsville, MD.

Newhouse, P. A., Potter, A., & Lenox, R. (1993). The effects of nicotinic agents on human cognition: Possible therapeutic applications in Alzheimer's and Parkinson's diseases. *Medical and Chemical Research, 2,* 628–642.

Olpe, H.-R., & Lynch, G. S. (1982). The action of piracetam on the electrical activity of the hippocampal slice preparation: A field potential analysis. *European Journal of Pharmacology, 80,* 415–419.

Piercey, M. F., Vogelsang, G. D., Franklin, S. R., & Tang, A. H. (1987). Reversal of scopolamine-induced amnesia and alterations in energy metabolism by the nootropic piracetam: Implications regarding identification of brain structures involved in consolidation of memory traces. *Brain Research, 424,* 1–9.

Price, D. L., Borchelt, D. R., & Sisodia, S. S. (1993). Alzheimer's disease and the prion disorders amyloid β-protein and prion protein amyloidoses. *Proceedings of the National Academy of Science USA, 90,* 6381–6384.

Rybash, J. M., Hoyer, W. J., & Roodin, P. A. (1986). *Adult cognition and aging.* New York: Pergamon Press.

Sahakian, B., Jones, G., Levy, R., Gray, J., & Warburton, D. (1989). The effects of nicotine on attention, information processing, and short-term memory in patients with dementia of the Alzheimer's type. *British Journal of Psychiatry, 154,* 797–800.

Sarter, M., Hagen, J., & Dudchenko, P. (1992). Behavioral screening for cognition enhancers: From indiscriminate to valid tasting: Part I. *Psychopharmacology, 107,* 144–159.

Satoh, M., Ishihara, K., Iwama, T., & Takagi, H. (1986). Aniracetam augments, and midazolam inhibits, the long-term potentiation in guinea pig hippocampal slices, *Neuroscience Letters, 68,* 216–220.

Saunders, A. M., Strittmatter, W. J., Schmechel, D., St. George-Hyslop, P. H.,

Pericak-Vance, M. A. et al. (1993). Association of apolipoprotein E allele e4 with late-onset familial and sporadic Alzheimer's disease. *Neurology, 43,* 1467–1472.

Schneider, E. L., & Reid, J. D., Jr. (1985). Life extension. *New England Journal of Medicine, 312,* 1159–1160.

Trojanowski, J. Q., & Lee, V. M.-Y. (1994). Phosphorylation of neuronal cytoskeletal proteins in Alzheimer's disease and Lewy body dementias. *Annals of the New York Academy of Science, 747,* 92–109.

Wagstaff, A., & McTavish, D. (1994). Tacrine. A review of its pharmacodynamic and pharmacokinetic properties, and therapeutic efficacy in Alzheimer's disease. *Drugs and Aging, 4,* 510–540.

Watabe, S., Yamaguchi, H., & Ashida, S. (1993). DM-9384, a new cognition-enhancing agent, increases the turnover of components of the GABAergic system in the rat cerebral cortex. *European Journal of Pharmacology, 238,* 303–309.

Weindruch, R. (1984). Dietary restriction and the aging process. In D. Armstrong, R. S. Sohal, R. G. Cutler, & T. F. Slater (Eds.), *Free radicals in molecular biology, aging, and disease.* New York: Raven Press.

Whitehouse, P. J., Martino, A. M., Antuono, P. G., Lowenstein, P. R., Coyle, J. T., Price, D. L., & Kellar, K. J. (1986). Nicotinic acetylcholine binding sites in Alzheimer's disease. *Brain Research, 371,* 146–151.

Woodruff-Pak, D. S., Lavond, D. G., Logan, C. G., & Thompson, R. F. (1987). Classical conditioning in 3-, 30-, and 45-month-old rabbits: Behavioral learning and hippocampal unit activity. *Neurobiology of Aging, 8,* 101–108.

Woodruff-Pak, D. S., & Li, Y.-T. (1994). Nefiracetam (DM-9384): Effect on eyeblink classical conditioning in older rabbits. *Psychopharmacology, 114,* 200–208.

Woodruff-Pak, D. S., Li, Y.-T., Kazmi, A., & Kem, W. R. (1994). Nicotinic cholinergic system involvement in eyeblink classical conditioning in rabbits. *Behavioral Neuroscience, 108,* 486–493.

Woodruff-Pak, D. S., Li, Y.-T., & Kem, W. R. (1994). A nicotinic agonist (GTS-21), eyeblink classical conditioning, and nicotinic receptor binding in rabbit brain. *Brain Research, 645,* 309–317.

Zopf, P. E., Jr. (1986). *America's older population.* Houston, TX: Cap and Gown Press.

Index

"A" test, attention, 34
Abrahams, J. P., 176
acetylcholine, 100–1, 116–17, 121, 277
acetylcholine receptor antagonist, 124–5
Achenbaum, W. A., 198
Adolfsson, R., 102
age differences, 16; balance, 68, 69, 72; cohort effect, 14, 153, 197, 201–2, 203; deep information processing, 216; hearing, 30, 68, 74–5, 281–2; inhibition, 164–5, 167, 168; intelligence, 191; pain, 71–2; positron emission tomography, 59–60; reaction time, 174–5, 176; sensory changes, 68–9; sleep/arousal, 153–4; smell, 72–3; taste, 73; touch, 70–1; vision, 67–9, 76–80
aged population, 4–8, 15–16, 42, 44, 279
aging, 8–9, 11–12, 86–7; biological, 9, 16; cognitive, 18, 280–3; demographic factors, 4–8, 16; onset, 9–11; psychological, 9, 16; social, 9
aging effects, 25–31; aphasia, 239; arousal levels, 82; attention, 170, 172; behavior, 18; brain plasticity, 16–18; brain-wave rhythms, 49–51; cell loss, 87–99; cerebrovascular changes, 99; depression, 131, 132–44; electroencephalogram, 153–4, 162–3; event-related potential, 153, 163–4, 165; executive function,

259–62; hippocampus, 92–5; and intelligence tests, 194–207; language, 248–51; learning, 221, 229; memory, 215, 230–1, 264–5; molecular changes, 105–6; neuropsychology, 4–8, 12–15, 21–2, 42, 44, 178–83; neurotransmitter systems, 99–105; peripheral nervous system, 67–8; psychometrics, 26; sensory changes, 68–80; synaptic plasticity, 105–6
Albert, M. S., 168, 249, 257
Albertson, S. A., 221
alcoholism, 144, 217
Alprazolam, 142–3
Alsop, D., 113
Altman, H. J., 104–5
aluminum, 119
Alzheimer, Alois, 110–11
Alzheimer's disease, 109–12; β-amyloid plaques, 273–4; assessment, 24–5, 28, 123–6; behavioral signs, 115–18; causes, 118–22; computerized tomography, 56; depression, 136, 143; diagnosis, 113–15, 122; drugs treatment, 116–17, 276; familial, 127–8, 274; frontal lobes, 144; genetic studies, 120–1, 274; hippocampus, 227, 275; learning impairment, 113, 115; nerve growth factor, 276; neuronal loss, 90, 91; neuropsychology, 122–3; neurotransmitter systems, 100, 121–2;

nicotinic receptors, 277; onset, 112–
16, 274; P300 wave, 186–7; post-
mortem examination, 48, 60–2,
114–15; rotary pursuit learning, 222;
slow virus studies, 118–19; smell, 73;
sobbing, 115; sporadic, 112–26, 274;
trace metal studies, 119–20; working
memory, 264
Alzheimer's Disease Assessment Scale,
28, 121, 123–4
Alzheimer's Disease and Related
Disorders Association, 114
American Academy of Neurology, 113,
114
American Psychiatric Association, 136
American Psychiatric Association Task
Force on Nomenclature and
Statistics, 140
gamma-aminobutyric acid (GABA), 277
Aminoff, M. J., 186
Ammons Quick Test, 39
Ammons, R. B. and C. H., 39
amnesia, 259
amyloid plaques, 118; β-amyloid
plaques, 16, 61–2, 113, 273–4
amylotrophic lateral sclerosis, 119
Anastasi, A., 192
Ancoli-Israel, S., 159
Anderson, B., 80
Anderson, B. J., 225
Anderson, J. M., 257
angular gyrus, 242
animal studies: aging, 19–20, 263–4;
cerebellar cortex of monkeys, 96;
cerebellar cortex in rabbits, 97, 98;
cholinergic receptor binding in rats,
100; dentate gyrus in rats, 86–7;
eyeblink classical conditioning in
rabbits, 20, 223, 224, 226; life
expectancy, 280; locus coeruleus
neurons in rats, 104; nefiracetam in
rabbits, 277; neuronal loss, 91;
nicotinic receptors in rabbits, 277–8;
NMDA receptors in mice, 105–6;
nootropic drugs, 277; prefrontal
cortex of monkeys, 101; Purkinje
cells in rats, 96–8; sleep/arousal in
cats, 161; somatosensory cortex of
monkey, 18, 19; transgenic mice,
118–19
anterior cortex, 168–70
Anthropological Society, 237, 238
antidepressant drugs, 139
anxiety over test-taking, 28–9
aphasia: Broca's, 238–41;
comprehension, 246; left frontal lobe,
236; receptive, 243–4; Wernicke's,
239, 241–2, 243
apnea, sleep, 159–60
apolipoprotein E, 120–1, 274
Arajuo, D. M., 277
ARAS: *see* ascending reticular arousal
system
Arbuckle, T. Y., 154
arcuate fasciculus, 242
Arenberg, D., 174
Aretaeus, 133
Aricep, 117
Army Alpha Examination, 198
Arnstein, A. F. T., 101, 263, 264
arousal: aging, 82; ascending reticular
arousal system, 52, 71, 155, 160–4,
171; attention, 169; autonomic
nervous system, 80–4; behavioral
performance, 71; states, 153–4; *see
also* underarousal
Arriagada, P. E., 115
arteries, hardening of, 99, 107
ascending reticular arousal system, 52,
71, 155, 160–4, 171
Ashton-Jones, G., 103
Asia, population age/sex, 7
aspartate receptors, NMDA, 105–6
atropine, 125
attention: aging, 170, 172; and arousal,
169; cognitive, 255; divided, 265,
266, 268; selective, 265–6, 268;
sustained, 265; testing for, 32–3, 34
Attention/Concentration Index (WMS-
R), 34

Auburtin, Ernest, 237
auditory evoked responses, 51–2, 53, 164
autonomic nervous system, 67, 68, 80–4
axodendritic synapses, 154
axosomatic synaptic loss, 154
Azmitia, E. C., 105

Backman, L., 26, 265
Bahrick, H. P., 213
balance, sense of, 68, 69, 72
Ball, S. S., 186
Balota, D. A., 39
Baltes, P. B., 26, 153, 282
Baltimore Longitudinal Study of Aging, 75, 76
Barnes, C. A., 93
Barrows, C. H. Jr, 280
Bartus, R. T., 100, 100–1, 264
basal ganglia, 187
Bashore, T. R., 53, 54, 184, 187
Bayles, K. A., 248
Bayley, N., 248
Beatty, J., 183
Beck, A. T., 132, 133
Beck, E. C., 52, 163–4, 165
Beck Depression Inventory, 135
Beeson, M. F., 248
behavior: aging, 18; Alzheimer's disease, 115–18; arousal, 71; brain function, 24; brain structure, 56; frontal-lobe syndrome, 145; intelligence, 190; timing, 187–8
Bengston, V. L., 16
Benson, D. F., 257
Berg, C., 177
Berg, C. A., 26
Berg, E. A., 258
Berg, J. M., 125
Berger, Hans, 47, 162
Berger, T. W., 226
Berrios, G. E., 110
Berry, S. D., 227
Betty, J., 247

Beutler, L., 142–3
Bickford-Wimer, P. C., 103
Binet, Alfred, 191, 192
Bird, T. D., 128
Birren, J. E., 3, 10, 26, 50, 71, 76, 161–2, 163, 174, 176, 178, 179–80, 201, 207
Bismarck, Otto von, 15
Blaxton, T. A., 225
Blazer, D. G., 132, 134, 139
Blessed, G., 28, 32
Blessed Information Memory Concentration test, 28, 32, 125
Bliwise, Donald, 158, 159
Block Design subtest (WAIS), 35, 44
blood plasma, 83
Bloom, F. E., 102
Blumer, D., 257
Bogdonoff, M. D., 83
Bolton, C. F., 70
Bondareff, W., 86, 98, 102, 154
Bondi, M. W., 264
Borod, J. C., 249
Boston Diagnostic Aphasia Examination, 33, 39
Boston Naming Test, 44, 249
Botwinick, J., 35, 80, 82, 174, 176, 179–80
Bouillaud, Jean Baptiste, 236–7
Bowen, D. M., 122
Bowles, N. L., 249
Boyd, J. H., 132, 133, 134
Braak, E. and H., 109, 113, 131
brain: aging, 49–51, 86–106; emotions, 147; function, 10–11, 24, 48; GABA, 277; and language, 242–8; lateralization, 147, 149, 238; localization, 236–7, 242; measuring techniques, 47–62; post-mortem analysis, 89; response to injury, 121
brain damage, alcoholism, 217
brain death, 52
brain imaging, 21
brain implant surgery, 275
brain memory systems, 211–28

brain plasticity, 10, 16–18, 88, 105–6, 203
brain-wave rhythms: *see* electroencephalogram
brainstem, 51–2, 53, 104, 220
Brant, L. J., 75
Braun, H. W., 164, 224
Brazier, M. A. B., 49, 162
breathing, apnea, 159–60
Brizzee, K. R., 91, 93
Broadbent, D. E., 266
Broca, Paul, 238, 251
Broca's aphasia, 238–41
Broca's area, word retrieval, 59
Brody, H., 90, 91, 102
Brown, R. M., 101, 263
Brozoski, T. J., 101, 263
Bruce, D., 3
Buckner, R. L., 220, 221
Buonanno, F., 58
Busse, E. W., 49, 162
Butler, R. N., 134, 229, 231
Byrd, E., 73

Cain, W. S., 73
Caine, E. D., 136
Caird, W. K., 266
calcium, 105, 107–8
California Verbal Learning Test, 29, 30, 36–7, 211, 212
Callner, D. A., 165
Canestrari, R. E. Jr, 229
Cappeliez, P., 132
caregiver, support for, 144
Carlson, M. C., 170, 265
Carskadon, Mary, 158
Caspi, A., 206
cat, sleep/arousal, 161
cataracts, 79–80
catecholamine, 101, 139, 263–4
Cattell, R. B., 196, 202
cell loss, 87–99
Center for Epidemiological Studies Depression scale, 42, 133–4
central nervous system, reaction time, 182–7
cerebellar cortex, 95–9, 107
cerebellum, 61–2, 187–8, 225, 248
cerebral blood flow, 222
cerebral cortex, 220
cerebrovascular changes, 99, 239, 243
cerebrovascular dementia, 109, 227
Cerella, J., 26
Chamorra natives, Guam, 119
Channon, S., 227
Chapell, M. S., 196, 202, 203
Chapman, C. R., 71
Charness, N., 265
Cheng, H., 17
Chiarello, C., 221
choline acetyltransferase, 121
cholinergic deficits, 129
cholinergic system, 100–1, 121–2, 227, 277
Christensen, H., 28, 123
chromosomal aberrations, 128–9
Clark, J. E., 281
classical conditioning, 20, 82
Clayton, V., 207
Clifford, P., 176
Clock Test, 35, 36
clonidine, 264, 268
closed head injury, 18, 144
Coffey, C. E., 92, 257
Coffin, J. M., 93, 97, 226
Cognex, 116, 117
cognition: aging, 10, 18; alpha frequency, 162–3; brain function, 24; changes, 206; and depression, 42; flexibility, 257–8; impaired, 102; inhibition, 170–1; reintegrative, 207; timing, 187–8
cognition-enhancing compounds, 276–7
cognitive aging, 18, 280–3
cognitive neuroscience, 211
cognitive therapy, depression, 142, 143
cohort effect, 14, 153, 197, 201–2, 203
Coleman, P. D., 90, 91, 93, 226
Coleman, P. G., 232
Collier, T. J., 104

color vision, 78–9

computerized tomography, 21, 48, 54–7, 63

concentration, attention, 32, 136

conduction velocity, 179–80

Connelly, S. L., 170, 265

contingent negative variation, anterior cortex, 168–70

Controlled Oral Word Association Test, 44

"cookie-theft" test, 239–40, 241, 242–3

Cooper, R. M., 73

Corkin, S., 58

Cormack, A. M., 55

Cornelius, S. W., 206

Corso, J. F., 75

Corwin, J., 73

Coslett, H. B., 33

Cotman, C. W., 105–6

Court, J. A., 100–1

Coyle, J. T., 100, 121, 122

Craig, T. J., 132

Craik, F. I. M., 211, 214, 216, 261, 262, 266

Cranston, M., 266

Crapo, L. M., 279, 280

Crawford, F., 120, 274

Creutzfeldt–Jakob disease, 118

Creutzfelt, O. D., 183

Critchley, M., 250

Cronholm, J. F., 98

Crook, Thomas, 115

Cross, C. K., 132

Crossman, E. R. F. W., 183

CT: *see* computerized tomography

Cutler, R. G., 280

Dai, X., 202

Damasio, A. R., 146, 222

Damasio, H., 144–5, 146

Daniel, L., 232

Daum, I., 165, 225, 227, 228

Davidson, R. J., 147

Davies, D. R., 183

Davies, P., 122

Davis, H. P., 221

Davis, P. A., 162

Dax, Marc, 237

Dayan, A. D., 98

Decker, M. W., 103

Delis, D. C., 36

Delong, M. R., 275

Dement, W. C., 157, 158, 159

dementia, 109–12; alpha rhythms, 162; chromosomal aberrations, 128–9; early detection, 124; single gene effects, 126–8

Demming, J. A., 206

demographic factors, aging, 4–8, 16, 279

Dempster, F. N., 257

dendritic branching, 155

dentate gyrus, 86–7, 154

depression, 42, 232; aging, 131, 132–44; Alzheimer's disease, 136, 143; Angry/Self Haters, 232; antidepressants, 139, 142–3; cognition, 42; defined, 132–4; life review, 232; memory loss, 109, 136; neurobiological aspects, 139–40; neuropsychological assessment, 136–8; psychological/social causes, 140–1; psychotherapeutic treatments, 141–4; self-rating scales, 135; symptoms and diagnosis, 135–6; therapy, 149

Deser, T., 251, 252

Desmedt, J. E., 53

developmental task theory, 231

DeVries, H. A., 176

Diamond, A., 256

Diamond, M. C., 10

Dickson, D. W., 115

Diehl, M., 206

diencephalon, 217–19, 233

dietary restriction, cognition, 280

Dietsche, L. M., 232

Digit or Letter Cancellation, 34

Digit Span subtest, WAIS-R, 33, 34, 44

Digit Symbol subtest (WAIS), 44, 176–7

discontinuity hypothesis, Birren, 163

disinhibition, 145

Disterhoft, J. F., 105

Dixon, R. A., 26, 211

dizziness, 72

Doar, B., 256

Dobbs, A. R., 260

Donchin, E., 53, 168, 184

dopamine, 87, 100, 101, 263–4, 274, 275

Doty, R. L., 73

Down's syndrome, 113, 128–9, 166, 227

Down's syndrome/Alzheimer's disease patients, 61, 113, 124–5, 129, 227

Drechsler, F., 168

drug treatment: Alprazolam, 142–3; antidepressants, 139–40, 142–3; Aricep, 117; clonidine, 264, 268; Cognex, 116–17; L-dopa, 274; nefiracetam, 277, 282; Prozac, 139–40; scopolamine, 121–2; tacrine, 116–17, 122, 123, 276, 282

DSM-III diagnostic system, 136, 140

Duncan-Johnson, C., 53

Durkin, M., 61, 222, 223, 225

Dustman, R. E., 11, 52, 163–4, 165, 166–7, 281

Dustman, R. W., 176

dysphonia, 246

Eames, N., 135

ear structures, 74; *see also* hearing

Eeg-Olofsson, O., 162

ego integration, 229

Eisdorfer, C., 83–4

electroencephalogram, 21; age changes, 153–4, 162–3; alpha rhythm, 49, 50–1, 62–3, 160, 162–3, 182; beta frequency, 49, 160; brain functions, 47; delta activity, 49, 157, 160; excitability cycle, 182–3; sleep stages, 47, 153, 156–9; theta activity, 49,

160, 183; *see also* event-related potential

electrophysiology, 49–51, 97–8

Ellis, R. S., 95

Emmers, R., 181

Emmerson, R. Y., 168, 281

emotion, 144–7, 149

Engen, T., 72, 73

epilepsy, 258

Erber, J. T., 214, 216

Erikson, Erik, 229–30

Esiri, M. M., 113

Eslinger, P. J., 222

Estes, E. H. Jr, 83

European population, age/sex, 7

Evans, D. A., 112

event-related potential, 21, 47; aging, 153, 163–4, 165; brainstem auditory evoked response, 51–2; computerized tomography, 56–7; Down's syndrome, 166; long latency potential, 52–4; P300, 63, 184–7, 189

evoked responses: auditory, 51–2, 53, 164; sensory, 52–4, 163; somatosensory, 53, 164; visual, 53, 164, 166–7; *see also* event related potential

excitability cycle, EEG, 182–3

executive function, 39–42; aging, 259–62; frontal lobes, 90–2, 256–6, 257–62; planning and organization, 20; tests for, 29–30

exercise, aging, 10–11, 176, 281

eyeblink classical conditioning: aging, 20, 223–8; Alzheimer's disease testing, 124, 126; cerebellar assessment, 188; inhibition, 164–5; learning and memory, 61; nicotinic receptor, 277–8; nootropic drugs, 277

Eysenck, M. W., 216

face recognition, 92

facial expression, 147–8

factor analysis, 193–4
Feier, C. D., 250
Feig, S., 105
Feinberg, I., 157, 158
Ferrante, L. S., 25, 124, 125
Ferraro, F. R., 39
Ferris, Steven, 115
fetal brain tissue, 275
Filion, D. L., 171
Finesinger, J. E., 49, 162
Finkbiner, R. G., 36, 37, 196, 203, 212
Fisher, C., 158, 159
Fisher, L. M., 174
Fisher, M. B., 78
Fleischman, D. A., 220, 221
flexibility, 257–8; reactive, 261, 267; spontaneous, 267
Floeter, M. K., 10
Flood, D. G., 91, 93, 226
Folstein, M. F., 31
Ford, J. M., 56–7
Foret, J., 158
forgetting, 213; *see also* memory loss
Foster, J. C., 248
Fox, J. H., 56
Fozard, J. L., 69, 76
Frank, R., 146
free fatty acid, in blood plasma, 83
Freedman, R. D., 103
French, J. D., 161
Fries, J. F., 279, 280
Froehling, S., 84
frontal cortex, 155, 168, 261
frontal-lobe syndrome, 144–7, 149
frontal lobes: aging, 106; Alzheimer's disease, 144; assessment of function, 39–42; attention, 32; deficits, 90, 212; dendritic layers, 170; divergent thinking, 41; emotion, 144–7; executive functions, 90–2, 255–6, 257–62; IQ scores, 190; neuronal loss, 155; role, 256–7; speech impairment, 237–8; Wisconsin Card Sorting Task, 258–9

functional MRI (fMRI), 21, 48, 58, 60, 63
Fuster, J. M., 155

"G" factor, 193–4
GABA, 277
Gabrieli, J. D., 220, 221, 227
Gage, Phineas, 144–5, 146, 149, 256
Galaburda, A. M., 146
Galbraith, G. C., 166
Gall, Franz Josef, 236
Gallagher, D., 135, 136, 142, 143
Galton, Sir Francis, 175–6, 191–2
galvanic skin response, 29, 80, 82
Gardner, E. F., 206
garrulousness, 145, 165
Gatz, M., 133, 141
Geiselhart, R., 164
gender differences: population aging, 7; suicide, 134, 135
genetic studies, 120–1, 126–8, 273–4
Gerard, L., 170
geroneuropsychology, 194
gerontology, 8, 11–12, 26
Gerstman, L. J., 250
Gerstman–Straussler–Scheinker syndrome, 119
Gertman, S., 73
Geschwind, Norman, 240, 246
Geula, C., 121
Giambra, L. M., 39
Gieselhart, R., 225
Gilbert, A. N., 73
Giurgia, C. E., 276
glaucoma, 79, 80
Glick, R., 98
Gliddon, J. B., 166
Glosser, G., 251, 252
Gold, D. P., 154
Gold, P. E., 101
Golden, J. C., 32
Goldfarb, W., 177
Goldman-Rakic, P. S., 101, 170, 256, 263, 264
Golgi–Kopsch sections, 96

Golomb, J., 95, 212, 221, 226
Good, P. F., 119
Goodglass, H., 33, 39, 239, 240, 243
Goodin, D. S., 54, 184, 186
Goodman, R. M., 125
Gordon, E., 186
Gordon, T. J., 279
Grabowski, T., 146
Grady, C. L., 59, 60, 92
Graf, P., 221
Grafton, S. T., 220, 222, 225
Granick, S., 75, 174
Gray, J. A., 227
Green, E. J., 10
Greenough, W. T., 10, 17, 88
Gregory, M., 266
grief, and loss, 134, 135, 231
Groll, E., 183
Grossman, J. L., 260
Grossman, M., 246
group therapy, 142, 143
Growden, J. H., 58
Grzegorczyk, P. B., 73
Guilleminault, C. C., 159
Gurland, B. J., 134
gustation, 68, 69
Gutman, G. M., 222

Haaland, K. Y., 258
Haber, D., 16
Halgren, E., 184
Hall, C. S., 223
Hall, T. C., 96, 226
Halstead–Reitan Neuropsychological
    Battery, 30
Hamilton, M., 42, 136
Hamilton Psychiatric Rating Scale, 42,
    135–6
Hanson, C., 16, 86
Harasymieu, S., 239
Hardy, J., 113, 120, 274
Harkins, S. W., 52, 71, 82
Harlow, J. M., 144–5
Harmatz, J., 135
Harms, J. W., 96

Harris, W. S., 125
Harter, M. R., 183
Hartley, A. A., 154
Harvey, J. A., 226
Hasher, L., 154, 165, 170, 266
Hashtroudi, A., 222
Haug, H., 91
Havighurst, R. J., 198, 230
Hayslip, B., 204
Head Start Project, 197
health, longevity, 279–80
hearing acuity, 74–5; age changes, 30,
    68, 74–5, 281–2; brain stem auditory
    evoked responses, 52; language
    comprehension, 250–1, 253–4
heart-rate reactivity, 82
Heaton, R., 257, 258
Hebb, Donald O., 3
Hellige, J. B., 147
Henderson, G., 257
Hendricks, L., 232
Heron, A., 266
Hertzog, C., 176
Hicks, L. H., 176
Hill, C., 138
Hinchliffe, R. M., 126
hippocampus: aging, 92–5; Alzheimer's
    disease, 227, 275; impairment, 90;
    memory, 59–60, 106–7; tissue
    shrinkage, 212, 226; working
    memory, 262–3
Hippocrates, 133
Hirschfeld, R. M. A., 132
histology: double-staining techniques,
    61–2; microtomes, 60; post-mortem
    examination, 48, 64
history-taking, 42–3
Hodges, J. R., 217–19
Holden, C., 5, 7
Hollingworth, H. L., 196
Horn, J. L., 202
Hounsfield, G. N., 55
Howard, D. V., 221
Hoyer, W. J., 177, 221
Hsiao, K., 118–19

Hubbard, O., 162
Huckman, M. S., 56
Hudson, Thomas, 273
Hughes, G., 73
Hughlings-Jackson, John, 256
Hugin, R., 176
Hulicka, I. M., 206, 213, 260
Hultsch, D. F., 211, 221
Human Genome project, 273–4
Huntington's disease, 109, 127, 144,
   228
Hybels, D. C., 140
Hyman, B. T., 73

infarction: *see* stroke
information processing, 26, 175, 214–
   17
Inglis, J., 266
Ingram, D. K., 280
inhibition: age differences, 164–5, 167,
   168; arousal, 154; cognitive
   approach, 170–1; neurophysiology,
   165–70; psychophysiology, 171
Institute of Medicine, 159
intelligence: age difference, 191, 282–3;
   assessment, 38–9; defined, 190–1;
   fluid/crystallized, 202; longitudinal
   studies, 192; misperceptions about
   aging, 198–200; optimizing, 202–5;
   psychometric assessment, 191–4;
   stability/decline with aging, 200–2;
   triarchic theory, 26; wisdom, 205–7
intelligence quotient (IQ), 190, 193
intelligence tests: for aged, 206;
   assessment of normal aging, 194–207;
   ecological validity, 205–6;
   neuropsychological assessment, 25–
   31, 190; practice, 204; relevance,
   206, 217; standardized scores, 192–3
ischemia, 243
Ivry, R., 187, 188

Jaeger, M., 188, 225, 226
Janowsky, J. S., 262
Jenkins, W. M., 18, 19

Jensen, A. R., 191
Jensen, R. A., 210
Jerome, E. A., 164–5
Johnson, S. H., 175
Jones, G. M. M., 277
Jones, H. E., 200, 248

Kahn, E., 158, 159
Kales, A., 157, 158
Kandel, E. R., 242
Kane, M. J., 266
Kaplan, E., 33, 39, 168, 239, 243,
   257
Kastenbaum, R., 203
Kaszniak, A. W., 56
Katzman, Robert, 112
Kaufmann, A., 176
Kausler, D. H., 213, 214–16, 217
Kawas, C., 112
Keane, M. M., 221
Keele, S. W., 187, 188
Kemper, S., 250
Khachaturian, Z., 48, 105, 115, 123
Kieley, J. M., 154
Kimble, G. A., 164, 225
kinesthesis, 69
Kinomura, S., 160
Kinsbourne, M., 266
Kirchner, W. K., 266
Knapp, M., 276
Knight, R., 184
Knorring, L. von, 166
Knox, C. A., 93
Koga, Y., 175, 176, 179
Kokkonen, G. C., 280
Kolb, B., 3, 18, 146, 147, 148, 190,
   238, 239, 256, 258
Konkle, D. F., 39, 250
Kornetsky, C., 80, 82
Kornfield, C. M., 183
Korsakoff's syndrome, 144, 217–19,
   233
Kosnik, W., 79, 265
Kraepelin, Emil, 111–12
Kramer, A. F., 154

Kramer, D. A., 206–7
Krkovic, A., 183
Krupa, D. J., 225
Kuhlen, R. G., 26, 196, 201
kuru, 118
Kusnerz, P. A., 198
Kutas, M., 53
Kwong See, S. T., 250

L-dopa, 274
La Rue, A., 33, 35, 40, 136–7, 138, 249
La Voie, D., 221
Labouvie-Vief, G., 26, 205
Lachman, J. L., 228
Lander, Eric, 274
Langston, J. W., 274, 275
language: acquisition, 236–48; aging, 248–51; brain function, 242–8; comprehension, 250–1, 253–4; macrolinguistic abilities, 252; neuroanatomy of, 241–2; neuropsychology, 20
language and communication, 39
Lashley, Karl S., 3
lateralization, brain, 147, 149, 238
Lauer, P. A., 216
Lavond, D. G., 225
Lawrence, A., 261
learning: classical conditioning, 61; declarative, and memory, 211–17; drug-enhanced, 277; and memory, 35–8, 101, 104, 210–11, 220–8, 282; nondeclarative, 211, 220–8; paired associate, 229
learning impairment, Alzheimer's disease, 113, 115
Lecours, A. R., 164
Lee, V. M.-Y., 118, 274
Lenhardt, M., 52
Lesher, E. L., 258
Lesse, H., 179
letter-reading paradigm, 170–1
Levitt, P., 101, 263
Lewis, M. I., 231, 232

Lewy bodies, 16
Li, Young-Tong, 61, 62, 277
Libon, D. J., 147, 258, 259
Lieberman, M. A., 139
life expectancy, 279–80
life review, 229–32
Light, K. C., 176
Light, L. L., 221
Lindsley, D. B., 47, 71, 160, 182
Lindvall, O., 275
Lindzey, G., 223
linguistic functions: *see* language
lipid mobilization, 83
Lippa, A. S., 100
Lipton, P., 105
localization of function, 236–7, 242
Lockhart, R. S., 214
locus coeruleus neurons, 102, 104
Logan, C. G., 225
Logical Memory subtest (WMS), 30, 37, 44
longevity, 279–80
Loranger, A. W., 258
loss: depression, 139, 140–1; grief, 134, 135, 231
Loveless, N. E., 169
Luria–Nebraska Neuropsychological Battery, 30
Lynch, G. S., 277

McCarthy, G., 184
McCarthy, R. A., 217–19
McDowd, J. M., 170, 171, 266
McFarland, R. A., 78, 79
McGaugh, J. L., 103
McGeer, E. G., 102
McIntyre, J. S., 261, 262
McKee, A. C. K., 115
McKhann, G., 114, 122
McTavish, D., 276
Madden, D. J., 171, 177
magnetic resonance imaging, 21, 48, 57–8, 63, 96
Magnusson, K. R., 105–6
Magoun, H. W., 160

malnutrition, 89
Maloney, A. J. F., 122
Mamo, H., 92
Mani, R. B., 93
Mann, D. M. A., 93, 113
Mann, J. J., 139
Manning, F., 276
Manton, K. G., 134
Marcopulos, B. A., 136
Marcusson, J., 104
Marsh, G. R., 53, 54, 82, 162, 169, 183, 184
Marsiske, M., 26
Marsolek, C. J., 221
Marwaha, J., 98, 102, 103
Marx, J., 275, 276
Masliah, E., 92
Mason, S. E., 216
Masoro, E. J., 280
Matsuyama, H., 114
Means, L. W., 277
medial temporal lobe memory, 100–1, 259
Meertse, K., 264
Meissner's corpuscles, 70, 71
melancholia, 132–3
memory: declarative, 211–19, 259–60; and diencephalon, 217–19; episodic, 215–16; hippocampus, 59–60, 95, 106–7; and learning, 35–8, 101, 104, 210–11, 220–8, 282; life review, 229–32; long-term, 214; medial temporal lobe, 100–1, 259; for past, 230–1; primary/secondary, 214; prospective, 259–60, 267; short-term, 169, 214; source, 261–2; storage, 215; working, 170, 174, 255–6, 262–5, 267–8
memory loss, 131–2; Alzheimer's disease, 113, 115, 122; age-related, 259; cholinergic block, 122; depression, 109, 136
Mental Control subtest, WMS-R, 33, 34
Merriam, S., 232

Merritt, F. L., 83
Merzenich, M. M., 18, 19
Mesulam, M.-M., 86, 100, 121
metamemory, 228–9
mice: life expectancy, 280; NMDA receptors, 105–6; transgenic, 118–19
Michalewski, H. J., 155, 169
microscopy techniques, 60–2
microtomes, 60
midbrain reticular formation, 160
Miles, L. E., 157, 158, 159
Miles, W. R., 178
Miller, A. K. H., 93
Miller, M., 141
Milner, B., 148, 169, 258, 261, 263
Mini-Mental State Exam, 31, 44, 136
mirror tracing, 222–3
Misiak, H., 258
Mistretta, C. M., 70
Mitchell, D. B., 221, 262
Mittenberg, W., 259
MMPI Depression Scale, 135
Molander, B., 265
Molchan, S. E., 225
molecular genetics, 273–4
Monge, R. H., 206
monkeys: aging/working memory, 263–4; cerebellar cortex, 96; prefrontal cortex, 101; somatosensory cortex, 18, 19
monoamine oxidase, 157
monoamines, inhibition, 166
Montoye, H. J., 178
Moore, J. W., 226, 227
Morant, G. M., 175, 176, 179
Morrell, L. K., 183
Morrow, D. G., 265
Mortimer, J. A., 112
Moruzzi, G., 160
Moscovitch, M., 222, 260
Mouritzen Dam, A., 93
movement time, 178
MRI: *see* magnetic resonance imaging
Mullan, M., 120, 274

Murphy, C., 73
Murphy, M. D., 36, 228–9
Murrell, F. H., 177

Nabeshima, T., 105
Nakamura, J., 277
naming errors, 249–50
Nandy, K., 96
National Academy of Sciences, 198
National Center for Health Statistics, 134, 135, 281
National Institute on Aging, 5, 112–13, 174
National Institute of Neurological and Communicative Disorders and Stroke, 114
Navarro, M., 67
Nebes, R. D., 177
nefiracetam, 277, 282
nerve growth factor, 274, 276
nervous system, 256; autonomic, 67, 68, 80–4; central, 182–7; peripheral, 67–8
Neugarten, B. L., 198
neural noise hypothesis, 183–4
neuro-imaging, Alzheimer's disease, 114
neurobiology, skills, 10
neurofibrillary tangles, 16, 32, 48, 111, 113, 114–15, 118
neuronal loss, 16, 87–91, 102, 107, 113, 155
neurophysiology, inhibition, 165–70
neuropsychological tests: aging, 4–8, 12–15, 21–2, 42, 44; Alzheimer's disease, 122–3; assessment, 16, 25–31, 69, 278–83; attention, 32–3, 34; depression, 42, 136–8; intelligence, 38–9; language and communication, 39; learning and memory, 35–8; mental status, 31–2; norms, 27; planning and executive function, 39–42; visuospatial ability, 33, 35
neuropsychologists, 4, 5; rapport with patients, 29–30, 42–3

neuropsychology: human/animal studies, 18–20; origins, 3–4; phase model of intelligence, 197–8
neurotransmitter systems, 99–100; acetylcholine, 100–1; age related changes, 107; Alzheimer's disease, 100, 121–2; dopamine, 87, 101, 263–4; molecular level changes, 105–6; norepinephrine, 101–4; serotonin, 104–5
neurotrophic agents, 276
Newhouse, P. A., 277
nicotinic receptors, 277
Nilsson, L., 214
NMDA receptors, 105–6
nootropic agents, 276–7
norepinephrine, 100, 101–4, 139
Normile, H. J., 104–5
Norris, A. H., 179
Nowlin, J. B., 82, 169
nucleus basalis, nerve cell loss, 121
number manipulation tasks, 264

Object Memory Evaluation, 44
Obler, L. K., 239, 250
O'Brien, C., 111, 112
Obrist, W. D., 49, 162
Oden, M. H., 192, 248
Ogden, Jenni A., 4, 144, 243–6
O'Hanlon, J. F., 183
Ojemann, G. A., 247
Older Americans Act (1965), 196
olfaction, 68, 69, 72–3, 119
Olpe, H.-R., 277
ordering, temporal, 261
Ordy, J. M., 93
Oseas-Kreger, D. M., 170, 266
Osler, William, 3
overarousal, 82–4
Owens, W. A. Jr, 200, 248

P300 wave, 52–4, 57, 184–7, 189
pain, 71–2
Paired Associate Learning subtests (WMS), 37–8, 40

Paired Associates (WAIS), 211
Palfreman, J., 274, 275
Papka, M., 227, 228
paraphasia, 244
parietal lobe, 33, 190
Parkin, A. J., 258, 259, 260, 261, 262
Parkinson's disease: brain surgery, 275;
    dementia, 109; dysphonia, 246;
    frontal lobes, 144; histological
    techniques, 60–2; skill learning, 222;
    substantia nigra, 87; tissue transplants,
    274; working memory, 264
Parmelee, P. A., 132
Pascual-Leone, A., 222
patients, rapport with, 42–3, 29–30
Patterson, R. D., 174
Pavlov, Ivan, 154, 164, 266
Payne, R. B., 222
Peach, R. K., 39, 250
Pennypacker, H., 164, 225
perception, and sensation, 281–2
peripheral nervous system, 67–8
Perl, Daniel, 119
Perlmutter, M., 216, 228
Perris, C., 166
PET: *see* positron emission tomography
Petersen, S. E., 242, 248
Petrides, M., 261, 263
Pfefferbaum, A., 56–7, 155, 170
phrenology, 236, 237
physical health and fitness, 10–11, 176,
    281
Piaget, Jean, 191
Piercey, M. F., 277
Pierson, W. R., 178
Pineda, J., 184
piracetam, 276–7
Pittman, R. N., 103
planning function, 39–42
plaques: amyloid, 118; β-amyloid, 16,
    61–2, 113, 273; senile, 32, 48, 111,
    113, 118, 121
plasticity: *see* brain plasticity
Plude, D. J., 171, 177
Poirier, J., 121

Polich, J., 184
Polkey, C. E., 227
Poon, L. W., 217, 249
population factors, 4–8
positron emission tomography, 21, 48,
    58–60, 63, 92
Posner, M. I., 58, 242, 248
Post, F., 138
post-mortem analysis, brain, 89
potentiation, frequency/long-term,
    105
Potter, H., 125
Powell, A. H. Jr, 83
prefrontal cortex, 101, 262–3
presbycusis, 74–5
presbyopia, 79
Pressey, S. L., 206
Price, D. L., 113, 120, 274
Prinz, P. N., 155, 157, 158, 159, 165
prion, 118
problem solving, 206
Prozac, 139–40
Prusiner, Stanley, 118–19
pseudodementia, 138
psychometrics, 26, 191–4
psychomotor speed, 174, 179
psychophysiology, inhibition, 171
psychotherapy, individual, 142
pupil dilation response, 124–5, 126
Purkinje cells: cerebellar, 95, 96–7,
    102–3; dendrites, 61–2; loss, 90, 107,
    225–6
pyramidal cells, hippocampus, 93, 94–5,
    157

Quilter, R. E., 82
Quinn, J. F., 6

rabbits: cerebellar cortex, 97, 98;
    eyeblink classical conditioning, 20,
    223, 224, 226; nefiracetam, 277;
    nicotinic receptors, 277–8
Rabbitt, P., 171
Radloff, L. S., 42
Raichle, M. E., 58, 242, 248

Raskind, M. A., 139, 140

rats: cholinergic receptor binding, 100; denate gyrus, 86–7; life expectancy, 280; locus coeruleus neurons, 104; Purkinje cells, 96–8

Raz, N., 92, 99

reaction time, 175–8; age differences, 176; central nervous system, 182–7; conduction velocity, 179–80; locus for slowing, 178–87; movement time, 178; neural noise hypothesis, 183–4; P300, 184–7, 189; sensory acuity, 179; synaptic delay, 180–2

recall, recognition, 92, 216, 217, 261, 262

recognition and consciousness awareness paradigm, 260

recruitment, hearing, 75

Regan, M. M. S., 250

Reichard, S., 232

Reid, J. D. Jr, 280

Reisberg, Barry, 115

repetition priming, 220, 221, 233

research design, 12–15

Research Diagnostic Criteria, 142

response speed, 174–5, 250, 281; delayed, 263–4; *see also* evoked responses

reticular formations, shrinking, 164, 168

retirement, 155, 232

Riegel, K. F., 198

Roberts, J. C., 80

Robertson, B. A., 214

Roca, R. P., 31

Rogers, J., 96, 97–8, 102, 103

Romano, S. J., 126

Ronge, H., 70

Roodin, P. A., 207

Rosen, W. G., 28

Roses, A., 120

rotary pursuit learning, 222

Roush, W., 5, 8

Rovee, C. K., 72

Rowe, M. J., 52

Ruch, F. L., 222

Ruhling, R. O., 176

Rule, B., 260

Ryan, E. B., 250

Rybash, J. M., 175, 283

Sacks, B., 125

Sacks, Oliver, 219

Saffran, E. M., 33

Sahakian, B., 277

Salt Lake City Laboratories, 52, 163–4

Salthouse, T. A., 26, 174, 176, 177, 264

Salvatierra, A. T., 227

Salzman, C., 135

sampling, 15, 200–1

Sanford, A. J., 169

Sara, S. J., 103

Sarter, M., 277

Satoh, M., 277

Saunders, A. M., 120, 274

Scabini, D., 184

Schacter, D. L., 59, 60, 92, 211, 220, 221

Schaie, K. W., 15, 26, 33, 39, 75, 153, 207

Schanne, F. A., 105

Schedule for Affective Disorders and Schizophrenia, 42, 136

Scheibel, A. B., 155, 168, 257

Scheibel, M. E., 93, 155, 168, 257

Schenkenberg, T., 52, 163–4, 165

Schluderman, E., 71

Schmahmann, J. D., 99, 187

Schmaltz, L. W., 227

Schneider, E. L., 280

Schonfield, D., 214

Schroeder, M. M., 53

Schugens, M. M., 165

Schwab, L., 79

Scinto, L. F. M., 124, 125

scopolamine, 121–2

scrapie, 118

search, attention, 32

self-monitoring, 260

Selkoe, D. J., 113

senses, proximal/distal, 70
sensory acuity, 68–80, 179, 281–2
sensory evoked potentials, 52–4, 163
sensory receptors, 69, 70
serotonin, 100, 104–5, 139–40, 157
Shader, R. I., 135
Shaps, L. P., 214
Shaw, T. G., 92
Shearer, D. E., 168, 281
Sheffield, J. B., 98
Sheridan, J., 39, 250
Shimamura, A. P., 257, 259, 262
Shock, N. W., 179
Simon, E., 216
Simon, Theodore, 192
Singer, W., 17, 88
Singh, A., 221
Sinnott, J. D., 206
skill learning, 220, 222–3
Skinner, B. F., 249
Skinner, J. E., 155
sleep, 156–60; age differences, 153–4;
    apnea, 159–60; delta activity, 49,
    157; electroencephalogram, 47;
    frontal cortex, 155; mental function,
    158–9; napping, 158, 159–60; stages,
    153–4, 156–9, 171–2; work/
    retirement, 155
sleeping pills, 159
smell, 68, 69, 72–3
Smith, A. D., 216
Smith, D. B. D., 165
Smith, S., 125
Snyder, E. W., 165–6
social attitudes, aging, 196, 197
Social Security Act (1935), 196
Solomon, P. R., 61, 124, 225, 226,
    227
somatosensory evoked responses, 53,
    164
Somberg, B. L., 177
Spar, J. E., 138
spatio-temporal organization, 261
Spearman, Charles, 193
speech comprehension, 38, 39

speech impairment, 237–8
spindle activity, 157
Spirduso, W. W., 176
Spitzer, R. L., 142
Sprague–Dawley rats, 97–8
Spreen, O., 27
Squire, L. R., 93, 211, 220, 261
Stanford–Binet Intelligence Test, 192
Stankov, L., 32
Starr, A., 184
Stein, Lincoln, 274
Steinmetz, J. E., 225
stereological analyses, 93
Stern, R. G., 28, 123
Stern, William, 192–3
Sternberg, R. J., 26
Stevens, J. C., 73
stimulus, conditioned/unconditioned,
    82
Stoltzfus, E. R., 266
Stookey, B. A., 238
Storandt, M., 134
Straumanis, J. J., 165
Strauss, E., 27
stroke, 18, 144, 239, 243
Stroop, J. R., 33
Stroop Color-Word test, 32–3
substantia nigra, 87, 100, 274
suicide, 134–5, 141, 148, 232
superior temporal gyrus, 90
Surwillo, W. W., 82, 182–3
Sutton, S., 184, 185
Suzman, Richard, 5
synapses: axodendritic, 154; axosomatic,
    loss of, 154; delay, 180–2; plasticity,
    105–6
Szafran, J., 174, 178, 183, 265

Tachibana, H., 92
tacrine, 116–17, 122, 123, 276, 282
Talamo, B. R., 73
Talland, G. A., 178, 217
tapping, 178, 187–8
taste, 68, 69, 73
Taylor, G., 248

Taylor, H. R., 79
Tecce, J. J., 155, 169
temporal lobe, 90
Teri, L., 143–4
Terman, Lewis, 191, 192, 193
Terry, Robert, 90, 92
testing of aged patients: anxiety, 28–9; excess difficulty, 29–30; fatigue, 30; relevance, 30–1; sensitivity/ specificity, 24–5; vision/hearing difficulties, 30; withdrawal, 138
thalamic intralaminar nuclei, 160
Thase, M. E., 129
Theios, J., 227
thinking: abstract, 191; adaptive, 191; divergent, 41
Thompson, L. W., 28–9, 53, 82, 162, 169, 176, 183, 184
Thompson, R. F., 10, 61, 211, 220, 223, 225, 227
Thornbury, J., 70
Thorndike, E. L., 194
Timed Interval Tapping, 188
"tip-of-the-tongue" phenomenon, 249, 253
Tipper, S. P., 266
tissue transplantation, 274–5
Tomlinson, B. E., 102
Topka, H., 225
touch, 70–1
trace metal studies, 119–20
Trail Making Test, 30, 40–1, 44
Trojanowski, J. Q., 61, 62, 118, 122, 274
Troyer, W. G. Jr, 83
Tucker, D. M., 147
tumor, 144
Tun, P. A., 249
Tuokko, H., 35
Turner, A. M., 10, 17, 88

UK, depression in elderly, 134
Ulatowska, H. K., 250
underarousal, 80–2, 161–4, 183
United States Bureau of the Census, 279

US: Alzheimer's disease, 112–13; cataracts, 79–80; depression in elderly, 134; population age/sex, 6, 16

Van Natta, P. A., 132
variability: cohort effect, 14; interindividual, 14, 27–8
Veith, R. C., 139, 140
vigilance, 32, 33, 82
Vijayashankar, N., 102
visual acuity, 76–80; aging, 67–9; dark adaption, 76, 78; search problems, 265; test conditions, 30; treatments, 282
visual monitoring, 178
Visual Reproduction subtest (WMS), 44
Visual and Verbal Paired Associate tests (WMS), 37–8, 40
visually evoked responses, 53, 164, 166–7
visuospatial ability, 33–5
Vizi, E. S., 103
vocabulary, 206, 248
Vocabulary subtest (WAIS), 44

Wagman, I. H., 179
Wagstaff, A., 277
WAIS: see Wechsler Adult Intelligence Scale
Wall, P. D., 179
Walter, B. M., 260
Walter, W. G., 168–9
Warrington, E. K., 227
Watabe, S., 277
Watson, John B., 194
Watson, Y., 35
Wayner, M. J., 181
Webb, W. B., 158
Wechsler, David, 191, 199
Wechsler Adult Intelligence Scale (WAIS-R), 33, 34–5, 38–9, 44, 158, 190, 199, 211

Wechsler–Bellevue Intelligence scales, 199
Wechsler Memory Scale (WMS-R), 27, 33, 37–8, 40, 44, 159
Weindruch, R., 280
Weiskrantz, L., 227
Weissler, A. M., 83
Weissman, M. M., 132, 133, 134
Welford, A. T., 82–4, 183, 266
Wenk, G. L., 104
Wernicke, Carl, 241–2, 246, 251, 253
Wernicke–Geschwind model of brain/ language function, 242–8, 253
Wernicke's aphasia, 239, 241–2, 243
Wernicke's area, 38, 39
West, M. J., 88, 90, 93–5, 221, 226
West, R., 260
Wheilihan, W. M., 258
Whishaw, I. Q., 3, 146, 147, 190, 238, 239, 256, 258
White, J. D., 250
White, S., 216
Whitehouse, P. J., 100, 104, 277
Wickelgren, I., 88, 90, 91
Wiegersma, S., 264
Williams, H. L., 183
Wingfield, A., 249
Winograd, E., 216
Wisconsin Card Sorting Task, 29, 30, 40, 257–9
wisdom, 205–7, 230
Wisniewski, K. E., 129
withdrawal, depression, 138

WMS: *see* Wechsler Memory Scale
Wolf-Klein, G., 35
Wong, D. F., 104
Woodruff, D. S., 3, 10, 49, 51, 82, 162
Woodruff-Pak, D. S., 16, 20, 24–5, 26, 36, 37, 61, 62, 86, 88, 97, 124, 125, 165, 188, 194–6, 203, 212, 225, 226, 227, 228, 231, 277, 278
word-association, 164–5
words: accessing, 249, 253; fluency, 41; retrieval, 92; *see also* language; speech
working memory, 170, 174, 255–6, 262–5, 267–8
Wright, B. M., 222
Wysocki, C. J., 73

Yakovlev, P. V., 164
Yates, C. M., 129
Yerkes, R. M., 198–9
Yingling, C. D., 155
Young, W., 17

Zacks, R. T., 165, 170
Zec, R. F., 28, 123, 124
Zemore, R., 135
Zopf, P. E. Jr, 278, 279
Zornetzer, S. F., 101, 103
Zubek, J. P., 71
Zung, W. W. K., 134, 135
Zung Self-Rating Depression Scale, 135